PUBLISHER'S PREFACE TO
THE STUDY EDITION

Since the publication of the first English translation of *Church Dogmatics I.1* by Professor Thomson in 1936, T&T Clark has been closely linked with Karl Barth. An authorised translation of the whole of the *Kirchliche Dogmatik* was begun in the 1950s under the editorship of G. W. Bromiley and T. F. Torrance, a work which eventually replaced Professor Thomson's initial translation of *CD I.1*.

T&T Clark is now happy to present to the academic community this new *Study Edition* of the *Church Dogmatics*. Its aim is mainly to make this major work available to a generation of students and scholars with less familiarity with Latin, Greek, and French. For the first time this edition therefore presents the classic text of the translation edited by G. W. Bromiley and T. F. Torrance incorporating translations of the foreign language passages in Editorial Notes on each page.

The main body of the text remains unchanged. Only minor corrections with regard to grammar or spelling have been introduced. The text is presented in a new reader friendly format. We hope that the breakdown of the *Church Dogmatics* into 31 shorter fascicles will make this edition easier to use than its predecessors.

Completely new indexes of names, subjects and scriptural indexes have been created for the individual volumes of the *Study Edition*.

The publishers would like to thank the Center for Barth Studies at Princeton Theological Seminary for supplying a digital edition of the text of the *Church Dogmatics* and translations of the Greek and Latin quotations in the original T&T Clark edition made by Simon Gathercole and Ian McFarland.

London, April 2010

HOW TO USE THIS
STUDY EDITION

The *Study Edition* follows Barth's original volume structure. Individual paragraphs and sections should be easy to locate. A synopsis of the old and new edition can be found on the back cover of each fascicle.

All secondary literature on the *Church Dogmatics* currently refers to the classic 14-volume set (e.g. II.2 p. 520). In order to avoid confusion, we recommend that this practice should be kept for references to this *Study Edition*. The page numbers of the old edition can be found in the margins of this edition.

CHURCH DOGMATICS

For further resources, including the forewords to the original 14-volume edition of the *Church Dogmatics,* log on to our website and sign up for the resources webpage: http://www.continuumbooks.com/dogmatics/

KARL BARTH
CHURCH DOGMATICS

VOLUME III

THE DOCTRINE
OF CREATION

§ 50–51

THE CREATOR AND HIS CREATURE II

EDITED BY
G. W. BROMILEY
T. F. TORRANCE

t&t clark

Published by T&T Clark
A Continuum Imprint
The Tower Building, 11 York Road, London, SE1 7NX
80 Maiden Lane, Suite 704, New York, NY 10038

www.continuumbooks.com

Translated by G. W. Bromiley, J. W. Edwards, O. Bussey, Harold Knight, J. K. S. Reid, R. H. Fuller, R. J. Ehrlich, A. T. Mackey, T. H. L. Parker, H. A. Kennedy, J. Marks

Copyright © T&T Clark, 2010

Authorised translation of Karl Barth, *Die Kirchliche Dogmatik III*
Copyright © Theologischer Verlag Zürich, 1945–1951
All revisions to the original English translation and all translation of Greek, Latin and French
© Princeton Theological Seminary, 2009

British Library Cataloguing-in-Publication Data
A catalogue record for this book is available from the British Library

ISBN13: 978-0-567-61332-5

Typeset by Interactive Sciences Ltd, Gloucester, and Newgen Imaging Systems Pvt Ltd, Chennai
Printed and bound in Great Britain by CPI Antony Rowe, Chippenham, Wiltshire

CONTENTS

§ 50–51

GOD AND NOTHINGNESS*

Under the control of God world-occurrence is threatened and actually corrupted by the nothingness which is inimical to the will of the Creator and therefore to the nature of His good creature. God has judged nothingness by His mercy as revealed and effective in Jesus Christ. Pending the final revelation that it is already refuted and abolished, God determines the sphere, the manner, the measure and the subordinate relationship to His Word and work in which it may still operate.

1. THE PROBLEM OF NOTHINGNESS

There is opposition and resistance to God's world-dominion. There is in world-occurence an element, indeed an entire sinister system of elements, which is not comprehended by God's providence in the sense thus far described, and which is not therefore preserved, accompanied, nor ruled by the almighty action of God like creaturely occurrence. It is an element to which God denies the benefit of His preservation, concurrence and rule, of His fatherly lordship, and which is itself opposed to being preserved, accompanied and ruled in any sense, fatherly or otherwise. There is amongst the objects of God's providence an alien factor. It cannot escape God's providence but is comprehended by it. The manner, however, in which this is done is highly peculiar in accordance with the particular nature of this factor. It is distinct from that in which God's providence rules the creature and creaturely occurrence. The result is that the alien factor can never be considered or mentioned together in the same context as other objects of God's providence. Thus the whole doctrine of God's providence must be investigated afresh. This opposition and resistance, this stubborn element and alien factor, may be provisionally defined as nothingness.

So far we have only perceived on the margin that something of this kind [290] exists, that in view of it we must reckon with a serious complication of our knowledge and exposition of the divine providence, and that amplification is perhaps required in this direction. We do, of course, remember one occasion

---

* Many terms have been considered for *das Nichtige*, including the Latin *nihil* which has sometimes been favoured. Preferring a native term, and finding constructions like "the null" too artificial and "the negative" or "non-existent " not quite exact, we have finally had to make do with "nothingness." It must be clearly grasped, however, that it is not used in its more common and abstract way, but in the secondary sense, to be filled out from Barth's own definitions and delimitations, of "that which is not."—Ed.

at least when the alien element in question had already to be expressly named, i.e., when we were trying to understand the divine preservation of the creature. We saw this to be God's preservation of His creature from being overthrown by the greater force of nothingness. We then considered how God confirms and upholds the separation between His creature and nothingness as effected in creation, halting the threatened and commencing enslavement of the creature. We saw that He does this because His will for His creature is liberation for a life in fellowship with Himself, because He wills to be known and praised by the creature as its Liberator and because He thus wills its continuation and not its destruction. He preserves the creature. For He has executed His will. He Himself has become a creature in Jesus Christ. And therefore He has set Himself in opposition to nothingness, and in this opposition was and is the Victor. Nothingness then met us as this total peril which is not actual in this form but is warded off by God's preservation. In that context, however, we gave only an incidental account of its existence and nature. We considered it only in the form in which it is a final peril warded off by the divine preservation. We did not consider it in the other form in which, though unable to overwhelm and destroy the creature, it constantly threatens and corrupts it. We did not take into account that it is not only inimical to the creature and its nature and existence, but above all to God Himself and His will and purpose. Neither did we answer the question how there can exist side by side the will and purpose of God and this opposition and resistance, the providence of God and the menace and actual operation of this alien factor, and even more radically the divine creation and the fact that this alien factor can exist and operate at all. All these questions must now be asked and answered.

It would be comparatively easy to understand and state the doctrine of God's providence if it involved no more than the relationship between the lordship of God and creaturely occurrence as such. So far we have understood and stated the doctrine in this basic form. There would be no difficulty if only creaturely occurrence, though ruled by God, did not also stand under the determination of this alien factor, of nothingness. There would be no difficulty if only a careful consideration of this factor which also determines creaturely activity were not absolutely unavoidable if the doctrine of God's providence is not to ignore its most urgent question and to desist from giving its most important answer. Perpendicular lines from above can render it in some measure intelligible and clear, as we have already demonstrated, what [291] takes place between God the Creator and the creature as God's royal dominion on the one side, and creaturely existence, life and occurrence under this dominion on the other. "Of him and through him, and to him are all things: to whom be glory for ever. Amen" (Rom. 11[36]). This thought has already been developed. With regard to the good Creator and Lord, and the creature created good by Him, it could indeed be developed in straight (or apparently straight) lines. The truth of this scriptural saying must stand. Yet what does "of him, through him, and to him" mean in view of the fact that "all things," i.e.,

2

man first, but through him and for him all things, are also affected by nothingness, being enmeshed in and bound up with it, sharing its nature, bearing its marks, and in some degree, directly or indirectly, actively or passively, overtly or covertly, being involved in the existence and operation of this alien factor? What is the meaning of "of him, through him, to him" from this standpoint? Is not the question of what is meant by God's lordship posed afresh and very differently against this background? Can the question be regarded as answered as long as it remains open to enquiry in this respect? Does not even the best which emerges from God's Word concerning His lordship over the creature remain unsaid if it is not also stated from the particular standpoint that it also belongs to the existence of life and activity of the creature to be involved in nothingness, and always to be partly determined by it in its present form?

We again recall the exemplary answer of the *Heidelberg Catechism* to the question of God's providence, and the writings of Paul Gerhardt, and all the classic hymns of trust and comfort of the older Protestantism. The strength of these texts obviously lies in the fact that they do not evade but face that which might destroy or at least disturb and weaken trust in God's providence and the comfort of its knowledge, namely, the whole complex of sin, guilt and punishment, the whole reality of calamity, suffering and death in the world-process, in short, the factor of nothingness. They bear witness to the lordship of God not by concealing but by openly acknowledging the dreadful fact that this factor exists. These texts are obviously based on the insight that only if this fact is taken into account with genuine sighing, in "confident despair" but also "despairing confidence," can the lordship of God be attested, but that in this way it may and must be proclaimed the more powerfully and triumphantly. In face of this fact the question of God's providence is obviously a serious one and their witness to it is real and credible. Apart from it the question cannot be seriously put nor can a significant answer be given. It has thus been realised in the dogmatics of all confessions that here more than anywhere a special account of the faith is due to the community and the world, and that here more than anywhere special attention to God's Word is unavoidable.

In this instance, however, we do not make any advance by drawing straight lines from above, i.e., by thinking and speaking in direct statements concerning the action of the Creator on and with His creature. It is true that here also there is involved a repetition and confirmation, i.e., a particular application, of the simple recognition that God is Lord over all. But the peculiar factor now to be considered is that between the Creator and the creature, or more exactly [292] the creaturely sphere under the lordship of the Creator, there is that at work which can be explained neither from the side of the Creator nor from that of the creature, neither as the action of the Creator nor as the life-act of the creature, and yet which cannot be overlooked or disowned but must be reckoned with in all its peculiarity. The simple recognition that God is Lord over all must obviously be applied to this third factor as well. Where would be the real situation of the real man or the real way of real trust of the real Christian, where would be the decisive truth and power of the doctrine of God's providence, if the knowledge that He is Lord over all were not applied especially to this element? But if God's lordship is applicable here too, how are we to avoid

3

error on the one side or the other? We stray on the one side if we argue that this element of nothingness derives from the positive will and work of God as if it too were a creature, and that the Creator Himself and His lordship are responsible for its nothingness, the creature being exonerated from all responsibility for its existence, presence and activity. But we go astray on the other side if we maintain that it derives solely from the activity of the creature, in relation to which the lordship of God can only be a passive permission and observation, an ineffectual foreknowledge and a subsequent attitude. In the one case, the obvious error is to misinterpret the fact that God is Lord, to fail to understand that for that reason His lordship cannot be affected by nothingness. In the other case, the error is to misinterpret the meaning of lordship, namely, that God rules in sublime and unlimited majesty over every sphere, and therefore over that of nothingness as well. But how is it possible to avoid the one error without falling into the other? How can justice be done both to the holiness and to the omnipotence of God when we are faced by the problem of nothingness? How can the simple recognition that God is Lord over all be applied to this sphere?

We may well understand the sighs of many of the older dogmaticians as they take up this subject. This is a *quaestio perceptu difficillima*^{EN1}, says F. Burmann (*Syn. Theol.*, 1671, I, 44, 52). It is a *quaestio intricatissima et maxime ardua*^{EN2}, complains F. Turrettini (*Instit. Theol. el.*, 1679, VI, 7, 1). And A. Heidan (*Corp. Theol.*, 1686) says: *Maximus labor restat, ut dispiciamus, quomodo, providentiae divinae sua tum veritas tum certitudo constare possit, etsi malum et peccatum sit in mundo*^{EN3}. They saw the difficulty precisely in the dilemma to which we have alluded: of failing either *in excessu*^{EN4} or *in defectu*^{EN5}; of either speaking, with Manichaeans, Priscillianists and similar early heretics, of a *causalitas mali in Deo*^{EN6} and thus violating the holiness of God (a possibility Calvinists were particularly careful to guard against), or of joining with Pelagians old and new in ascribing evil solely to the creature, thus putting evil more or less outwith the providence and lordship of God and becoming guilty in consequence of an overt or covert denial of the omnipotence and omnicausality of God; in short, of vitiating either one way or the other the nerve-centre of the doctrine of divine providence, the recognition of God Himself as Lord over all.

[293] Yet it is also possible to go astray here in an entirely different manner. For it is clearly wrong to apply the basic recognition of God's lordship in such a way that nothingness in its relation of opposition and resistance to God's world-dominion assumes the form of a monster which, vested with demonic qualities, inspires fear and respect instead of awakening the Easter joy that even in all its power as sin and evil it is no more than the nothingness which as such is already judged in Jesus Christ and can therefore injure but no longer kill or

---

^{EN1} most difficult matter to grasp
^{EN2} matter that is most perplexing and extraordinarily difficult
^{EN3} The greatest work is required to understand how it is possible to affirm both the truth and trustworthiness of divine providence in light of the fact that there is evil and sin in the world
^{EN4} in saying too much
^{EN5} too little
^{EN6} source of evil in God

destroy. Again, it is no less clearly wrong if this victorious might of faith is treated as if it were a principle at our own disposal, or if it is forgotten that the victory over nothingness can be ours only through hope in Jesus Christ, or if we think and speak of this adversary, who was certainly not defeated by us, in any other way than in the fear of God and the seriousness of faith. We describe the same dilemma when we say that in considering the manner in which God disposes even of nothingness, letting it have its course and yet overruling it for good, there is the danger either of an uneasy, bleak and sceptical overestimating of its power in relation to God, or of an easy, comfortable and dogmatic underestimation of its power in relation to us. How are we to avoid both an easy pessimism on the one side and a no less easy optimism on the other? How are we to think and speak of God's lordship even over nothingness with the necessary confidence and yet also the required humility, the required humility and yet also the necessary confidence? Nor is the truth to be sought in a central position of neutrality between these claims; for all are of equal urgency. Nor can we overcome the contrast between God's holiness and His omnipotence by mediation. How, then, is this matter to be seen and stated? How can the simple recognition of God's lordship be rightly applied?

It may be said at least that it can be so only as we soberly acknowledge that we have here an extraordinarily clear demonstration of the necessary brokenness of all theological thought and utterance. There is no theological sphere where this is not noticeable. All theology is *theologia viatorum*[EN7]. It can never satisfy the natural aspiration of human thought and utterance for completeness and compactness. It does not exhibit its object but can only indicate it, and in so doing it owes the truth to the self-witness of the theme and not to its own resources. It is broken thought and utterance to the extent that it can progress only in isolated thoughts and statements directed from different angles to the one object. It can never form a system, comprehending and as it were "seizing" the object. That is true of all theological assertions. It is true even of the perpendicular lines from above in which we have developed the general doctrine of God's providence with regard to the relationship between the good Creator and His good creature. But if we failed to see this there and elsewhere, here at last we must surely see and acknowledge that our knowledge is piece-work, and that only as such can it stand and make sense in relation to its theme. But why is this true here, and therefore universally? The reason is obvious. The existence, presence and operation of nothingness, which we are here concerned to discuss, are also objectively the break in the relationship between Creator and creature. The existence, presence, and operation of nothingness are not only the frontier which belongs to the nature of this relationship on both sides and which is grounded in the goodness of the Creator and that of the Creature. They are also the break which runs counter to the nature of this relationship, which is compatible with neither the goodness of the Creator nor that of the

[294]

[EN7] theology on the way

5

creature and which cannot be derived from either side but can only be regarded as hostility in relation to both. We are not now dealing with the break itself, but with God's relation to it, with His providence and the extent to which it comprehends this break as well. In this context, however, this break is our particular concern. For theology as a human activity, and under the presuppositions of the present dispensation, knows its object solely under the shadow of this break. Objectively, it must always receive it from beyond this break. Hence it cannot even be aware of its object without also being aware of this break. And this means that theological thought and utterance must always be broken. Not even objectively is the relationship between Creator and creature a system. It is always disrupted by this alien element. Hence there can be no system in the subjective knowledge of this relationship, and therefore in theology. Does not this emerge with particular clarity when we have to deal specifically with God's providence in its relation to the nothingness with which His creature is involved? Here if anywhere it is imperative that theology, which is also a creaturely activity, should acknowledge that it is bound up with nothingness, and cannot and must not try to escape it. Here if anywhere theology as the subjective reproduction of objective reality ought not to impose or simulate a system. Here especially theology must set an example for its procedure generally, corresponding to its object in broken thoughts and utterance.

When P. van Mastricht (*Theol. pract. theor.*, 1699, VI, 10, 18) treats of this particular problem, he says, not without a hint of complaint, that it is the *imbecillitas captus nostri*[EN8] which prevents us from unifying what really ought to be unified. He is thinking especially of the unification of God's holiness and omnipotence, which is so difficult in face of the existence and presence of nothingness. But what ground is there for saying that here we have something which ought to be unified? What ground is there for saying that a sober and radical acknowledgment of the *imbecillitas captus nostri*[EN9] which reveals our incapacity to achieve and demonstrate certain unifications is not more in keeping than all the alleged or real cleverness and skill which might permit us to achieve these unifications?

[295]   This does not mean, of course, that we ought not to proceed here and everywhere with the greatest intellectual probity and with rigorous logic and objectivity. Here however—and not only here, but here with particular urgency by reason of the particular aspect of the theological object—the meaning of objectivity is that we must be prepared simply and without diminution to accept and take into account, each in its own place and manner, all the conflicting claims: the claim that God's holiness and omnipotence should be equally respected; the claim that we should think and speak of this matter with joy and also with seriousness; the claim that the power of nothingness should be rated as low as possible in relation to God and as high as possible in relation to ourselves. If we do this, it does not mean that we shall be led to a system nor to the complete and compact sequence of thoughts and statements yielded by

---

[EN8] the feebleness of our understanding
[EN9] the feebleness of our understanding

a principle. On the contrary, the break itself and as such will be reproduced and reflected in our knowledge and its presentation; and not only the break, but in, with and above it the history in which it is after all—for God is Lord— no more than an alien, disruptive and retarding moment—the history of the Creator's dealings with His creature, of the doing of His will as it was in His counsel and as it will finally and ultimately be fulfilled. This history, in the course of which this break occurs, is the object of theology. Theology is the record of this history. Hence it must consider all those claims in their place and manner. It must not be intent on unifications or mediations which are not to be found in the history. It must not degenerate into a system. It must always be related to that history. It must always be a report. It must not strain after completeness and compactness. Its aim must simply be to make the right report. This is the general and formal answer to the question how the simple recognition of God's universal lordship is rightly to be applied in view of the presence of nothingness as opposition and resistance to that lordship.

But what is the nature of this opposition and resistance? What exactly is nothingness? It is to this question that we must now address ourselves.

2. THE MISCONCEPTION OF NOTHINGNESS

We must indicate and remove a serious confusion which has been of far reaching effect in the history of theology. Light exists as well as shadow; there is a positive as well as a negative aspect of creation and creaturely occurrence (cf. *C.D.*, III, 1 § 42, 3). When the first biblical account of creation distinguishes and opposes day and night, and land and water, it unmistakeably indicates this twofold character and aspect of creaturely existence. Viewed from its negative aspect, creation is as it were on the frontier of nothingness and orien-   [296] tated towards it. Creation is continually confronted by this menace. It is continually reminded that as God's creation it has not only a positive but also a negative side. Yet this negative side is not to be identified with nothingness, nor must it be postulated that the latter belongs to the essence of creaturely nature and may somehow be understood and interpreted as a mark of its character and perfection. It belongs to the essence of creaturely nature, and is indeed a mark of its perfection, that it has in fact this negative side, that it inclines not only to the right hand but also to the left, that it is thus simultaneously worthy of its Creator and yet dependent on Him, that it is not "nothing" but "something," yet "something" on the very frontier of nothingness, secure, and yet in jeopardy. It thus follows that though its existence is under doubt and shadow it is not of itself involved in opposition and resistance to God's creative will. On the contrary, this will is fulfilled and confirmed in it. The creature is natural and not unnatural. It is good, even very good, in so far as it does not oppose but corresponds to the intention of God as revealed by

7

Him in the humiliation and exaltation of Jesus Christ and the reconciliation of the world with Himself effected in Him. For in Him God has made Himself the Subject of both aspects of creaturely existence. And having made it His own in Jesus Christ, He has affirmed it in its totality, reconciling its inner antithesis in His own person. The creature does not have the character of nothingness as and because it is a creature and partakes in this antithesis. On the contrary, this is its perfection and the proof of its creation in and for Jesus Christ. In this it is determined for its place in the covenant of God. In this it is energized and equipped for life in fellowship with its Creator, for work in His service, for faith, obedience and prayer. In this it is given a place for its praise For God Himself has revealed and shown that this is the determination of His will by Himself becoming a creature under this determination. There is thus no common ground between it and nothingness, the power inimical to the will of the Creator and therefore to the nature of His good creation, the threat to world-occurrence and its corruption. To be sure, the negative aspect of creation is a reminder of this threat and corruption. But it is not the case that because creation has this shadowy side it is itself their victim and therefore belongs to nothingness. When Jesus Christ shall finally return as the Lord and Head of all that God has created, it will also be revealed that both in light and shadow, on the right hand and on the left, everything created was very good and supremely glorious.

[297] It is difficult to attack a slander on creation which is so old, multiform and tenacious. Yet it is imperative that we should do this at the very outset. No protest can be too sharp or emphatic. It is true that in creation there is not only a Yes but also a No; not only a height but also an abyss; not only clarity but also obscurity; not only progress and continuation but also impediment and limitation; not only growth but also decay; not only opulence but also indigence; not only beauty but also ashes; not only beginning but also end; not only value but also worthlessness. It is true that in creaturely existence, and especially in the existence of man, there are hours, days and years both bright and dark, success and failure, laughter and tears, youth and age, gain and loss, birth and sooner or later its inevitable corollary, death. It is true that individual creatures and men experience these things in most unequal measure, their lots being assigned by a justice which is curious or very much concealed. Yet it is irrefutable that creation and creature are good even in the fact that all that is exists in this contrast and antithesis. In all this, far from being null, it praises its Creator and Lord even on its shadowy side, even in the negative aspect in which it is so near to nothingness. If He Himself has comprehended creation in its totality and made it His own in His Son, it is for us to acquiesce without thinking that we know better, without complaints, reproach or dismay. For all we can tell, may not His creatures praise Him more mightily in humility than in exaltation, in need than in plenty, in fear than in joy, on the frontier of nothingness than when wholly orientated on God? For all we can tell, may not we ourselves praise Him more purely on bad days than on good, more surely in

sorrow than in rejoicing, more truly in adversity than in progress? It can, of course, be otherwise. But need it always be? If not, if there may also be a praise of God from the abyss, the night and misfortune, and perhaps even from the deepest abyss, the darkest night and the greatest misfortune, why should we doubt the hidden justice which apportions the distinctions and contrasts to ourselves and others? How surprised we shall be, and how ashamed of so much improper and unnecessary disquiet and discontent, once we are brought to realise that all creation both as light and shadow, including our own share in it, our puny and fleeting life, was laid on Jesus Christ as the creation of God, and that even though we did not see it, without and in spite of us, and while we were shaking our heads that things were not very different, it sang the praise of God just as it was, and was therefore right and perfect. We aspire to be Christians, and no doubt in some small measure we are, but is it not strange that only in our few better moments can we make anything either theoretically or practically of the truth that the creation of God in both its aspects, even the negative, is His good creation?

I must again revert to Wolfgang Amadeus Mozart. Why is it that this man is so incomparable? Why is it that for the receptive, he has produced in almost every bar he conceived and composed a type of music for which "beautiful" is not a fitting epithet: music which for the true Christian is not mere entertainment, enjoyment or edification but food and drink; music full of comfort and counsel for his needs; music which is never a slave to its technique nor sentimental but always "moving," free and liberating because wise, strong and sovereign? Why is it possible to hold that Mozart has a place in theology, especially in the doctrine of creation and also in eschatology, although he was not a father of the Church, does not seem to have been a particularly active Christian, and was a Roman Catholic, apparently leading what might appear to us a rather frivolous existence when not occupied in his work? It is possible to give him this position because he knew something about creation in its total goodness that neither the real fathers of the Church nor our Reformers, neither the orthodox nor Liberals, neither the exponents of natural theology nor those heavily armed with the "Word of God," and certainly not the Existentialists, nor indeed any other great musicians before and after him, either know or can express and maintain as he did. In this respect he was pure in heart, far transcending both optimists and pessimists. 1756–1791! This was the time when God was under attack for the Lisbon earthquake, and theologians and other well-meaning folk were hard put to it to defend Him. In face of the problem of theodicy, Mozart had the peace of God which far transcends all the critical or speculative reason that praises and reproves. This problem lay behind him. Why then concern himself with it? He had heard, and causes those who have ears to hear, even to-day, what we shall not see until the end of time—the whole context of providence. As though in the light of this end, he heard the harmony of creation to which the shadow also belongs but in which the shadow is not darkness, deficiency is not defeat, sadness cannot become despair, trouble cannot degenerate into tragedy and infinite melancholy is not ultimately forced to claim undisputed sway. Thus the cheerfulness in this harmony is not without its limits. But the light shines all the more brightly because it breaks forth from the shadow. The sweetness is also bitter and cannot therefore cloy. Life does not fear death but knows it well. *Et lux perpetua lucet* (sic!) *eis*^{EN10}—even the dead of Lisbon. Mozart saw this light no more than we do,

[298]

---

^{EN10} light perpetual shines upon them

but he heard the whole world of creation enveloped by this light. Hence it was fundamentally in order that he should not hear a middle or neutral note, but the positive far more strongly than the negative. He heard the negative only in and with the positive. Yet in their inequality he heard them both together, as, for example, in the Symphony in G-minor of 1788. He never heard only the one in abstraction. He heard concretely, and therefore his compositions were and are total music. Hearing creation unresentfully and impartially, he did not produce merely his own music but that of creation, its twofold and yet harmonious praise of God. He neither needed nor desired to express or represent himself, his vitality, sorrow, piety, or any programme. He was remarkably free from the mania for self-expression. He simply offered himself as the agent by which little bits of horn, metal and catgut could serve as the voices of creation, sometimes leading, sometimes accompanying and sometimes in harmony. He made use of instruments ranging from the piano and violin, through the horn and the clarinet, down to the venerable bassoon, with the human voice somewhere among them, having no special claim to distinction yet distinguished for this very reason. He drew music from them all, expressing even human emotions in the service of this music, and not *vice versa*. He himself was only an ear for this music, and its mediator to other ears. He died when according to the worldly wise his life-work was only ripening to its true fulfilment. But who shall say that after the "Magic Flute," the Clarinet Concerto of October 1791 and the Requiem, it was not already fulfilled? Was not the whole of his achievement implicit in his works at the age of 16 or 18? Is it not heard in what has come down to us from the very young Mozart? He died in misery like an "unknown soldier," and in company with Calvin, and Moses in the Bible, he has no known grave. But what does this matter? What does a grave

[299]   matter when a life is permitted simply and unpretentiously, and therefore serenely, authentically and impressively, to express the good creation of God, which also includes the limitation and end of man.

I make this interposition here, before turning to chaos, because in the music of Mozart—and I wonder whether the same can be said of any other works before or after—we have clear and convincing proof that it is a slander on creation to charge it with a share in chaos because it includes a Yes and a No, as though orientated to God on the one side and nothingness on the other. Mozart causes us to hear that even on the latter side, and therefore in its totality, creation praises its Master and is therefore perfect. Here on the threshhold of our problem—and it is no small achievement—Mozart has created order for those who have ears to hear, and he has done it better than any scientific deduction could. This is the point which I wish to make.

But there is another and very different reason for rejecting this confusion. The confusion itself and as such is a masterpiece and even a triumph of nothingness. This is so not merely because it entails a slander on creation, and an act of stupidity and ingratitude towards the Creator who seeks His own likeness, but also because it implies a most subtle concealment of genuine nothingness, because in this confusion with what is not null but perfect the latter fabricates a kind of alibi under cover of which it cannot be recognised and can thus pursue its dangerous and disruptive ways the more unfeared and unhampered. For what happens when we wrongfully indict the Creator and the creature? What happens when we seek, localise and apprehend the real source of danger and distress to the creature, perhaps lamenting and bewailing and taking it tragically, but openly or secretly adapting and preparing to use it, at a point where in actual fact no more is involved than this negative aspect of creation and existence? What obviously happens is that we neither perceive nor evaluate it as true nothingness, but accept it, incorporate it into our philosophical outlook, validitate and exculpate it, and thus, if we are consistent, finally justify it, not regarding and treating it as null, but as an essential and necessary part of existence. This is inevitable, for no reality corresponds to this confusion. Though we may err and deceive ourselves and others by seeking nothingness in the negative side of creation, this does not alter the fact that this negative side also belongs to God's good and perfect creation. It does not alter the fact that the real or supposed antithesis between the negative and the positive side is a relative and provisional one which is basically not only innocuous but even salutary in view of the orientation of creation on Jesus Christ. Our confusion is wrecked on the rock of this truth. But this means that, no matter how serious and solemn and tragic we may be, and even if we may identify ourselves theoretically or practically with Marcion and Schopenhauer (and *Auch Einer**), we do not really come to grips with true nothingness, with the real adversary which menaces and corrupts us so long as we look in this direction. Entangled in this confusion, we can never achieve the seriousness which is required in face of true nothingness. What is not dangerous *in re*[EN11] simply cannot be treated as if it were *in cognitione*[EN12]. However serious we may pretend to be, and even in the spasms of real seriousness occasioned by this great deception, we shall still come to terms with it somehow. We shall encounter it as an adversary with whom we contend but may at a pinch capitulate and come to terms, indeed, with whom we must come to terms, because with it we are "in the same boat" as the whole of creation and finally the good Lord Himself. We shall encounter it with a bad conscience and without joy, yet temporarily lulled by these considerations; whereas Mozart encountered the inner antithesis with joy and a good conscience. What we wrongly regard as nothingness will be considered in the context of God's good creation, or rather what we arbitrarily think to be good in it. We shall then find some way of showing that it stands in a dialectical relationship to the so-called good, and therefore assume that we can see a higher unity of both. On the wrong assumption that it is genuine nothingness, we shall then be able to ascribe to it a certain goodness, a certain participation in good. In short, nothingness suddenly becomes something which is ultimately innocuous, and even salutary. Real sin can then be regarded as a venial error and mistake, a temporary retardation, and *comprendre c'est pardonner*[EN13]. Real evil can then be interpreted as transitory and not intolerable imperfection, and real death as "rest in God." The devil can then be denied or described as the last candidate for a salvation which is due to him too by reason of a general *apokatastasis*[EN14]. Nothingness can then

[300]

---

* *Auch Einer* is a novel by F. T. Vischer—Translator's note.
[EN11] in fact
[EN12] with respect to our experience of it
[EN13] to understand is to forgive
[EN14] restoration

be tidily "demythologized," although in actual fact what is in question is not real nothingness, but only the misconceived negative side of creation, which is not null *in re*EN15. Nor must we fail to realise that, while we indulge in this formidable confusion, real nothingness, real sin, evil, death and the devil, are no less present and active, although not where man in his folly seeks and thinks to find them. The whole trouble is that they are overlooked, forgotten, unnoticed, unexpected and disregarded. While we look in the wrong direction, and there hope to hear ultimate harmonies and to accomplish ultimate syntheses, they are not taken seriously in their reality. Is not the consequence clear? Do not all the seriousness in face of sin and the grave, all the tragedy, all the fear of the devil, to which we think we must give way in virtue of this confusion, seeking the adversary where he is not to be found, and not seeking him where he is, constitute not only an empty calumniation of the Creator and creature, but also direct co-operation with what is attempted against them by true nothingness? The more tidily the latter is "demythologized," i.e., the more it is interpreted as an element in a philosophical system in which things are not really so dangerous, and what is dangerous is only what occasions a little fear and sadness, tragedy and remorse, the more this confusion estab-

[301] lishes itself; or, conversely, the more the strange mystery of the true nothingness between Creator and creature is reduced to fantasy, the more freely and surely nothingness can take its course and exercise its power. Is it not manifest that in the masquerade and camouflage of this confusion and the concurrent insult offered to Creator and creature, in the infamous trick which is played upon us and which we ourselves help to play, we have the most palpable self-revelation and self-demonstration of genuine nothingness? The very existence and essence of the latter is that this can and does happen. In this way nothingness deceives us, we let ourselves be deceived by it, and we deceive ourselves. In this way true nothingness irrupts into God's good creation. In this way we ourselves come to have a part in its nullity.

Where is the error in this confusion, and why must we avoid it? We call it an insult to Creator and creature because it contradicts God's self-manifestation in Jesus Christ. Since God's Word became flesh, He Himself has acknowledged that the distinct reality of the world created by Him is in both its forms, with its Yes and its No, that of the world which He willed. He has thus revealed its right to this twofold form, and therefore the goodness of creation. We cannot believe in Jesus Christ and repudiate this right of the Creator and creature proclaimed in Him. We cannot ignore the fact that in Jesus Christ God has again and expressly claimed the whole of creation as His work, adopting and as it were taking it to heart in both its positive and negative aspects. In the knowledge of Jesus Christ we must abandon the obvious prejudice against the negative aspect of creation and confess that God has planned and made all things

---

EN15 in fact

well, even on the negative side. In the knowledge of Jesus Christ it is inadmissible to seek nothingness here.

But in this confusion an error is also made in relation to nothingness itself. Being sought where he is not to be found, the enemy goes unrecognised. He assumes a form, a relatively and ultimately innocuous form, to which he has no right and in which he cannot be taken seriously. Being understood as a side or aspect or distinctive form of creation, nothingness is brought into a positive relationship with God's will and work. Its nature and existence are attributed to God, to His will and responsibility, and the menacing and corruption of creation by nothingness are understood as His intention and act and therefore as a necessary and tolerable part of creaturely existence. We cannot really fear and loathe nothingness. We cannot consider and treat it as a real enemy. We have already decided to make terms with it, and thus unconsciously to give it power and honour. Without desiring to do so, we already serve it most effectively, for how could we better serve it than by this misapprehension? But why must we avoid this confusion as a misconception of nothingness itself? Why is a very different seriousness demanded in face of nothingness from that which is required in face of the negative aspect of creation and which, because God's [302] creation is good even on this side too, can only be a relative seriousness and can have nothing whatever to do with real fear or loathing?

3. THE KNOWLEDGE OF NOTHINGNESS

To answer this question we must revert to the source of all Christian knowledge, namely, to the knowledge of Jesus Christ, though now in a different sense. For in Him there is revealed not only the goodness of God's creation in its twofold form, but also the true nothingness which is utterly distinct from both Creator and creation, the adversary with whom no compromise is possible, the negative which is more than the mere complement of an antithetical positive, the left which is not counterpoised by any right, the antithesis which is not merely within creation and therefore dialectical but which is primarily and supremely to God Himself and therefore to the totality of the created world. This antithesis has no substantive existence within creation, i.e., it is not a creaturely element confronted by others as elements of good. It is the antithesis which can be present and active within creation only as an absolute alien opposing and contradicting all its elements, whether positive or negative. It is the antithesis which the creature (which it does of course greatly concern) cannot possibly envisage, comprehend and explain within creation, even though it is present and active within it. It is the antithesis which cannot be synoptically viewed, or reduced to a common denominator, or reconciled, with what is opposed to it. It is the antithesis whose relationship to creation is real but absolutely negative, offering only menace, corruption and death, so that it must never be expressed in terms of synthesis. For a real synthesis, which must always be the criterion of an ideal or intellectual, cannot be effected except by the surrender of creation to the negation, menace and corruption offered by this antithesis. It is the antithesis which is only comprehensible in correlation with creation not as an equilibrating but an absolute and uncompromising No. For it is in opposition primarily and supremely to God Himself, and therefore necessarily and irrevocably to all His work and creation. Yet God Himself comprehends, envisages and controls it. This is the insight which in the context of the doctrine of providence we seek to attain in this whole section. For God is Master of this antithesis. He overcomes and has already overcome it. The negative content and significance of His saving decree and act in Jesus Christ are that this antithesis should be finally routed and the creature liberated from it, as His sovereignty requires. But we have not yet reached this point. God alone, the God who from all eternity has decreed its defeat, transcends the antithesis, comprehending, envisaging and controlling it. For us it remains the antithesis which we can neither conquer nor comprehend, neither envisage nor master and control either in theory or practice. It is the antithesis which is impatient of any legitimate synthesis. God, but He alone, can deal with it and has already done so, in accordance with the fact that He transcends it from all eternity in His essence as God. But it must be clearly understood that He has treated it as His adversary, as the No which is primarily and supremely addressed to Himself, as the nothingness which is the true nothingness in opposition to Himself and His will and work. But if this is the relationship between God and nothingness, we cannot and must not include it in the creaturely world, in the divine creation, or in any way relativise or subtly minimise it. Any theoretical synthesis we contemplate between creaturely existence and genuine nothingness can only be a description of its triumph over creaturely existence, and therefore blasphemy. Our only option is to refrain from any such attempt in the radical fear and abhorrence which alone are appropriate. In face of this antithesis, this adversary, genuine nothingness, there is place only for the seriousness which we cannot exercise even in face of the negative side of creation. For here we are confronted by what is not only abhorrent to ourselves but also primarily and supremely to God Himself, and therefore terrifying to His creature faced with its ultimate and mortal threat. If we are weak and inclined to conciliation or appeasement, we treat God's enemy as our friend, thus renouncing our one hope of deliverance from the danger which overhangs us. For the sake of God nothingness can only be nothing worth. Against it, God is our one hope. For it is His enemy no less than ours.

[303]

How do we know this? How do we know that nothingness really exists, and does so in such a way, in such radical superiority, that it cannot be legitimately incorporated into any philosophical system, that we must not try to treat it as one element in the world among others? We know all this clearly, directly and certainly from the source of all Christian knowledge, the knowledge of Jesus

Christ. It must be clearly grasped that the incarnation ef the Word of God was obviously not necessary merely to reveal the goodness of God's creation in its twofold form. To be sure, it gives us this revelation too. When God Himself became a creature in Jesus Christ, He confirmed His creation in its totality as an act of His wisdom and mercy, as His good creation without blemish or blame. Yet much more than this was involved. It is written that "the Word became flesh," i.e., that it became not only a creature, but a creature in mortal peril, a creature threatened and actually corrupted, a creature which in face and in spite of its goodness, and in disruption and destruction of its imparted goodness, was subject not to an internal but to an external attack which it could neither contain nor counter. The Word became a creature which had fallen under the sway of a possessive and domineering alien, and was therefore [304] itself alienated from its Creator and itself, unable to recover or retrace its way home. The Word became a creature to which it was of no avail to be the creature of God, or to receive confirmation of its creation by Him, or to remember the wisdom and mercy in which it was created, because it was betrayed and *nolens volens*[EN16] subjected to a determination inimical to its creation in wisdom and mercy. That the Word became flesh means that the Word became a creature of this kind, a lost creature. That God's Word, God's Son, God Himself, became flesh means no other than that God saw a challenge to Himself in this assault on His creature, in this invading alien, in this other determination of His creature, in its capture and self-surrender. It means that God took to heart the attack on His creature because He saw in it an attack on His own cause and therefore on Himself, seeing His own enemy in this domineering alien, intruder, usurper and tyrant. God therefore arose, and in His Son gave and humbled Himself, Himself becoming flesh, this ruined and lost human creature, setting Himself wholly in the place of His work and possession. To be sure, He did this in confirmation of His goodness as Creator and of that of His creature. But for this reason He did so in His own most proper cause, repelling an injury and insult offered to Himself. He did so in necessary and righteous wrath, not against His creature but against its temptation and destruction, against its deviation, defection and consequent degeneration. He did so as a Judge asserting His own right and therefore restoring that of His creature. And therefore in His Son He exposed Himself with it to this assault, to this alien, to this hostile determination, yielding to this adversary in solidarity with His creature, and in this way routing it, achieving what the creature, who was and is only secondary in this matter, could not accomplish but yet required for its deliverance.

Our present interest in all this is that it is obviously the decisive ground of our knowledge of the whole problem with which we are concerned. Here we can see what nothingness is. Here we can see its true nature and reality. Here we can see that it is an antithesis not only to God's whole creation but to the

---

[EN16] willing or unwilling

Creator Himself. What challenged Him and provoked His wrath, what made Him come forth as the Judge, what made Him yield to nothingness in order to overcome it, was obviously nothing that He Himself had chosen, willed or done. It was nothing that He would or could previously have affirmed. It was nothing—day or night—that He as Creator had declared to be very good. It was nothing that could be considered the end and aim of His creation. That which rendered necessary the birth of His Son in the stable of Bethlehem and His death upon the cross of Calvary, that which by this birth and death He smote, defeated and destroyed, is that which primarily opposes and resists God

[305]   Himself, and therefore all creation. It is obvious that this neither can nor may be understood as something which He Himself has posited or decreed, and that it cannot be subsumed under any synthesis. It thus demands on our part a wholly different seriousness from that imposed by life and the world—the seriousness of a radical fear and loathing founded on hope in the God who is primarily affected but who is omnipotent and supreme and therefore our only hope. What is nothingness, the real nothingness which is not to be confounded with the negative side of God's good creation behind which it seeks to shelter for greater strength? What is nothingness unmasked and deprived of that camouflage by which it seeks to deceive us, and we ourselves? In plain and precise terms, the answer is that nothingness is the "reality" on whose account (i.e., against which) God Himself willed to become a creature in the creaturely world, yielding and subjecting Himself to it in Jesus Christ in order to overcome it. Nothingness is thus the "reality" which opposes and resists God, which is itself subjected to and overcome by His opposition and resistance, and which in this twofold determination as the reality that negates and is negated by Him, is totally distinct from Him. The true nothingness is that which brought Jesus Christ to the cross, and that which He defeated there. Only from the standpoint of Jesus Christ, His birth, death and resurrection, do we see it in reality and truth, without the temptation to treat it as something inclusive or relative, or to conceive it dialectically and thus render it innocuous. From this standpoint we see it with fear and trembling as the adversary with whom God and God alone can cope. But it is to be noted that in this we see it where our one real hope against it is grounded and established. If there is confusion concerning it, we obviously do not see it from the standpoint of Jesus Christ.

It is evident that the concept may at once be developed in many different ways against this background. We can and must ask and say what real evil is, real death, the real devil and real hell—questions to which we can give only the most summary answers in this context. Above all, although it is not our present theme, our eyes are opened to the most important of all its forms, i.e., the real sin of man, its source and its several manifestations and consequences. When seen in the light of Jesus Christ, the concrete form in which nothingness is active and revealed is the sin of man as his personal act and guilt, his aberration from the grace of God and its command, his refusal of the gratitude he owes to God and the concomitant freedom and obligation, his arrogant

16

attempt to be his own master, provider and comforter, his unhallowed lust for what is not his own, the falsehood, hatred and pride in which he is enmeshed in relation to his neighbour, the stupidity to which he is self-condemned, and a life which follows the course thereby determined on the basis of the necessity thus imposed. In the light of Jesus Christ, it is impossible to escape the truth [306] that we ourselves as sinners have become the victims and servants of nothingness, sharing its nature and producing and extending it.

Nevertheless we must be careful not to relinquish the position that the objective ground of our knowledge of nothingness is really Jesus Christ Himself. We must be careful not to transfer this ground to the consciousness of our own existence and sin as though this were our direct consciousness of nothingness. We must be careful not to postulate a knowledge of human sin, whether immediate or mediated or occasioned by an abstract law, as the real source of the truth required.

For the knowledge of sin it is formally decisive that it should be recognised as man's personal act and guilt, that man should be and be made responsible for it, and this in such a way that he can neither renounce his liability nor impute it to others nor to an inexorable fate. It is essential that the direct climax should be seen which compels man to confess that alien and enemy, and to acknowledge his own treachery in giving entrance to the enemy. This is indeed the only serious knowledge of nothingness. But this knowledge is assured only if God Himself, and God in His Word and work, and therefore Jesus Christ, is its basis. We must remember that what we know of ourselves is necessarily relative to our creatureliness. Therefore even our most sincere and serious self-consciousness, even our profoundest experience of our own existence, cannot reveal sin except as an element in our creatureliness. The consciousness of sin of which we are immediately capable in mere self-understanding can consist only in the ultimate realisation that the twofold determination of creation runs through our own lives, that in us, too, the Yes is confronted by the No, the light by shadow. It can consist only in this realisation because the consciousness of sin itself cannot amount to more than an awareness of the deficiency of our spontaneity and activity, and therefore of our action, and to that extent of our existence in the true sense. But this deficiency is not our true sin. Even when we are conscious of our deficiency we are still able to take a detached view of ourselves, and to correlate the evil in us with the good which is certainly not lacking. We are still able to make favourable comparisons of ourselves with others, and to reflect on the general contrariety of creaturely existence, its intrinsic tension and distinctive dialectic. When the knowledge of sin derives from man's self-communion it cannot possibly be a knowledge of real nothingness, of real sin, because in the knowledge of sin acquired in this way there can be no indictment of the existence of man in its totality, including its Yes and No and light and shadow, as one which involves a repudiation of the grace of God and its command, a breach with the neighbour, and a perversion of creaturely nature. Why should man accuse himself?

[307]   Why should he accept this accusation? What we say to ourselves on this ground can never be this total indictment, nor consist in the saying: "Thou art the man." I can and will be told that I am a real sinner, responsible for the reality of nothingness because I am its bearer and doer, only when I am told it by God Himself. And it can be told me by God Himself only as He reveals Himself to me in His opposition to real nothingness, to sin, as His real adversary, so that I see that He Himself is contradicted and resisted by this enemy and opposes to him His own more powerful contradiction and resistance, and thus abolishes and overcomes him. No abstract law of God, if such were possible, could reveal this to me—only the law of His grace and judicial action, the law of His covenant. These alone can speak to me of sin, of my real sin, which is not an attribute or defect of the creature, but an insult to the Creator and therefore its guilt. This guilt cannot be estimated, assessed, evaluated or classified by the creature, since the creature itself permits and participates in it, bearing and committing the offence against God. It can be revealed to me only by the God who Himself became flesh in His Word, yielding to the adversary in the flesh and judging sin in the flesh (Rom. 8³). It can be revealed to me only by Jesus Christ, because in Him alone and in His light real nothingness, the real sin that wages war with God and is assailed and overcome by Him, stands revealed as the sin of man, and so revealed that I may no longer regard it as a defect or as something natural but must rather recognise in it the alien and adversary to whom I myself have given place. Again, only in Him did the Word of God become flesh, flesh of my flesh, to judge sin in the flesh, executing this judgment for me as my Brother. Only in relation to Him as my Substitute do I know myself as the man who is also smitten by this judgment. Only in relation to what reality is in or in face of Him can and must I confess myself to be such a man, and acknowledge that I am a sinner, a real sinner before God. In relation to Him I can and must do this. But we must be clear that all our knowledge and acknowledgment of sin can be genuine and related to our own real sin, to true nothingness, only when it is clearly apprehended that sin and nothingness are primarily and properly known in Jesus Christ and acknowledged by Him, so that in this respect, too, we can only follow Him, adding our indirect and secondary knowledge and acknowledgment to His. Unless Jesus Christ is their objective basis, our own knowledge and acknowledgment will bear no real relation to the alien and adversary here involved, nor to the insult which it is his very nature to offer to God; and we ourselves shall certainly accept no responsibility for this insult. This is the first and formal reason why, to understand the nature of nothingness, we must not turn elsewhere than to the heart of the Gospel. But there are also two material reasons.

[308]   The reality of nothingness is not seen sharply enough, even in its concrete form as sin, if sin is understood only generally as aberration from God and disobedience to His will. This is true enough, but we cannot stop at this generalisation. Otherwise we might escape and extricate ourselves with the assertion that we are men, creatures, and not God, and that therefore our aberration

from God, and to that extent our disobedience, and therefore sin and noth-ingness, are basically no more than our essential and natural imperfection in contrast with His perfection. Even in the bitterness of self-accusation we might still excuse and even justify ourselves by arguing that there can obviously be no real conformity between creature and Creator, and that this cannot be expected, so that the divine demand for obedience is robbed of its ultimate rigour and its transgression is not quite so serious a matter. In sin as the con-crete form of nothingness we should then be dealing again with merely the negative aspect of creation. This is the point where it becomes particularly clear and definite that, even if such be possible, no abstract law of God, whether revealed or natural, can possibly be the objective ground of the know-ledge of real sin. An abstract law can no more make us conscious of the true nature of our sin or the seriousness of our situation than the most conscien-tious self-examination. In face of a stark demand of God we might well be conscious of the imperfection of our actions, but we should not find our escape cut off. This is the case only when we realise that as disobedience to the will of God sin is a repudiation of His grace and its command, and therefore on the one hand a refusal of the gratitude which is naturally due to the gra-cious God, and on the other a rupture of the relationships with our neigh-bours which are normal and natural because this gracious God is our Creator. In relation to his gracious Creator man ought to be both free and bound by nature, not to a divine or even a heavenly but to a creaturely and earthly per-fection, corresponding though not equal to the perfection of his Father in heaven. In relation to his gracious Creator man could and should live in this righteousness. His sin consists in the fact—and this is why it is so real and inexcusable—that he repudiates this possibility and imperative, and therefore the grace of God and its command. Hence he can no longer claim that he is only human and therefore fallible and not God. He cannot interpret his sin as mere retardment. God has not required too much of him, nor was he unable to meet His demand. God in His goodness required no more of him than his adherence to this goodness, and man was free and bound by nature to meet this demand. In all its majesty, the sovereign will of God which he resisted was His merciful, patient and generous will. It was this will that he rejected, preferring to go his own way. This is what gives such seriousness to the oppos-ition between God and human sin, between God and the sinner. This is what reveals the true nature of sin and nothingness as our repudiation of the good-ness of God.

But how can we maintain that this is the case? How do we have knowledge of the gracious Creator? How do we know, then, that our fellowship with Him is our true and natural state? How do we have consequent knowledge of our real sin and real nothingness? How do we perceive that the command or law against which we sin is the command or law of God's grace? How does this command or law so judge us that we are left with no avenue of escape? The answer is obvious if Jesus Christ is the objective ground of knowledge of sin [309] and nothingness. For the incarnation of the Word of God was not the revelation of a mere requirement or abstract divine law, and therefore of an abstract indictment and condemnation which man might evade by pleading the severity of God and his own human frailty. But when the Word of God became flesh, God took up the cause of sinful man enslaved to nothingness and subject to sin, putting His creative will into operation and revealing it as the will of His mercy. In the incarnate Word God has shown that His goodness to His creature is His persistent attitude. With His right to the creature He has vindicated and restored its own natural right. Himself becoming a creature, and attacking and overcoming that which offended Him, He has dealt with it as also an offence to His creature, and completely destroyed it. The cause which He assumed in the flesh as the Judge of sin was the cause of man as well. Thus the incarnation of His Word is the new and ultimate revelation of His grace, the ratification of the faithfulness which He pledged to the creature when He made it. It proves that His mercy is not conditional but unconditional, and that it cannot be reversed even by sin and nothingness. But all this is proved in His confrontation with sin and in the confrontation of sin with Himself as the One who is essentially the gracious God. Yet it is only in Jesus Christ and not in an abstract divine law, however founded and formulated, that we have a revelation of real sin, of its nature as real enmity against the grace of God, and of man's refusal of the gratitude natural to him. The sickness is disclosed with the cure. How else could we see it? As the grace of the covenant, i.e., as the requirement which results from the covenant established, maintained and fulfilled by Him, as the command imposed on us by God's faithfulness and mercy, the Law in this concrete form confers the knowledge of sin. It "worketh wrath" and "killeth" with the irrefutable verdict that the disobedience of man does not consist in imperfection but in guilt. If it were not the command of the gracious God, how could man be conscious of his guilt, indeed how could he be guilty at all? Why should he not justifiably plead the weakness of his humanity? But he cannot do this in face of the command of the gracious God, the God who is unconditionally for him, who from the very outset is his God and Father. He cannot do it in face of the command of [310] the God revealed in Jesus Christ. The command of the gracious God invalidates any such plea, convicting man of an opposition and resistance for which there can be no explanation, excuse or justification. This command which exposes the real nothingness served and effected by man is the command of Jesus Christ. No shifts or turns can alter the fact that without this objective ground of knowledge there can be no real insight in this matter, and the result will necessarily be some form of that major confusion.

The other material reason for strict adherence to this source of knowledge is as follows. We have called sin the concrete form of nothingness because in sin it becomes man's own act, achievement and guilt. Yet nothingness is not exhausted in sin. It is also something under which we suffer in a connexion with sin which is sometimes palpable but sometimes we can only sense and sometimes is closely bidden. In Holy Scripture, while man's full responsibility for its commission is maintained, even sin itself is described as his surrender to the alien power of an adversary. Contrary to his will and expectation, the sin of man is not beneficial to him but detrimental. He is led astray and harms himself, or rather lets himself be harmed. He is not merely a thief but one who has himself fallen among thieves. Sin as such is not only an offence to God; it also disturbs, injures and destroys the creature and its nature. And although there can be no doubt that it is committed by man, it is obviously attended and followed by suffering, i.e., the suffering of evil and death. It is not merely attended and followed by the ills which are inseparably bound up with creaturely existence in virtue of the negative aspect of creation, but by the suffering of evil as something wholly anomalous which threatens and imperils this existence and is no less inconsistent with it than sin itself, as the preliminary experience of an absolutely alien factor which is radically opposed to the sense and purpose of creation and therefore to the Creator Himself. Nor is it a mere matter of dying as the natural termination of life, but of death itself as the intolerable, life-destroying thing to which all suffering hastens as its goal, as the ultimate irruption and triumph of that alien power which annihilates creaturely existence and thus discredits and disclaims the Creator. There is real evil and real death as well as real sin. In another connexion it will fall to be indicated that there is also a real devil with his legions, and a real hell. But here it will suffice to recognise real evil and real death. "Real" again means in opposition to the totality of God's creation. That nothingness has the form of evil and death as well as sin shows us that it is what it is not only morally but physically and totally. It is the comprehensive negation of the creature and its nature. And as such it is a power which, though unsolicited and uninvited, is superior, like evil and death, to all the forces which the creature can oppose to it. As negation nothingness has its own dynamic, the dynamic of damage and destruction with which the creature cannot cope. Knowledge of these import- [311] ant features is attained when it is seen in these forms, i.e., the forms of evil and death. Evil and death may be distinguished from sin in so far as they primarily and immediately attack the creature but indirectly and properly the Creator, whereas sin primarily and immediately attacks God and only indirectly the creature. Yet both attack the creature no less than God. And it is also a common feature that they are necessarily incomprehensible and inexplicable to us as creatures. It is absolutely essential that nothingness should be seen in all these forms and aspects if we are to understand what is at issue and to what we refer.

But in this totality, in the form in which it is not merely evil but the supreme adversary and assailant, in the mode in which it must be suffered by the creature, nothingness is to be known only at the heart of the Gospel, i.e., in Jesus Christ. In the incarnation God exposed Himself to nothingness even as this enemy and assailant. He did so in order to repel and defeat it. He did so in order to destroy the destroyer. The Gospel records of the miracles and acts of

Jesus are not just formal proofs of His Messiahship, of His divine mission, authority and power, but as such they are objective manifestations of His character as the Conqueror not only of sin but also of evil and death, as the Destroyer of the destroyer, as the Saviour in the most inclusive sense. He not only forgives the sins of men; He also removes the source of their suffering. He resists the whole assault. To its power He opposes His own power, the transcendent power of God. He shows Himself to be the total Victor. He works as the perfect Comforter. This emphasis is unmistakeable in the New Testament, and if for any reason we erase it we necessarily annul its testimony and silence the voice of Him to whom it testifies. For here there not only speaks but acts the One who has come to hurl Himself against the opposition and resistance of nothingness in its form as hostile and aggressive power. Here there speaks and acts the One who for the salvation of the creature and the glory of God has routed nothingness as the total principle of enmity, physical as well as moral. He is not only the way and the truth; He is also the life, the resurrection and the life. If He were not the Saviour in this total sense. He would not be the Saviour at all in the New Testament sense. It is a serious matter that all the Western as opposed to the Eastern Church has invariably succeeded in minimising and devaluating, and still does so to-day, this New Testament emphasis. And Protestantism especially has always been far too moralistic and spiritualistic, and has thus been blind to this aspect of the Gospel. In this respect we have every cause to pay more attention rather than less. We certainly cannot afford to make arbitrary demarcations, and therefore not to see, or not to want to see, the total Saviour of the New Testament. According to the New Testament, the last and true form in which Jesus exposed Himself to this total enemy is that of His crucifixion. He did it by suffering death, this death, the death of condemnation. The New Testament says that He suffered death for the forgiveness of the sins of many, but it also says, and the two statements must not be dissociated, that He did so in order to take away the power of death, real death, death as the condemnation and destruction of the creature, death as the offender against God and the last enemy. In His resurrection from the dead God reveals that He has done this. His resurrection sums up the whole process of revelation. It is the manifestation of the divine act which according to the New Testament was effected in His work, the work of His person. According to this witness, it shows that His death is God's own reconciling and liberating act against nothingness, in all its scope and dimensions. But since this may be affirmed only of Him, only of the divine act which, according to the witness of the New Testament, was effected and revealed in Jesus Christ, from this standpoint too the only knowledge which includes a knowledge of true nothingness is that of Jesus Christ. In Him, i.e., in contradistinction to Him, nothingness is exposed in its entirety as the adversary which can destroy both body and soul in hell, as the evil one which is also the destructive factor of evil and death that stands in sinister conflict against the creature and its Creator, not merely as an idea which man may conceive and to which he can and does give allegiance

[312]

22

but as the power which invades and subjugates and carries him away captive, so that he is wholly and utterly lost in face of it. In the incarnation Jesus Christ, God Himself, has exposed Himself to this real nothingness. And He has proved Himself to be its Victor. In so doing He has disclosed and revealed its true nature and threat, its impotence against the creature, and its utter impotence against the Creator. This being the case, we have every reason to adhere to the truth that Jesus Christ Himself is the objective ground of our knowledge even of nothingness.

In dealing with this whole question of the objective ground of our knowledge of nothingness, I have been engaged in implicit controversy with the most significant literary work which has as yet been specifically devoted to this difficult theme. I refer to the famous book by the Halle theologian Julius Müller first published in 1838–44, *Die Christliche Lehre von der Sünde* (E.T. *The Christian Doctrine of Sin*, 2 Vols., 1885). In this work we have one of those phenomena in 19th-century Protestant theology which reflect a partial yet very definite movement in opposition to the general trend. J. Müller was of the view that there is a point at which contemporary Christian Monism, the synoptic view of God and the world, God and man and sin and redemption classically represented by Schleiermacher and Hegel, comes up against a frontier where it either ceases to be Christian or must cease to be monistic. Other theological individualists of the time found the same frontier at different points. Kohlbrügge found it in the problem of justification in Christ; the elder Blumhardt in that of Christian hope; Vilmar of Marburg in that of ecclesiastical order. But the specific point where Müller found it, where as a Christian theologian he felt obliged to employ Christian and not monistic categories, was the problem of sin. At this point he largely repudiated the widely adopted views and ideas of his time, accepting a Christian doctrine of evil only as a "conception of its inconceivability" (E.T. II, p. 172), only as the assertion of an utterly alien factor which is radically opposed and resistant to the nature of God and of man and their mutual relationship, for the existence of which man alone must bear responsibility, and the derivation and explanation of which from a higher principle are to be resolutely rejected. It is another matter that Müller does not remain wholly true to his own insight when in the second volume he introduces the curious theory of a "pre-temporal fall" of which the temporal reality of human sin must be regarded as a consequence or at least an epiphenomenon. But, as we shall see, it is difficult and even impossible to make any meaningful final or initial pronouncement on this alien and entirely negative reality without incurring the suspicion of covertly seeking to expound it in a "speculative" manner, incorporating it into a system and thus misrepresenting its nature. We may ignore these doubtful features in Müller's exposition in view of the fact that he so sharply perceived and propounded the problem itself, and that he was the first and only scholar of his day to do so. [313]

The implicit controversy with him in my own statement is in respect of the decisive and objective ground of knowledge normative in this question. Müller was a product of his age, and followed almost all earlier tradition, in accepting it as axiomatic and incontestable that the reality and nature of the factor which separates God and man can be established and discussed as it were in a vacuum, in the mere analysis of evident facts. His apparent rule is that, if we consider human existence in its psychological, sociological and historical reality, a little serious reflection will necessarily lead us to the conclusion that man is a sinner. The words with which he introduces his great exposition (I, p. 28) plainly characterise what he regards as a self-evident procedure: "It requires no special profundity of reflection but only a moderate degree of moral earnestness to prompt us thoughtfully to pause before one great phenomenon of human life, and ever and anon to turn towards it a scrutinizing look. I refer to the phenomenon of evil; the presence of an element of disturbance and discord in a sphere where the demand for harmony and unity is felt with peculiar emphasis. It meets us at every turn as the history of the human race in the course of its development passes before us; it betrays its presence in manifold forms when we fix our eyes upon the closest relationships of society; and we cannot hide from ourselves its reality when we look into our own hearts. It is a dark and dismal shadow, casting a gloom over every department of human life, and continually pervading its fairest and brightest forms." The lofty moral earnestness which like so many before and after him Müller exhibited in discussing this phenomenon is indubitable. He was deficient neither in deep and comprehensive insight into human reality nor in scrupulous consideration of earlier thought and opinion. In this regard the monograph he devoted to this unrewarding theme leaves nothing to be desired. On the contrary, the outstanding and enduring significance of his work is that he confronts this dark stain on the psychological, sociological and historical picture of man with greater thoughtfulness, perplexity and alarm, that he investigates and explores this sphere with greater thoroughness, and that he weighs and evaluates the dialectics and limitations of the various ancient and modern theories with greater exactitude, not only than his contemporaries, but also than most of the representatives of the earlier tradition. There is only one question which he apparently neither contemplates nor pursues. It is the radical question whether this dark stain can be so directly perceived, identified, analysed and assessed as though it were one phenomenon among others, or whether knowledge of this phenomenon is not a question of faith and therefore in the strict sense a theological question. Müller assumes the existence of sin as a matter of common knowledge, and he believes that a conscientious and comprehensive investigation and consideration must inevitably conduce to a knowledge of its nature. By this apparently direct approach he can come to the conviction that sin is that which stands in absolute opposition, and that as such it cannot have its source or justification either in the nature of God or in that of the creature or in their natural inter-relation, but can and must be understood only as man's evil act and guilt. Even before Müller, at the beginning of his *Religion within the Limits of Pure Reason* and on or even outwith the periphery of his own system, Kant claimed to be capable of demonstrating sin as a reality of this kind. He speaks, for example, of the "indwelling of the principle of evil alongside that of good." He refers to the evil which opposes good very differently from the way in which sensuousness opposes reason or folly wisdom. He says that its foundation is not inherent in the natural instincts of man, but in the "malice of the human heart." He speaks of the "bias" towards evil; of the "inscrutable reason for the acceptance of unlawful maxims"; of the corruption of the loftiest subjective ground of all maxims which is characteristic of man and his whole species, which in its way is just as much a matter of his freedom as of his obedience to the law, and for which he is responsible. He speaks of "radical evil." Kant does not state the source of his knowledge of this curious, perverted "freedom." Probably he would not have called it a "phenomenon," as Müller does. But he assumes that this perverted freedom is as patient of direct perception as true freedom, the freedom for good. And this is also the view of Müller. The remarkable accuracy of their main thesis invites the conjecture that perhaps their only failure is not to see that they actually accept the Christian insight and look from the heart of the Gospel. Since even a theologian like Müller was guilty of a radical failure at this point, and could not exploit all the possibilities offered, there are inevitably some serious gaps and weaknesses in his investigation and presentation.

[314]

1. He did, of course, try to understand evil as "absolutely alien and repugnant to our nature, to whose existence no higher standpoint and no clearer perception can ever reconcile us" (I, p. 30), so that we can only explain and acknowledge it as our guilt. In this respect, contrary to the prevalent trend of his age, he formally returned to the fundamentals of the Reformation and older Protestant theology. But when asked: "Whence knowest thou thy

misery?", older Protestant theology could give a plain answer like that of the *Heidelberg Catechism*: "From the Law of God" (*Qu.* 3). Müller, too, refers at once to the Law, but for him it is only the idea of human life as voluntarily conditioned, so that the impression made upon an unbiassed mind is necessarily that of transcendent majesty. It is the "moral law," and in opposition to it evil is revealed as the deviation and perversion of the actual orientation of the will. "In this sense" (I, p. 43) he then seeks to apprehend what the Bible calls Law, sin and the knowledge of sin. But Müller does not make clear that the Bible speaks of the Accuser and Judge who transcends and confronts man, of God the Lawgiver (Christ according to the *Heidelberg Catechism, Qu.* 4) whose judgment reveals sin as sin and whose Word compels man to acknowledge himself a sinner. Therefore, although Müller's intrinsically correct assertions concerning the absolute enmity of sin and man's responsibility for its commission are impressive and important, they remain mere assertions and no more. They lack the authority which such exceptional declarations require and which alone can give weight to such unusual intelligence concerning the reality of this alien element. We can only surmise and suppose that both Müller and Kant based their theses on postulates which they suppress but which would give them the strict validity that a mere reference to the "moral law" is quite unable to do. However emphatic Müller's presentation and defence of his view, the result may simply be to estrange, as happened in the case of Goethe when confronted by Kant's assertion of "radical evil."

2. Conversely, Müller was only too faithful to the general trend of older Protestant theology in failing to understand the Law which reveals sin in the light of the Gospel. He con [315] ceived of it as a stark abstract imperative rather than the Law of the covenant and grace. And it was in the light of this imperative that he then showed sin to be disobedience to God, selfishness, worldly affection etc., and finally guilt. He did not ask, however, how far God and man are so related that this imperative is reasonable, possible and necessary, and its nonobservance is abhorrent and absurd. He was thus unable to show the true incomprehensibility, iniquity and culpability of sin. He was unable to show that sin is no mere formal but a material transgression, that it is not the breach of a high and difficult but a near and easy command—the requirement of the gratitude which is natural to man because the God who requires it is beside him, is covenanted to him in His mercy, has identified Himself with him and has freed and bound him to do His will. Müller was unable to show that it is the goodness of God which makes His Law binding on man, and therefore makes sin abhorrent as a loathsome product of nothingness. He was unable to show the invalidity of the familiar excuse that God is too exalted and his command too excessive and extraordinary for man in his frailty to fulfil it. He was unable to show the fact and extent that even as a sinner man is still indebted to the Law (i.e., in virtue of God's faithfulness), or that this is not so much a threat as a promise. He persisted in the dialectic of Law and sin, which, if they were based on a genuine understanding of the Epistles to the Romans and the Galatians, could only lead to the conclusion that Paul's experience on the road to Damascus did not consist in a manifestation of Christ but in a revelation of the Old Testament Law as understood by the Pharisees—the very thing from which Paul assures us again and again that he was then delivered. Müller completely obscured the fact that only the sweetness of the Old and New Testament Gospel and its command can make man conscious of the bitterness of his transgression, whereas a command which is wrongly called bitter, and is thus godless from the biblical standpoint, may certainly embitter man against an unknown and exalted God, but cannot reveal to him his personal bitterness, the bitterness of his transgression.

3. Again in agreement with theological tradition, at any rate in the West, Müller did not realise that human sin is not an isolated phenomenon but only one important aspect of the fundamental phenomenon of nothingness. Among the older theologians Polanus (*Synt. Theol. chr.*, 1609, VI, 7) was an exception when he devoted a special treatise to the *malum*

afflictionis[EN17], and even placed it before his discussion of the *malum peccati et culpae*[EN18]. In Müller the question of the *malum afflictionis*, of evil and death, arises only in connexion with the judgment and punishment of sin. He does not really seem to see anything but the *malum peccati et culpae*. For him the New Testament accounts of the acts of Jesus on behalf of the sick, the bewildered, the hungry, the dying and even the dead, and indeed the resurrection of Jesus Himself, seem to have no significance. It seems never to have occurred to him that in the physical evil concealed behind the shadowy side of the created cosmos we have a form of the enemy and no less an offence against God than that which reveals man to be a sinner. Hence Müller was incapable of any serious recognition of the power of this adversary of of this adversary as a power. He was entirely unaffected by the discovery made in this matter by the elder Blumhardt in his own lifetime. He thus restricted his monograph to the doctrine of sin. Nor could it have been otherwise. When the total Saviour and perfect Comforter is not the primary source of knowledge, it cannot be expected that there will be knowledge of the full misery of the creature, or of the absolute negation which is the source of this misery.

There are, of course, excuses for Müller, particularly in respect of the second and third points, for neither his contemporaries nor the authoritative tradition in which he stood had anything better to offer, and in his attempt to understand sin as a given factor apart from Jesus Christ he was simply following the general tendency. If I dissociate myself from Müller in his attempt and the resultant inferences I do so because he does not go to the heart of the matter, because one might have expected a new and better approach to the basis and to these three questions in view of the material accuracy of his main thesis, and because his conclusions especially show that a new and better approach is imperative.

[316]

We shall now consider some of the most important of the historically influential theories which we have implicitly rejected in our discussion. And first we must recall the mighty figure of G. W. Leibniz (cf. *C.D.*, III, 1, p. 388 ff.), who in his *Theodicy* and kindred works elaborates the following view of this matter. To the absolutely perfect God as the being who is self-consistent and who integrates in Himself absolute wisdom, power, freedom and goodness, there corresponds in perfection, although a relative perfection, this actual world of ours which, created and governed by Him, has been selected from an infinite range and is thus the best of all possible worlds. Yet while this is the case, and in this sense it is relatively perfect, the world still presents us with a problem. In short, it confronts us with the fact of metaphysical evil, and more extensively with the facts of physical suffering, moral evil, and death. These facts are as such incontrovertible. Yet they do not constitute a final or insoluble enigma, but one which is patient of satisfactory explanation.

The explanation offered is as follows. Metaphysical evil, as the sum and source of all others, is simply the essential non-divinity of the creature. That the divinely created world is the best possible world does not exclude but includes this imperfection, for the world is not God. God could not endow the world with absolute perfection except by making it another god. He has really blessed the creature and endowed it with an appropriate perfection by refraining from performing what is impossible for Himself. Thus the creature is perfect within the limitations of its non-divinity. If this non-divinity entails imperfection, this merely consists in creaturely limitation. It is not, then, a positive evil, nor should it be described as evil but only as a deficiency or "privation" proper to the creature. Privation is so conjoined by God to creaturely perfection as not to diminish but rather to augment it. The possible and actual evils of sorrow, sin and death proceed from this necessary metaphysical evil (which is not really an evil) and are explicable in like terms.

Sorrow is the pain which is no less unavoidable to the human spirit than pleasure, because

---

[EN17] evil of suffering
[EN18] evil of sin and error

the spirit is what it is only in conjunction with a material body and therefore, in conjunction with its perfection, shares all the positive and negative sensations of this body. Sorrow is meted out to human life and individual persons in accordance with the innate excellence and salutary benevolence of the cosmic order. It may be a just punishment or more generally a profitable educational process. But reason and patience will always make it essentially endurable. And in any case, in relation to the total realisation of the world order, there are more and greater grounds for pleasure than for pain, for joy than sorrow. As a later poet sang: "Hand in hand joy and woe, Together down the ages go." Finally, it must be said of sorrow that it is merely a partial and passing privation in the intrinsically though relatively perfect cosmic order governed by the absolutely perfect God. In the light of this, we must realise that sorrow is supportable even when and where we cannot understand its wider setting or see how it is to be endured in any particular instance.

The case is ultimately the same with moral evil and therefore with sin. God has made man capable of sin. He had to do so, for otherwise He would have deprived him of free will, thus denying him his spiritual and moral nature and therefore his distinctive perfection. Evil arises because the limitation innate in the creature emerges also in the region of the will. Naturally God does not will this. He does not will that man should sin. He does not cause or compel him to do so. Leibniz did not teach a necessity of sin in this sense. Yet God allows man to sin, and He does so in His beneficence. Man could not be a free and reasonable creature, living dutifully and to the glory of God; he could not be the man whom the grace of God encounters and assists, if he were not a creature which can and does sin. Grounded in the innate imperfection of the creature, sin is likewise conjoined with its creaturely or relative perfection. This is possible because it, too, is in itself a mere privation which is not grounded in a *causa efficiens*[EN19] but only in a *causa deficiens*[EN20], only in the defective clarity of our conception and the defective certainty of our decisions, or again only in a natural inertia, so that the good and bad attributes and actions of men may be likened to a number of boats which, though conveyed by the same current (that of the divine activity), still move downstream at greatly differing rates because they carry different weights of cargo and therefore the force of inertia inhibits their motion to varying degrees. But again, the relationship between sin and creaturely perfection is an actual one because there can and must be sin within the context of the whole. Without the possibility of sin there could be no creaturely good. By its inexcusable and culpable committal it necessarily serves to augment the sum total of good in the creaturely order in a way which would otherwise be impossible. If this specific man did not now commit this specific sin, the whole world order would be entirely different. It would no longer be this real order which is the best. God Himself, its Creator and Governor, would then necessarily be different, and could not be the absolutely perfect being. This means that it is indispensable that God should create and posit the possibility of sin and allow its realisation.

[317]

The case is also finally the same with death. For individual souls and their physical organisms subsist eternally, and are therefore indestructible. At the beginning of life there is expansion, and at its end merely contraction. Hence the latter, and consequently death, is merely a passing privation, an unfortunate compression of life, the disintegration of a distinct and notable function of the living creature. Yet the creature survives this transformation both in soul and body, and thus attains to a new life. Hence even in death there is no real disruption or disintegration of the continuity of creaturely existence, so that even on the ground of mortality no rational objection may be raised to the perfection of the created world.

[EN19] efficient cause
[EN20] lack of any cause

Now it must be allowed that Leibniz' view has an obvious advantage over those of a critic like J. Müller and most other theologians. It is universal, and does not restrict itself to the moral problem but tries to take a loftier synoptic view of sin, evil and death and therefore to understand the whole of what we mean by nothingness. In this sense the *Theodicy* might be regarded as a masterly Western representation of the Eastern conception. But unfortunately this is its only praiseworthy characteristic.

For it would be a mistake (cf. *C.D.*, III, 1, p. 406 ff.) to think that, though Leibniz is obviously guilty of confusing nothingness with the intracosmic antithesis or negative side of creation, he is at least right in relation to this negative aspect, so that his doctrine is illuminating and useful in our approach to this preliminary problem. The fact remains that, even if his doctrine is applied only to the preliminary problem, it necessarily results in a repudiation and abrogation of the antithesis, i.e., in the absorption or at least the assimilation of the negative aspect of creation by the positive. The negative side becomes the mere periphery of the positive. This is of a piece with the fact that there is in Leibniz' system no adequate criterion by which to establish that which opposes it, namely, the "perfection" which is obviously the positive aspect. There is clear lack of a higher principle by which to select, decide and discriminate between the two, and therefore to say an unequivocal Yes which includes and expresses but also overcomes and transcends the unequivocal No. For Leibniz' concept of God is a resplendent reflection of the strong human self-sufficiency which later found even more massive expression in the philosophy of Hegel. But it is no more than this. It does not describe the real God who is the Lord of creation but the man who aspires to be. Yet this man cannot even visualize the intracosmic antithesis. The man who conceives this idea of God, or rather this idea of his own self-sufficiency, and who with the help of it considers and judges the perfection and imperfection of God's creation, is a spectator and observer of God and His creation, and even of himself. He is not a properly cited and sworn witness to the truth. Clarity to distinguish between the right and the left, and positive perception that this is essential, are lacking in his vision and judgment. That is why even in the region of this preliminary problem Leibniz' *Theodicy* cannot be an adequate instrument.

[318]

Yet the *Theodicy* makes an even greater claim. It purports to offer an explanation of real sin, evil and death, and therefore of real nothingness. Confusing it with the twofold aspect of the world, it has in view the antithesis in which God and the totality of the world created by Him stand on the one side and the counterpart of both on the other. It could be conceded that Leibniz had this counterpart in view and in his own fashion took it seriously. We can as little contest this as that in formulating his concept of God and of the world he had God and His creation in view and was anxious to magnify them both to the best of his ability. But from the Christian standpoint it is impossible to say that the adversary is in any sense recognisable in Leibniz' exposition. With what may be described as a truly fantastic thoroughness the great Leibniz successfully undertook to domesticate the adversary. This domestication is such that the wolf not only dwells with the lamb, as depicted in Is. 11[6], but actually becomes a lamb. There can be no thought of redemption or liberation, since there is nothing or no one from whom the created world needs to be redeemed and liberated. Again, there is no place for a reconciliation of the world with God, since the peace between them has never been broken. The decisive concept of privation makes this clear. He took it from Augustine: *malum est privatio boni*[EN21]. Augustine used the term quite correctly to define the purely negative character of evil, i.e., the nullity of sin, evil and death, its nature as opposition both intrinsically and in relation to God and His creature. For Augustine privation is *corruptio* or *conversio boni*[EN22]. It is not only the absence of what really is, but the assault upon it. Evil is

---

[EN21] evil is a privation of the good
[EN22] corruption or inversion of the good

related to good in such a way that it attacks and harms it. It seeks to destroy and consume it, *tendit ad non esse*[EN23], as the fire threatens to consume fuel, and is in process of doing so. It is another matter whether evil has the power to succeed, whether good is actually destructible as that which really is. Augustine rightly replies in the negative. Nevertheless, evil in its relationship with good has this aggressive and hostile character. But when Leibniz took over the Augustinian concept, privation became in fact mere negation; the creaturely imperfection which consists in the fact that the creature is a creature and not God, and does not therefore possess the divine attributes. Because of this essential metaphysical imperfection, the creature may be and is subject to suffering, sin and death. But this metaphysical imperfection is natural to the creature. There can thus be no question of disruption, deprivation and corruption, and therefore of privation in the Augustinian sense. Anxiety, fear and especially despair, are superfluous in face of what is natural to the creature as such. And Leibniz consistently and necessarily proceeded yet a stage further on his chosen path when he saw in the negation to which the creature is subject one of the determinations of its perfection. For him evil is so related to good that it is only a particular form of good, not opposing, disrupting or threatening it, but rendering it an indispensable service, contributing to it as the necessary vacuum which permits its fuller expansion, the indispensable darkness which it needs to shine forth as light. For Leibniz nothingness cannot have the character of true nothingness in the sense of that which has been and is thus consistently to be rejected, of a danger to be constantly shunned and avoided, of an awful thing to be continually deplored. It cannot be real nothingness. For as sorrow it is only passing and partial pain, as evil only deficient intellectual perspicuity and power of moral decision, as death only the transition of a being intrinsically indestructible from one state of existence to another. Under all these aspects it is something which is necessarily allowed by God and may and must therefore be [319] accepted by us. Hence only a limited dejection, opposition and resistance are legitimate in face of it. For Leibniz it cannot have the character of an originating and active force. For it is not just nothingness but nothing, i.e., the absence of something, the absence of divine perfection, and therefore pain, the lack of good, and in the form of death a mighty contraction of creaturely existence, but not its destruction or extinction. It neither owns nor effects anything; it is merely a deficiency. It neither has nor is a destructive, extinguishing or consuming energy. It has no position from which it can rebel against God and invade the world and establish "negative positions." It is purposeless and immobile. It cannot affront God. It cannot conquer or capture any one, enslave or victimise any one. It had absolutely no function. It has merely the force of inertia, so that the more heavily laden boats are conveyed by the same stream with less momentum than those whose load is lighter. Yet individually all these boats proceed in the same direction. It is not to be gainsaid that we do have here a feeble echo of the biblical message that God has brought to nought all the powers opposed to Him and His creation. But how faint and easily misheard this echo when the reference is to a powerless nothing which God cannot fight and overcome as a real enemy! How trite and jejune is that which in the New Testament is not at all self-evident but a costly reality and truth! Nothingness as understood by Leibniz cannot even be set aside or removed. For in spite of the use of the term it is not real privation at all but merely a necessary negation which is innate in the created world and therefore intrinsic to its perfection, which is not, and is not to be rejected, which has neither initiative nor function, neither power nor potency. A defeat of this nothing in the sense of its abolition by the Creator and the creature's liberation from it is not only unnecessary but even impossible. Its defeat in the sense of its abolition would mean that the creature becomes God and partakes of His absolute perfection, thus losing its own nature and therefore its own perfection. The most that can be

---

[EN23] it pushes it toward non-existence

considered and is actually entertained by Leibniz in this respect is only an infinite approximation to the abolition of creaturely imperfection. It is in this sense that he defines the created spirit as the "*asymptote* of the Godhead." Creaturely bliss presumably consists in the *progressus infinitus*[EN24] of this approximation. For it is clear that according to Leibniz what awaits us beyond death will not be a new life in the sense that the creature is no longer involved in the metaphysical imperfection natural to non-divine being and therefore ceases to carry within itself the seeds of suffering, evil and further death. Since man is an *asymptote* of the Godhead and the process of approximation is infinite, the consoling truth to which he may cling will be the same to all eternity, namely, that he must always be imperfect, and that his imperfection is necessary to his perfection. It is particularly clear at this point that the question whether or not nothingness is rightly understood is not in any sense peripheral but basically affects our understanding of the positive truth concerning the relationship between Creator and creature. Those who like Leibniz convert nothingness into something positive—and in this respect Leibniz is the classic representative of the many lesser men who followed him—need not be surprised if they can perceive and understand what is really positive only in the strange relativity to nothingness which characterises it in Leibniz' great exposition.

In further illustration of what we must repudiate we select the doctrine developed in §§65–85 of his *Glaubenslehre* (E.T. *The Christian Faith*, 1928) by F. E. D. Schleiermacher. These sections belong to the second main part of his work, in which he discusses religious self-consciousness antithetically determined as a consciousness of sin and grace. They constitute a sub-division on "the first aspect of the antithesis," namely, the "explication of the consciousness of sin," and are succeeded by a contrasting discussion of "the second aspect of the antithesis," namely, the "explication of the consciousness of grace."

[320] Since even our statements about sin have their source in our immediate self-consciousness, "which as the truth of our being cannot be in contradiction with itself" (§ 65), we must assume from the very outset that, whatever else may have to be said, there can be only an apparent contradiction between man's innate disposition to God-consciousness and the resultant statements concerning the eternity, omnipresence, omnipotence and omniscience of God and the original perfection of the world and man on the one hand, and what must be said about sin and consequent evil on the other. For seen from the standpoint of the consciousness of grace sin is simply that "which would not be unless redemption was to be" (§ 65). The crucial point with which we are confronted in Schleiermacher's teaching is the resolution of this "apparent antinomy."

What is sin? Schleiermacher's answer is that it is a particular determination of our self-consciousness by our God-consciousness, namely, the determination in which we are conscious of the relative impotence or obstruction of our God-consciousness, or, in other words, of the obstruction of the determinative power of the "spirit" by the continuing independence of the sensuous functions, of the incapacity of the "spirit" in relation to the "flesh," or of the more rapid development of our insight as compared with our willpower in relation to our God-consciousness. God-consciousness itself determines our self-consciousness as the consciousness of this condition as pain. It must thus be said at once that consciousness of sin never exists in the soul of the Christian without the consciousness of the power of redemption (§ 66). The awakening of God-consciousness in us renders us conscious of sin as resistance to it. But even prior to this awakening this resistance germinates in us, and to this extent it takes precedence of our God-consciousness. Yet just as a trace of sin-consciousness lurks in even the most exalted moments of religious experience as awakened God-consciousness, conversely the sinful condition anterior to the awakening of our God-

---

[EN24] unending development

consciousness presupposes an original perfection not abrogated by it. Moreover, the awakening of our God-consciousness, at all events in its Christian form as the knowledge of the absolute sinlessness and perfect spiritual power of the Redeemer, includes the assurance that the end of its development is sinless human perfection. From both standpoints sin must be conceived of as a derangement of human nature but no more (§§ 67–68). It offers a twofold aspect. We experience it both as our dependence on the form given to life by preceding generations, and therefore as "original sin," and also as our own self-grounded act, and therefore as "actual sin" (§ 69).

In its first form as "hereditary" or "original sin" it is universal human "sinfulness," i.e., the total incapacity for good which is prior to every act of the individual and which is thus grounded outside his being and can be removed only by the influence of redemption. "Incapacity for good" does not signify incapacity to appropriate redemption, as though man were born without human nature. It means incapacity to develop or even to desire the state of complete and victorious God-consciousness which is the goal of the process of redemption (§ 70). In this first form sin is not only already accepted and admitted but committed by every individual. His sinfulness perpetuates itself in his will and is thus his guilt. But in the first form sin is also the "corporate act and corporate guilt of the human race." Thus it is "in each the work of all, and in all the work of each." Every man sins in and with his own generation, and "what appears as the congenital sinfulness of one generation is conditioned by the sinfulness of the previous one, and in turn conditions that of the later." In this first form, therefore, consciousness of sin is a "corporate feeling," and is thus connected with the consciousness of the universal need of redemption (§ 71). The question how this universal sinfulness originated is irrelevant. It certainly did not originate in an alteration in human nature in our first parents, for it is surely inconceivable that "to such an extent God should have made the destiny of the whole human race contingent upon a single moment, the fortune of which rested with two inexperienced individuals who, moreover, never dreamt of [321] its having any such importance." This sinfulness must rather have been present along with original perfection in our first parents as the presupposition of their sinful act, as the "idiosyncrasies" of sex were already present in them and they were subject to "changes of mood" (§ 72).

In its second form sin is the sinful act, or "actual sin," which, beginning with a sensuous appetite or sloth, derives in all men from that universal sinfulness. In some individuals the first form of sin is more predominant, in others the second, but apart from redemption no individual is wholly secured against any of its forms (§ 73). All sins rank equal as manifestations of universal sinfulness and momentary or partial victories of the flesh over the spirit, though the power of the God-consciousness obstructed in them and the force of the external attraction to sin and occasion for it can be greater or less. But involved in all forms of sin is the reciprocal action of a predominant desire or sloth and a vitiation of the God-consciousness. A real distinction of degree between different sins only arises because man's relationship to redemption may be positive or negative. In the first case the sin committed is venial, being already broken, shadowy, impotent, and no longer dominant but waning, while in the second it is the "sin of the unregenerate" and will grow and rule, consolidating and extending itself, though it must always be remembered that here, too, it will never occur without a deeper or fainter shadow of the good, without "an acquiescent presentiment or imagining of a state free from inner conflict" (§ 74).

Nothing could properly be reckoned as evil if there were no sin. It is sin alone, the repression of the God-consciousness, which destroys the harmony between originally perfect man and the originally perfect world, and makes an evil of those aspects of the world which limits man's spatial and temporal existence. If there were no sin, what we know as "natural" evil, e.g., disease, or "social" evil, i.e., the obstruction imposed by one man on the life of another, might well be understood partly as inevitable imperfection and partly as incentive to future control of natural forces and intensive amelioration of the social order (§ 75). Since it is because of sin that they both seem to be evils, they are its direct and indirect punishments (§ 76). But sin and evil involve the whole structure of corporate human life, so that the evils experienced by an individual must not be traced back directly to his sins as their cause (§ 77). The godly resignation which endures "evil" on account of its connexion with sin will necessarily include and not exclude resistance to sin as the cause of evil, together with practical measures in the realm of nature and society (§ 78).

Even as we trace the annulment of sin by redemption to the divine causality, so we are bound to ascribe attributes to God in virtue of which even sin, not in abstract isolation but in so far as redemption from it is due to Him, is ordained by Him as its author (§ 79). To be sure, God is the author of sin in a very different way from what He is of redemption. Yet there is no doubt that we know the power of the God-consciousness and therefore of redemption only in co-existence with our continuing incapacity for good, so that we can understand the good will of God only if we conceive of the sin which yields before grace as posited in it and therefore by God. Both these points must be seen and stated. The practical interest of religion in the integrity of the divine will must be conserved no less than its theoretical interest in the divine omnipotence (§ 80). It is to be particularly noted that even sin does not entail a complete cessation of the God-consciousness, that even in sinful nature evil is always accompanied by good, that no moment is entirely pervaded by sin. Why should not the limitation of grace, and therefore sin, be grounded in the same divine will as its impartation? Why should not the shortcoming in us, and again therefore sin, be grounded in God's efficient as distinct from His commanding will (§ 81, 1)? Sin could not be grounded in human freedom if it had no divine causality. Sin, too, is posited with free self-development and therefore in virtue of the divine ordination, just as it proceeds as man's guilt from the universal sinfulness that is part and parcel of the principle of his individual will (§ 81, 2). Purely from the standpoint of God and His omnipotence, there is no divine causality of sin; it simply does not exist for God. But in so far as the consciousness of sin is a true element in our being, and to that extent sin is a reality for us, it is ordained by God as that which makes redemption necessary. It comes from God, not only in the form of the sensuous natural impulse which rests on divine causality and with the ascendancy of which it gains an entry, not only in the form of the God-consciousness which rests on the same divine causality and which yields before it, and not only in the form of the weakness of this God-consciousness, but also in the sense that, although the God-consciousness is impotent in face of the sensuous impulse, to the extent that it is effected in us by God as the recognition of His commanding will, and as the consciousness of this will, it negates this impotence and thus makes it sin to us. It is due to God's decree that "the continually imperfect triumph of the spirit should become sin in us," a state of weakness which must be transcended, a state of opposition which must be annulled, a state which ought not to be, and must therefore end. Is sin not to be attributed to the divine causality merely on the ground that it is a negation? It has this in common with all finite nature, which is as such a blending of being and not-being but even in its not-being rests on the efficient will of God. Or is it not of God because it does not correspond to the divine will which commands the good? But it has this in common with all the good undoubtedly effected by God, in which there are always elements of evil and yet it is no less the work of God. Only if sin were an absolute contradiction of the commanding will of God, and thus utterly annulled this will in us, would it be impossible to think of the efficient will of God in relation to it. But the commanding will of God still remains within us, and it is by this that the weakness of our God-consciousness is made sin, and sin is thus ordained by God (§ 81, 3), but with a view to the redemption in whose light it cannot even be regarded as injurious,

[322]

since "the merely gradual and imperfect unfolding of the power of the God-consciousness is one of the necessary conditions of the human stage of existence" (§ 81, 4).

What has been said concerning the divine causality with regard to sin also applies to evil in virtue of its connexion with sin. The notion that the entrance of sin caused a pejorative change in the physical world is, of course, "fantastic." But the religious self-consciousness advances two equally essential propositions. We must ascribe evil to ourselves as the consequence of our sins, and therefore not to God as the Author of the original perfection of the world. And we must acquiesce in all the evils of life as an expression of a divine decree passed upon us, seeing them so far as possible in relation to the atoning sufferings of Christ. When viewed in this light they cease to be evils for us, but become calls and incentives to a spiritual activity to be embraced with joy. An "origin in God" is obviously to be ascribed to evil itself in its relationship to sin. Evil too, to the extent that like sin it is grounded in our freedom, is ordained of God. In the measure in which God-consciousness is not yet dominant in us, and we are doers of the "corporate action" of evil, we must regard natural and social imperfections as evils and share in "corporate suffering" (§ 82).

The holiness and righteousness of God are to be understood as the divine attributes which correspond to our consciousness of God as the Author of sin and evil, as the modes of the divine causality in this particular respect (§82 postscript).

The holiness of God is the "divine causality through which conscience is found conjoined with the need of redemption." It is the conscience by which, as already described, a certain state is made sin for us as our own act. Conscience is the voice of the commanding will of God within us. It is thus "the sole and whole causality which sin as such implies." Conscience is related to man's need of redemption, and is therefore to be ascribed to the whole human race for which redemption is ordained through Christ. Yet it is also related to redemption itself, for it is through conscience as consciousness of their incapacity that men are held for [323] and to redemption. Conscience can cease to exist only in a consciousness in which the will is perfectly at one with the God-consciousness, which means that Christ Himself can have had a conscience only in the form of fellow-feeling and not as something personally His own. Through the operation of God's holiness, conscience belongs to the human consciousness as antithetically determined by grace and sin. As it appears in corporate life, it is identical with the moral law. The holiness of God, in so far as it is effectual in man as grace, redemption and the power of God-consciousness, is man's displeasure at his own sin as effectuated by means of conscience and law. But if God's holiness is also directly apprehended as His own absolute displeasure at sin, it inevitably follows that sin cannot exist or be a divine thought as the object of the divine displeasure opposed to the good. Thus there is no reality nor idea of sin. For finite being cannot generate sin of itself. Therefore sin as a real antithesis to the good has no existence at all, and strictly speaking our displeasure at sin as effected by God is merely our displeasure at the fact that the effective power of the Godconsciousness falls short of the clearness of the apprehension it gives us (§ 83).

The righteousness of God is the divine causality through which, in the state of universal sinfulness, a connexion is ordained between evil and actual sin. At this point Schleiennacher understands by God's righteousness only His retributive or punitive justice. This justice consists in the fact that the whole constitution of the world, to the extent that evil is also conditioned in it, is related in a particular way to the sin grounded in human freedom, and that this relationship is also present in our consciousness in such a manner that all sin, corporate as well as individual, is reflected in evil, and evil is explained by sin. In this sense evil is the operation of God's punitive justice, but the latter has nothing to do with retribution for an offence. "What has all along been preached, sometimes with apparent profundity, regarding the mysterious nature of the divine wrath and the fundamental necessity of divine retribution cannot be made clear to the mind." God's ordination of evil as an activity of divine justice is simply the preservation of man with a view to a future strengthening of the God-consciousness : "the object being to prevent his dominant sensuous tendencies from meanwhile attaining complete mastery through mere unchecked habits." But as a real opposition to the original perfection of the world, evil cannot exist at all. Divine holiness and justice are both essential elements in our God-consciousness, for we can know the absolute power and predominance of the latter only as we know the state and culpability of sin as removed by redemption (§ 84).

On the other hand, Schleiermacher holds that the concept of divine mercy is more appropriate to the language of preaching and poetry than to that of dogmatic theology. The reason is that this concept speaks of "a state of feeling specially evoked by the sufferings of others, and finding outlet in acts of relief." Being definitely anthropopathic, it cannot be applied to God without bringing Him under the antithesis of the agreeable and disagreeable. In any case, we do not speak of mercy in a close fellowship such as that between father and children, and therefore the object of God's mercy cannot be those who are already enjoying their part in redemption. Finally, mercy could mean "the repression of jealousy by compassion," and therefore "readiness to remit punishment." But apart from the fact that God is neither wrathful nor jealous, the punishment in question is ordered by the divine justice. Mercy would have to begin where justice ceased and *vice versa*, "a relation that cannot subsist between divine attributes." In short this concept cannot be used in relation to sin and evil and the divine being and attitude towards them (§ 85).

Schleiermacher's doctrine of sin and evil has been frequently and severely criticised. Older writers such as K. Rosenkranz, J. Müller and W. Bender reduced it to shreds, and E. Brunner has condemned it outright. It is true that his teaching is untenable as a whole and thus contains much that is obscure and artificial. His answer to the problem of nothingness is no more satisfactory than that of Leibniz. But it is also true that merely to indicate the failings of his teaching is insufficient. A careful study of his doctrine is rewarding, though this may not be apparent after the destructive criticism to which it has been subjected. In certain respects this destructive criticism was unjustified, for his teaching (like that of Leibniz) has certain definite and positive merits. Once these are recognised, we can still reject it, and the reasons for our rejection will be better understood. I shall begin by mentioning some of the points in Schleiermacher's teaching which have been most unjustly criticised.

[324]

We cannot object that what he calls sin is only the consciousness of sin, and therefore no true reality. Schleiermacher's procedure was to examine and expound the religious self-consciousness of the Christian. He was unable to avoid the perils of this procedure, but it must not be disregarded that his doctrine might well be adapted and developed in a very different direction as a theology of the subjective reality and possibility of revelation which is not exclusive but inclusive of its objective reality and potentiality—a theology which, beginning with man, is intended as a theology of the Holy Spirit. To be sure, Schleiermacher himself did not regard his theology of the consciousness in this way but viewed it wholly subjectively as an historical exposition of specific states, the inner religious states of the Christian. These were for him realities as such. Grace was real as the consciousness of grace, and he attributed a definite reality to sin as the consciousness of sin. For him sin had reality within the framework of his theology of consciousness—and therefore not as it should and would have done if he had realised that the grace which confronts it in objective transcendence is the grace of God in Jesus Christ, and that therefore sin is opposition to God. Yet it is not to be denied that, within the limitation of his purely subjective examination of Christian consciousness, sin was for him a reality. His error is not that he confounded sin with consciousness of sin, but that he failed to interpret the Christian self-consciousness first as a consciousness of grace and then of sin, in the antithesis in which grace and sin manifest themselves in the work of the Holy Spirit in man as a subjectivisation of the objective Word of God, or, if we must use the term, in the "Christian self-consciousness." He was thus unable to exhibit the peculiar reality of sin, for he was unable to exhibit the reality of grace. But it must not be denied that he did exhibit as a reality that which he was able to apprehend as sin in contradistinction to grace.

Moreover, the common charge cannot be sustained that he equated sin with sensuality ("beloved sensuality," Rosenkranz), as the essence of the natural appetites in opposition to the higher spiritual life of man; or that he erroneously identified sensuality with the Pauline concept of "flesh," thus overlooking the fact not only that sensuality is not intrinsically sinful, but also that the higher spiritual as well as the natural being of man is involved in sin. For sensuality as Schleiermacher understands it is not only man's specifically natural impulses, but the whole of his being or consciousness including his capacity and activity of mind and will, in so far as it may be distinguished as his world-consciousness from his God-consciousness. And what he calls sin is world-consciousness as opposed to God-consciousness, for which he here employs the Pauline term "spirit." This is certainly rather confusing, since by "spirit" he usually understands the higher spiritual life which is here classified in the category of sensuality or world-consciousness. World-consciousness is to be regarded as sinful, and therefore called "flesh" in the Pauline sense, to the extent that it dissociates itself from God-consciousness (the Pauline "spirit") and thus opposes it instead of being governed and pervaded by it. Sin is sensuality paramount and predominant but— because will is outstripped by knowledge—inwardly divided. It is world-consciousness evading or resisting the majesty and claim of God-consciousness or spirit, and therefore falling into disorder and becoming flesh. Augustine had already portrayed sin in this way. And even in Schleiermacher sin is definitely not identical with sensuality, i.e., with world-consciousness [325] as such. In view of his plain assertions in this respect, and of his basic dialectics of nature and spirit, the physical and the ethical, it is rather surprising that any other opinion can ever have been entertained.

Again, it cannot be that for Schleiermacher sin merely consists in the fact that man is "not yet spirit," or that it is "nature which is not yet spirit." According to the presuppositions of Schleiermacher, it is impossible that nature should ever become spirit, for this would entail the transformation of man's world-consciousness into pure God-consciousness. But Schleiermacher's ideal of human consciousness is not pure God-consciousness or purely spiritual being. It is world-consciousness governed, pervaded, filled and fashioned by God-consciousness, i.e., world-consciousness with all the attributes and tokens of God-consciousness. His concern is that man should cease to be "flesh," i.e., to be implicated in his world-consciousness, in that opposition to God-consciousness. According to Schleiermacher, sin is man's continuing implication in this opposition.

Again, it is wrong to attack Schleiermacher on the ground that he defines sin, and especially original sin, as a mere condition, and the "incapacity for good" as a natural determination of man. He certainly describes sin as something "original" in man, innate in our first parents even before their evil deed. It may well be that this is an unfortunate suggestion. But it must not be overlooked that on his own presuppositions Schleiermacher could not entertain a merely passive conception of the "sinfulness" which precedes all actual sin, or think of sin as simply a condition. On the contrary, he expressly described this "hereditary" or original sin as a specific form of the human will, as act and therefore guilt. Although the "corporate act and corporate guilt of the human race," these are none the less real act and guilt, and although in "each the work of all," they are none the less "in all the work of each."

Hence the absurd accusation falls to the ground that Schleiermacher discards the concept of sin as guilt, replaces it by "the psychological concept of voluntary action," and transfers it from the individual to the entire race. That he so emphatically indicated men's universal solidarity in sin, and therefore did not see the individual only in isolation but in the sequence of the generations of men, surely does not restrict the definition of sin as guilt. In line with the general Christian tradition, this insight is intended rather to emphasise and strengthen it. To anticipate any misapprehension, he describes sin (§ 69, 2) as not only grounded outwith the life of the individual but also as his own "voluntary action." As he himself explains, Schleiermacher's purpose is to state that as individual sin it has the basis of its reality in the man himself. What else could sin as guilt be, within his system of theology of consciousness, but voluntary action (the self-grounded action of the individual) in opposition to the God-consciousness? Do we not have here the misunderstanding as merely "psychological," and lacking in ethical content, of a statement in Schleiermacher which, if not exhaustive, is not inaccurate as an exposition of the point at issue, and cannot really be avoided in any description of the matter or definition of "guilt"?

It is also manifestly unjust to argue that Schleiermacher tries to "evade" the issue of punishment. His whole doctrine of evil and divine retribution refutes this. He is open to criticism on the ground that he links the concept of evil too closely to that of sin, envisaging it exclusively from the standpoint of retribution and handling it in such a way, i.e., as the mere misapprehension (in sin) of an intrinsically perfect world, as ultimately to deny its existence. But he cannot be accused of blindness to the gravity of evil in the form of this misapprehension, and even less of evasion of the issue of punishment. For as he sees it, this misapprehension is the inevitable result of sin, and it is God's punitive justice that it must establish itself in the consciousness of sinful man. Schleiermacher's contention in the passage (§ 71, 4) against which this indictment is preferred is simply a Christian truth which we must all uphold, namely, that fear of punishment cannot in itself either awaken or deepen man's sense of the need of redemption, because the desire to liberate the God-consciousness from obstruction, and therefore to obtain what redemption offers, differs from the desire to attain to certain conditions of sensuous self-consciousness and to avoid their opposites (i.e., to exclude evil), so that it is impossible to have a genuine sense of the need of redemption which derives solely from a consciousness of the culpability of sin.

[326]

It is a considerable testimony both to the formal originality and the material value of Schleiermacher's conception that, though its rejection is patently necessary, this cannot be accomplished without conceding its great merit and following up as it were some of its insights. We are forced, indeed, to agree with Schleiermacher against himself, as J. Müller once said in a very different sense and on very different grounds (I, p. 359). If we look closely, and dismiss every false accusation, the remaining objections present themselves as a vast complex which curiously enough confronts us at the exact point where we cannot but first and foremost acknowledge and admire his positive achievement. In other words, he is extremely weak where he is so very strong; he is catastrophically wrong where he is most convincingly and instructively right. One is tempted to say that controversy with him, and the implied relationship of acceptance and rejection is almost forced to reflect his own dialectical views of the relationship between grace and sin. Yet the important difference remains that controversy with him demands a differentiation and decision between acceptance and rejection which are unfortunately impossible in his doctrine of grace and sin.

We must first state what is to be learned from Schleiermacher, and rather strangely from Schleiermacher alone. It may be reduced to a proposition with two cognate parts—that the nature and being of nothingness consists in the fact 1. that God in His omnipotent grace has negated it, and therefore 2. that it exists only in this relationship to His grace.

We may begin with the first point that it is that which God has negated. And at once we remember Schleiermacher's doctrine of sin. Consciousness of sin is not fortuitous. It is not a determination of our world-consciousness nor generated by ourselves. We are conscious of sin because our God-consciousness determines our self-consciousness in a particular way, as displeasure at self. We are conscious of sin because we are conscious of our implication in a "positive antagonism of the flesh against the spirit," and consequently must be displeased at ourselves. We have here a definite being and action of man that is realised in a particular relationship between his "sensuality," i.e., his world-consciousness and his God-consciousness. Why and how far are this being and action sinful in this relation, and man himself within it? Schleiermacher's answer is that man is sinful because the relationship is made sin as the tyranny of his sensuality and the weakness, impotence and obstruction of his God-consciousness. But why is it made sin? Schleiermacher's answer is that this weak, impotent and obstructed God-consciousness, not in virtue but in spite of its impotence, i.e., in the power which it has as God-consciousness even in its impotence, negates the being and action of man. In its very impotence it does not cease to command, to own and exercise the power of the commanding will of God which makes demands on men. It is consciousness of the divine holiness. How does God-consciousness do this? Schleiermacher's answer is that the holy God in His omnipotence has given conscience to man as a sign of the God-consciousness of which the "moral law" is the corresponding universal human form. Because God-consciousness exists in the form of conscience, because in God's omnipotence God-consciousness is indisputably and irrefragibly conscience as well, it negates the being and action of man and determines that this particular relationship between human worldconsciousness and God-consciousness is sin, man's incapacity for good and his evil act. In this way God "makes" his being and action sin. In this way it "becomes" sin. Schleiermacher clearly states that conscience, or the divine causality operative in it, is the "whole and sole causality which sin as such implies," and that beside it there is no other (§ 83, 1). This assertion of Schleiermacher's has often been overlooked, and his formally most audacious proposition that God is the Author of sin has been taken quite wrongly and in a sense quite contrary to his intention. God is its Author as He negates it. He is its Author solely because consciousness of Him is the cause of our displeasure at ourselves, of our being and action. In this sense He is certainly the Author of sin. The fact that we are sinners and commit sin is not in dispute. We become conscious of the sinfulness of our being and action by reason of the negation to which we are subjected through our God-consciousness. That our being and action are sinful and we ourselves sinners, that the relationship between our sensuality and God-consciousness is discordance, opposition and resistance and therefore culpable and punishable, is neither explicable in terms of human nature nor is it caused by ourselves, but it is "ordained" for us, and ordained by God in the form of this negation, in the omnipotence of His holiness in which He has posited conscience. Without this divine ordinance sin would be incapable of either reality or being. In Schleiermacher's view and exposition, this ordination is not to be abstractly apprehended in isolation from the fact that God's will for men is redemption and therefore good. Why, then, does God make this negation? The answer of Schleiermacher is that He does so to hold man firmly for and to redemption; to make and keep him aware of the need of redemption without which he would be incapable of attaining to or continuing in the consciousness of redemption itself. Hence the negation is in fact an additional decree of salvation. It is made by the omnipotent grace of God. Sin has reality and being by reason of this decree of salvation, i.e., of this irrefutable and irrefragible negation to which we and our being and action are subjected by our God-consciousness but which by the omnipotent grace of God is positive in its end. Sin in itself is our being and action in the relationship between sensuality and God-consciousness which we can only understand, in the light of our God-consciousness, as the superiority of the former and the corresponding weakness of the latter, as the victorious antagonism of the flesh against the spirit, so that it inevitably becomes the object of our self-disapproval of which we can be conscious only in the form of a "displeasure" which will be emphasised and augmented by the evil which corresponds to this relationship and is entailed by it as its punishment. Sin exists as our being and action are actually determined in this way by our

[327]

37

God-consciousness, and are thus negated by the omnipotent grace of God. It exists as we ourselves exist.

Do we not have to say: So far so good? Within the most dangerous limits of Schleiermacher's basic outlook and terminology, we may certainly do so. As we shall see later, the limits were not only dangerous, but there took place within them a theological catastrophe of the first magnitude. Yet it is not only right but also rewarding to affirm that Schleiermacher has here made a contribution to the apprehension of sin and nothingness which we usually seek in vain even in orthodox theology, but which is absolutely indispensable in relation to the doctrine of providence. Nothingness is what it is, and is real as such, because it, too, owes its existence to God in the sense that He has not elected and willed, but ignored, rejected, excluded and judged, or, as Schleiermacher would say, "negated" it. Whatever else must be said of nothingness, e.g., that it opposes and resists God, or disturbs and destroys man and world, is a corollary of the initial truth that it is that which is first opposed by God. This is the Alpha and Omega of what Schleiermacher says in his hundred and twenty pages on sin. He introduces other necessary matters, but they follow on this initial statement. He makes it within the limits prescribed for or selected by him. But within these limits he might well have described sin, like Leibniz, as mere negation and therefore as a mere imperfection which as such necessarily conduces to the perfection of all creation. Why [328] was Schleiermacher incapable of such a simplification of his thesis? Why did he attribute or at least try to attribute a certain substantiality and gravity to sin by consistently expounding it not only as that which negates but also as that which is negated by the God-consciousness and has reality by reason of this divine negation? Is this not obviously related to the fact that in spite of everything, and in contrast with Leibniz' *Theodicy*, we have here a real doctrine of the Christian faith, and one in which Christology is given the important place, the function of one pole in the whole discussion, which Schleiermacher accords it? To be sure, the compulsion of his monistic thinking is such as to inhibit him from according to Christology even the complementary significance which is his obvious intention. The first pole, the religious experience of the individual, is from the very outset stronger than the second. In his teaching Christology ultimately becomes a purely transitional point, a kind of objective reflection of the portrayal of subjective Christian experience. Thus the defect of his Christology is its ultimate superfluity. For Jesus Christ is in no sense adapted to function as the second pole in Christian thought. If He is treated in this way, He can only disappear as in Schleiermacher's systematics. Nevertheless, in contrast with his contemporaries Schleiermacher does try to honour Christ by making Him the historical point of connexion with the religious consciousness of the Christian. He reckons with Him in a manner in which Leibniz does not do, at least in his system. And it is to be suspected that, though Schleiermacher himself was unconscious of it, this was of great consequence for his distinctive doctrine of sin. Christology can indeed show that sin must first and foremost be apprehended from the standpoint of God, namely, as the work of a powerful divine negation, as a reality which is not created but posited or, as Schleiermacher says, "ordained," by God's opposition to it. In the light of Jesus Christ, this reality may be perceived as that which is excluded by omnipotent grace, so that, while it has no basis in itself, it acquires and temporarily enjoys a sinister basis in and through this antithesis, and can work itself out as the basis, origin and sum of all the contradiction in which alone it exists like all evil opposition, being subjected from the very outset, as mere nothingness, to the omnipotent grace of God and finally succumbing and falling to it at the end of the way on which God accompanies His creature and its adversary. Schleiermacher does not put it like this. Christology is not the real point of departure in his development of the doctrine of sin. All that can be asserted is that on the one hand he actually intended to exalt the position and significance of Christology more than was possible on his premises, and that on the other the form actually assumed by his doctrine of sin is only explicable in terms of a Christological point of departure. But although Schleiermacher does not formulate it as we do, he actually say it. And it cannot be denied that within the limits prescribed and adopted by him his statement is supremely true and important.

Unfortunately however—and this brings us to our first criticism—he did actually succumb to the danger of his limits, and made a further assertion, or rather a definite denial, which inevitably compromises the whole truth and importance of the first insight. In other words, he tried to understand the divine "ordination" of sin in the form of its negation—this is where his monism betrayed him—as an inner process effectuated only in the Christian religious consciousness and therefore exclusively subjective. There was no recollection of the Jesus Christ who is more than the embodiment of a serene and supremely potent human God-consciousness pervading and governing world-consciousness. There was no recollection of the Jesus Christ in whom God covenants with man and therefore genuinely confronts him, negating, judging and condemning sin and thus opposing it as an objective reality. Just as Schleiermacher denies that real encounter and real history are involved in the relationship between God and man, or God and creation, so he refuses to admit them in the relationship between God and sin. It is not, of course, fortuitous that the concepts of transgression. rejection and judgment are absent from his exposition of sin, and that he [329] almost entirely avoids the term "evil" to denote that which resists God and is negated by Him. In Schleiermacher's teaching, the negation and therefore the ordination of sin are real only in our consciousness of God. For God Himself they are unreal and irrelevant, and are treated accordingly. As Schleiermacher sees it, God has no part in this matter, but stands inviolate above it. He merely sees to it that we become conscious of it, of His grace and therefore in contradistinction of our sin. In virtue of His holiness, He causes the discordance of our existence to become sin for us through conscience. God Himself has neither adjutant nor adversary. He is not assailed. He is neither offended, nor does He suffer. He is neither wroth against sin nor merciful to sinners. He is merely the Physician who prescribes a medicine for the patient with no intention of testing or taking it Himself. We and we alone are really implicated in sin. It is instructive to note what Schleiermacher says concerning Jesus Christ. As the vehicle of supremely potent God-consciousness, He possesses no personal conscience of His own, but simply a fellow-feeling with those who must needs have one because they are actually implicated in sin. Do we not have to conclude that there is no place for the holiness of God in the supremely potent God-consciousness of Jesus? Is there really a place for holiness in God Himself? The case is naturally the same, and even more so, with evil. Divine justice ordains that as a misapprehension due to sin evil should be very painful to us. But from God's standpoint and for Him it has no existence. In creation itself there is no alien element capable of being the result or object of His wrath. Evil is operative in our consciousness simply as opposition, as disruption of the perfection of the world, and as the inevitable subjective consequence of the disunity of our nature which is made sin for us. Again God has no part in it, nor is there any question of the divine mercy as "a state of feeling specially evoked by the sufferings of others finding outlet in acts of relief." J. Müller has rightly seen and described (I, 35f.) the resultant dilemma in the following terms.

If it is really God who "ordains" sin for us; if it is true that as sinners we must become and be conscious before Him of the culpability of our being and action; if God has actually "shut up all unto disobedience" (Rom. 11[32]), justly indicting and branding them for their disobedience; if men must acknowledge this to be true and just; if there can be no escape except by the avenue of His grace, how can all this be the case unless sin is first and foremost a reality for God Himself? Has He or has He not accomplished anything by its mighty negation? But if He has, and His act is not without purpose but of real significance for us, how can it have no significance for Him? How can His holiness and justice be described as divine attributes which we attribute to Him, not because they are characteristic or essential, but because we find that in our consciousness we are confronted by the truth of the disunity of our existence and are negated, judged and punished by Him in consequence? How can any place be found for the proviso that God is untouched by what we apprehend as the antagonism between our sensuality and our God-consciousness?

On the other hand, if it is really the case that God is untouched by our sinfulness and actual sin; if it is not primarily God's own adversary who is at work; if He Himself is not engaged; if there is neither wrath nor mercy in God; if the work of His holiness and justice is simply to render us conscious of our need of redemption, why is there any true need of this consciousness? Can anything less than God Himself, can our mere consciousness of God, suffice to make this need clear and certain, especially when we are clearly informed that God has no personal interest in the matter but is concerned only as the Author of our consciousness, for whom it is suggested that neither sin nor evil has any reality. Where, then, is the veracity of God to which we must be able to cling if we are to take the accusation of our conscience seriously? How can anything have reality for us if we are convinced that it has [330] none for God? Does not the fact that it has no reality close the question? How can anything have existence if it is nothing for God? How, then, can we be capable of a real consciousness of our sin as guilt, and of the evil to which we are subject as punishment? Why, then, should we have any real desire for grace and redemption? If this is how matters stand, how can dogmaticians speak of an essential, serious and stringent insight? On these presuppositions is not the insight nullified even before it presents itself as a problem? How can anything move us either theoretically or practically to anxiety and repentance, prayer or even consideration, if we are informed that God views it not only as nothingness but as nothing, as in no sense an object, but for some reason seems to think that it should be of concern to us? Surely if it is of no concern to Him, it cannot be to us!

This is the great dilemma which Schleiermacher's doctrine cannot avoid as he himself propounded it.

If it is his serious contention that God Himself is not concerned with sin and evil, then man need not take them seriously nor acknowledge his own need of redemption from them.

But if he believes in man's need of redemption, in the culpability and punishment of sin, in the divine holiness which imputes it to him, and the justice which subjects him to evil as its consequence, then God Himself is supremely involved in this mighty negation of nothingness, it is His own most intimate concern. He is holy and righteous not merely for us but in Himself, and He is the God of wrath and mercy.

If Schleiermacher cannot be understood in the sense of the second alternative, i.e., if he cannot be radically rectified by the elimination of the first, then it is hard to see—and this is the crucial point—why the grace and redemption of God should not also be regarded as mere phenomena of the consciousness, as a sense of exaltation and deliverance which is communicated by God in opposition to the sense of sin and its consequence, but in the experience of which we accept the fact that God Himself is not involved, that He is self-evidently not gracious in Himself, but remains aloof from our conflicting senses. He is certainly their Author, but has in Himself no fundamental reality corresponding to them and making them genuinely necessary for us. It is unfortunate that we cannot take Schleiermacher in the sense of the second alternative. But if his doctrine were radically rectified in this way, and the first alternative eliminated, he would cease to be Schleiermacher. The limits of his theology are such that he was neither able nor willing to look beyond the facts and emotions of the Christian consciousness; that even Jesus Christ was for him merely one, though a most important, subjective fact and emotion among others; that "God Himself," even in relation to Jesus Christ, could not be for him a necessary, let alone a decisive theological concept, but only an enigmatical figure who stands above the human emotions He

40

causes and of whom it can basically be said only that He is alien to the antithesis of our emotions. Within these limits Schleiermacher's doctrine of nothingness as that which is negated by the omnipotent grace of God cannot be developed as a Christian perception which is tenable by the biblical standard. Therefore we can only state that within these limits he does offer the remarkable beginning of a true Christian understanding.

But we should be well advised to consider the matter in the light of the fact that Schleiermacher has expressed that which makes his doctrine so remarkable within its limits in a second form, namely, that nothingness does not exist at all except in relation to redemption. In other words, since there is a consciousness of redemption, and this contains a consciousness of our original human perfection, then, estimated in relation to the end held out to us with the consciousness of redemption, and to the origin thus revealed, there are such things as sin and evil. As by our God-consciousness we become simultaneously aware of a future victory over the disunity of our existence and of its original unity, we also become aware of the disunity itself and its culpability, and we thus come under the negation which is as it were [331] a mere addendum to the affirmation to which we must primarily accede. The consciousness of sin follows that of grace, and serves it by conducing to our sense of the need of redemption. The negation is not in fact injurious to us. On the contrary, it is provisionally and incidentally advantageous. The same is true of the punishment meted upon us in the form of our great misconception of the intrinsically perfect world, i.e., in the form of evil. Indeed, punishment is only our preservation for and in redemption. It was to demonstrate this that Schleiermacher defined sin in terms which are decisively negative—that it is not so much the resistance and rule of the flesh (though in fact it is this too) but the state of the spirit no longer or not yet capable of ruling, subduing and renouncing the flesh as flesh. Sin is the impotence, obstruction, limitation, withdrawal and non-development of our God-consciousness. The consciousness of sin, the dissatisfaction with it, the "displeasure" which our knowledge of it entails, is decisively the dissatisfaction of our God-consciousness with itself, with its weakness and impotence, with its failure to pervade and sanctify our world-consciousness instead of being denied by it. Strictly speaking, then, there is no essence or idea of sin. As it is only that which is negated by our God-consciousness, it has reality only in so far as it constitutes the frontier of our God-consciousness, and as we become conscious of it in that capacity.

Again we might say: So far so good. For it cannot be contested that Schleiermacher has seen and said here something which is true and important. And within the limits of his theology he has seen and said it in such a way that we are forced to listen and able to learn from him, even though a more scrupulous study must reveal that the standpoint which he assumed is untenable. Here, too, he has perceived something which the majority of the exponents of a purer doctrine failed to perceive, to the detriment of themselves and of the Church. We are again surprised that it did not occur to him to establish his view Christologically. But we must immediately add that his own Christology rendered this impossible, and that if he had established it on another and better Christology it would have been embodied in another and less fallacious form than that in which it exists. Yet it is a no less astonishing fact that on another and better Christology, and in another and more valid form, we necessarily come to the same view of the relationship between grace and sin as that of Schleiermacher. If at the outset we realise that we are not free to formulate our own serious and profound opinions on the whole complex of nothingness and therefore on sin, evil and death, nor to determine the existence, nature and importance of this matter in a vacuum, i.e., speculatively, as is finally the case with the otherwise rigorous Müller; if we must maintain that here, too, Jesus Christ the incarnate Word of God is the only objective ground of knowledge, then the conclusion is inevitable that real nothingness does not reveal its existence to us at random points, e.g., in an abyss within ourselves, or in face of a personal or

41

general calamity, or in our pretended understanding of transience and death. It is an error to suppose that we can seek and find nothingness in this way. We encounter it in the relationship that God has established between Himself and us and all creation by becoming man to deliver us and creation. We encounter nothingness as the reality that God confronted in Jesus Christ. It is real in relation to God, and not with an absolute reality. And its nature is also revealed at this point. Nothingness is not something malign, sinister and monstrous. It is not endowed with invented negative qualities, but with the specific and authentically evil character of the antithesis to the grace of God. That which it wills to be it cannot, and therefore here too it is not absolute. Its nature corresponds to the relationship in which it exists. It is the antithesis to the good, kind, benevolent will of God which He exercises and manifests by not abandoning His creature but by identifying Himself with it in His Word. What confronts Him in us and all creation, what is alien and opposed to His gracious will—

[332] that and that alone is true nothingness, sin, evil, death in their true form as that which is bad. And this relationship also reveals the scope and therefore the limitation of its power. The extent of our gravity and fear in face of nothingness is not to be determined by our free choice and opinion. When nothingness is seen in this relationship, in its opposition to Jesus Christ, it cannot be for us either a legendary monster of unlimited power or a second and negative God. In this respect, too, it is not absolute. God is first and last in action against it. It exists only through God, in the power of the divine negation and rejection, of the divine judgment. Its place is given it by God. It is never over God, but always under Him. It does not limit God, but is limited by Him. God's grace is mightier than sin, evil and death. They are together the enemy of whom it can be said: "One word shall quickly fell him." No morality however earnest, no pessimism however sincere, can possibly exonerate us here. We do not honour the truth but compound a falsehood and make common cause with the enemy if even momentarily we fail to see nothingness otherwise than in its relativity. Schleiermacher is quite right to maintain that from the standpoint of creation and the covenant the total force of the enemy is far from absolute. It is only the object of the victory which God has gained over it. To be sure, Schleiermacher did not and could not express it in this way. But in his own terminology and within his own limits, did he not assert the same thing? Before any objection to the development of his idea is advanced, must he not be credited with the fact that he justly opposed a foolish dualism in the consideration of the relationship between sin and grace, an unbiblical absolutisation of nothingness by Christian theology as though it could be apprehended and existed in a vacuum? Did he not try to exhibit against this the sovereignty of the grace of God? When he says that "evil is only correlative to good," is this statement false because it is actually reminiscent of Leibniz' conception, or because it is unfortunately a statement in his monistic philosophy and is thus accompanied in his teaching by other propositions which completely compromise its Christian character? We cannot accept the other propositions, but are forced to say that evil is the one entity in Christian knowledge and confession which cannot be affirmed absolutely but only in relation and subordination to the grace of God. Nothingness is radically but not autonomously opposed to the creation and covenant of God. It does not exist in itself, but only in this state of antithesis. It is thus merely "correlative to good." This proposition is not in itself the doubtful element in Schleiermacher's teaching. On the contrary, his powerful advocacy of it is the illuminating feature which must not be ignored or denied even in the most necessary and justifiable criticism.

The criticism which we are forced to bring is that Schleiermacher understood this intrinsically correct proposition in such a way that he thought he could reverse it like an hourglass and say that good is only correlative to evil. He was thus guilty not only of a serious consolidation of evil but of an even more serious disintegration of good quite contradictory to what the proposition that evil is only correlative to good should signify in a truly Christian sense.

What does he affirm? He affirms that the power of our God-consciousness, of our consciousness of grace and redemption, subsists only in relation to our incapacity for good and our sin yielding before grace. It is in some sense essential that sin should also be posited as an element in human development, which without it would be inhibited. Were it not so, man would not be a free agent and therefore would not be man. All being as divinely caused is a compound of being and non-being. There is evil in all the good wrought by God. Therefore, in virtue of relationship to redemption, sin can be no true "injury," because "the merely gradual and imperfect unfolding of the power of the God-consciousness is one of the necessary conditions of the human stage of existence." Because of this necessity sin was posited and ordained for man by God. We cannot possibly accept this view. While sin may justifiably be regarded as relative in confrontation with grace, Schleiermacher's proposition goes further. It includes sin in the same category as grace, and thus esteems, justifies and even establishes it as the counterpart and concomitant of grace. Sin is given a legitimate standing in relative grace. It presents itself as an agent whose reaction to grace fulfils a function no less accredited than that of grace, and just as lawful and necessary and divinely ordained. This is a real return to Leibniz. Sin is now understood positively. Without sin grace could not exist. That evil is correlative to good now means that it balances it. At this point we can only protest. When sin is understood positively, when it is esteemed and justified and established, when it counterbalances grace and is indispensable to it, it is not real sin. For real sin cannot be vindicated in this way. We cannot say of it that it is in any sense necessary to a stage of human existence and therefore willed and posited by God. How can sin be grounded in human freedom, the freedom of man created perfect by God? How can it be indispensable to man? But our protest goes even deeper. For the grace which is conditioned by the presence of sin, living by its antithesis and therefore bound to it, is not real grace. Grace cannot possibly be subject to this necessity, require to be counterbalanced in this undesirable way, or need this indispensable "accomplice." How can it ever be averred of the real grace of God that it can be true only in conjunction with our incapacity for good and the resultant evil actions? What kind of a grace is it which is obviously unable to cover, forgive and cancel sin? What does the justification of the sinner mean if his sin is already justified as sin? At this point we are confronted by an abysmal error in Schleiermacher's teaching. For he either does not see or completely forgets that the relationship between grace and sin in which sin can have only a relative existence and power is not a positive relationship but one of opposition and conflict, of the victorious conflict of grace against sin and the futile conflict of sin against grace, but of real conflict, and therefore not in any sense of peace. In Schleiermacher's teaching the nature and character of the two concomitants are forgotten, and it is thus overlooked that there can be no mediation nor arrangement between these two adversaries. It goes unheeded that their relationship is an encounter and history in which all the honour and justice and dignity pertain to the first partner, whereas the existence and being and power of the second have no basis, so that they cannot competently be classified together, and first and last theology can define their interconnexion only in terms of a conflict which is favourable to the first and not to the second. How could Schleiermacher fail to see this? How could he venture to reverse his proposition, and thus give nothingness the favourable report of being essential to man's existence, though injurious to it? How could he dare compromise in this way the cause of God in relation to it? Well, he not only could do this, but his presuppositions left him no alternative. We understand the whole tragedy when we consider that, faithful to his historico-psychological methodology, Schleiermacher means by grace and sin no more than two corresponding states in the religious consciousness of the Christian. It is true indeed that in our consciousness the antithesis exists only as a variable juxtaposition and not an exclusive encounter of good and evil. The good in our consciousness is always correlative to evil, and *vice versa*. The grace of God is

[333]

43

never present with us as absolutely antagonistic to or triumphant over our sin, but sin is always too firmly entrenched against it. We cannot actually know grace without a simultaneous acknowledgment of our sin. In our own consciousness, and in relation to that of the race as a whole, there are good grounds for the notion that the impotence of our God-consciousness is a prerequisite of our existence and is thus divinely ordained. The fallacy of Schleiermacher was to absolutise the historico-psychological actuality of the Christian religious consciousness, and therefore to regard the sin apprehended within its limits as real. If he had been free to transcend the self-imposed limitations which circumscribe his conception, and to consider sin where it can be recognised as real sin in its relativity to real grace, he

[334]   would have been compelled to take seriously his own definition of sin as that which is negated by our God-consciousness and is only real as such, and therefore to refrain from minimising it. Even the religious consciousness itself, opened to the Word of God and instructed by it, should have given him a different view of sin. Even in relation to this subjective sphere, it should have been possible to speak of sin with far greater dismay and of grace with far deeper joy. The trouble is that the religious consciousness as Schleiermacher understood it was not opened to the Word of God. In the restricted sphere in which Schleiermacher was cramped the divine No to sin could not be revealed as God's own No, nor the divine Yes as His Yes. In this sphere, therefore, the threat of sin, the nullity of nothingness and the glory of grace could not be seen in their reality, i.e., in their encounter and history, but only in a peace which is really spurious and not the peace of God that passes all understanding.

It is on these grounds that, for all the credit due to Schleiermacher and our debt to him, we must categorically repudiate his concept of nothingness.

We may conclude our review by turning to two contemporaries, Martin Heidegger (b. 1889) and Jean-Paul Sartre (b. 1905). Although their work is not yet complete, the main features are already distinct, and are highly pertinent to our present investigation. I am aware that exception might be taken to classifying Heidegger and Sartre together (cf. Max Müller, *Existenzphilosophie im geistigen Leben der Gegenwart*, 1949). It is true enough that they only stand together as it were back to back; yet the fact remains that they do stand together. And both must be heard if we are to wrestle with the view of nothingness which, approximately two centuries after Leibniz and one after Schleiermacher, has emerged as characteristic of our own time, the decades of the two world wars. Modernity with its obtrusion of seemingly indispensable viewpoints and criteria is not the measure of all things. And the so-called existentialism of our own day, in this or any other form, is certainly not the philosophy *par excellence* which will have no successor and therefore merits our special or even exclusive attention. Let it not be forgotten that in the time of Hegel it was held with even greater conviction, and perhaps with greater internal justification, that a similar delusion might be entertained regarding the conclusive significance of his teaching. And the position which Roman Catholicism gives to Aristotle as the philosopher *par excellence* was and is a very remarkable but also a very questionable matter. In theology, at least, we must be more far-sighted than to attempt a deliberate co-ordination with temporarily predominant philosophical trends in which we may be caught up, or to allow them to dictate or correct our conceptions. On the other hand, there is every reason why we should consider and as far as possible learn from the typical philosophical thinking of the day. As we have listened to Leibniz and Schleiermacher, so now we listen to these modern thinkers at a point which is particularly important for them and in which they may be able to teach or warn us in our own understanding of the theme.

With regard to Martin Heidegger we are in the fortunate position of being able to consult the short essay which he delivered as his inaugural lecture at Freiburg in Breisgau in 1929,

3. The Knowledge of Nothingness

Was ist Metaphysik? (E.T. *What is Metaphysics?* in *Existence and Being*, 1949). This is a summary of what he says on the present theme in his greater work *Sein und Zeit* (or rather in the first and so far the only volume published in 1927). I shall not try to follow Heidegger's process of thought, but to describe the concept which dominates his exposition and then to show how it is developed in his teaching and how an answer is finally given to the question under discussion.

The predominant concept is that of nothing. According to Heidegger, the question of nothing is raised, and ultimately already resolved, by the fact that science repudiates and rejects nothing as nothingness (the only time this term is used), but in so doing admits it (p. 358). Science is related to the world as to that which is, and to nothing more (p. 358). That which is determines its attitude, and nothing more. It deals with that which is, and nothing more (p. 358). Science seeks no knowledge of nothing. We know nothing by seeking no knowledge of it (p. 359). The question: "What is nothing?" is meaningless, and even more so is any answer which might try to begin: "Nothing is ... " Nothing is merely admitted and repudiated as that which "is not" (p. 359). It is the negation of the totality of that which is. It is that which is not absolutely (p. 361). On the other hand, it is not grounded either in our rational act of negation or in our "not." It does not exist because of this negation. Our negation can only be subsequent to our rational act. In this act we acknowledge nothing (in the form of its admission and repudiation). Nothing itself is prior to our "not" and negation. Heidegger believes that he may justifiably regard this thesis as crucial (p. 361). While he offers neither ground nor proof for it, it is obvious that as he advances it he regards "nothing" not only as a "something," a factor, which has to be reckoned with, but as an original factor which precedes our negation and affirmation, which is dynamic and active, and which operates with an original dynamism and activity. We cannot set ourselves before it by our own resolution and willpower (p. 374), but it "obtrudes" upon us as being as a whole escapes in a mood of dread. In face of it, it is impossible to say "is" (pp. 366–367). It thus discloses itself in dread, not as a being or object, nor in isolation from that which is, but in unity with it. In dread that which is falls away altogether. It is not annihilated, but it eludes us (p. 368). In dread nothing is manifested as that which essentially refers aside, but yet which refers us to elusive and evanescent being. It is this work of nothing Heidegger calls its "nihilating." But as it nihilates, rejecting and reprimanding elusive being, it discloses that which is in all its hitherto undisclosed alienation as that which is absolutely other, in its utter differentiation from itself, as that which really is and is not nothing. The essence of nothing as original nihilation thus consists in the fact that it sets the existence of man face to face with being as such, confronting man with that which is (p. 369). Only on the basis of the original disclosure of nothing can the existence of man approach that which is. Apart from the original disclosure of nothing existence can have neither self-hood nor freedom. Not only, then, does nothing belong to the essence of being—since the nihilation of nothing occurs in the being of that which is—but existence, which is essentially related to that which is, derives always from manifested nothing. "Existence means being projected into nothing" (p. 370). It is indeed true that we do not always but only very occasionally live (or are "suspended ") in a state of dread because of it. The primary reason is that nothing is continually "distorted" out of its original state by the fact that we wholly immerse ourselves in that which is, not allowing it to elude us, and thus intruding ourselves into the "open superficies" of existence. Yet this perpetual if equivocal aversion from nothing "accords within certain limits with its own essential meaning." Nothing itself refers us to that which is. But this does not alter the fact, unapprehended by ordinary perception, that it continuously nihilates (p. 371). In sum, it can be generally agreed with Hegel that "pure being and pure nothing are one and the same." The older affirmation: *ex nihilo nihil fit*[EN25] must be amended to read: *ex nihilo omne ens qua ens fit*[EN26] (p. 377). On this basis we shall now try to understand the details.

The initial question concerns (human) existence. We are informed that there is a "basic event" in which all that which is is disclosed to existence. The basic event in which this occurs is comprehensively described as the "affective state" (p. 364). It is of interest to observe that this basic event is assumed to be identical with metaphysics (p. 379). The mood involved in the disclosure of all that which is might be joy. But for Heidegger another form of this disclosure seems to be more significant, namely, "true boredom." "Profound boredom, drifting hither and thither in the abyss of existence as in a silent fog, gathers all things and all men, and oneself with them, into a strange indifference. This boredom is the totality of that which is." Yet when our moods thus bring us face to face with this totality, they still conceal nothing. Materially, the revelation of nothing which is truly constitutive for existence occurs prior to this revelation and as it were at a deeper level. It, too, occurs in a mood, but in the basic mood of dread (pp. 364–365). On the very basis of the revelation of nothing which occurs in the mood of dread, existence itself, being projected into nothing, reaches the stage of approaching and entering that which is, but also passes beyond the totality of being, thus "transcending it" (p. 370). "Projection into nothing on the basis of hidden dread is the overcoming of the totality of that which is—transcendence" (p. 374). Projected into nothing, existence has self-hood and freedom (p. 370). As existence is not only capable of logical negation, but more generally is pervaded by a nihilating attitude, being constantly engaged in the acrimony of opposition, the violence of loathing, the painful responsibility of refusal, the cruelty of interdiction and the bitterness of renunciation, there is present the constant but much concealed revelation of nothing (p. 373). Finally, it falls to be said of man, whose existence is involved, that the projection of his existence into nothing on the basis of hidden dread makes him "the *locum tenens*[EN27] for nothing" (p. 374). Necessarily brought into the question concerning nothing, existence itself is inevitably called in question by this question (p. 378).

[336]

But what is the basic mood of dread which is so obviously decisive for the basic event of existence as well as for the action and revelation of nothing? We have seen that nothing itself stands as the agent behind this key-mood into which we are brought, if only very occasionally, by it. This mood is not to be confounded with fear, which is always the fear of this or that. Dread is not this confusion of fear. On the contrary, it is pervaded by a peculiar kind of peace. Dread is dread of the indefinite as that which is essentially impatient of definition. In dread, "one feels something uncanny." But what is meant by "something " and "one"? We cannot say what occasions this uncanny feeling. "One just feels it generally." Everything merges into a kind of indifference. Yet this does not mean that everything disappears, but that in the very act of withdrawing it returns to us. It is the withdrawal of the totality of that which is which oppresses us in dread as it surges around us. There is nothing to cling to. That which is eludes us, and we can cling only to this nothing. What happens? Dread reveals nothing. In dread we are suspended, or more exactly dread holds us in suspense by causing the totality of that which is to elude us. This is because we ourselves, as these men who are, elude ourselves in the midst of that which is. Hence it is not thou or I but one who has this uncanny feeling. In the trepidation of the suspense where there is nothing to cling to, the only thing which remains is pure existence. Dread strikes us dumb. In the uncanniness of dread we may often try to break the silence by random words, but this only proves the presence of nothing. And what happens when we have overcome our dread? We are forced to say

---

[EN25] nothing comes from nothing
[EN26] every being as being comes from nothing
[EN27] place-holder

46

that that of which we were afraid was "actually"—nothing! Indeed, we are forced to say that nothing itself and as such was there (pp. 365–367). And what happened as dread was there? What happens as it is basically always present? Although it is powerless as dread in face of the totality of that which is, nothing declares itself in it in and with that which is, and that which is reveals itself in it as a totality which eludes us (p. 368). Again, we ourselves in dread are engaged in a withdrawal which is not a flight but a conjured rest. That before which we withdraw, or by which we are conjured to rest, is nothing. Our withdrawal or rest in dread thus proceeds from nothing, from its nihilation (p. 369). It is true that only in the clear night of dread does the original "disclosure of that which is, and is not nothing, emerge." It is true, then, that we "distort" nothing as we follow its reference to that which is, and lose ourselves in it (p. 371). But this does not alter the fact that dread is present, and with it nihilating nothing in its original disclosure. Dread is always present, though sometimes dormant. Its breath palpitates through all existence, most feebly through the pusillanimous, imperceptibly through the active, most readily through the introverted, and most firmly [337] through the valiant. The dread felt by the valiant, which is the most real dread, is not patient of contrast with joy, or even with the easy enjoyment of life in tranquillity. Beyond all such contrasts, it stands in mysterious union with the serenity and tenderness of all creative longing. Yet it is always there as dread, and can awaken at any moment. It needs no extraordinary event to awaken it. Its action is so deep that the shallowness of its possible cause genuinely corresponds to it. If it seldom plunges, it is always on the brink, so that when it does plunge it drags us again into the state of suspense (pp. 373–374).

That which is, then, is to be apprehended from the standpoint of the revelation of nothing which occurs in dread. In the mood of joy, or supremely in that of boredom, that which is discloses itself to us in totality. But it is still not manifested to us in its actuality, i.e., in its distinction from nothing. For the manifestation of that which is nothing and its nihilation are indispensable, since it is in virtue of this nihilation that that which is discloses itself as recessive, elusive and evanescent, yet in this way as that which is. Only as nothing is disclosed at the basis of existence is it possible for the utter strangeness of that which is to dawn upon us. Only when this utter strangeness intrudes itself upon us does it excite our wonder, and the question of its ground and its nature springs to our lips, so that we can ask and answer, i.e., prove and explain, and therefore investigate (pp. 369; 378–379). Nothing is that which renders the disclosure of that which is possible for human existence. It is nothing, therefore, which makes science possible. Nothing belongs to the essence of that which is. It is in the being of that which is that the nihilation of nothing takes place (p. 370). Under this determination there is not only an attitude of (human) existence to that which is, but there is to be ascribed to that which is itself a definite dynamism and activity which is very real even if secondary in its relationship to that of nothing. There is thus attained in the objectivity of scientific enquiry, definition and proof a subjection of existence to that which is in which the latter must disclose itself. What is achieved in science, then, is not only the irruption of a particular entity called man into the totality of that which is, but also in and through this irruption an eruption of that which is itself, so that in its own way science as an "erupting irruption" helps that which is to itself (pp. 357–358). All this rests, of course, on the original disclosure of nothing in which that which is is revealed as elusive and evanescent, but in this way as that which is.

The rational act of negation is also to be apprehended from the standpoint of the revelation of nothing which takes place in dread. It does not lead to nothing, since, as the rational negation of a theory, of a conception of the totality of that which is, it offers only the formal concept of an hypothetical nothing and not real nothing itself (p. 363). Nothing itself is of necessity prior to our negation; the latter can only follow it. In this way our negation attains significance and justification. The fact that in negating we repeatedly utter a Not which is not generated by our own negation, since that which is to be negated must as a negative entity precede our negation, is more impressively demonstrative than anything else of the revelation of nothing in our existence. That they may utter the Not our negation and human cognition are already expecting a Not—a Not which can only manifest itself with the disclosure of its source in the great nihilation of nothing and therefore in nothing itself. Thus negation is based on the Not which derives from the nihilation of nothing. Thus it is merely a mode of the nihilating behaviour of our existence based on the nihilation of nothing itself. The rational act of negation is not alone. Nor is it a chief witness either for the disclosure of nothing which is an essential part of existence, nor for its nihilation which shakes our existence everywhere. More abysmal is the multitude of negations unrelated to rational acts— opposition, loathing, refusal, interdiction, renunciation. In short, the exact apprehension of [338] the rational act of negation demonstrates precisely that the sovereignty of reason in the field of enquiry into nothing and being is demolished, and that the fate of the rule of logic in philosophy is determined. "The very idea of logic disintegrates in the vortex of a more fundamental questioning" (pp. 372–373).

On the basis of these propositions, we now come to Heidegger's answer to his thematic question: What is metaphysics? In his exposition he was trying to raise and answer one metaphysical question in order to make metaphysics possible. Metaphysics consists in the investigating and therefore the passing beyond being which takes place in the essence of existence, in its basic event which we have learned to know as the "affective mood." Metaphysics is transcendence. The enquiry concerning nothing is an enquiring and passing beyond of this kind in which we men are already actually engaged. Enquiry concerning nothing is therefore a metaphysical question (p. 374) which, though it is only one, embraces and occupies all metaphysics because it is obviously concerned with the being of that which is (pp. 374–377). It is a genuinely metaphysical question because it integrates our questioning existence with itself and thus calls our existence in question; for scientific existence is not possible unless "projected at the outset into nothing." Existence can only apprehend its own nature if it does not repudiate nothing. The pretended sobriety and superiority of science become ludicrous if they fail to take nothing seriously. Science can exist only on the basis of metaphysics, indeed on the basis of the metaphysics which is penetrated and embraced by this particular metaphysical question concerning nothing and which in so doing takes science into itself (pp. 374–378). The task of philosophy is to instigate metaphysics, this metaphysics. But philosophy itself is only instigated when the philosopher plunges his own being into the basic possibilities of being as a whole. In this plunge these points are of vital importance: first, to allow room for the totality of that which is; secondly, to let oneself go into nothing; and finally, to give free play to this suspense "so that it may continually revert" to the basic question of metaphysics wrested from nothing itself: Why is there being at all and not just nothing?

In relation to Jean-Paul Sartre we again have the advantage of having his own commentary on the position and message advocated by him in *L'Etre et le Néant* (1943) and other works, for the most part literary. This commentary is *L'Existentialisme est un humanisme* (1945), in which he not only answers his opponents but also offers an exact and definitive statement of his system, discarding the intentionally exasperating attitude of his other works and clearly adumbrating his essential interest. If by reason of the consistently exasperating attitude of the author, or our exasperated failure to take his part, we have not seen it in his other works, in this work we cannot but realise that Sartre presents us with a view which is completely self-consistent and finally simple, and for all the differences very much of a piece with that of Heidegger.

In passing from Heidegger to Sartre our first main impression is that Sartre has behind him (as though obsessed by nothing and unable to see anything except in the light of it) what Heidegger still has before him (as though obsessed by nothing and unable to look to any other goal). In other words, while nothing is the basic concern of both, there is this difference in their respective attitudes towards it. In Heidegger we are concerned with the premise of Sartre, in Sartre with Heidegger's conclusion. Both deal with nothing as a principle, dimension and imperative. But whereas Heidegger's purpose is almost entirely to demonstrate the potency of nothing against existence, that of Sartre is almost entirely to demonstrate human existence as conditioned by it. In both cases I have said "almost entirely," for naturally there is overlapping. Heidegger's own teaching foreshadows the inevitable and ultimate tendency of the development of his thought if his conclusions regarding the constraint and compulsion of nothing are accepted and human existence is positively interpreted in accordance with his view. Indeed, this tendency is already evident in his own thought. But his true passion is revealed in relation to the "disclosure" of nothing which is [339] ready to leap out in the basic mood of dread and which is always on the verge of possible awakening. It is thus revealed in connexion with the evanescence of that which is and the concomitant dubiety of human existence itself. Sartre again does not fail to indicate his point of departure, i.e., the absolute impotence of what lies behind human existence. He even gives to the initial perception of nothing a sharpness which is implicit and necessary but not explicit in the thinking of Heidegger. Sartre's decisive presupposition is a regretful but emphatic and forceful denial of the existence of God. For this reason he has a radical awareness of dread, *délaissement (expression chère à Heidegger*[EN28], p. 33), and despair. In 1938, when the French were faced by a probable war which was only postponed, Sartre depicted it in *Le Sursis* in all the colours of a mythical monster: *on était solidaire d'un gigantesque et invisible polypier*[EN29]. His description of hell in *Huis Clos* is overpowering just because it is ultimately no more than a portrayal of the dreadful banality that prevails in man's relationship with man. And many more examples might be given. Because he is so eloquent and illuminating on this subject Sartre has often been misunderstood. It has often been thought that he could be dismissed with the assertion that—like a second Zola—his sole concern was the realistic exposure of the sordid, ugly and base side of human life. Though there is no ambiguity in either his writings or his explicit defence of them, it has been completely overlooked that his passionate concern is to be sought in his description of man: the man whose point of departure and therefore background is nothing with its constraint and compulsion; the man who realises that he must live without God; the man who knows dread, *délaissement*, despair, war and hell; the man who knows and reckons with all that to which Heidegger looks as though he were obsessed, and who in this way and for this reason is man, and is absolutely resolved to be and become and remain such. As though he also were obsessed Sartre looks forward from this point. If the source of Heidegger's philosophy is to be found in the First World War in retrospect, Sartre is a very definite and in his way magnificent type of the man of the French Resistance in the Second. But even before the Second World War Sartre was a *résistant*—one who saw the adversity of the age and was fully resolved to reveal it to the blind, but who also meant to assert himself, to caution others against all collaboration and to inculcate in them a similar self-assertion. He emerged from the Second World War immeasurably purified and strengthened in this positive purpose. The awful No derived from nothing is an actuality, but out of it there strangely grows the peculiar and categorical Yes of human existence. This Yes is Sartre's concern. In my view, he is the most virile of modern existentialists. The core of his teaching is not that man must be somewhere "in suspense," or vacillate in the famous "frontier situations," but that he should stand and advance to a goal.

[EN28] dread (a term of which Heidegger is fond)
[EN29] we are entangled in a huge and invisible octopus

We can understand his derivation from Heidegger and the relationship of the two if we also consider the connexions in Heidegger's teaching, in which we are surprised to learn that the real dread in which nothing is revealed to us is not without a "peculiar peace," not being a flight but a "conjured rest" in mysterious union with the serenity and tenderness of creative longing," or that the valiant experience dread most surely and the introverted most readily, or that this dread is not patient of contrast with joy, "the easy enjoyment of life in tranquillity." We must also remember that Heidegger's ultimate intention in his doctrine of dread and nothing was to establish a positive basis not only for metaphysics but also for the quiet purpose, outlook and labour of science. Heidegger is not and never was a "Nihilist." His statement that man is the "*locum tenens*[EN30] for nothing" can be interpreted positively. This is where Sartre comes in, but on a broader basis. He does not ignore dread, and the nothing which underlies it. He submits them to a careful scrutiny. But he will not allow them to prepossess, hamper, or obstruct him. He performs at this point a resolute *volte face*[EN31]. He turns to his true theme, i.e., the depiction of man as he comes from dread and nothing, and the positive message of the existence of this man. Is his intention already tantamount to what Heidegger condemns as "distortion" of nothing? Be that as it may, the all-embracing question and questionability which form the horizon for Heidegger are not ultimate for Sartre. To be sure, his writings speak with eloquence and agony of the *ignominie humaine*[EN32], of the intolerable confusion of weakness, brutality, triviality, folly, mendacity and dread which we call human life, and of the inevitable impasses and labyrinths into which man ineluctably wanders, however noble his intentions and efforts may seem to be. Yet there is always somewhere in Sartre the sudden flash of a kind of Nevertheless, a defiance which is defeated yet does not accept defeat, but always reveals in some way that man has finally grasped and overcome everything with a smile, and is sovereignly transcendent. It is precisely this sovereign transcendence of lost but self-reliant man which is, if I understand him aright, the existential viewpoint of Sartre, and the call to final resolution for this movement is the core of his teaching. To put it summarily, Sartre contrasts with the ponderously reflective German Martin Heidegger as a type of the perennial French *débrouillard*[EN33]. It is for this reason and in this sense that he can and must make what many find the surprising explanation: *L'Existentialisms est un humanisme.*

For Sartre existentialism—and this is what he means by *humanisme*[EN34]—is *une doctrine, qui rend la vie possible*[EN35] (p. 12). His existentialism is a doctrine of freedom. Man *hic et nunc*[EN36]—this or that particular man—cannot and may not find freedom anywhere at all. But he can and may exercise and therefore possess it. Indeed, he can and may become it himself. Hence his freedom is not an idea. It is not a potentiality which he controls. It is not a gift which he is granted. It is not an assumption on which he may proceed. It is not a capital sum on which interest accrues and with which he can start something. He cannot start anywhere or with anything. There is no corresponding something. He can start only with nothing. The ground is taken from under his feet. For as there is no God, so there is no human nature. There are no eternal and historical realities, nor conventions and ideals, to which he may cling, which he may believe and respect, which can help, secure or deliver him. He cannot take others as examples and imitate them. He is given no directives. Even in himself he is and has and finds absolutely nothing of any significance, authority, power or value, so

[EN30] place-holder
[EN31] about-face
[EN32] ignominy of human existence
[EN33] problem-solver
[EN34] humanism
[EN35] a doctrine that makes life possible
[EN36] here and now

[340]

that he cannot even fall back upon himself. There is nothing on which he can fall back. What is behind him is always nothing. In the light of what is behind he has no prospect but hell. *Continuons!*[EN37]—as he says just before the final curtain in his *Huis Clos*. There remains only one true case of precedence in which life is possible and there is prospect of a genuine future. This is existence itself: *l'existence précède l'essence*[EN38] (p. 17). But man is the being who can live and be this case of precedence. He can first be nothing and then something. He can be as he wills to be, as he imagines and makes himself (p. 22). What is man? *Ce qui se jette vers un avenir et ce qui est conscient de se projeter dans l'avenir*[EN39]. What is man? *Un projet, qui se vit subjectivement, au lieu d'être une mousse, une pourriture ou un choux-fleur; rien n'existe préalablement à ce projet; rien n'est au ciel intelligible*[EN40]. Let it be clearly understood that he is not what he wills. What he wills (e.g., to join a political party, to write a book, to marry etc.) is only the manifestation of a more original decision. He is that as which he wills himself (p. 23 f.)—himself before all his thoughts, inclinations, passions and decisions, and self-evidently before all the external circumstance of his life, and above all before what is usually called his "destiny." He has not created himself. He is "projected into the world." But he is projected in order that he may choose, will and create himself. *L'homme est condamné*[EN41], but *condamné à être libre*[EN42]. (p. 37). He has no advisers. Even to choose possible advisers he must first have chosen himself, and every true and genuine adviser can only say to him: *Vous êtes libre, choisissez, c'est-à-dire inventez*[EN43]. (p. 47). It is to be noted that even the *essence* before him can only be what he can and will choose, will, invent and create as he chooses himself. *La vie n'a pas de sens a priori; avant que vous ne viviez la vie, elle n'est rien*[EN44]. (p. 87). Man has no future prospect apart from what he is, lives and does. For example, he cannot take part in a general kind of "progress." All that he can and may do is to act. *Il n'y a pas de réalité que dans l'action*[EN45]. (p. 55). What is man? He is *l'ensemble de ses actes;*[EN46] he is *sa vie*[EN47]; he is *une série d'entreprises*[EN48] (p. 58). *Ce qui compte c'est l'engagement total*[EN49]. (p. 62). It is always on man himself that there is laid the ineluctable necessity of this *engagement total* with every positive or negative possibility, with every acceptance and self-assertion, with every great or small decision, with all that is called either good or bad. This is inevitably the case. *Autour de lui les choses s'étaient groupées en ronde; elles s'attendaient sans faire signes, sans livrer la moindre indication, il était seul, sans aide et sans excuse, condamné à décider sans retour possible, condamné pour toujours à être libre*[EN50] (from *L'âge de raison*).

[341]

[EN37] let us continue!

[EN38] existence precedes essence

[EN39] One who projects himself into the future and is aware that he does so

[EN40] A project which one lives out deliberately instead of being froth, mold, or a cauliflower; nothing exists prior to or as a precondition of this project; nothing has a meaning written in the heavens

[EN41] The human beings is condemned

[EN42] that to which he is condemned is freedom

[EN43] You are free: choose, that is, invent

[EN44] Life has no pre-given meaning: before you live life, it is nothing

[EN45] Only in action is there reality

[EN46] the totality of his acts

[EN47] his life

[EN48] a series of undertakings

[EN49] It is one's total engagement in life that counts

[EN50] Things cluster round the individual in a circle: they await his decision without providing any clues, without giving him any indication how to act; he is alone, without help and without excuse, condemned to make a decision that allows no going back, condemned always to be free

Sartre denies the charge that his existentialism is naturalism. He is not concerned with how man is, but with how as such he is the being which freely chooses himself in his life. He also maintains that his existentialism is not materialism, but the only doctrine which does not make man into an object: *nous voulons constituer précisément le règne humain comme un ensemble des valeurs distinctes du règne matériel*[EN51]. (p. 65). Again, he claims that his existentialism is not pessimism, but points to the freedom of man and thus a genuine humanistic optimism. Above all, it is not libertinism. This is the point at which he has been most widely misunderstood, and therefore close attention must be paid to his own explicitly expressed desire that his concept of freedom should be understood as responsibility. One might, of course, ask to whom man is responsible? Who calls him to account for the life he has actually lived? But we must not overlook the fact that Sartre wishes the freedom of his new man to be ethically understood. In his strictly subjective action man is responsible for all men (p. 24). *En se choisissant il choisit tous les hommes*[EN52]. With each of his actions—and here his agreement with Kant cannot but be observed—he creates an image of man as he thinks he ought to be (*une image de l'homme tel que nous estimons qu'il doit être*). *Choisir d'être ceci ou cela c'est affirmer de même temps la valeur de ce que nous choisissons*[EN53]. What we choose is never the worse but the better, and can anything be "better" for us unless it is better for all? In consequence, our action at any time is a commitment not only of ourselves but of the whole of mankind (p. 24 f.). We ought always to ask ourselves: What would happen if everyone did as I am doing just now? This question provides the standard of truth according to which we choose and will ourselves (p. 29). Finally Sartre definitely repudiates the charge of subjectivism. For a man does not discover himself only in himself, but in relation to his fellows. And in himself he does not only discover himself, but his fellows too. *Pour obtenir une vérité quelconque sur moi il faut, que je passe par l'autre. L'autre est indispensable à mon existence, aussi bien d'ailleurs qu'à la connaissance que j'ai de moi … la découverte de mon intimité me découvre en même temps l'autre comme une liberté posée en face de moi …. Aussi découvrons-nous tout de suite un monde que nous appellerons l'inter-subjectivité et c'est dans ce monde que l'homme décide ce qu'il est et ce que sont les autres*[EN54] (p. 65 f.). What, therefore, Sartre desires is not merely individual freedom, *la liberté pour la liberté*[EN55], but freedom which depends entirely on the freedom of others and on which the freedom of others depends. Only within this corporate freedom does the individual act *de bonne foi*[EN56]; otherwise he acts *de mauvaise foi*[EN57] and is *un lâche*[EN58] or even *un salaud*[EN59] (p. 83 f.). While there is nothing that can be called "human nature," there is nevertheless an *universalité humaine de conditions*[EN60]. There are the great unvarying necessities of being in the world, of having to labour, to live with other men and to die (p. 67 f.). Freedom is

---

[EN51] we wish precisely to establish the human realm as a collection of values that is distinct from the material realm

[EN52] In choosing himself he chooses all people

[EN53] (an image of the human being as we think he ought to be). To choose to be this or that is to affirm in that very act the value of that which we choose

[EN54] To obtain any true understanding of myself it is necessary that I proceed by means of the other. The other is indispensable to my existence every bit as much as he is to whatever knowledge I have of myself … the discovery of my own inwardness reveals at the same time the other as a form of freedom over against me … Thus we discover immediately a world that we may call that of intersubjectivity, and it is in that world that the individual decides both what he is and what others are

[EN55] freedom for freedom's sake

[EN56] in good faith

[EN57] in bad faith

[EN58] a coward

[EN59] bastard

[EN60] a universality of the condition of being human

freedom within the order of these conditions. But what man is or shall be under these conditions is not a given reality but always requires (and this is what his existence means) to be [342] imagined, produced and built up (p. 70). It is to this that every man is committed: *Chaque homme se réalise en réalisant un type d'humanité …. Chacun de nous fait l'absolu en respirant, en mangeant, en dormant ou en agissant d'une facon quelconque*[EN61]. (p. 71 f.). In short, *il n'y a aucune différence entre être librement, être comme projet, comme existence qui choisit son essence et être absolu; et il n'y a aucune différence entre être absolu temporairement localisé, c'est-à-dire qui s'est localisé dans l'histoire et être compréhensible universellement*[EN62]. (p. 72).

Sartre clearly wishes existentialism to be understood as *un effort pour tirer toutes les conséquences d'une position athée cohérente*[EN63] (p. 94). Unlike the radicals of the 18th and 19th centuries, he is not particularly concerned to demonstrate the non-existence of God. He can even say *qu'il est très gênant, que Dieu n'existe pas*[EN64] (p. 35). The existence of God simply falls away because nothing of value, significance and capacity can precede human existence. Even if a proof of the existence of God were possible it could not alter the fact that there is nothing to precede the existence of man, to keep him from the "damnation of freedom," to spare him his responsibility for himself and for mankind, to deprive him of the magnificent defiance or defiant magnificence with which he conquers the nullity of everything which is not of his own will and invention, leaves all else behind and below, and fashions a new world, his own world, the world of his own human values. *L'existence précède l'essence*[EN65]. Even a God whose existence could be proved could only be added as an element in the essence which follows existence. Sartre shows real discernment in the fact that he cannot admit God even at this point, as a *valeur*[EN66] among other *valeurs*[EN67]. The real conclusion of his case against the existence of God is that He is absolutely superfluous where He should matter most, i.e., prior to human existence. For every "prior" can only be human existence itself. Hence God's place is already filled. The man who is projected into the world, who is necessarily active in it, who necessarily lives among his fellows, who is mortal, but who is free, who imagines, chooses and wills himself, who lives reasonably—this man is himself God. I cannot imagine how Sartre's existentialism can possibly be understood without the realisation that from first to last it involves the extraordinary but typically mythological spectacle of a theogony. To be sure, it is a strange, short-lived and stunted God who is conceived and born—a God for whom many allowances must be made before the claims which he advances, the powers which he assumes and the role which he tries to fill can be accepted. Nevertheless the position and significance claimed—*l'existence précède l'essence*[EN68]—are indisputable evidence that we are confronted by a God, or at least by something resembling the conventional Western conception of God. To be sure, this being is only man. Yet we see something of the passion of a monotheistic conception of God in the way in which man excludes and rejects the existence of God, of any other God. Sartre thought that in this way he could give man his proper place. But this obviously means that he gives him the place and function of God, i.e.,

---

[EN61] Each person realises himself in realising a form of humanity …. Each of us performs the absolute in breathing, in eating, in sleeping,or in doing anything whatsover

[EN62] there is no difference between existing freely, existing as a project, as an existent which chooses its essence, and absolute existence; and there is no difference between absolute existence that is temporally localised (that is, which is located in history) and existence universally conceived

[EN63] an attempt to draw out all the consequences of a coherent atheist position

[EN64] that God does not exist is very unfortunate

[EN65] Existence precedes essence

[EN66] value

[EN67] values

[EN68] Existence precedes essence

of the true God as distinct from all others. Naturally, we hardly ever find in his writings a specific equation of man with God. There are times when he almost makes this equation, e.g., when he says: *si j'ai supprimé Dieu le père, il faut bien quelqu'un pour inventer les valeurs*[EN69] (p. 89). But he only borders upon it. For all that he despises the positivism of the older French radicals, he is too deeply imbued with it to be speculative or even dialectic at this point. He can accomplish the apotheosis of man without God. It is as man that man assumes the functions of deity, and in spite of the strangeness of his form is clotted with the attributes of at least the conventional Western conception of God, existing of and by and for himself, constituting his own beginning and end as absolute actuality without potentiality, unique, omnipotent, and certainly omniscient. If I am not mistaken, not even the favourite attribute of infinity is lacking, for it may be seen in the unlimited nature of the claim which Sartre's

[343]   man-God advances for himself. All that is lacking is the slightest trace of the biblical concept of God. Yet the conventional Western figure of God is almost completely delineated, with the one difference that the existence of God is denied, and "atheistic" man, man discarding acknowledgment of any Supreme Being other than himself, stands forth clothed in the garments of the conventional figure of God.

Our first question concerns the position of God in these thinkers. We shall put it to Heidegger first, whose starting point is not quite the same as that of Sartre. Sartre regards Heidegger as a fellow-representative of atheistic existentialism (p. 17). It is to be noted, however, that Heidegger has recently denied that his doctrine is atheistic. Nevertheless, if he is no atheist, in the same sense although in a different way Sartre is not one either. He is perhaps an atheist in the sense that it is difficult to envisage any possible function and place for a God outside his threefold postulate of that which is (human) existence and nothing. But he is not an atheist in the sense that in his teaching the nature and functions of deity are not absent but are in fact transferred to another dimension. He, too, has not made an actual equation. But he cannot be understood unless it is realised that his teaching involves such an equation, not identical with but corresponding to that of Sartre. In Heidegger nothing is actually the pseudonym which conceals the Godhead. He considers it from the standpoint of man, whereas in Sartre it is itself the standpoint from which man is considered. In what is Heidegger a believer in the sense that Sartre is undoubtedly a believer in man? We have already seen that the basic question of metaphysics as wrested from nothing is why there is anything at all and not nothing. We have seen the underived and comprehensive dynamism and activity of this nothing: how it actually compels, obtrudes, repels and nihilates; how it can never be discovered by us, yet reveals itself in dread as the basic mood of existence; how our existence itself is a projection into nothing and is constituted by our enquiry into it; how to be open to nothing is the fundamental virtue of existence, and "distortion" of nothing its fundamental sin; and finally how even that which is, is only as nothing pervades and is present with it, and discloses itself to existence only as it becomes elusive and evanescent. We have seen that it is nothing that exhibits the nature and mode of that which is, and the fact that it is. We have seen that it is the whence and whither of transcendence, the basis and pure content of human science. We have seen that "pure being and pure nothing are one and the same," and that *ex nihilo omne ens qua ens fit*[EN70]. Must we not say that just as it is irrelevant that Sartre explicitly denies the existence of God, His place being taken and filled by man, so it is irrelevant that Heidegger does not explicitly deny it. His place being fully and finally taken and filled by the all-dominant and dynamic depth of nothing? We might easily say that if Sartre were not to deny God, and Heidegger to deny Him, it would not modify in either the

---

[EN69] though I have excluded God the Father, it nevertheless remains necessary for someone to establish a scale of values

[EN70] every being as being comes from nothing

essential fact that God is not dead, but that a substitute is provided and therefore He is suppressed, and put as it were "on the retired list." Heidegger differs from Sartre only in choosing a different substitute for God: "My cause on nothing is founded."* But in his teaching this substitute has actually arrogated the place and function of deity. Thus his doctrine, too, is really a mythological theogony. He is not concerned to interpret it in this way, or to make the express equation: "Nothing is God." He is content with nothing itself without the apotheosis of this designation. Nevertheless, after the suppression of God the Father he, too, required someone *pour inventer les valeurs*EN71. The "someone" that Heidegger discovered, approved and adopted to fulfil this function is nothing. Nothing is the basis, criterion and elucidation of everything, and in relation to it that which is can be only elusive and evanescent, and man can only be a *locum tenens*EN72. In Heidegger's thought, nothing seems lacking in none of the essential features of the conventional figure of God (aseity, uniqueness, omnipotence, omniscience, infinity etc.), but nothing has of course no relation to the biblical concept of God, which is not taken into account by either Heidegger or Sartre in their respective mythologies. It might well be said, then, that the God of the Bible, the living God, is entirely unaffected by the suppression and pensioning off of "God" in terms of these two mythologies. In the "God" whom Heidegger and Sartre suppress by providing a substitute for Him, the Church cannot possibly recognise the One whom it calls God. Nor can it recognise Him in the positive aspects of these mythologies, in their proposed substitutes for Him, whether it be said that man or that nothing is the first and the last word, the being from which all things derive and in which they find their end. From the standpoint of the biblical conception of God these alternative postulates between which we have to choose are only mythological fabrications in respect of the character, place and function attributed to them by Heidegger and Sartre.

[344]

But in our present discussion of Heidegger and Sartre we are concerned to learn about nothingness rather than God. It would seem that with the necessary reservations already made Heidegger turned towards and Sartre away from nothingness in order to press on in their different ways to absolutisations and therefore to their substitutes for God. What is this nothingness which is Heidegger's goal and Sartre's starting-point? What do they know of that which is obviously the conclusion for the one and the premise for the other? Is it or is it not identical with the nothingness with which we are here concerned in its relation and opposition to God? Is there anything to be learned from them, and if so, what?

We have observed that Heidegger and Sartre alike have remarkably little to say about God. And the God whom explicitly or implicitly they deny, or at least try to ignore and actually replace, is not the God whose relation and opposition to nothing we are considering. Even less so is the substitute for God which they venture to offer either in the form of man emerging from nothing or of nothing itself claiming man, in both cases with an actual though not an explicit identification. We are thus tempted to assume that, though Heidegger and Sartre are both in different ways concerned with nothing, they are concerned with something very different from the nothingness which we have here considered as nothingness before God. And indeed, in view of the state of their knowledge of God, we cannot expect from these two philosophers a knowledge of nothingness which is finally acceptable. But it would be an error to leave out of account the compulsion of the thing itself operative to some extent, and sometimes with remarkable force, in all human systems, and therefore the fact that for all the speculation something instructive and worth while is introduced. We can surely see its

---

* Parody of Johann Leon's Hymn: "Ich hab' mein Sach' Gott heim estellt" (My cause on God is founded).—Trans. note.

EN71 to establish a scale of values

EN72 place-holder

compulsion in the fact that even in their atheistic blindness Heidegger and Sartre could not escape the problem of God, that they could not remove, let alone deny Him with their actual replacement and denial. In this respect do they not see something they would rather not? And in view of that which confronts both the one and the other as nothing, are we not forced to ask whether they do not see something of that which, because of their ignorance of God, they could not really see, but which still seems in some sense to be quite manifest to them? I should like to call it the pure presence and operation of nothingness, in correspondence with what I have said about both seeming to be obsessed by it, so much so that it is for one the only end and for the other the only startingpoint. It may well be that what they know in this obsession, and what they have to say about it, is all false and ineffectual. It may well be that their knowledge of nothingness is vitiated by the fact that both are unable freely to direct their thoughts towards God, or to think from His standpoint, and are thus obsessed, constrained and captivated by and to this subject. But, the fact remains that from their thought and its expression as determined by this obsession an inference may be drawn which cannot [345] be drawn from the teaching of Leibniz or Schleiermacher, namely, that nothingness is really present and at work. It is no mere fiction or theme of discussion. It is no mere product of our negations to be dismissed by our affirmations. It is there. It assails us with irresistible power as we exist, and we exist as we are propelled by it into the world like a projectile. We are forced to consider it, for it already confronts us. We experience nothingness, and in so doing we experience ourselves and all things as well. Heidegger's astonishment is no less eloquent of this than Sartre's defiance, nor does the latter bear lesser witness. Their thought is determined in and by real encounter with nothingness. They may misinterpret this encounter and therefore nothingness, but not for a moment can they forget it. They misunderstand what they read, but this is the text which they undoubtedly read. Their thought and expression are determined in and by the considerable though not total upheaval of Western thought and expression occasioned by two world wars. They have completely abandoned the optimism and pessimism, the quietism and activism, the speculation and positivism of the 18th and 19th centuries. While the "road back" may not be closed altogether to them, for we cannot tell what the ultimate development of their systems will be, it is nevertheless heavily barred. For the moment at least they cannot deny that nothingness—and it might well be the true nothingness—has ineluctably and unforgettably addressed them, that the question of nothingness has emerged from the plenitude of problems and that it has become for them the real problem. We may certainly learn from them, if we have not learned it already, a more intense and acute awareness. In this sense, whether taught by Heidegger and Sartre or elsewhere, no one to-day can think or say anything of value without being an "existentialist" and thinking and speaking as such, i.e., without being confronted and affected by the disclosure of the presence and operation of nothingness as effected with particular impressiveness in our day. Whoever is ignorant of the shock experienced and attested by Heidegger and Sartre is surely incapable of thinking and speaking as a modern man and unable to make himself understood by his contemporaries. For we men of to-day have consciously or unconsciously sustained this shock. In our time man has encountered nothingness in such a way as to be offered an exceptional opportunity in this respect. More than that may and must not be said, for at all times man has his being within this encounter, and no more than an exceptional opportunity of realising this is offered us even to-day. Even to-day we have no reason to boast that "we have looked in the face of demons." Although an exceptional opportunity is offered us to-day of recognising nothing in encounter with it, it does not follow that this has actually taken place. There are grounds for believing that it has not really done so in the case of Heidegger and Sartre. But it cannot be denied that in an outstanding way they have grasped an outstanding opportunity to do so. And their positive value is to direct their age to this outstanding opportunity, to introduce the subject of nothingness with such urgency. In this respect they reach a point unreached in much ancient and modern—and even Christian—literature.

But in spite of our indebtedness to them for bringing us to the point, to *this* point, we cannot agree that, with their doctrine of nothing, our existentialists have even entered the dimension in which nothingness is to be seen and described as true nothingness by Christian insights. This is naturally of a piece with their ignorance of God, in consequence of which they cannot adopt the standpoint from which one must see and think and speak in this matter. They see and think and speak as true, alert and honest children of our time who have experienced themselves the shock sustained by modern man. Yet they still resemble Leibniz and Schleiermacher in the fact that they do so from an arbitrary human standpoint and in the unshakeable confidence that they themselves can and should assume such a standpoint, that they are free to choose it, and that, from it they are able to see things as they really are. In a fine sentence Heidegger says of science that "its distinction lies in the fact [346] that, in an altogether specific manner, it and it alone explicitly allows the object itself the first and last word. In such objectivity there is a submission to what is, so that this may reveal itself" (p. 357). But in respect of the choice and assumption of the scientific standpoint there is no such "submission to what is" by Heidegger and Sartre. At this point "the object itself" has neither a first nor a last word nor anything at all to say to them. The one thing that has not been affected, let alone broken, by the upheaval of the age—and it cannot be effected by purely secular upheavals—is the self-reliant assurance of the *ego cogito*[EN73] as the presupposition of their whole systems. From the standpoint of the *ego cogito*[EN74] true nothingness cannot be discerned, no matter how powerful the impression of its presence and operation may be. From this standpoint nothingness cannot be interpreted in any other way than it has been and always will be when the Christian basis of knowledge is left out of account. It is futile to deny that what the existentialists encounter and objectively perceive is real nothingness. Yet it must be stated most emphatically that seeing they do not really see. What they see, describe and proclaim is not real nothingness, just as the God whom, denying or not denying, they ignore and replace by surrogates is not the real God.

We shall first take the case of Sartre. We have said that nothing is behind him. He has definitely apprehended it as evil and bad. He has really recognised it as calamity and misery. He has experienced so powerfully its actuality that he constantly reverts to it and confronts himself and his contemporaries with it. He is so deeply engrossed in it that one might easily misunderstand his position and think that his only concern is to "debunk" man and the world. Yet nothing is actually behind him. His threefold advantage is that he sees it (1) in its reality, (2) in its actuality, and yet also (3) as behind and beneath. Here a distant recollection of Christian perception might almost be seen. Badness and evil exist in full actuality, yet in such a way as to be behind and below, sterilised, vitiated and overthrown. We cannot but admire the virile address and resolution with which Sartre sets this matter behind him. But at the same time it is here that the most serious problem confronts his system. For who is it that sets the matter behind him? It is the man who in the midst of corruption and ruin defiantly chooses, imagines and wills himself; who, projected into the world, projects himself into the future, his own future; who undertakes to live his life in full and sole responsibility for himself. We are moved to say to this man: "Well done, we are with you." But have we not heard the same before? Was not the ancient watchword of the Stoics: *si fractus illabatur orbis impavidum ferient ruinae*[EN75]? There is not much to be said against this slogan, and a good deal for it. But it is to be noted that real nothingness cannot be set aside by a pinch of

---

[EN73] thinking self
[EN74] thinking self
[EN75] if the world were to crumble to fragments, they would strike undaunted at the ruins

indifferent resolution. If "I" can cope with it, opposing "myself" to it victorious in defeat; if I can acknowledge and resist it by defying it, it is not true nothingness. It may well be significant, violent, threatening and extremely aggressive, but if I can confront it with sovereign power, if I can deal with it, if I can even play with it in changing situations, if I can set it behind me, I cannot convince myself that I have to do with the true and deadly dangerous adversary of myself and man and life. As I project myself into my future, disposing of the enemy who can be disposed of in this way, i.e., of adverse circumstances, of human folly and evil and their consequent entanglements, of all the calamities of the age, might it not be that in the course of this most courageous and successful conflict of St. George with the dragon, the true and deadly dangerous enemy quietly leers over my shoulder from behind and mocks my manliness, the more secure because I have obviously forgotten him in learning and then happily outgrowing a little terror? As I project myself into my future, might it not be that the true enemy accompanies my flight, and easily overhauls me, and is at the goal before me? Might it not be that in real nothingness I have an adversary who is quite unim-

[347] pressed by my vaunted sense of responsibility for myself and mankind, the more so as I do not know to whom I owe this responsibility, and who is my judge? Might it not be that I have to do with a refutation and abolition of the very existence which I boldly assert to precede all essence? This enemy and adversary, this one who refutes and abolishes my existence, this No which strikes and brackets the Yes with which I try to overcome it, might well be real nothingness. And Sartre does not have the slightest inkling of it. Otherwise he could not have fabricated the myth in which man is in effect the God who can master and control nothingness. The paltriness of this God, or rather the fact that Sartre is capable of thinking that he is not paltry but a majestic deity well equipped to fight the dragon, indicates that the dragon envisaged by him is comparatively innocuous. In the conflict with it a truce is possible, but decisive victory can never be gained. This dragon may be handled as Sartre handles it. It may be made a subject of literary elegance. It may be continually presented and represented as a spectacle which affords the public enraptured dread or dreadful rapture. The public may be taught how to overcome it. Or with a cynical sneer the attempt may be made to teach it. Those who have the gift, like Sartre, can make existentialism fashionable as a humanism, as the old but ever new gospel of the free sovereignty of man. By this existentialism some slight encouragement may be given to man as with two world wars behind him he faces the second half of the strange concluding century of the second Christian millennium. The intention is good. So, too, is the act. To inject morphia is often a good act. Yet the fact that it can be effected or attempted is itself evidence that the case is not as severe as at first supposed. If it were realised that this is a case of "sickness unto death," a syringe of morphia would not be used. That Sartre uses it is evidence that the sickness unto death, real nothingness, is as unknown to him as the true God.

We return to Heidegger. His case is different to the extent that nothingness, or what might seem to be such, is before him. He is in no sense a *débrouillard*[EN76]. He has not mastered this factor, neither does he trifle with it. He handles it with religious solemnity. The effect which he produces is therefore immeasurably more serious than that of Sartre. His apparent aversion to Sartre is thus comprehensible, as is the indignation of his friends at the idea that he should even be named in the same breath as Sartre, let alone be considered beside him. We are undoubtedly in a different milieu. But when we address to him the same question as to Sartre, enquiring concerning nothingness, we can only say that his blindness regarding it is as great as Sartre's. Although it cannot be without significance in a writer so word-conscious as Heidegger, the fact might easily escape our notice that only once in his study on metaphysics does he explicitly define nothing as nothingness, and this only by way of introduction and

---

[EN76] problem-solver

in definition of its a-logical nature. For him it is in no sense nothingness. That it discloses itself in the basic mood of dread might indicate a trend in this direction. But in its most real form this dread (and this is a direct agreement with Sartre) is already overcome. It is peace, serenity and even daring. And that as which nothing reveals itself in dread, Heidegger's nothing in itself and as such, has no power to awaken dread at all. Otherwise how could it arrogate the functions of God and become a substitute for Him, as in Heidegger's myth? Otherwise Heidegger would surely have had to say that the devil is the true God. But he never dreams of saying this, because for him nothing is not a dreadful, horrible, dark abyss but something fruitful and salutary and radiant. In face of Heidegger's nothing, acceptance and not exclusion is demanded. For without such acceptance there can be no metaphysics or science. Indeed there can be no existence except as a projection into nothing. What possible relationship can there be between the nothing which in this positive sense can replace God and arrogate and exercise His functions, and true nothingness? Heidegger's nothing is an ambivalent concept. Heidegger was quite serious when as early as 1929 he accepted the Hegelian identification of nothing with being. In this writing the leading concept might well be replaced throughout by that of being without modifying in any way the [348] sense and substance of his exposition. In a letter on humanism written in 1946 to one of Sartre's French followers, and published in 1947 in the appendix to *Platons Lèhre von der Wahrheit*, Heidegger does in fact effect this replacement, introducing the "truth of being" as the subject of exactly the same assertions as in 1929 were made concerning nothing. In place of the "nihilation of nothing" there now emerges with equal intensity and like effect the "affirmation of being" (*das Lichten des Seins*), and existence as projection into nothing is now "ecstatic" *ek-sistere*, "entry into the truth of being." All the negative inferences drawn by disciples or critics of the earlier form of his teaching in respect of humanism, logic, values, transcendence, the highest and holiest good of men, and even God, are now dismissed as false with an air of contempt for such pedantries of logic (p. 95 f.). Indeed, a place is now found for God (or at least for "God and the gods" p. 85) as a dimension of being, namely, the "dimension of the Holy" (p. 102), and in the history of being there is the prospect or possibility of the dawning of a "day of the saints" (p. 85). We are tempted to say: "Behold all things are made new," but this would involve another and more radical misunderstanding of Heidegger. For if the earlier work is intelligently read, it is obvious that even there nothing is also being, that in some dimension it may be the holy or even God, and that it does actually arrogate and exercise a divine function. On the other hand, his concept of being in 1946 is still ambivalent, and therefore does not cease to comprehend the nothing of 1929. When being asserts itself positively, wholeness is accompanied by that which is evil and horrible. Being itself is "that which is disputed." "In it is concealed the origin of the essence of nihilation from which every Not derives and which gives to every genuine negation its legitimacy and necessity" (p. 112). There is really nothing new. Heidegger is thoroughly consistent. In 1946 he merely reverses his concept of nothing. But even in 1929 is not the concept reversible and actually reversed? Nor is there anything original in this. Heidegger himself tells us that in his dialectic he is pursuing the path of older philosophy, gnosticism and mysticism. It is not for us to estimate the legitimacy of this dialectic. But one conclusion is inevitable. The nothing of Heidegger, which may also be called being and under either title arrogates the function of God, can never be identified with nothingness in the Christian sense. Whatever it may be that Heidegger perceives and expounds (and he and the tradition which he obviously follows must accept responsibility for this), it is absolutely certain that his nothing is not real nothingness, but is comparatively innocuous as compared with it. The concept of real nothingness is in no sense ambivalent. If Heidegger had perceived real nothingness, he would not have described the dread in which his nothing discloses itself as though it were not basically dread but peace, serenity and daring. The sickness unto death in which man is confronted by real nothingness has a different aspect. The dialectic in which nothing may reveal itself as being and being as nothing is a useless instrument in face of it. If Heidegger had seen it, he might well have spoken of the relativity, inferiority, subjugation and vitiation of nothing, and shown that in spite of its nature it can be subordinated to the service of being and brought under its control. But in so doing he would have established and authenticated it as nothing, and could not have conceived of its identification with being, nor even dreamt of attributing to it of all things the sovereign role and function constitutive of being and existence. He would have realised that to do this is to proclaim the devil to be the principle of all being and existence. The unhesitating confidence with which he did what he could not possibly have done if he had perceived real nothingness is conclusive evidence that he did not perceive it. Thus by a different route we reach the same conclusion as in the case of Sartre.

[349] Credit must be given to both that in so striking a way they looked and pointed in the direction in which real nothingness can actually be perceived in other circumstances. Yet we cannot but say of both that their accounts of what they have seen in this direction have so far been a false alarm.

4. THE REALITY OF NOTHINGNESS

Forearmed and forewarned by these discussions, we may now attempt a comprehensive statement. What is real nothingness?

1. In this question objection may well be taken to the word "is." Only God and His creature really and properly are. But nothingness is neither God nor His creature. Thus it can have nothing in common with God and His creatures. But it would be foolhardy to rush to the conclusion that it is therefore nothing, i.e., that it does not exist. God takes it into account. He is concerned with it. He strives against it, resists and overcomes it. If God's reality and revelation are known in His presence and action in Jesus Christ, He is also known as the God who is confronted by nothingness, for whom it constitutes a problem, who takes it seriously, who does not deal with it incidentally but in the fulness of the glory of His deity, who is not engaged indirectly or mediately but with His whole being, involving Himself to the utmost. If we accept this, we cannot argue that because it has nothing in common with God and His creature nothingness is nothing, i.e., it does not exist. That which confronts God in this way, and is seriously treated by Him, is surely not nothing or non-existent. In the light of God's relationship to it we must accept the fact that in a third way of its own nothingness "is." All conceptions or doctrine which would deny or diminish or minimise this "is" are untenable from the Christian standpoint. Nothingness is not nothing. Quite apart from the inadmissibility of its content, this proposition would be self-contradictory. But it "is" nothingness. Its nature and being are those which can be assigned to it within this definition. But because it stands before God as such they must be assigned to it. They cannot be controverted without misapprehending God Himself.

2. Again, nothingness is not simply to be equated with what is *not*, i.e., not God and not the creature. God is God and not the creature, but this does not

mean that there is nothingness in God. On the contrary, this "not" belongs to His perfection. Again, the creature is creature and not God, yet this does not mean that as such it is null or nothingness. If in the relationship between God and creature a "not" is involved, the "not" belongs to the perfection of the relationship, and even the second "not" which characterises the creature belongs to its perfection. Hence it would be blasphemy against God and His work if nothingness were to be sought in this "not," in the non-divinity of the creature. The diversities and frontiers of the creaturely world contain many "nots." No single creature is all-inclusive. None is or resembles another. To each belongs its own place and time, and in these its own manner, nature and   [350] existence. What we have called the "shadow side" of creation is constituted by the "not" which in this twofold respect, as its distinction from God and its individual distinctiveness, pertains to creaturely nature. On this shadow side the creature is contiguous to nothingness, for this "not" is at once the expression and frontier of the positive will, election and activity of God. When the creature crosses the frontier from the one side, and it is invaded from the other, nothingness achieves actuality in the creaturely world. But in itself and as such this frontier is not nothingness, nor has the shadow side of creation any connexion with it. Therefore all conceptions and doctrines which view nothingness as an essential and necessary determination of being and existence and therefore of the creature, or as an essential determination of the original and creative being of God Himself, are untenable from the Christian standpoint. They are untenable on two grounds, first, because they misrepresent the creature and even the Creator Himself, and second, because they confound the legitimate "not" with nothingness, and are thus guilty of a drastic minimisation of the latter.

3. Since real nothingness is real in this third fashion peculiar to itself, not resembling either God or the creature but taken seriously by God Himself, and since it is not identical either with the distinction and frontier between God and creation or with those within the creaturely world, its revelation and knowledge cannot be a matter of the insight which is accessible to the creature itself and is therefore set under its own choice and control. Standing before God in its own characteristic way which is very different from that of the creature, the object of His concern and action, His problem and adversary and the negative goal of His victory, nothingness does not possess a nature which can be assessed nor an existence which can be discovered by the creature. There is no accessible relationship between the creature and nothingness. Hence nothingness cannot be an object of the creature's natural knowledge. It is certainly an objective reality for the creature. The latter exists objectively in encounter with it. But it is disclosed to the creature only as God is revealed to the latter in His critical relationship. The creature knows it only as it knows God in His being and attitude against it. It is an element in the history of the relationship between God and the creature in which God precedes the creature in His acts, thus revealing His will to the creature and informing it about Himself. As this

occurs and the creature attains to the truth—the truth about God's purpose and attitude and therefore about itself—through the Word of God, the encounter of the creature with true nothingness is also realised and recognised. Of itself, the creature cannot recognise this encounter and what it encounters. It experiences and endures it. But it also misinterprets it, as has [351] always happened. Calumniating God and His work, it misrepresents it as a necessity of being or nature, as a given factor, as a peculiarity of existence which is perhaps deplorable, perhaps also justifiable, perhaps to be explained in terms of perfection or simply to be dismissed as non-existent, as something which can be regarded as supremely positive in relation to God, or even as a determination of God Himself. All these conceptions and doctrines, whatever their content, are untenable from a Christian standpoint if only because they are contingent upon an arbitrary and impotent appraisal of what can only make itself known in the judgment of God, and is thus knowable only as God pronounces His sentence, while its malignity and corruption find supreme expression in the assumption of the creature that of itself and at its own discretion it is able to discover its nature and existence.

4. The ontic context in which nothingness is real is that of God's activity as grounded in His election, of His activity as the Creator, as the Lord of His creatures, as the King of the covenant between Himself and man which is the goal and purpose of His creation. Grounded always in election, the activity of God is invariably one of jealousy, wrath and judgment. God is also holy, and this means that His being and activity take place in a definite opposition, in a real negation, both defensive and aggressive. Nothingness is that from which God separates Himself and in face of which He asserts Himself and exerts His positive will. If the biblical conception of the God whose activity is grounded in election and is therefore holy fades or disappears, there will also fade and disappear the knowledge of nothingness, for it will necessarily become pointless. Nothingness has no existence and cannot be known except as the object of God's activity as always a holy activity. The biblical conception, as we now recall it, is as follows. God elects, and therefore rejects what He does not elect. God wills, and therefore opposes what He does not will. He says Yes, and therefore says No to that to which He has not said Yes. He works according to His purpose, and in so doing rejects and dismisses all that gainsays it. Both of these activities, grounded in His election and decision, are necessary elements in His sovereign action. He is Lord both on the right hand and on the left. It is only on this basis that nothingness "is," but on this basis it really "is." As God is Lord on the left hand as well, He is the basis and Lord of nothingness too. Consequently it is not adventitious. It is not a second God, nor self-created. It has no power save that which it is allowed by God. It, too, belongs to God. It "is" problematically because it is only on the left hand of God, under His No, the object of His jealousy, wrath and judgment. It "is," not as God and His creation are, but only in its own improper way, as inherent contradiction, as impossible possibility. Yet because it is on the left hand of God, it really "is" in this para-

doxical manner. Even on His left hand the activity of God is not in vain. He [352]
does not act for nothing. His rejection, opposition, negation and dismissal are
powerful and effective like all His works because they, too, are grounded in
Himself, in the freedom and wisdom of His election. That which God
renounces and abandons in virtue of His decision is not merely nothing. It is
nothingness, and has as such its own being, albeit malignant and perverse. A
real dimension is disclosed, and existence and form are given to a reality *sui
generis*[EN77], in the fact that God is wholly and utterly not the Creator in this
respect. Nothingness is that which God does not will. It lives only by the fact
that it is that which God does not will. But it does live by this fact. For not only
what God wills, but what He does not will, is potent, and must have a real
correspondence. What really corresponds to that which God does not will is
nothingness.

The first and most impressive mention of nothingness in the Bible is to be found at the
very beginning in Gen. 1^2 (cf. *C.D.*, III, 1, p. 101 f.), in which there is a reference to the chaos
which the Creator has already rejected, negated, passed over and abandoned even before
He utters His first creative Word, which He has already consigned to the past and to oblivion
even before the beginning of time at His command. Chaos is the unwilled and uncreated
reality which constitutes as it were the periphery of His creation and creature. It is that
which, later depicted in very suitable mythological terms and conceptions, is antithetical
both to God Himself and to the world of heaven and earth which He selected, willed and
created. It is a mere travesty of the universe. It is the horrible perversion which opposes God
and tempts and threatens His creature. It is that which, though it is succeeded and overcome
by light, can never itself be light but must always remain darkness. Note that the first creative
work (Gen. $1^{3f.}$) is simply separation—the separation of light from darkness, of the waters on
the earth from the threatening waters above the firmament, of the dry land from the seas.
Note also that with this separation there arises even within the good creation of God a side
which is as it were the neighbour and frontier of chaos. But chaos is not night, or the waters
above the firmament, or the earthly sea. It still remains not merely distinct from the works of
God, but excluded by the operation of God, a fleeting shadow and a receding frontier. Only
in this way can we say that it "is." But in this way it undoubtedly "is," and is thus subject to the
divine sovereignty. In this way it is present from the very outset with God and His creature. In
this way it is involved from the very outset in the history of the relationship between God and
His creature, and therefore from the very outset the biblical witness to this history takes its
existence into account. The sin of man as depicted in Gen. 3 confirms the accuracy of our
definition. It is purely and simply what God did not, does not and cannot will. It has the
essence only of non-essence, and only as such can it exist. Yet the sin of man also confirms
the real existence of nothingness. Nothingness is a factor so real that the creature of God,
and among His creatures man especially in whom the purpose of creation is revealed, is not
only confronted by it and becomes its victim, but makes himself its agent. And all the subsequent history of the relationship between God and His creature is marked by the fact that
man is the sinner who has submitted and fallen a victim to chaos. The issue in this whole
history is the repulse and final removal of the threat thus actualised. And God Himself is
always the One who first takes this threat seriously, who faces and throws Himself against it,
who strives with chaos, who persists in His attitude, who cortinues and completes the action
which He has already undertaken as Creator in this respect, negating and rejecting it. As He

---

[EN77] in its own category

[353] affirms and elects and works His *opus proprium*[EN78], the work of His grace, God is always active in His *opus alienum*[EN79] as well. And He is always holy. Therefore He always wills that His creature should be holy. He wills to take part in its conflict. Since it is really His own cause, He wills to place Himself alongside it in this conflict.

Nothingness "is," therefore, in its connexion with the activity of God. It "is" because and as and so long as God is against it. It "is" only in virtue of the fact that God is against it in jealousy, wrath and judgment. It "is" only within the limits thus ordained. But within these limits it "is." From the Christian standpoint, therefore, any conception must be regarded as untenable if it ascribes to nothingness any other existence than in confrontation with God's non-willing. It would be untenable from a Christian point of view to ascribe autonomous existence independent of God or willed by Him like that of His creature. Only the divine non-willing can be accepted as the ground of its existence. Equally untenable from a Christian standpoint, however, is any conception in which its existence in opposition to the divine non-willing is denied and it is declared to be a mere semblance. Within this limit nothingness is no semblance but a reality, just as God's non-willing in relation to it, and the whole *opus alienum*[EN80] of the divine jealousy, wrath and judgment, is no semblance but a reality.

5. The character of nothingness derives from its ontic peculiarity. It is evil. What God positively wills and performs in the *opus proprium*[EN81] of His election, of His creation, of His preservation and overruling rule of the creature revealed in the history of His covenant with man, is His grace—the free goodness of His condescension in which He wills, identifying Himself with the creature, to accept solidarity and to be present with it, to be Himself its Guarantor, Helper and King, and therefore to do the best possible for it. What God does not will and therefore negates and rejects, what can thus be only the object of His *opus alienum*[EN82], of His jealousy, wrath and judgment, is a being that refuses and resists and therefore lacks His grace. This being which is alien and adverse to grace and therefore without it, is that of nothingness. This negation of His grace is chaos, the world which He did not choose or will, which He could not and did not create, but which, as He created the actual world, He passed over and set aside, marking and excluding it as the eternal past, the eternal yesterday. And this is evil in the Christian sense, namely, what is alien and adverse to grace, and therefore without it. In this sense nothingness is really privation, the attempt to defraud God of His honour and right and at the same time to rob the creature of its salvation and right. For it is God's honour and right to be gracious, and this is what nothingness contests. It is also the salvation and right of the creature to receive and live by the grace of

---

[EN78] proper work
[EN79] alien work
[EN80] strange work
[EN81] proper work
[EN82] alien work

God, and this is what it disturbs and obstructs. Where this privation occurs, nothingness is present; and where nothingness is present this privation occurs, [354] i.e., evil, that which is utterly inimical first to God and then to His creature. The grace of God is the basis and norm of all being, the source and criterion of all good. Measured by this standard, as the negation of God's grace, nothingness is intrinsically evil. It is both perverting and perverted. In this capacity it does not confront either God or the creature neutrally. It is not merely a third factor. It opposes both as an enemy, offending God and threatening His creature. From above as well as from below, it is the impossible and intolerable. By reason of this character, whether in the form of sin, evil or death, it is inexplicable as a natural process or condition. It is altogether inexplicable. The explicable is subject to a norm and occurs within a standard. But nothingness is absolutely without norm or standard. The explicable conforms to a law, nothingness to none. It is simply aberration, transgression, evil. For this reason it is inexplicable, and can be affirmed only as that which is inherently inimical. For this reason it can be apprehended in its aspect of sin only as guilt, and in its aspect of evil and death only as retribution and misery, but never as a natural process or condition, never as a subject of systematic formulation, even though the system be dialectical. Being hostile before and against God, and also before and against His creature, it is outside the sphere of systematisation. It cannot even be viewed dialectically, let alone resolved. Its defeat can be envisaged only as the purpose and end of the history of God's dealings with His creature, and in no other way. As it is real only by reason of the *opus Dei alienum*[EN83], the divine negation and rejection, so it can be seen and understood only in the light of the *opus Dei proprium*[EN84], only in relation to the sovereign counter-offensive of God's free grace. It "is" only as the disorder at which this counter-offensive is aimed, only as the non-essence which it judges, only as the enemy of God and His creation. We thus affirm that it is necessary to dismiss as non-Christian all those conceptions in which its character as evil is openly or secretly, directly or indirectly, conjured away, and its reality is in some way regarded or grouped with that of God and His creature. Where God and His creature are known, and His free grace as the basic order of their relationship, nothingness can only be understood as opposition and resistance to this basic order and cannot therefore be regarded or grouped with God and His creature.

6. The controversy with nothingness, its conquest, removal and abolition, are primarily and properly God's own affair. It is true of course, that it constitutes a threat to the salvation and right of the creature, but primarily and supremely it contests the honour and right of God the Creator. It is also true that in the form of sin nothingness is the work and guilt, and in the form of evil and death the affliction and misery, of the creature. Yet in all these forms it is first

---

EN83 the alien work of God
EN84 God's proper work

[355] and foremost the problem of God Himself. Even the man who submits to nothingness and becomes its victim is still His creature. His care for His creature takes substance as its work and guilt and affliction and misery engender such rebellion and ruin, such disturbance and destruction. It is true, again, that God does not contend with nothingness without allowing His creature a share in the contention, without summoning His creature to His side as His co-belligerent. Yet the contention remains His own. His is the cause at stake, His all the power, His all the wisdom, His every weapon profitable and effectual in the strife. His free grace alone is victorious even where it is given to His creature to be victorious in this conflict. Everything depends upon the performance of His *opus proprium*[EN85]. Only with the operation of His election and grace, and only as its converse, is His *opus alienum*[EN86] also performed, and the sovereign No pronounced by which nothingness is granted its distinctive form and existence. Only within the limit of His No does nothingness have its reality, and in its reality its character as that which is evil, alien and adverse to grace, and therefore without it. And the limit of His No, and therefore of nothingness, is His Yes, the work of His free grace. As God performs this work, espousing the cause of the creature, He engages in controversy with nothingness, and deals with it, as is fitting, as that which separated, passed over and abandoned, as the eternal yesterday. He exercises the non-willing by which it can have existence, and His jealousy, wrath and judgment achieve their purpose and therefore their end, which is also the end and destruction of nothingness. It is God's *opus proprium*[EN87], the work of His right hand, which alone renders pointless and superfluous His *opus alienum*[EN88], the work of His left. This penetration and victory of His free grace as the achievement of the separation already recognisable in creation, and therefore as the destruction of chaos, is the meaning of the history of the relationship between God and His creature. He alone, His activity grounded in His election, can master nothingness and guide the course of history towards this victory. God alone can defend His honour, ensure His creature's salvation, and maintain His own and His creature's right in such a way that every assault is warded off and the assailant himself is removed. God alone can summon, empower and arm the creature to resist and even to conquer this adversary. This is what has taken place in Jesus Christ. But it has taken place in Him as the work of the creature only in the strength of the work of the Creator. The creature as such would be no match for nothingness and certainly unable to overcome it.

It is not insignificant that the story of the creature in its relationship to God begins in Gen. 3 with a disastrous defeat, and that in the terrible form of human sin the chaos separated by God becomes a factor and secures and exercises a power which does not belong to it in relation to God but can obviously do so in relation to His creature. The creature had neither

---

EN85 proper work
EN86 alien work
EN87 proper work
EN88 alien work

the capacity nor the power to effect that separation. It neither could nor should be God, judging between good and evil. It could and should live only by the grace of God and in [356] virtue of the judgment already accomplished by Him. It could not and should not deal with nothingness as God did, nor master and overcome it like God. Only in covenant with God could it and should it confront nothingness in absolute freedom. And even in covenant with God, where God never fails, there could be and has been failure on the part of the creature. It is worth noting that in Gen. 3 the failure of the creature consisted in the fact that, succumbing to the insinuations of nothingness, it desired to be like God, judging between good and evil, itself effecting that separation, unwilling to live by the grace of God and on the basis of the judgment already accomplished by Him, or to persist in the covenant with God which is its only safeguard against nothingness. It did evil by desiring to do in its own strength the good which cannot be done save by God alone and by the creature only in covenant with Him. The creature sinned by thinking, speaking and acting in a way alien and adverse to grace and therefore without it. We are certainly not to say that man was capable of sin. There is no capacity for nothingness in human nature and therefore in God's creation, nor is there any freedom in this direction as willed, ordained and instituted by God. When man sinned he performed the impossible, not acting as a free agent but as a prisoner. We can and must say, however, that the creature in itself and as such did not and does not confront nothingness in such a way as to be exempt from its insinuation, temptation and power. It cannot, then, be secured against it apart from the grace of God, nor is it a match for it in its own strength. If it tries to meet and fight it in its own strength, as in Gen. 3, it has already succumbed to it. This is the disastrous defeat of the creature by nothingness as typically described in Gen. 3.

The incredible and real mystery of the free grace of God is that He makes His own the cause of the creature which is not even the equal of nothingness, let alone its master, but its victim. There is a grain of truth in the erroneous view that in virtue of His Godhead God Himself has absolutely done away with nothingness, so that for Him it is not only nothingness but nothing. In Him there is room only for its negation. And as the Creator He has effected this negation once and for all. In creation He separated, negated, rejected and abandoned nothingness. How, then, can it still assail, oppose, resist and offend Him? How can it concern Him? But we must not pursue this thought to its logical end. We have not to forget the covenant, mercy and faithfulness of God, nor should we overlook the fact that God did not will to be God for His own sake alone, but that as the Creator He also became the covenant Partner of His creature, entering into a relationship with it in which He wills to be directly and primary involved in all that concerns it. His grace as the basis of His relationship with His creature means that whatever concerns and affects the creature concerns and affects Himself, not indirectly but directly, not subsequently and incidentally but primarily and supremely. Why is this so? Because, having created the creature, He has pledged His faithfulness to it. The threat of nothingness to the creature's salvation is primarily and supremely an assault upon His own majesty. That is to say, He whom nothingness has no power to offend is prepared on behalf of His creature to be primarily and properly offended and humiliated, attacked and injured by nothingness. [357] For the sake of the creature which of itself can be no match for it, He Himself is willing not to be an easy match for it. He thus casts Himself into this conflict which is not necessarily His own. Where His creature stands or succumbs, He comes and exposes Himself to the threat of assault, to the confrontation with nothingness which the creature cannot escape and in which it falls an easy prey. God is not too great, nor is He ashamed, to enter this situation which is not only threatened but already corrupted, to confess Himself the Friend and Fellow of the sinful creature which is not only subject to the assault but broken by it, to acknowledge Himself the Neighbour of the sinful creature stricken and smitten by its own fault, and to act accordingly He Himself inaugurates the history of His covenant with this impotent and faithless partner. His grace does not stop short because it sees that, in spite of the nature which He has given it and the freedom for which He has determined it, the creature is alien and adverse to grace and therefore without it. Though Adam is fallen and disgraced, he is not too low for God to make Himself his Brother, and to be for him a God who must strangely contend for his status, honour and right. For the sake of this Adam God becomes poor. He identifies His own honour and right, which nothingness is obviously unable to contest, with the salvation and right of His creature, which is not only exposed but has already succumbed to its threat. He lets a catastrophe which might be quite remote from Him approach Him and affect His very heart. He makes this alien conflict His very own. He does this of His free grace. For He is under no compulsion. He might act as the erroneous view postulates. He might remain aloof and detached from nothingness. He need not involve Himself. Having given free course to His jealousy, wrath and judgment once and for all in creation, He might have refrained from any further exercise of them. He might have been a majestic, passive and beatific God on high. But He descends to the depths, and concerns Himself with nothingness, because in His goodness He does not will to cease to be concerned for His creature. He thus continues to act in relation to nothingness with the same holiness with which He acted as the Creator when He separated light from darkness. He continues to be the Adversary of this adversary because His love for the creature has no limit nor end. He does not will to be faithful to Himself except as He is faithful to His creature, adopting its cause and therefore constantly making the alien problem of nothingness His own.

Thus it follows that the controversy with nothingness, its conquest, removal and abolition, is primarily and properly the cause of God Himself. At first sight we might regard the converse as true. Nothingness is the danger, assault and menace under which the creature as such must exist. Therefore the creature as such is surely the hero who must suffer and fight and finally conquer this adversary, and the conflict with it is the problem of his destiny and decision, his tragedy and courage, his impotence and comparative successes. But there can be no greater delusion nor catastrophe than to take this view. For it would not be real nothingness, but only an ultimately innocuous counterfeit, if the attack were primarily and properly directed against the creature, and its

[358]

68

repulse could and should be primarily and properly the creature's concern. And while the creature is preoccupied with the assault and repulse of these counterfeits, it is already subject to the attack of real nothingness and its defence against it is already futile. In face of real nothingness the creature is already defeated and lost. For, as Gen. 3 shows, it regards the conflict with it as its own cause, and tries to champion it as such. It tries to be itself the hero who suffers and fights and conquers, and therefore like God. And because this decision is a decision against the grace of God, it is a choice of evil. For good—the one and only good of the creature—is the free grace of God, the action of His mercy, in which He who has no need to do so has made the controversy with nothingness His own, exposing Himself to its attack and undertaking to repel it. He knows nothingness. He knows that which He did not elect or will as the Creator. He knows chaos and its terror. He knows its advantage over His creature. He knows how inevitably it imperils His creature. Yet He is Lord over that which imperils His creature. Against Him, nothingness has no power of its own. And He has sworn fidelity to His threatened creature. In creating it He has covenanted and identified Himself with it. He Himself has assumed the burden and trouble of confrontation with nothingness. He would rather be unblest with His creature than be the blessed God of an unblest creature. He would rather let Himself be injured and humiliated in making the assault and repulse of nothingness His own concern than leave His creature alone in this affliction. He deploys all His majesty in the work of His deepest condescension. He intervenes in the struggle between nothingness and the creature as if He were not God but Himself a weak and threatened and vulnerable creature. "As if"—but is that all? No, for in the decisive action in the history of His covenant with the creature, in Jesus Christ, He actually becomes a creature, and thus makes the cause of the creature His own in the most concrete reality and not just in appearance, really taking its place. This is how God Himself comes on the scene.

But it is really God who does so in His free grace. And therefore it is He as the first and true and indeed the only man, as the Helper who really takes the creature's place, lifting from it all its need and labour and problem and placing them upon Himself, as the Warrior who assumes the full responsibility of a substitute and suffers and does everything on its behalf. In the light of this merciful action of God, the arrogant delusion of the creature that it is called and qualified to help and save and maintain itself in its infinite peril is shown [359] to be evil as well as foolish and unnecessary. So, too, is the arrogant illusion that it is the principal party affected, that its own strength or weakness, despair or elation, folly or wisdom, modicum of "existential" insight and freedom, is the problem in solution of which there takes place the decisive encounter with nothingness, the repelling of its assault, and perhaps its defeat. In the light of the merciful action of God, only God Himself, and trust in Him, and perseverance in His covenant, can be called good, even for the creature too. Hence the creature has only one good to choose, namely, that it has God for it, and that it is thus opposed by nothingness as God Himself is opposed, the God who can so easily master it.

In this way, in this trust and perseverance, in this choice of God's help as its only good, the creature can and will have a real part in the conflict with nothingness. It is certainly no mere spectator. But only in this way does it cease to be such. Only in this way is it rescued from illusory struggles and strivings with what are only counterfeits of nothingness, and from inaction in the event in which the onslaught of nothingness is real but its repulse is effective and its conquest in sight. In this way alone is the situation of the creature, its fall and rehabilitation, its suffering, action and inaction, full of meaning and promise. As the action of God is primary, the creature can and will also play its part. For it is the salvation of the creature which God makes a matter of His own honour. It is for the right of the creature that He establishes and defends His own right. The *opus alienum*[EN89] of divine jealousy, wrath and judgment is no less for the creature than the *opus proprium*[EN90] of divine grace. For it is the sin and guilt, the suffering and misery of the creature that God makes His own problem. The creature is not its own. It is the creature and possession of God. It is thus the object of His concern. And therefore conflict with nothingness is its own problem as it is the cause of God. The full intervention of God is needed, and this action of His mercy is the only compelling force, to make the creature willing and able to act on its own behalf in the conflict with nothingness. As God takes action on its behalf, the creature itself is summoned and empowered. It has no arrogant illusion as to its own authority or competence. It really trusts in God, perseveres in His covenant and chooses His help as the only effective good. But if it does this it can and will take action in the conflict with nothingness. It is not under the wings of divine mercy but in the vacuum of creaturely self-sufficiency that the laziness thrives which induces man to yield and succumb to nothingness. And it is not in the vacuum of creaturely self-sufficiency but under the wings of divine mercy that the fortitude thrives in which man is summoned and equipped to range himself with God, so that in his own place he opposes nothingness and thus has a part in the work and warfare of God.

[360]   The concluding delimitation which must be made is self-evident. We must reject as non-Christian all conceptions of nothingness which obscure or deny the fact that God Himself is primarily affected by its contradiction and opposition and primarily confronts it with His own contradiction and opposition. There are few heresies so pernicious as that of a God who faces nothingness more or less unaffected and unconcerned, and the parallel doctrine of man as one who must engage in independent conflict against it. We know well enough what it means to be alien and adverse to grace and therefore without it. A graceless God would be a null and evil God, and a self-sufficient, self-reliant

---

[EN89] alien work
[EN90] proper work

creaturely subject a null and evil creature. If a doctrine of nothingness is not unyielding on this point, nothingness itself will triumph. But from another angle, too, we are here at the heart of the whole question. If God Himself were not the primary victim and foe of nothingness, there would be no reason for the unyielding recognition (1) that nothingness is not nothing but exists in its own curious fashion, (2) that it is in no way to be understood as an essential attribute of divine or creaturely being but only as their frontier, (3) that we are capable of knowing nothingness only as we know God in His self-revelation, (4) that nothingness has its being on the left hand of God and is grounded in His non-willing, and (5) that it is evil by nature and therefore we cannot regard or group it in any sense with God and His creature. All these insights, and therefore the whole theological concept of nothingness, depend upon the fact that the primal antithesis or encounter in which it has its being is its confrontation with God Himself, which God freely allows because His freedom is that of His grace and love and faithfulness, and His glory is that of His condescension, to His creature. Everything ultimately depends on this one point, and we remember that it is not a theory or notion but the concrete event at the core of all Christian reality and truth—the self-giving of the Son of God, His humiliation, incarnation and obedience unto death, even the death of the cross. It is here that the true conflict with nothingness takes place. And it is here that it is unmistakeably clear that it is God's own affair. All the statements and delimitations which we have made rest on this point and can be made only on this noetic and ontic basis.

7. On this one point, again, rests our final and decisive insight that nothingness has no perpetuity. God not only has perpetuity, but is Himself the basis, essence and sum of all being. And for all its finiteness and mutability even His creature has perpetuity—the perpetuity which He wills to grant it in fellowship with Himself, and which cannot be lacking in this fellowship but is given it to all eternity. Nothingness, however, is not created by God, nor is there any covenant with it. Hence it has no perpetuity. It is from the very first that which is past. It was abandoned at once by God in creation. He did not even give it time, let alone any other essence than that of non-essence. As we have already [361] pointed out, in all the power of its peculiar being it is nothing but a receding frontier and fleeting shadow. It has no substance. How can it have when God did not will to give it substance or to create it? It has only its own emptiness. How can it be anything but empty when it is only by God's non-willing that it is what it is? It is thus insubstantial and empty. Only in this way does it have being, form and space on the left hand of God as the object of His *opus alienum*[EN91].

But this *opus alienum Dei*[EN92] is jealousy, wrath and judgment. It does not confer substance and fulness on nothingness but prevents it from assuming them. It gives it only the truth of falsehood, the power of impotence, the sense

---

[EN91] alien work
[EN92] the alien work of God

of non-sense. It establishes it only as that which has no basis. It admits it, but only as that which can have no perpetuity. Nor is this *opus alienum Dei*[EN93] an interminable process. It moves towards a definite goal and end. It is not effected for its own sake. Unlike the *opus proprium Dei*[EN94], the work of His grace, it does not take place by an inner and autonomous necessity. On the contrary, it is subsidiary and complementary to the divine *opus proprium*[EN95]. The *opus alienum Dei*[EN96] can have only the significance, weight and scope proper to it as the inevitable divine negation and rejection. If it is inevitable, i.e., as the obverse of the divine election and affirmation, it is nevertheless as such a basically contingent and transient activity. As God fulfils His true and positive work, His negative work becomes pointless and redundant and can be terminated and ended. It is of major importance at this point that we should not become involved in the logical dialectic that if God loves, elects and affirms eternally He must also hate and therefore reject and negate eternally. There is nothing to make God's activity on the left hand as necessary and perpetual as His activity on the right. It takes place only with the necessity with which it can take place according to its nature and meaning—not with the higher, true and primary necessity with which God is gracious to His creature, but only with the subordinate and transient necessity with which, in virtue of His grace, and to establish its rule, He wills to keep it from evil and save it from its power, and has thus to reckon with evil and take it seriously. This negative activity of God has as such, in accordance with its meaning and nature, a definite frontier, and this is to be found at the point where it attains its goal and accomplishes its purpose. With the attainment of the goal the *opus alienum*[EN97] of God also reaches its end. God is indeed eternally holy, pure, distinct and separated from the evil which is nothingness. But this does not mean that He must always strive with this adversary, enduring its opposition and resistance, and Himself exercising His jealousy, wrath and judgment upon it. Surely He will also be holy, and all the more so, when judgment is executed, when the triumph of His love is unchallenged and boundless, and therefore when He is the God who no longer has to do with an enemy but only with His creature. If He now has to do with nothingness, it is only that He may have to do with it no more, but only with His creature in eternally triumphant love. No eternal enemy is needed for this. And because nothingness is *His* enemy, because it is *He* who allows it to be this, because He has made the controversy with it *His* affair, it cannot be an eternal enemy or have perpetuity.

[362]

It is true that God concerns Himself with it. How else could He take up the cause of the creature which is menaced by and subjected to it? He does this by giving Himself in His Son, by Himself becoming a creature and as such taking

---

[EN93] the alien work of God
[EN94] God's proper work
[EN95] proper work
[EN96] the alien work of God
[EN97] alien work

on Himself the sin, guilt and misery of the creature. It is true that in the person of the man Jesus He becomes the bearer of the creature's guilt and shame, and as such causes His burning jealousy and kindling wrath and righteous judgment on nothingness to concern and affect Himself. It is true that in what befalls this man God pronounces His No to the bitter end. But it is no less true that this divine *opus alienum*^{EN98}, the whole activity of God on the left hand, was fulfilled and accomplished once and for all, and therefore deprived of its object, when it took place in all its dreadful fulness in the death of Jesus Christ. Nothingness had power over the creature. It could contradict and oppose it and break down its defences. It could make it its slave and instrument and therefore its victim. But it was impotent against the God who humbled Himself, and Himself became a creature, and thus exposed Himself to its power and resisted it. Nothingness could not master this victim. It could neither endure nor bear the presence of God in the flesh. It met with a prey which it could not match and by which it could only be destroyed as it tried to swallow it. The fulness of the grace which God showed to His creature by Himself becoming a threatened, even ruined and lost creature, was its undoing. In the encounter with God Himself it could only fulfil its true destiny of having no perpetuity, of ceasing to be even a receding frontier and fleeting shadow. This is what happened to it in the death of Jesus Christ, in the justification and deliverance of sinful man in this death. If it is true that in humbling Himself in the man Jesus God had to do not only with His creature but with nothingness for the sake of His creature, it is also true, and even more so because definitively and conclusively, that in the exaltation of the same man Jesus God has to do only with His creature and no longer with nothingness. The purpose of His *opus proprium*^{EN99} is the termination of His *opus alienum*^{EN100} and therefore the elimination of its object. Where God exercised His jealousy, wrath and judgment, He does so no more; but where He does so no more there is no enemy against whom to do so. Where God has said No, He has done so and need do so no more; but where He no longer does so that which He negates no longer exists. Nothingness is deprived of even the transient, temporary impermanent [363] being it had. Even the truth of falsehood, the power of impotence, the sense of non-sense and the possibility of the impossible which it is accorded on the left hand of God are withdrawn from it in the victory of God on the right. Even the permission by which it existed there is revoked. This is what has already been fulfilled in Jesus Christ, in the exaltation of this creature to the right hand of God. However audacious it may seem to be, we cannot deviate from it by a hairsbreadth. In the light of Jesus Christ there is no sense in which it can be affirmed that nothingness has any objective existence, that it continues except for our still blinded eyes, that it is still to be feared, that it still counts as a

---

EN 98 alien work
EN 99 proper work
EN100 alien work

cogent factor, that it still has a future, that it still implies a threat and possesses destructive power.

What is nothingness? In the knowledge and confession of the Christian faith, i.e., looking retrospectively to the resurrection of Jesus Christ and prospectively to His coming again, there is only one possible answer. Nothingness is the past, the ancient menace, danger and destruction, the ancient nonbeing which obscured and defaced the divine creation of God but which is consigned to the past in Jesus Christ, in whose death it has received its deserts, being destroyed with this consummation of the positive will of God which is as such the end of His non-willing. Because Jesus is Victor, nothingness is routed and extirpated. It is that which in this One who was both very God and very man has been absolutely set behind, not only by God, but in unity with Him by man and therefore the creature. It is that from whose influence, dominion and power the relationship between Creator and creature was absolutely set free in Jesus Christ, so that it is no longer involved in their relationship as a third factor. This is what has happened to nothingness once and for all in Jesus Christ. This is its status and appearance now that God has made His own and carried through the conflict with it in His Son. It is no longer to be feared. It can no longer "nihilate." But obviously we may make these undoubtedly audacious statements only on the ground of one single presupposition. The aspect of creaturely activity both as a whole and in detail, our consciousness both of the world and of self, certainly do not bear them out. But what do we really know of it as taught by this consciousness? How can this teach us the truth that it is really past and done with? The only valid presupposition is a backward look to the resurrection of Jesus Christ and a forward look to His coming in glory, i.e., the look of Christian faith as rooted in and constantly nourished by the Word of God. The knowledge and confession of Christian faith, however, inevitably entails the affirmation that by the divine intervention nothingness has lost the perpetuity which it could and must and indeed did have apart from this intervention. It can no longer be validly regarded as possessing any [364] claim or right or power in relation to the creature, as though it were still before and above us, as though the world created by God were still subject to and dominated by it, as though Christians must hold it in awe, as though it were particularly Christian to hold it in the utmost awe and to summon the world to share in this awe. It is no longer legitimate to think of it as if real deliverance and release from it were still an event of the future. It is obvious that in point of fact we do constantly think of it in this way, with anxious, legalistic, tragic, hesitant, doleful and basically pessimistic thoughts, and this inevitably where we are neither able nor prepared to think from the standpoint of Christian faith. But it is surely evident that when we think in this way it is not from a Christian standpoint, but in spite of it, in breach of the command imposed with our Christian faith. If our thought is conditioned by the obedience of Christian faith, we have only one freedom, namely, to regard nothingness as finally destroyed and to make a new beginning in remembrance of the One who has destroyed it. Only if our thought is thus conditioned by the obedience of Christian faith is it possible to proclaim the Gospel to the world as it really is, as the message of freedom for the One who has already come and acted as the Liberator, and therefore of the freedom which precludes the anxiety, legalism and pessimism so prevalent in the world. We need hardly describe how throughout the centuries the Christian Church has failed to shape its thought in the obedience of Christian faith, to proclaim it to the world in this obedience, to live in this freedom and to summon the world to it. For this reason and contrary to its true nature, so-called Christianity has become a sorry affair both within and without. It is shameful enough to have to admit that many of the interpretations of nothingness which we are forced to reject as non-Christian derive their power and cogency from the fact that for all their weakness and erroneousness they attest a Christian insight to the extent that they do at least offer a cheerful view and describe and treat nothingness as having no perpetuity. It ought to be the main characteristic of the Christian view that it can demonstrate this more surely because on surer ground, more boldly because in the exercise and proclamation of the freedom granted to do so, and more logically because not in a venture but in simple obedience. We must not imagine that we serve the seriousness of Christian knowledge, life and proclamation by retreating at this point and refusing to realise and admit that the apparently audacious is the norm, the only true possibility. The true seriousness of the matter, and we may emphasise this point in retrospect of the whole discussion, does not finally depend upon pessimistic but upon optimistic thought and speech. From a Christian standpoint "to be serious" can only mean to take seriously the fact that Jesus is Victor. If Jesus is Victor, the last word must always be secretly the first, namely, that nothingness has no perpetuity.

Our only remaining task is briefly to indicate how the reality of nothingness [365] as we have expounded it is to be conceived in relation to the doctrine of God's providence and world-government. We began by defining it as the sinister alien factor in the sphere of the fatherly rule of God. Our fuller enquiries have confirmed the fact that it must indeed be regarded as an alien factor, that it cannot be anything else, but that even as such it cannot be envisaged and apprehended as outside the jurisdiction of the fatherly rule of God, but only as within it. A few remarks must still be made on the final formulation.

The problem of nothingness primarily arises in a consideration of the relationship between Creator and creature, and therefore of general world-occurrence under the rule of God. In this connexion there comes to the forefront a disturbing and destructive element which casts doubt on the goodness and the being of either the Creator or the creature or possibly of both. The resultant problem of theodicy is usually presented as follows. God is either good, but obviously neither divine nor omnipotent in relation to this element, or He is divine and omnipotent, but obviously not good in relation to this element. And the problem of the perfection of the creature, of being as distinct from God, is presented in this way. The creature is either good, but obviously imperfect in relation to this element, or perfect, but obviously good only in a limited sense in this regard. And the problem of the co-existence of Creator and creature is given the following form. This co-existence is either orderly, but not good in relation to this element, or it is good, but disorderly at this point. But where does it lead us to pose these alternatives? We obviously pose them in this way only if the relationship between Creator and creature, general world-occurrence under the divine government, is considered abstractly and as it were detachedly, in forgetfulness of the fact that this relationship and general world-occurrence under the divine government are centred in the history of the covenant, grace and salvation, that decisions concerning the meaning of this relationship and the goodness and right of Creator and creature, and their co-existence, are taken at this central point, and that therefore truth will be attained in this matter only as we take this concrete centre as our starting point and goal. What reason have we to disregard this fact and to begin with an abstraction?

The older orthodoxy is vitiated at the very outset by the fact that it begins with this abstraction and thus admits these alternatives in all their captiousness, which indeed is inevitable if this centre is not accepted as our starting-point and goal. The older orthodoxy did not make use of the simple and obvious possibility of considering this matter from a Christian standpoint, but treated Creator, creature and their co-existence, and the intrusion upon them of the undeniable reality of nothingness, as if they were philosophical concepts which had to be resolved or brought into a tolerable relationship. The result was that even its most careful [366] labour could not produce definitive statements and acceptable findings in any respect, whether in respect of Creator, creature and their coexistence, or even in respect of nothingness itself, its nature, recognition, ground, character, location and final conquest. It necessarily lost itself in academic discussions which from the very first were of doubtful value for theology and the Church and which as a general consideration of the relationship between God and the world could not even claim any final originality over later philosophical developments, let alone superiority as an authentic interpretation of the revelation committed to the Christian community.

Here we ourselves have tried to avoid this abstraction. We have not sought to apprehend the relationship between Creator and creature philosophically and therefore from without, but theologically and therefore from within. Hence we have not accepted the alternatives posed by an abstract and external view. Even in the general relationship between Creator and creature, even in general world-occurrence under the divine government, we have sought the problem of nothingness where it is raised in its true form and is authentically answered. It is in the mighty act of salvation in Jesus Christ as attested by Holy Scripture that the question of the reality, nature and function of this alien factor is seriously raised and seriously answered. Only what is shown to be true there in the central fact of all history is true in relation to this alien factor even in world-occurrence generally.

From this standpoint—and our final word must really be the first—we must say first and supremely of nothingness that basically it can be reviewed and interpreted only in retrospect of the fact that it has already been judged, refuted and done away by the mercy of God revealed and active in Jesus Christ, or, in other words, that basically it can be reviewed and interpreted only in prospect of the fact that this refutation and termination will be generally revealed in the return of Jesus Christ. Nothingness has its reality and character, and plays its past, present and possibly future role, as the adversary whom God has regarded, attacked and routed as His own enemy. All that makes it threatening and dangerous, all that it can signify as disturbance and destruction in the relationship between Creator and creature, all its terrible features, all the hostility to God and nature which characterises and proceeds from it, can be summed up in the fact that it is that which God did not will and therefore did not tolerate but which He has Himself removed. Indeed, we may say that if nothingness is not viewed in retrospect of God's finished act of conquest and destruction, it is not seen at all. It is confounded with the negative side of God's creation, and viewed only in its negative and not in its privative character. A notion of the dreadful is feared but not the thing itself. And strangely enough, the dreadful is feared only when it is realised that God has denied and deprived nothingness of perpetuity and therefore it is no longer to be feared. It is to be really feared only in retrospect and prospect of Jesus Christ, and therefore only in the fearlessness which is founded on the act of God.   [367]

But secondly it also follows that no true or ultimate power and significance but only a dangerous semblance of them are to be attributed to the existence, menace, corruption, disturbance and destructiveness of nothingness as these may still be seen. Whatever its actuality and potentiality, that which it is and does is only in the power of a fragmentary existence. It is only an echo, a shadow, of what it was but is no longer, of what it could do but can do no longer. For the fact that it is broken, judged, refuted and destroyed at the central point, in the mighty act of salvation accomplished in Jesus Christ, is valid not merely at that point but by extension throughout the universe and its activity. This is not yet visible or recognisable, but it cannot be doubted and does not need to be repeated, fostered, augmented or extended. It took place once and for all, and is universally effective. Nothingness may still have standing and assume significance to the extent that the final revelation of its destruction has not yet taken place and all creation must still await and expect it. But its dominion, even though it was only the semblance of dominion, is now objectively defeated as such in Jesus Christ. What it still is in the world, it is in virtue of the blindness of our eyes and the cover which is still over us, obscuring the prospect of the kingdom of God already established as the only kingdom undisputed by evil.

Third, it follows that nothingness can have even its semblance of validity only under the decree of God. What it now is and does, it can be and do only in the hand of God. How can it be otherwise when it can never escape the divine grasp? There is a legitimate place here for a favourite concept of the older dogmatics—that of permission. God still permits His kingdom not to be seen by us, and to that extent He still permits us to be a prey to nothingness. Until the hour strikes when its destruction in the victory of Jesus Christ will be finally revealed, He thus permits nothingness to retain its semblance of significance and still to manifest its already fragmentary existence. In this already innocuous form, as this echo and shadow, it is an instrument of His will and action. He thinks it good that we should exist "as if" He had not yet mastered it for us—and at this point we may rightly say "as if."

Finally, because in this form still left to it nothingness exists and functions under the control of God, we must say that even though it does not will to do so it is forced to serve Him, to serve His Word and work, the honour of His Son, the proclamation of the Gospel, the faith of the community, and therefore the way which He Himself wills to go within and with His creation until its day is done. The defeated, captured and mastered enemy of God has as such become His servant. Good care is taken that he should always show himself to be a strange servant, and therefore that his existence should remind us who and what he used to be, and therefore that at the sight of him we can never cease to flee to the One who alone has conquered him and has the keys to his prison. Yet it is even more important to reflect that good care is taken by this One that even nothingness should be one of the things of which it is said that they must work together for good to them that love Him.

[368]

THE KINGDOM OF HEAVEN, THE AMBASSADORS OF GOD AND THEIR OPPONENTS

God's action in Jesus Christ, and therefore His lordship over His creature, is called the "kingdom of heaven" because first and supremely it claims for itself the upper world. From this God selects and sends His messengers, the angels, who precede the revelation and doing of His will on earth as objective and authentic witnesses, who accompany it as faithful servants of God and man, and who victoriously ward off the opposing forms and forces of chaos.

1. THE LIMITS OF ANGELOLOGY

The dogmatic sphere which we have to enter and traverse in this section is the most remarkable and difficult of all. Why do we have to give ourselves at all to this part of biblical and ecclesiastical tradition? And if we do, how are we even to put the right questions, let alone give the right answers? And if we are successful in putting the right questions and giving the right answers, what results, what lessons, what enrichment of Christian knowledge and proclamation, what solid gains for the Christian life, are we to expect from it? In this sphere there has always been a good deal of theological caprice, of valueless, grotesque and even absurd speculation, and also of no less doubtful scepticism. *Vestigia terrent*[EN1]—the lack of any sense of humour on the part of those who know and say too much, and the equal lack of any sense of humour on the part of those who deny or ignore too much. How are we to steer a way between this Scylla and Charybdis, between the far too interesting mythology of the ancients and the far too uninteresting "demythologisation" of most of the moderns? How are we to advance without becoming rash, exercising discretion without overlooking what has to be seen, not saying too much and yet not failing to say what has to be said? How are we to be both open and cautious, critical and naive, perspicuous and modest? There are no spheres of dogmatics where we are not well advised to take note of these questions. But there are reasons why they are particularly dark and oppressive in the doctrine of angels which must now concern us.

At all events, this sphere brings us to the very limit of what can be the subject of necessary, sure and helpful Christian impartation and therefore of Church

---

[EN1] the footsteps frighten

[370]   dogmatics. The limit is to be seen in the fact that the name and concept of angels denotes a reality which is distinct both from God and man, and therefore distinct from the true and central content of the Word of God although intimately related to it. The problem of angelology, the character of the kingdom of God as the kingdom of heaven, and the being and activity of heavenly messengers of God border on problems which are necessarily alien to the task and purpose of a dogmatics grounded on the Word of God. The step over this frontier is undoubtedly a step into the sphere of the superfluous and uncertain, which as such might also be both dangerous and even corrupt. But it is illegitimate, and it might be equally dangerous and corrupt, if we allow a fear of failing to halt at this frontier to exclude from our dogmatic investigation the remarkable sphere of the kingdom of heaven, ignoring and even denying it. We have thus no option but to take up the questions which crowd so thickly upon us at this point.

Traces of an awareness of this frontier are clearly discernible in the Early Church at any rate in the centuries prior to the epoch-making *Hierarchia coelestis* of Pseudo-Dionysius. Even Origen (*De princ.*, I, *praef.* 10) said of angels that although they belong to the proclamation of the Church (*ecclesiastica praedicatio*) there is no sure knowledge *quando isti creati sint, vel quales aut quomodo sint*[EN2]. Similarly Gregory of Nazianzus(*Or.*, 28, 31) said that it is difficult to find the right words in which to speak of angels. Similarly Augustine (*ad Oros*, 11, 24) admitted that it is difficult to say how matters stand with the orders of the angelic world (concerning which Pseudo-Dionysius thought that he knew so much)—*quo me contemnas, quem magnum putas esse doctorem, quaenam ista sint et quid inter se differant nescio. Dicant, qui possunt, si tamen possunt probare quod dicunt; ego me ista ignorare confiteor*[EN3] (*Enchir.*, 15, 58). And Thomas Aquinas could also concede: *Nos imperfecte angelos cognoscimus et eorum officia*[EN4]. (*S. theol.*, I, *qu.* 108, *art.* 3c). But there could, of course, be no question of abandoning the problem. At a later date Calvin was even more radical and pointed (*Instit.*, I, 14, 4), claiming that most of what *ille Dionysius, quicunque fuerit*[EN5] wrote concerning the nature and order and number of angels was ματαιώματα *absque Dei verbo tradita*[EN6], the *mera garrulitas*[EN7] of one who seemed to imagine that he had come to earth with first-hand knowledge of heaven, in sharp contrast to the apostle Paul, who according to 2 Cor. 12[2f.] had really been caught up into the third heaven, yet nowhere spoke of it in this way, but expressly stated that we have to do here with mysteries which it is not appropriate for man to discuss. But this does not mean that Calvin was trying to avoid the task of speaking of angels according to the guidance and rule of Scripture (*ib.*, 14[3]): *quia si Deum ex operibus suis agnoscere cupimus, minime omittendum est tam praeclarum et nobile specimen*[EN8]. How far the limit of theology generally must form that of angelology in particular was finally and almost classically stated by Calvin, both negatively and positively, in the dictum (14, 4): *Theologo autem non garriendo aures oblectare, sed vera, certa,*

[EN2] when they were created, what sort of beings they are or how they exist

[EN3] you many disdain me for not knowing what they are and how they differ from one another, since you imagine me to be a teacher. Let they who can teach these things, if they are able to prove what they teach; but I confess that I am ignorant of these matters

[EN4] Our knowledge of angels and their activities is imperfect

[EN5] that Dionysius, whoever he may have been

[EN6] empty concepts delivered without regard to God's word

[EN7] mere chattering

[EN8] because if we desire to know God from His works, this glorious and noble example should by no means be omitted

1. *The Limits of Angelology*

utilia docendo conscientias confirmare propositum est[EN9]. As we address ourselves to this theme we cannot pay too much attention to the restraint as well as the compulsion to which he made reference.

But there is another and more specific reason why the questions are so urgent in this connexion. As we have seen, it belongs to the nature of the case that the doctrine of angels, unlike that of predestination, creation, or man, has in the strict sense no meaning and content of its own. Angels are not independent and autonomous subjects like God and man and Jesus Christ. They cannot, therefore, be made the theme of an independent discussion. Directed to God and man, and belonging particularly to the person and work of Christ, they are only the servants of God and man. They are, only as they come and go in this service. They are essentially marginal figures. This is their glory. It is in their subordination to the great events enacted between God and man that they are that *praeclarum et nobile specimen*[EN10] of the creaturely world. Hence they have to be considered in our present context, namely, in the consideration of God's lordship over the creature, which has its meaning and centre in its exercise in Jesus Christ. And this is the task which we must now take up. But in this context they can only be considered together with other things. Strictly speaking, every angelological statement can only be an auxiliary or additional statement, an explanation and elucidation of what is not to be said properly and essentially of angels but—corresponding to the ministerial nature and work of angels—of the divine action in Jesus Christ and therefore of the divine lordship in the creaturely world. The only thing is that, since angels belong to the divine action and lordship in this incidental and ministerial fashion, we cannot omit this explanation and elucidation, but have to make it as definitely and precisely as possible.

[371]

I hope that I understand Erich Schick correctly if in this connexion I refer to the fact that on p. 9 of his book *Die Botschaft der Engel im N.T.²*, 1946, he says that he wishes to speak of the relevant truths only "incidentally and in passing" and "very softly," "just as there is something essentially fleeting and transitory about the beings under discussion." I do not think that the same general validity can be ascribed to the saying of Kierkegaard which he adduces, and which is to the effect that in religious matters the speaker is always a whisperer. Even the speech of angels never seems to take the form of a whisper. Yet there is no doubt that what is intended is right enough in this particular sphere. When we undertake to think and speak about angels we have to remember that they are not leading characters and that we can thus speak of them only incidentally and softly. And the "incidentally" and "softly" have to be taken with the greatest seriousness and force. After all, it makes a great difference whether we treat a theme independently or in connexion with something else. And it is the latter which must obtain in relation to the kingdom of God as the kingdom of heaven and therefore to angels as the heavenly messengers of God.

[EN] 9 For it is not the assignment of the theologian to entertain the ears by chattering, but to confirm consciences by teaching what is true, certain and useful

[EN10] glorious and noble example

From this standpoint, too, it should be obvious that all the questions of appropriate procedure on both sides, of what to do and not to do, of what not to do and to do, are particularly pressing in the sphere of dogmatics to which we now turn, so that we have no option but to allow them to be put.

In the first sub-section, then, we shall attempt some basic and methodological clarifications in relation to these questions.

[372] 1. The first of these clarifications must necessarily consist in the proposition that the teacher and master to which we must keep in this matter can only be the Holy Scriptures of the Old and New Testament, that we must not accept any other authority, that we must listen exhaustively to what this guide has to tell us, and that we must respect what it says and what it does not say. It will be seen that; in this matter we have to claim a specific freedom in relation to all tradition both orthodox and liberal in order to be the more obedient to Holy Scripture. What we mean is Holy Scripture as the human and historical but unique and normative witness to the revelation and work of God in His dealings in Jesus Christ and therefore in His lordship in the creaturely world. According to the witness of the Old and New Testaments, to this revelation and work of God there belongs also the character of the kingdom of God as the kingdom of heaven, and the angels as His heavenly messengers. They belong to it in a particular way, not as leading but subsidiary characters, and these not as autonomous subjects but merging as it were into their function, which is wholly and exemplarily that of service. It is only in this way that they belong to it. But in this way they do belong to it. Concerning the basis and reach and meaning and importance of the fact that they do so we shall have to speak when we take up the theme itself. For the moment it is enough to maintain that in certain contexts the biblical witness to the revelation and work of God includes the witness to angels, and that in the sense of its authors it would not be right, but a definite dimension would be lacking, if this witness were lacking. This is the fact which forms our starting-point. The dogmatics of the Christian Church has no other reason or cause to enter the sphere apart from this fact, which is not merely indisputable but springs at once to our notice and demands that we take up some sort of attitude to it. We are not concerned with angels in general, or with higher angelic beings which may be possible or actual, postulated or in some way confessed. We are dealing wholly and exclusively with what are described and introduced as angels in the witness of Scripture and in connexion with the revelation and work of God. In this respect our procedure is similar to that which we had to follow in relation to God, where we were not concerned with a real or supposed deity, a personal of impersonal cosmic or redemptive principle, but only with the One who is attested as God and Saviour in Holy Scripture under the name of Father, Son and Holy Ghost; and also in relation to man, where we were not dealing with a generalised picture of man but only with the real man who according to the witness of Holy Scripture is the reflection of Jesus Christ. The fact which is our starting-point is co-extensive with the fact that according to the witness of Holy Scripture the

revelation and work of God also have this dimension, that this witness also includes the strange existence or function of angels, and that it thus presents it unavoidably for discussion, no matter how it is to be understood or explained. [373] So far as the task of dogmatics is concerned, we cannot imagine that we have any knowledge of this sphere of ourselves or on the basis of any philosophical freedom or compulsion. We can only keep to the fact that the biblical witnesses say that they know something of this sphere: something which stands in what is for them a necessary connexion with their true theme, God and man and the history of God with man; and something which in this context is very definite and contrasts with all philosophical parallels. It is with this alone that we must concern ourselves at this point.

I again quote Calvin (*Instit.*, I, 14, 4): *Meminerimus hic, ut in tola religionis doctrina, tenendum esse unam modestiae et sobrietatis regulam, ne de rebus obscuris aliud vel loquamur, vel sentiamus, vel scire etiam appetamus quam quod Dei verbo fuerit nobis traditum*[EN11]. And negatively Quenstedt is even clearer (*Theol. did pol.*, 1685, I, *cap.* II, *sect*, 1, *th.* 3): *Existentia angelorum nititur non tam argumentis probabilibus ex philosophia petitis sive a gradibus entium et complemento universi … sive a testimoniis humanis sive ab experimentis variis, quam apodictico, clara nimirum et crebra scripturae assertione*[EN12].

2. In this respect we do really have to wrestle with the witness of Holy Scripture. That is to say, we have to ponder what it presents for our consideration, understanding and explaining it so far as the limits of the matter itself and of our own capacity allow. There can be no question of a blind acknowledgment and acceptance of something perceptible in the Bible. If it would be bad biblical scholarship to stop at this kind of acknowledgment and acceptance, this type of attitude is totally impossible in relation to the special task of dogmatics. If according to the witness of the Bible the function of heavenly messengers belongs incidentally to the revelation and work of God, and therefore incidentally to the faith of the Church, and incidentally and softly to its proclamation, we do not have here a *pistis*[EN13] which does not press forward to *gnosis*[EN14], a *fides*[EN15] which is not as such a *fides quaerens intellectum*[EN16]. We cannot, then, merely affirm the fact and describe it as such. We must really *start* from this fact. That is to say, we must press on to what is denoted by this witness. And we must do so to the point of exhausting its knowability and therefore our own possibility of knowing what we say when we are not silent concerning it, when

---

[EN11] Let us remember here that in the teaching of religion there is a rule of modesty and sobriety to which we must adhere, lest we speak or think or desire to know anything of obscure matters beyond what has been handed down to us in God's word

[EN12] The existence of angels is not established by probable arguments derived from philosophy, or by speculations on possible levels of creaturely being and the structure of the universe .... or by human testimony or by various experiencs, but apodictically, by the absolutely clear and repeated assertion of Scripture

[EN13] faith

[EN14] knowledge

[EN15] faith

[EN16] faith seeking understanding

we do not deny or ignore it, but try to say something about it. We do not honour the authority of Scripture with due obedience, indeed, we are not dealing with its authority at all, if on its authority we try to hold a biblical doctrine of angels without taking the trouble to ask what it is that we really hold and how far we do so. The Church has no right to appeal to this authority for continually speaking about angels in its songs and prayers and pictures if it is not prepared to consider what this means, sparing dogmatics the effort involved, or concluding that it is not worth while. Even to-day the Church gives

[374] many signs that it has not accepted a simple denial of angels. But if we agree that the effort is worth while it must obviously be made, not merely for reasons of personal honesty and conscientiousness, but even more so for the sake of the credibility of the Church's proclamation. How can this be credible to the world and itself if, because there is some correlate in the Bible, it proceeds to say something—even if only on this margin—without knowing, or perhaps trying to know, what it is saying? To be sure, an angelology which is dogmatic as well as historico-exegetical is a difficult and dangerous undertaking. But a dogmatics which tried to escape the task of angelology would be guilty of an indolent omission which might well jeopardise the whole Church. A *sacrificium intellectus*[EN17] is thus the very last thing which is justified or demanded by the reference to the witness of Scripture in this matter. On the contrary, we are summoned to ponder what the witness of Scripture presents for our consideration in this respect.

In saying this, we take consciously and expressly into account the fact that when the Bible speaks of angels (and their demonic counterparts) it always introduces us to a sphere where historically verifiable history, i.e., the history which is comprehensible by the known analogies of world history, passes over into historically non-verifiable saga or legend. That is to say, when it is a matter of angels in the Bible, we are in the sphere of the particular form of history which by content and nature does not proceed according to ordinary analogies, and can thus be grasped only by divinatory imagination, and find expression only in the freer observation and speech of poetry.

There is real, spatio-temporal history which has this form or that of transition to it. The fact that it has this form is not a compelling argument for rejecting, as less valuable or even worthless its narration in the corresponding genre of saga or legend. Why should not imagination grasp real history, or the poetry which is its medium be a representation of real history, of the kind of history which escapes ordinary analogies and cannot therefore be verified historically, but is real history all the same? Not all saga or legend deals with real history, nor can this be said of all narratives which cannot be verified historically. But there is true saga or legend as well as false. To turn to the Bible, if we have reason to see in a history narrated in the Bible an element in the revelation and work of divine grace, and therefore real—we might almost say the most real—history in time and space, then the fact that we must regard the account as a saga or legend does not mean that we can deny the history this character. Whether it can be verified historically or is saga or legend does not affect its

---

[EN17] sacrifice of the intellect

credibility in this respect. If we believe it, it is because we see that it has happened as the revelation and work of divine grace, and this is the gift of our enlightenment by the Holy Spirit. If this recognition and gift be presupposed only for a moment, the fact that a biblical history cannot be verified historically but has only the form of saga or legend cannot deprive it of this character or make it incredible as real history. Thus, although we must regard the relevant sphere as saga or legend, we must accept it as true and not false legend in the relevant sense, and therefore treat this history too as credible in its distinctive form. Once this is grasped, it obviously makes no odds that in the construction of these accounts the [375] active imagination of the biblical authors, as is only to be expected, lived with images and conceptions which were stamped by the outlook and mythology of their day and which we can no longer accept, but which it was not the purpose of the texts in question to impart or to force on us. If it is a matter of scholarly understanding, we may always try to translate them, so far as possible, into the current images and conceptions of our own outlook and mythology. But if we really want to know and understand the accounts, it will not help us to translate them into the language of the outlook and mythology of any age either present or future, but we too shall have to make that divinatory crossing of the frontier of historicism and enter the sphere of imagination and poetry. It cannot be a question of translating the saga or legend into verifiable history, but of repeating (in whatever language) the saga or legend as such, of a renewal of the form commensurate with the history envisaged in these accounts. On the pretext of a translation from antiquated to more modern language we cannot put another history in the place of this history. Otherwise the translation is a falsification. And it is a safe rule in cases of doubt to narrate this history in a language which is less clearly understood to-day than to narrate another history in a language which is supposedly or actually better understood. The history of the revelation and work of God recounted in the Bible, while it intends to be and is real spatio-temporal history, passes over into the sphere in which (in whatever language) we can obviously think and speak only in the form of saga or legend. At all events, it will always have this form in a faithful translation of the biblical account, and every faithful rendering of what is narrated by it will necessarily reveal the historical sphere into which it passes.

To this sphere there undoubtedly belong all the biblical passages in which angels appear. On grounds still to be discussed, we are even forced to say that the appearance of angels is always a distinctive sign of the basically continuous proximity of the biblical history to this sphere, and of its continual secret tendency in this direction. There is reason for surprise that angels are not more frequently mentioned in the Bible. The whole history of the Bible, while it intends to be and is real spatio-temporal history, has a constant bias towards the sphere where it cannot be verified by the ordinary analogies of world history but can be seen and grasped only imaginatively and represented in the form of poetry. How can it be otherwise when it is the history of the work and revelation of God, which as such, as the history of the action and lordship of the Lord of heaven and earth, although it can also take place in the comparatively narrow sphere of historically verifiable occurrence, is not confined to the sphere of ordinary earthly analogies? To some extent the angels mark this transition, this reaching of the incommensurable into the commensurable, of mystery into the sphere of known possibilities. For this reason they particularly are figures of biblical saga and legend. This does not count against them. It is a factual explanation of their distinctive being and action. Nor is it a concession

[376]

to modern thought. The distinction between documented history and saga is a possibility of modern thought. We make use of it. But we do so in the very free sense indicated, and only because it is peculiarly adapted to set the nature of the object under discussion in a light in which it could not stand for the older theology which did not know this distinction. In general and formal terms, the angels are the particular representatives of the mystery of the biblical history. If we are to understand this history as the work and revelation of divine grace, even on this general and formal ground we cannot dismiss the angels as of no consequence. It is to this that we point when we describe them as figures of biblical; saga and legend.

But this assertion cannot mean that *fides quaerens intellectum*[EN18] has to halt at the angels, or that the question of theological truth has not to be raised in this matter. If this were the case, there would be no question of theological truth at all, and therefore no theology, no *fides quaerens intellectum*[EN19]. For in some way, we repeat, almost the whole of the biblical history is engaged in that transition to saga or legend, and the angels in particular can only make this clear. But in dogmatics it is a matter of trying to understand both the fact and the extent that in the whole sphere of biblical history—whether it be documented history or saga—we have to do with the work and revelation of divine grace, and to that extent with real, with the most real history. To understand this, and to put the question of truth in this sense, is our task in relation to the angels too. Hence we are not released from this task by the fact that we regard the angels as figures of biblical saga or legend. This does not mean that we are in the sphere of Red Riding Hood and her grandmother and the wolf, or the stork which leaves babies, or the March Hare and Father Christmas; in a sphere in which the biblical authors gave free rein to their poetic imagination, and in which we can give ourselves up with abandon to the same indulgence. This is not the case. For there can be meaningful as well as meaningless imagination, and disciplined as well as undisciplined poetry—this is the difference between good saga and bad. Both imagination and poetry can be ordered by orientation on the subject and its inner order. Both can be truthful, and in their own way the knowledge of the truth, in virtue of the truth of the subject. But the subject of the imagination and poetry of the biblical authors is not an ocean or mist of obscure possibilities. It is the spatio-temporally real history of the revelation and work of divine grace. This subject orders what they think and say in terms of saga no less than in terms of history. It establishes the meaning and discipline of their divination, of their imagination and poetry. This subject is the truth which in all circumstances they seek to attest and to which in some form they subject themselves. If we really hear them, we hear them speak of this subject. And if we accept their witness, it can only be for us the witness to the truth of this subject. As and because the question for us can

---

[EN18] faith seeking understanding
[EN19] faith seeking understanding

only be that of repeating the history narrated by them as the history of the work and revelation of God, we are summoned to think and speak as they did, not without the divination, imagination and poetry which they found necessary in view of the fact that this history is continually engaged in that movement of transition, yet not with any divination, imagination and poetry, but like them with the divination, imagination and poetry which are ordered and filled with meaning and disciplined by this particular history. Even in relation to the angels we are not left without any thoughts at all, or in the sphere of dreams or day-dreams, but we are summoned to think with the true theological knowledge in which it will be shown that no indolence is possible in this sphere, that divinatory thinking and speech are indispensable, but that we are not allowed to think and speak anything and everything, that the angels and the March Hare are two different things, that in relation to the angels we are commanded to think and say something very definite—*vera, certa*[EN20] and *utilia*[EN21], to use once again the terminology of Calvin.

[377]

It may be instructive to give a particularly bad example of what we must not do. For this purpose, I select the doctrine of angels which Carl Hase, a church historian distinguished not least of all by his gushing style, presented in the volume of dogmatics to which he gave the title *Gnosis* (1827, 2nd edit. 1869). His biblical disquisitions concerning angels are completely devoid of any deeper understanding, and his historical observations are amused and in their own way amusing (Vol. I pp. 485 f.). He crowns them with the following concluding judgment. Beings of a spirituality by nature and grace higher than that of man, and which may be either angels or demons, are certainly conceivable but problematical. Yet the conception is unfortunately quite impossible, having perished with a "past and childlike outlook," of a heaven with the throne of God surrounded by singing angels ("and surely on this view it must have been very wearisome for the Lord to let His praises be sung so continually.") Whether they exist or not, these beings do not really belong to religion, and so "faith does not need to decide concerning them any more than it does concerning other heavenly bodies or the man in the moon." "If we confidently entrust ourselves to the providence of God, what does it matter to us whether or not it is exercised through an angel?" Goethe was right when he wrote to Lavater: "Let me call nervous calm what you call an angel." What place is there then for these problematical beings? "By their possible existence, their poetic content, their religious associations and the manner in which they have been handed down they constitute a circle of sacred saga." If there is no religious interest in the question whether they exist, they embody certain ideas which are either religious or related to religion, and hover in the pleasant twilight between poetry and history. "Those who have a heart for the beautiful and the ideal will gladly think of angels. It was the desire for a living creature better than ourselves yet benevolently participating in our human joys and sorrows which first heard the angel-song in the quiet night: ' Glory to God in the highest ... '." In particular the belief in a personal guardian angel is not regarded by Hase as completely reprehensible. "In intercourse with oneself, the protection of one's own spirit presents itself to youthful phantasy. High above every worthy man there stands his idea. The man usually contemplates it in self-awareness and sees himself in it; the maiden, in unconscious innocence as regards her own spiritual beauty, is disposed to love it in the man." The philosopher

---

[EN20] true, certain
[EN21] useful

F. H. Jacobi is quoted: "The object of the noble love of Heloise certainly deserved this love; for he formed her tender soul, adorned her and gave her wings—and it was not Abelard!" But Hase knows better: "And yet it was Abelard! Not the one whose aspiring spirit was torn in the conflict with his age, but a higher, eternal spirit which in both his theology and his love gave only an inkling of what he was and was to be." And again: "Our own future, and the conception of transfigured friends, take on angelic form. The thought of a mother, or some other loved one, becomes a guardian angel in the hour of temptation." It is objected against the scholastic doctrine of angels that in it the angels became "metaphysical bats," and in face of all biblical and ecclesiastical tradition it is finally taught that "the angels belong to the poet and painter for the ideal representation of youthful and childlike beauty. The angels of Thomas Aquinas cut a poor show compared with the two heavenly children which resting on their little arms look pensively on Raphael's virgin mother of God, reflecting in their child-like eyes the most beautiful thing that this world ever saw. Art can as little portray heaven without angels as spring without flowers." With similar eloquence Hase in a final burst of generosity found a place for the devil as a "heroic and humorous" figure of poetry, art, rhetoric and especially the forceful speech of the people.

What are we to say to all this? Naturally it represents the 19th century in full blast, as in the *Trompeter von Säckingen*. And we need hardly be surprised that, having dismissed the real angels and substituted these paper pomposities, Hase did not see how comical he himself was, and therefore saw no reason to apply his witticisms to himself and his own products. But there is a serious side to the matter. How did Hase reach this strange conclusion? The decisive point was that, although he knew the relevant texts of the Old and New Testaments, of "Hebraism" and "primitive Christianity," he merely recorded their contents without any interest in their relationship to the biblical message and without putting the question of theological truth, but with a superior smile which could only become broader as he turned to the statements of the Early Church, the Middle Ages, the Reformation, Orthodoxy, the Enlightenment and Romanticism, and everywhere with the inquisitive and ironical detach-ment of the pure historian making his discoveries, until at last he came to the conclusion which had been obvious from the very first, that philosophically and religiously there was nothing of any practical value in the whole history as he had unravelled it in the Bible and in previous ages in the Church. But in this particularly bad case of intellectual self-complacency Hase did not attempt either a speculative reconstruction like some of the theologians whom we shall consider later or a complete dismissal of the whole sphere like his contemporary D. F. Strauss or more ruthlessly R. Bultmann in our own day. What remains in his case is a doctrine of angels which is that of a not very bold but rich, home-baked, aesthetic enthusi-asm, the "circle of sacred saga" and the "pleasant twilight" in which the theologian, trying to improve on the Bible and Church history, lights on the idea which hovers above the worthy man, on Abelard and Heloise, on transfigured friends, on the thought of a mother, on the childlike eyes of Raphael's cherubs, and what have you. It was these new curiosities which he substituted for the old in solution of the problem. And if we are not to end in the same way we must take up a different attitude from the very beginning. The strange thing is that Hase gave to his dogmatics the title *Gnosis*. But if we are merely summoned by the Bible to record and not to ponder and understand, we shall necessarily regard what is said in the Bible and elsewhere on this topic as so much arbitrary nonsense, and we shall even more certainly demonstrate that we ourselves cannot do better than produce even more arbitrary and greater nonsense ourselves. If we are merely clever and are obviously not prepared from the very first to practise the *credo ut intelligam*[EN22], we are well advised not to venture into this sphere, or that of dogmatics generally. For we can have no prospect of success.

[EN22] I believe in order to understand

3. If the doctrine of angels is to be theological in character; if, then, it is to
be significant for the faith and proclamation of the Church; or more simply, if
it is to rest on solid ground, it is necessary that we should strictly respect the
sequence, relationship and consequence disclosed in the statement *credo ut
intelligam*[EN23]. It is not a matter of any *intelligere*[EN24], but of that whose theme is
the angels to the extent that they belong to the context of Christian faith, so
that the *intelligere*[EN25] does not arise from a general need to know but is
demanded by Christian faith, nor does it rest on any basis but on that which is
given to Christian faith in this respect as in all others. But this means that we
have to wrestle with the view and concept of angels as they come before us in
Holy Scripture as the witness to the work and revelation of God in Jesus Christ.
It is no use erecting on general grounds a conception of something that angels
might be, then persuading ourselves that these are the angels to which Holy
Scripture refers and of which we have to accept that their nature, existence
and action are related to the work and revelation of God and therefore to the
theme of Christian faith, and finally deducing that *credere*[EN26] means to have
some kind of belief in these beings and that the real task of theology, applying
the *intelligere*[EN27] consistently to these beings, is to understand and explain
them. We must not be guilty at this point of the $\pi\rho\hat{\omega}\tau\sigma\nu \ \psi\epsilon\hat{\upsilon}\delta\sigma\varsigma$[EN28], taking up
the matter with a preconception of what angels might be or must be which we
have formed on some very different grounds, no matter what these grounds
may be. But we must be ready to be instructed concerning them *ab ovo*[EN29]
from the source from which theology must always learn if it is not to degenerate into that gnosis in the bad sense which hovers either in the heights or the
depths. If we are guilty of that $\pi\rho\hat{\omega}\tau\sigma\nu \ \psi\epsilon\hat{\upsilon}\delta\sigma\varsigma$[EN30], we need not be surprised if
we are entangled in all kinds of questions and difficulties which secretly ham-
pered the angelology of older orthodoxy, which were merely increased by the
sun of the Enlightenment that lit up so many other things, and which have
finally brought the whole subject into the disrepute from which it still suffers
to-day. These do not derive from what is discernible in the Bible as a witness to
the work and revelation of God which also includes the existence and work of
angels, but from the preconception by means of which it was hoped even in
early days to provide rather than to facilitate an understanding of this witness
instead of applying the required concern for the *intelligere*[EN31] directly to the
witness itself. They derive from the false translation with which even in early
days, and with the best intentions, the biblical view and concept of angels were

---

[EN23] I believe in order to understand
[EN24] understanding
[EN25] understanding
[EN26] believing
[EN27] understanding
[EN28] first false step
[EN29] from scratch
[EN30] great number of angels and servants
[EN31] understanding

to be made more readily accessible. There is every reason to be particularly strict in our application of the Scripture-principle in this field because tradition has been unhelpful in this respect, not merely preparing the catastrophe which broke later and still affects us to-day, but doing something which was far worse, i.e., binding and obscuring the positive instruction to be gained in the [380] matter. We must avoid both these errors. The doctrine of angels is difficult to understand like all the other things that we have to understand in faith in the Word of God attested in Holy Scripture. It may even be said that, although it is not more difficult to understand, it is difficult in a particular way. Even if we keep strictly to Scripture, and make its witness the theme of our endeavour, we shall have our work cut out and find plenty of questions to engage us. But this legitimate, necessary and unavoidable difficulty is to be distinguished from that which besets us if in what we think and say about angels we look in a different direction from that to which we are directed by Scripture. We can and must jettison the ballast which has accumulated in consequence of the latter aberration, and we shall then see that there is no reason to take part in the stampede from the whole subject which has become general in our own day. But it is not merely a question of freeing ourselves from difficulties. It is a question of bringing to light the truth which has been buried not so much by that catastrophe and the common denial of the whole subject but by the way in which it was earlier affirmed and made the theme of positive discussion.

In both respects, however, our only course is to keep to the original form of the subject in our attempt to understand and explain it. The angels have an original form in the witness of Holy Scripture. In it they belong to the theme of Christian faith. In it they are not an absurdity or curiosity which we are at liberty to reinterpret, to deny, or to replace by curiosities of our own invention. In it they open up vistas of a dimension of Christian faith which this should not lack. At a pinch and in the forbearance of God, which sustains it in spite of its defects, the Church and its proclamation may well survive without this dimension of faith, although not without hurt, and not without an underlying awareness that something is missing. Yet when it opens up, the knowledge of this dimension will not be something to be evaded; it will be found to be a liberation and enrichment which once discovered is no longer dispensable. And it is hard to estimate what it might mean for Christianity and the world if in faith it could really become aware again of the distinctive reality of this thing which at best it does not abandon but somehow brings in for reasons of piety. But this depends upon its becoming aware again of its original form. It is to this, and therefore to the biblical witness to angels, that we must direct our attention and endeavours.

In this introduction we are well advised to consider some concrete instances of the possibilities which must be avoided.

In the Apologists of the 2nd century it is more than equivocal that in answer to the charge of atheism brought by pagans against the Church Justin (*Apol.*, I, 6) can give a reassuring account of the many divine authorities which Christians actually reverence and worship

1. The Limits of Angelology

(σεβόμεθα καὶ προσκυνοῦμεν): the true God as the Father of righteousness, prudence and all virtues, who is free from every taint of evil; the Son who teaches us, and the host of other angels which follow and resemble Him; and finally the prophetic Spirit. And Athenagoras is even more suspect when he says (*Leg. pro Christ.*, 10) that Christian theology is not exhausted in the confession of the triune God, but that we also confess the πλῆθος ἀγγέλων καὶ λειτουργῶν EN32 which God the Creator of the world set by His Word over the elements, the heavens, the cosmos, and all that is in it, and over the order of this totality, subordinating the latter to them. And in another place (*ib.*, 24) he says that as we confess God and the Son (His Word) and the Holy Ghost ... so we reckon with other δυνάμεις EN33 which rule in and over the ὕλη EN34. Already we have here many features which are new and strange in relation to the doctrine of angels in the Old and New Testaments. In Justin there is the conception of Christ as an ἄγγελος EN35 at the head of a host of similar beings (cf. *Dial. c. Tryph.*, 128). In Justin and Athenagoras there is the assumption that the angels are a subject of Christian confession, reverence and worship together with the triune God. And in Athenagoras there is the presupposition as self-evident (cf. also the *Shepherd of Hermas, Vis.* III, 4, 1) that angels have the function of mediatorial cosmic principles.

In the Church fathers there is a whole series of similar conceptions which plainly deviate from the Bible and obviously derive their nourishment from another source. Decisive for all that follows is the emergence and the rapid domination of the assumption that it is possible, legitimate and necessary to seek the existence and nature of angels elsewhere than in their function as God's heavenly messengers. Certainly this took place in answer to a natural requirement of formal logic. But it did not take place in the sense and according to the pattern of the biblical witness. It was under the sway of an alien interest that there was an increasing desire to know about the nature of angels and an increasing belief that it was possible to know what these beings are in themselves, and therefore prior to and apart from the fact that they are angeli, the messengers of God. The basic innovation involved, although not introduced by Augustine, receives at his hands its classical formulation (*Enarr. in Ps.* 103¹. ¹⁵): *Spiritus autem angeli sunt; et cum spiritus sunt, non sunt angeli; cum mittuntur fiunt angeli. Angelus enim officii nomen est, non naturae. Quaeris nomen huius naturae, spiritus est; quaeris officium, angelus est; ex eo quod est, spiritus est, ex eo quod agit, angelus est*EN36.

There was now an interest in angels as a particular species of creaturely being which at an earlier time it was thought possible to group in one genus with man according to his psychical components. Irenaeus (*Adv. haer.*, IV, 37, 1) thought that this common grouping was possible only for the one reason, maintained by all who followed, that angels and men are both endowed with freedom of choice (*potestas electionis*) between good and evil. Eusebius, however, took the wider view more typical of the age which followed that each is a λογικὴ κτίσις, a *rationalis creatura*EN37, created by God for fellowship with His own rational and spiritual being (*Demon. evang.*, IV, 1). This common rational and spiritual nature is imparted (according to Gregory of Nyssa, *De or. domin.*, 4) to the ἀσώματος EN38 and the

---

EN32 great numbers of angels and servants
EN33 powers
EN34 material world
EN35 angels
EN36 For the angels are spirits; and when they are considered as spirits, they are not angels; they become angels only when they are sent forth. For "angel" is the name of an office, not of a nature. If you seek the name of this nature, it is spirit; if you seek that of the office, it is angel. With respect to its being, this creature is a spirit; with respect to what it does, it is an angel
EN37 rational creature
EN38 bodiless

ἐνσώματος φύσις [EN39], i.e., to angels and men, who both have their true and supreme destiny (Gregory the Great, *Moralia*, IV, 3, 8) in the fact that they may know God. The peculiarity of the nature of angels as compared with that of men is that they are non-corporeal or non-material, or at least that this is almost the case (Greg. of Naz., *Or.*, 28, 31), i.e., that it is so in relation to us though not in relation to God, since God alone is absolutely non-corporeal and non-material (J. Dam., *De fide orth.*, III, 2). The fact that—with this reservation—they are purely spiritual and therefore self-evidently invisible and immortal now became the dominant view, and it was usual to compare them with the purity of fire. With both philosophical and mythical splendour Gregory of Nazianzus (*Or.*, 38, 9) described how

[382] the eternal goodness was not content to move alone in its own θεωρία [EN40]; how its good, corresponding to its nature as goodness, had to flow out and be spread abroad; how, active in the Logos and perfecting in the Spirit, it conceived angelic and heavenly powers; and how in the work of this conception of the Godhead, and subordinated to it, they were created as λειτουργοὶ τῆς πρώτης λαμπρότητος the νοερὰ πνεύματα, the *intelligentes spiritus* [EN41], which we have to think of as fire or as non-corporeal and non-material nature or something similar. And Augustine (*De Gen. ad lit.*, IV, 32, 49) characterised the reason of angels as one which clings in pure love to the Word of God because it is adapted to know all things first in this Word and therefore *a priori* [EN42] (as *cognitio matutina* [EN43]), and not merely as created by this Word and therefore *a posteriori* [EN44] (as *cognitio vespertina* [EN45]). Their reason embraces both these forms of cognition. As a created reason, it cannot, of course, know God as He is but only in accordance with its capacity (Cyril of Jerusalem, *Cat.*, 6, 6). Therefore right up to the days of Protestant orthodoxy (e.g., J. Wolleb, *Theol. chr. comp.*, 1626, I, *cap.* 5, 3) the definition could be accepted that angels are *spiritus intelligentes a corpore liberi* [EN46]. If in the later parlance of the Church God is often called the Creator of the *creatura spiritualis et corporalis* [EN47], the reference of the *creatura spiritualis* [EN48] is to the *creatura angelica* [EN49], according to the express elucidation of the Fourth Lateran Council of 1215 (*Denz.*, 428). But this basic definition obviously gave rise to further questions and the corresponding answers, and these could only lead even further away from the Bible. For example, how is it that these beings are holy and stand essentially in a particular relationship to God? A trace of biblical reminiscence may be found in the answer given by Basil (*De spir. s.*, 16, 38 etc.) and others, that this was not by nature but as they received and maintained a special sanctification by the Holy Spirit. Or again, what is their relationship to space? *Momento ubique sunt, totus orbis illis locus unus est* [EN50], was the rather over-confident assertion of Tertullian (*Apol.*, 22). But the view expressed by Athanasius (*Ad. Serap.*, 1, 26) became the dominant one, namely, that they are not omnipresent like God but for all their freedom of movement are always in one particular place. As J. Damascene put it (*De fide orth.*, II, 3), they are neither corporeal nor material, and therefore unlimited and unrestricted, yet they are always in a definite and therefore a limited place, in heaven and not on earth, or *vice versa*. According to

---

[EN39] embodied nature
[EN40] contemplation
[EN41] servants of the primal splendour, the intellectual spirits
[EN42] unconditionally
[EN43] "morning knowledge"
[EN44] conditionally
[EN45] "evening knowledge"
[EN46] intellectual spirits that are free of bodies
[EN47] spiritual and physical creatures
[EN48] spiritual creatures
[EN49] angelic creatures
[EN50] They are everywhere at any given moment, and the whole world is but one place to them.

1. *The Limits of Angelology*

Didymus Alex. (*De trin.*, II, 6, 2), they have a πέρας, an ὡρισμένη ποσότης EN51. Or again, are there differences and degrees of dignity and power as between these beings? Is there an order intrinsic to them? In the light of the different biblical descriptions of angels, and the biblical reference to angelic hosts (although not merely on these grounds), Dionysius Areopagita had long since answered this question in the affirmative, and if Augustine declared that he did not know this order Jerome (*Apol. adv. Ruf.*, I, 23) intimated that he knew something about it. There seems at first to have been a certain restraint in this matter, which the Areopagite was the first to penetrate. Again, if angels for all the difference of their nature were to be counted as part of the known constitution of that which is outside God and therefore of the creaturely world, the question arises why there is no mention of them in the Mosaic account of creation, and at what point in this account their creation is tacitly assumed. If appeal was not made to Gen.2¹ with its recapitulatory reference to heaven and earth "and all the host of them," or if their creation was not found in that of light in Gen. 1³, then it had to be explained, as by Ambrose (*Hex.*, I, 5, 19), that although as creatures they were not without beginning they were already present at the creation of the rest of the cosmos (as suggested by Job 38⁷: "When the morning stars sang together, and all the sons of God shouted for joy"). Or on the basis of the same text it was said (cf. Epiphanius, *Adv. haer.*, 65, 5) that although they could not have come into being after the stars they could not have preceded heaven and earth, because in the beginning God created heaven and earth, prior to which there was nothing apart from Himself. Or it was thought with Gennadius (*Libr. eccl. dogm.*, 10) that their creation should be put in the space of time when darkness was upon the [383] face of the deep in Gen. 1²: *ut non esset otiosa Dei bonitas, sed haberet in quibus per multa ante spatia bonitatem ostenderet*EN52. The final problem was to explain the existence of demons. This was usually done by the theory of the fall of a number of angels, created good like men but gifted with *liberum arbitrium*EN53, and their consequent corruption. This apostasy took place under the leadership of the *Diabolus* as the great *angelus apostata*EN54 (Irenaeus, *Adv. haer.*, V, 24, 3). What was his sin? Not licence, theft or the like, but pride, was the answer of Athanasius (*De virg.*, 5), and the wickedness of the other bad angels was that, although they should only be orientated on the supreme being, instead they *ad se ipsos conversi sunt*EN55 (Augustine, *De civ. Dei*, XII, 6). Following the first, and voluntarily forfeiting the blessedness they might have enjoyed, a greater or lesser number of other angels became transgressors and therefore bad angels—a final and irrevocable decision because quite inexcusable in view of the high nature of angels as compared with weaker man. On the other hand, those who did not do so stood fast in the truth in virtue of their *liberum arbitrium*EN56, being finally established after their victorious withstanding of this once-for-all temptation (Augustine, *De corr. et grat.*, 10, 27; *In Joann.*, 110, 7; Fulgentius, *De fide ad Petr.*, 3, 30; Gregory the Great, *Mor.*, IV, 3, 8). As Tertullian saw it (*De carne Chr.*, 14), the reason why Christ became a man and not an angel was because the Father could neither promise nor commission the redemption of fallen angels. Much later Anselm of Canterbury (*Cur Deus homo*, I, 16–18) could use this theory of the fall of angels, which he regarded as a revealed truth, as an argument in his doctrine of atonement. As he saw it, the original number of angels as citizens of the *civitas superna*EN57 had to be restored. The gap could not be filled by the creation

---

EN51 boundedness, a definite quantitative measure
EN52 so that God's goodness should not be idle, but might have occasion to show forth its goodness in many ways before the creation of the world
EN53 freedom of the will
EN54 apostate angel
EN55 were orientated to themselves
EN56 freedom of the will
EN57 exalted city

of new angels, because the number had been laid down in the plan of creation. Thus, to overcome this disruption of cosmic harmony, God had to elect a corresponding number of other rational beings, i.e., of men. Since they are elected and ordained to replace angels, they must themselves be like angels, i.e., freed from their sins. For this satisfaction was needed, and since God alone would supply this satisfaction He had to become man.

It is obvious—and it confirms the fact that what we have here is a basic aberration—that in the fathers relatively less attention is devoted to what claims the exclusive interest of the Old and New Testaments, namely, what Augustine called the *officium angelicum*[EN58], than to the far more widely discussed question of the *angelica natura*[EN59], in which the Bible seems to have no interest at all. Nor can we say of the comparatively few statements of the fathers on the former point that it follows the line of the biblical witness. We seem to be nearest to this when we read in Chrysostom in (*Ep. ad Hebr. hom.*, 3, 2) that the $\lambda\epsilon\iota\tau o\upsilon\rho\gamma\iota\alpha$[EN60] of angels consists in serving God to our salvation; that it is the $\dot{\alpha}\gamma\gamma\epsilon\lambda\iota\kappa\dot{o}\nu$ $\check{\epsilon}\rho\gamma o\nu$[EN61] to do everything to save the brethren; that this is the true work of Jesus Christ Himself; that He Himself as the Lord is the real Saviour; and that the angels can only be His servants in this work. In what does their $\delta\iota\alpha\kappa o\nu\epsilon\hat{\iota}\nu$[EN62] consist? According to Hilary (*Tract. sup. Ps.*, 129, 7), it consists in a *ministerium spiritualis intercessionis*[EN63] which was needed by man though not by God for the effectiveness of his prayer and meritorious work. The surest and most general conception is that of the guardian angel given to each individual on his way, of an *angelus in custodiam delegatus*[EN64] (Jerome, *In Matth.*, 3, 18, 10). This is to be found already in Origen (*In Luc. hom.*, 12), although with the dubious addition that we all have a bad angel as well. Then according to Hilary (*loc. cit.*), on the obvious basis of Rev. 2–3, there are also *spirituales virtutes ecclesiis praesidentes*[EN65], and according to J. Damascene (*De fide orth.*, II, 3) and others there are national angels which "keep watch over the different parts of the earth, presiding over nations and regions, controlling our history and giving us their aid." But even if this or that passage in the Bible seems to say something of this kind, the question arises where in the Bible the ideas of guardian and national angels are so substantial and important as to compel or even to allow us to understand the function of angels according to this norm.

[384]

A very different aspect of the angelic office is opened up if the theory developed by Erik Peterson (*Das Buch von den Engeln*, 1935, pp. 39–81) really represents the general conception of the Early Church. As he sees it, the decisive function of angels consists in the worship which they offer in heaven and in which the worship of the Church on earth has only an imitative part, although conversely the angels participate in the worship of the Church on earth. With the ascension of Christ, and as Christians have left the earthly Jerusalem and "come unto ... the heavenly Jerusalem, and to an innumerable company of angels, to the general assembly and church of the firstborn" (Heb. 12 [22f.]), the temple of Isaiah 6 has been transferred to heaven, and it is there that the glory of God and the Sanctus of the seraphim are now located. But all the angelic hosts now stand behind the seraphim, and that isolated cry has become an unceasing hymn. This is the worship which embraces the whole cosmos. Its central and most spiritual part is that of the angels in heaven. But the sun and moon and stars all have a share in it. And the worship of men can only be added to this worship of angels and all creation. The earthly liturgy can only be integrated and fused into the great

---

[EN58] angelic office
[EN59] angelic nature
[EN60] service
[EN61] angelic work
[EN62] serving
[EN63] ministry of spiritual intercession
[EN64] angel assigned for protection
[EN65] spiritual powers presiding over the churches

order of the heavenly. For this reason the worship of the Church has a tendency to change into a ministry similar to the worship of angels. And it is the hymn of monks (as distinct from the mere acclamation or *Sanctus*[EN66] of the people) which in its constant repetition of the offices, its unison, and its renunciation of any musical instruments apart from the human voice, is obviously closest to the worship of the angels and comes nearest to actualising that change. And there is a corresponding participation of the angels in the worship of the Church on earth, a sharing in the administration of the sacraments, a particular presence of angels in the services of monks, Church synods etc.—always with the particular intention of lending to the actions of the Church a public character in the emphatic and almost political sense of the term, the character of a participation in the worship of the cosmos. Peterson has been able to find support for this view in numerous passages, especially from the Egyptian Liturgy of St. Mark, but also from the Syrian Liturgy of St. James and many of the fathers and other ecclesiastical writers. But the question remains whether it will stand up to detailed scrutiny. Something which is so far-reaching, if it had been a dominant view, would surely have exercised a plain and general influence on the whole picture presented by patristic theology. Is it not surprising that a devotee and expert in this whole field of heavenly and ecclesiastical hierarchy like Pseudo-Dionysius, who actually wrote about the two hierarchies, while he certainly knew the relationship between the two and the imitation of the one by the other, should not really base his presentations on this mutual relationship, and that the specifically cultic or choral function of angels, although he certainly touches on it, does not seem to constitute for him the essence of their office? Again, how is it that neither Pseudo-Dionysius nor the other fathers seem to have thought of using the biblical passage (Rev. 4–5) to which Peterson makes basic reference on pp. 19–38 to explain the ministry of angels along the lines which he has propounded? Why have they not even exploited in this sense the verse in Heb. 1¹⁴ where angels are expressly called $\lambda \epsilon \iota \tau o \upsilon \rho \gamma \iota \kappa \grave{a} \ \pi \nu \epsilon \acute{\upsilon} \mu a \tau a$[EN67]? But I am in no position to contradict a scholar like Peterson. In the Early Church there may well have been such views and systems with many other secret traditions which are poorly attested from the literary standpoint. Yet if Peterson is right, and the angelology of the Early Church was really dominated by this aspect, we can only come to the unfortunate conclusion that it departed further from its biblical basis than was actually the case according to its clear pronouncements concerning the *natura*[EN68] and *officium*[EN69] of angels. For the basic term *angelus*[EN70], messenger, is reduced to almost utter insignificance in this system. Even in Pseudo-Dionysius the term is sometimes given its proper weight. But how can the task of a messenger consist decisively in the singing of hymns? And how can the sight and sound of [385] the choir office of the Benedictines give the impression that this can have anything whatever to do with the service of messengers? What is said in Revelation 4–5 will certainly call for consideration. But we can say already that even if these chapters do in some sense point in this direction we shall certainly not recognise the angels of the biblical witness in its entirety if we confine ourselves to a doctrine which looks abstractly in this direction.

But it is high time that we considered the most famous of all the early monographs on our present subject, the *De hierarchia coelesti* of the supposed Dionysius the Areopagite. This is the work of an unknown writer who probably lived and worked in Syria about 500 A.D. He pretended to be the disciple of the apostle Paul who bore the name of Dionysius in Acts 17³⁴. In reality, however, he was a Christian Neo-Platonist well-versed in the Greek fathers from

---

[EN66] Holy
[EN67] spirits appointed for service
[EN68] nature
[EN69] office
[EN70] angel

Clement to Cyril of Alexandria and particularly influenced by the philosopher Proclus. Under the same pseudonym he wrote a series of other writings of which the most important extant are *De hierarchia ecclesiastica* and *De divinis nominibus*. We have here the work of one of the greatest frauds in Church history (which seems to have had more than its share of this type of author), and one who made such a material impression on the ages which followed that for a long time he was recognised as one of the official saints of the Catholic Church and it was only in the period of Humanism that the first doubts were raised as to the authenticity of his writings—doubts which have now been confirmed even by Catholic scholars. But forged or otherwise his writing achieved a historical significance which it is impossible to contest and which remained long after the discovery of the imposture. For in it we have a first and epoch-making climax in the angelology of the Early Church.

As the title indicates, it is specifically concerned with a question which the earlier fathers had touched on but never developed—that of the hierarchy of the heavenly world. In the process, however, it gives us a very definite doctrine of angels generally.

The word "hierarchy" seems to have been given a new sense by this Dionysius. As he uses it, it means generally the order of salvation executed by God as the original and proper "Hierarch" or sacred Ruler. This order consists in the outpouring and outshining of the primal divine light. It is thus to be understood essentially as revelation, as intellectual illumination and irradiation for the purpose of knowing God and all things in Him and from Him and to Him. Its meaning and goal is to lead the beings which are reached by it, which receive it, and which become its active bearers and mediators, each at its appointed stage and to its allotted degree, to likeness to God, union with Him and participation in His work, i.e., to cause them to become mirrors of the primal divine light and therefore those who have genuine knowledge. In this process, according to the specific stage and in relation to those above and below, "some are purified and others purify, some are enlightened and others enlighten, some are perfected and others perfect," but all are made capable of contemplation and participant in knowledge, and therefore all are elevated to participation in God and co-operation with Him. In different ways this is true of every hierarchy, of the ecclesiastical and other terrestrial hierarchies. As used by Dionysius, hierarchy is not a static but a supremely dynamic general term to denote the manner in which the Godhead participates in manifold ways in the created world and the created world in the Godhead. But the specific hierarchy on which Dionysius proposes to inform us on the basis of Holy Scripture is the heavenly hierarchy—that of angels.

In the second chapter of his work he interposes a remarkable epistemological discussion. Holy Scripture speaks of angels, as of God, by means of images, thus taking into account our human capacities and at the same time concealing its mysteries from profane eyes. This [386] concealment with a view to true and legitimate disclosure consists sometimes in homogeneous images (e.g., word, spirit or essence), sometimes in less similar (e.g., light or life), and sometimes in those which are openly dissimilar and incommensurate (especially where the images are corporeal and material). The language is always to be understood and expounded anagogically, i.e., according to the spiritual sense, and not according to what is conveyed directly by the images. When we speak of "wrath" in relation to God, to spiritual natures and to angels, we mean their resolute wisdom and inflexibility; when we speak of "desire," their inconceivable divine love for the spiritual; when we speak of "excess," their undivided and unalterable love for divine beauty; and when we speak of "irrationality" (for some of the biblical images belong to the inorganic and animal world), their superiority as supraterrestrial spirits to our discursive rational and emotional capacities, which are tied to matter. The fact that these descriptions of the divine and heavenly have a discordant and offensive element not only conceals that which is holy from those who are not initiated, but prevents those who are from clinging to the truth of the images, frightening them off as it were, and directing them to the way of true knowledge, which in its purity is always apophatic, and therefore negative.

On this presupposition Dionysius believes and maintains that Scripture has taught him as follows. It corresponds to the goodness of God to call creatures according to their nature to participation in His own being: inorganic creatures to participation in His mere being as such; organic but irrational to participation also in His living power; and rational spirits to participation also in His eternal wisdom. It is obvious that the creatures are closest to Him which participate most diversely in Him. But of these rational beings those are closest of all to Him, i.e., the angels, which are engaged in forming His image in a way which is purely spiritual. They are called angels because it is to them first that the divine illumination comes directly, being mediated to all others only through them. In this connexion Dionysius thinks that he can refer to the statement in Gal. 3[19] that the Law was given by angels. On his interpretation this means that there was and is for man no direct manifestation or vision of God, but that this was and is always accomplished by the intervention of heavenly powers. Thus we men, as members of a lower order, are lifted up to the divine by angels as members of a higher. And this process necessarily finds consistent repetition in human orders, e.g., in that of the Church. Hierarchical order is thus essential to the Church. For instance, it was the angels who first learned of the incarnation of Christ, and they then communicated it to Zacharias, Mary, Joseph and the shepherds. Even the man Jesus subjected Himself to the directions of His Father and God as mediated by angels. "Angel" is a basic term to denote all heavenly spirits, even those of a higher order which in their particularity bear other names. In the stricter sense the "angels" are merely the spirits which stand at the foot of the heavenly hierarchy and are thus responsible for the direct conveyance of messages to us men. They do not have the prerogatives of higher spirits, and cannot therefore bear their names. But the general title is valid because the higher spirits all possess, and possess to a supreme degree, the illuminations and powers of all the lower and even these lowest spirits. All of them, therefore, can be described as angels.

In Chapter 6 there commences the famous detailed description of the angelic hierarchy as such. It is the names given to angels in the Bible which rightly understood declare the peculiarity of the different classes of angels and also their mutual order and relationship. A divine teacher—it is not quite clear whether the apostle Paul is meant or not—has introduced Dionysius to the resultant knowledge, and on the basis of this knowledge he is able to pass on the following information. There are in the Bible nine names of angels, and therefore nine angelic choirs, which are mutually related in three triads, each of which has also its own order. The first and highest of these consists of the three choirs of the seraphim, the [387] cherubim and the throne. These are the direct recipients of the divine revelations, outpourings and initiations: the seraphim as the flaming movers; the cherubim as those who first see and know; and the throne, it seems, as the principles of the relative sovereignty of these first three angelic choirs. For it is the particularity of the first order to be sovereign (relatively, of course, to God); to be removed from every suggestion of weakness and inferiority; to be incapable of any kind of lapse. It is filled with a light which surpasses even immaterial knowledge. It is the reflection of God in the sublimest sense. It is perfect because engaged in a direct upsoaring to primal deity. It is grouped immediately round God, and in unceasing praise the simple mediation of these supreme spirits is occupied in the eternal knowledge of God. As the first and supreme triad, raising the first *trisagion*[EN71], it is the direct witness of the triad and monad of the Godhead. The second and middle order consists of the dominions (κυριότητες), powers (δυνάμεις), and authorities (ἐξουσίαι). It is hard to extract from the fulness of his eloquence the details of what he has to say concerning this triad. It emerges,

---

[EN71] acclamation of God as thrice holy

97

however, that by these three choirs he means instruments of heavenly rule which exercise their power in noble freedom, with no taint of tyranny, yet inviolably, unconquerably and in perfect harmony. We have here spirits which are led mediately to perfection, and are therefore less full of light as compared with those of the first triad. But in their particular function and to their own degree they have indirectly both a passive and an active part in the divine irradiation. The third and lowest triad consists of the principalities (ἀρχαί), the archangels ἀρχάγγελοι and the angels in the stricter sense, which form the lowest choir of all. The transition from the second to the third order, and the distinctive features of this final triad, are not at all clear. But it is evident that at this point the order of heaven draws near to events on earth and the hierarchies which control them. Again it is a question of instruments of rule—and here as in the second order we have to remember that for Dionysius rule consists in an enlightenment, in an impartation of knowledge. But now we have to do with instruments of a more concrete kind. The principalities look to the source of all rule, seeking, finding and giving a certain orientation. The angels are heavenly interpreters in the sphere of the more visible and the earthly world. And the archangels occupy a midway position, reflecting the attitude of the principalities on the one hand and prefiguring, directing and co-ordinating the action of the angels on the other. It is indicative of the peculiar conception of Dionysius that he finds the direct activity of angels in earthly occurrence wholly in their influence on earthly hierarchies (ecclesiastical and otherwise), and not in their influence on individuals, so that for him guardian angels are exclusively national angels.

In nature, structure, task and function, touching Godhead at the one end and the human sphere at the other, yet distinct for all the intensity of the contact, the heavenly hierarchy is a harmonious whole, hovering as heaven between God and earth. All the angelic choirs are revealers, proclaimers and messengers, each from and for the others, all directly or indirectly from God, all directly or indirectly for the world of man, all engaged in descent and ascent. When by their mediation the illumination of divine revelation finally comes down to man, again by their mediation it mounts back to God as its origin. All angels of all degrees can be called heavenly powers as well as angels to the extent that on their level and to the appropriate degree they all participate in the distinctiveness and purpose of the whole dynamically motivated system. It is to be noted, however, that the law of hierarchical sequence admits of no exceptions. Although Isaiah 6 seems to speak of a direct encounter between the seraphim and the prophet, Dionysius takes this to imply that a vision was given to the prophet through a lower angel and that it was in this vision that he saw the supreme angels and God. His work concludes with a mystical analysis, on the basis of his earlier epistemological theory, of the corporeal and material images used by the Bible when it speaks of angels, concealing and disclosing at one and the same time.

[388]

What was it that Dionysius attempted and achieved? His work plainly claims to be a reduction of the angelology of the earlier fathers. It is to be noted that it leaves on one side the questions and answers of his predecessors concerning the relationship of angels to space, the fall of angels, or individual guardian angels. This is because he is not really interested in the existence and history of angels as such, but only in their existence and function in that heavenly hierarchy. And this orientation of interest allowed and demanded a remarkable concentration of the elements which he took over from the earlier angelology. What his predecessors said about the nature of angels as *spiritus intelligentes puri*[EN72], about their peculiar knowledge, about their gracious sanctification and about their ministry, is comprehended or rather subsumed or submerged into the one consideration and depiction of the heavenly hierarchy as that order of salvation, i.e., of revelation and knowledge, which proceeds from God. In this he was not, of course, absolutely original, for he made use of hints

---

[EN72] pure intellectual spirits

which he may have found in Gregory of Nazianzus, and he obviously borrowed a good deal from his Neo-Platonic teacher Proclus in respect of the famous triads in his system. Since the unmasking of the literary imposture of which he was guilty many justifiable objections have been raised against the bombast of his style and language and against the garrulous obscurity or obscure garrulity of his mode of presentation. But this does not alter the fact that within its limits his work is one of those original and masterly ventures which do not often occur in the history of theology. It was not by accident, nor due only to the pseudonym, that it made such an impression on its own age and the whole of the Middle Ages, whose thinkers had ultimately a good eye for quality. The one who made this venture was no ordinary man. He did not need to masquerade as a disciple of Paul to gain a hearing. As angelology his heavenly hierarchy is a remarkable and instructive enterprise. Nor is this a tribute merely to its formal aspects.

There are, of course, obvious material objections to his teaching. Nor do they relate only to his annoying—and in detail not very clear or helpful—omniscience concerning the three triads and their choirs, and the names and natures of the various classes of angels; nor to the arbitrariness of his spiritual exposition of the biblical terms and the images used in the Bible—a matter on which we have touched only briefly in the present context. They must be brought against his view of the heavenly hierarchy as such, against that wave of light which as revelation comes cascading down from above and as knowledge climbs up again from below, which in the last resort is obviously cyclic, and within which the angels after their manner are all transitional elements. That this intellectual cycle between deity and humanity is identical with what is described as God's revelation and the knowledge of this revelation in the Old and New Testaments is something which we can hardly accept, and this means that we cannot recognise the real angels attested by the Bible in the figures which bear this name in Dionysius, i.e., in the hypostatised transitional points in that ascending and descending wave. Was Dionysius trying to lay the metaphysical foundation for a definite cosmology, anthropology and above all noology alien to the witness of the Bible, and did he find it helpful to use certain fragments of the biblical revelation and its transmission, and therefore the figures of the biblical angels, in demonstration of this underlying system? Or was he trying to find and display a metaphysical basis for a definite hierarchical but again unbiblical conception of the Church, and in the establishment and development of this basis was forced to make what he did of the biblical revelation and especially the biblical angels? Who can say whether he was trying to do the one or the other, or perhaps with this or that emphasis both? The one thing which is incontestable is that in Dionysius the biblical concern for its subject and therefore for angels finds no place but is replaced by another. And since in his angelology we have to do with a joyfully and gratefully attempted reduction and [389] concentration of that of the Early Church in general, the problem of Dionysius is that of all early angelology. For what kind of an angelology is it if it can culminate in his teaching, and if in the period which follows right up to the Reformation, and in Roman Catholic circles right up to our own day in spite of agreement on the literary question, Dionysius can be regarded as the outstanding representative of primitive angelology? Does not this mean that from the very outset unbiblical and materially unchristian attitudes, questions and answers dominate this whole doctrine? If its interests and concerns are the same as those of Dionysius, are we not forced to ask whether in this whole teaching we do not have either a metaphysical speculation—we might almost say a secular myth—or the justification by means of such a myth or speculation of a conception of the Church and revelation and faith whose authenticity is brought under suspicion by the very fact that it needs this basis or justification?

But when all this is said against Dionysius, we cannot deny him the specific merit of having tackled this doctrine. It is a truth which has to be asserted in relation to the history of theology that none of the many philosophical systems which have been brought in as a foundation, and have always come to dominate and determine it, has ever failed to damage and corrupt it, enticing it away from its orientation by the Word of God and falsifying it in its processes of thought and forms of representation, but that on the other hand none has ever served only to damage and corrupt and not also to provide a very real opportunity. Both these things are true of the Neo-Platonism of Dionysius. It sounds strange, but it is true, that his heavenly hierarchy gives us easier access to the biblical witness to angels than what was written on this subject either by the earlier fathers before him or Thomas Aquinas after him. The reduction and concentration to which he subjected the tradition of the 3rd to the 5th centuries was a good thing to the extent that it removed the figures of the angels from the isolation in which they were then conceived and understood. According to Dionysins it is no longer the case that somewhere below God (or suspiciously near Him according to the Apologists) and above man, with their own nature and history and a function which does not rightly correspond to their elevation, there are angels. But according to him they appear in a great and necessary context which, even though it is neo-platonically conceived, seems to be, or to be seen in the place of, that of the divine work of salvation on behalf of man, the economy of grace. The hierarchies of Dionysius in their totality unmistakeably represent or caricature or replace what the Bible in a narrower circle describes as the history of the covenant of grace between God and man and in a wider circle as the rule of divine providence. Seen in this context, the angels lose their interest as distinctive beings existing for themselves and acquire instead a genuinely necessary function as dynamic factors in that occurrence between God and man, thus becoming really interesting. Even in the Bible account has to be taken of the created heaven between God and man, and the problem of angels is that of the participation of this sphere of creation in the history of the covenant and salvation as it concerns man, and in this context of the divine governance of the world in general. Dionysius did not see this, but he saw something very like it, whereas the earlier fathers may have suspected it in part but did not really see or state it. And because he saw it, for him the angels were not just heavenly beings which God willed to create and did create as He also created earthly creatures, and concerning the nature, meaning and history of which theology has the task and the capacity to seek information. In and with what he called the heavenly hierarchy, he saw something corresponding formally to the participation of heaven in God's action and work on earth as attested in the Bible. And therefore, in a way which was impossible both for his predecessors and his successors, he was not only able to make use of the biblical concept of angels as servants and even revealers, announcers, witnesses and [390] messengers, and therefore of the basic understanding of Scripture, but also, within the sphere of his Neo-Platonic view of the cyclic movement of intellectual being, and for all the remarkable arbitrariness of his development of it, to reproduce something of the significance and dignity which it enjoys as the predominant motif in the Bible. In spite of all our reservations in respect of the form and content of his doctrine, this is a serious point in favour of Dionysius.

The Neo-Platonic key which he used was unsatisfactory. But it was not unserviceable. The Neo-Platonic temptation to which Christian theology was acutely exposed in Dionysius also gave it a definite opportunity. It was not impossible to move back from the view of Dionysius to the Bible and therefore to the matter itself, to the knowledge of angels in the context of the divine work of salvation. And the great aberration of which he was undoubtedly guilty both in detail and (as the representative of ancient angelology) in general, is less lamentable than the fact that the period which followed did not accept the summons to move in this direction. What happened both in the age which immediately followed with Gregory the

1. *The Limits of Angelology*

Great and John Damascene, and throughout the Middle Ages when he was quoted as so eminent an authority, was that he was used as a kind of quarry for all kinds of treasures of knowledge in respect of the difference and gradations in the angelic sphere as expansively described by him, so that his triads in particular came to constitute the central core of the Church's doctrine of angels. Moreover, his reduction and concentration of the whole problem was tacitly abandoned and the dynamic purpose of his hierarchy forgotten, the discarded elements in tradition being readopted, and his doctrine being understood as if he had made to the description of the heavenly cosmos and its inhabitants—even "hierarchy" was now taken to suggest a static reality—a contribution which was particularly interesting and which it surpassed the work of his predecessors in a way which was highly significant. With the remarkable addition that their names and degrees were now known, the angels were again given a particular and rather curious place in the inventory of the created world, and their meaning and necessity could be considered as far as possible in the light of selected standards. Materially, the way proposed by Dionysius was itself alien to the biblical witness. But it had the advantage that for all its alien character it still indicated the way in which thinking must proceed in this matter. In the Middle Ages his Neo-Platonism was limited, if not replaced, by the Aristotelian counter-movement. In the process, however, the important stimulation which might have come from Dionysius was completely lost. Even the Reformation made no decisive difference in this respect. In its controversy with mediaeval Scholasticism, orthodox Protestant dogmatics was content to jettison the extravagancies of Dionysius and other repellent and over-subtle elements, and it spoke of angels very much after the matter of the fathers before Dionysius and much mediaeval theology. But unfortunately it was not merely the shock of the discovery of the literary fraud which prevented Evangelical theology from asking whether there was not to be learned from Dionysius something which his successors and the Scholastics did not learn from him—an understanding of the existence of angels in the context of the history of salvation as the basis and order of their ministry.

In view of developments after Dionysius, it is only with the gravest anxiety that we can turn to the other great climax in the history of angelology, i.e., the doctrine developed by Thomas Aquinas in relation to this question (*S. theol.*, I, qu. 50–64, 106–114, and *S. c. gent.*, II, *cap.* 91–101). The distinction of his treatment is to be found in the scholarly acuteness, fulness and comprehensiveness of the investigation which he pursues and the information which he gives concerning the questions which are to be posed in respect of angels, the answers which can be given either in logical development of the concept or its application, and that which is to be gleaned from Scripture and tradition with reference to their nature, history and function. If the *Hierarchy* of Dionysius reads more like a dithyramb, in the two [391] *Summae* of Thomas we enter the sphere of the most calm and sober enquiry and teaching, of the strictest method and of corresponding statement—a sphere where nothing unnecessary, but everything necessary is said, and what is said is controlled by everything else and by its more immediate and remote contexts, so that there are no mere assertions, but every statement ventured is proved with refreshing conscientiousness. But in this respect Thomas Aquinas is too great to need any particular praise from us.

In relation to his doctrine of angels, two things are clear from the very outset. The first is that consciously and of set purpose he pursues an abstract angelology. In considering the world created by God, either primarily as in the *S. theol.* or finally as in the *S. c. gent.*, we must think of these beings which are called angels, and investigate and portray their particular being and nature and activity. As God is after His own manner, and physical things and psychico-physical men after theirs, so too it is with the angels. It is with them as such that the doctrine of angels has to do. This is assumed as self-evident. Many very acute questions are posed, and handled in great detail. But the decisive question is not even seen whether a

Christian understanding of this matter can pursue an abstract investigation, or reach any useful goal if it attempts to do so. The second point is that with relentless determination a definite conception in respect of the nature of angels, a particular definition, is presupposed, introduced and applied as a canon to the whole material, being assumed to be self-evident and tirelessly repeated and victoriously confirmed at each stage in the investigation and presentation. Again the central question (perhaps the question of all questions) is not even perceived, let alone considered, whether this is really the Christian conception, and therefore really in keeping with a *Summa theologica* or a *Summa contra gentiles* bearing the subtitle: *De veritate catholicae fidei.* Both decisions emerge at once at the beginning of both tractates on the theme as irrevocable and indisputable decisions. *S. theol.*, I, *qu.* 50, *art.* 1 is an answer to the question: *Utrum sit aliqua creatura omnino spiritualis et penitus incorporea?*[EN73] i.e., whether and to what extent there really is a creature of this kind beside God and among other creatures. And *S. c. gent.*, II, *cap.* 91 stands under the thesis: *Quod sint aliquae substantiae intellectuales corporibus non unitae*[EN74]. The existence of these substances among others, under God and above man and purely physical things, can and will be proved. They exist as do the others. There are such beings, created but distinctive. The task is thus to see and explain them in their autonomy. What kind of beings are they? And it is clear that we have to do with purely spiritual, intellectual and non-corporeal creatures, with "substances " (autonomous beings) which have this peculiarity. In the *S. theol.* they bear from the very first the accepted name of *angeli*[EN75]. But it is only incidentally in *qu.* 112, which speaks of the *missio angelorum ad homines*[EN76], that attention is drawn to the material significance of this name. Elsewhere it merely covers what is indicated by a definition which does not in the very least correspond to it. And in the *S. c. gent.*, perhaps out of regard for the *gentiles*, the name is used only on very few occasions, while the abbreviated designation of the subject treated, in closer correspondence with the matter as envisaged by Thomas, is simply *substantiae separatae*[EN77]. These are the considerations which compel us first and last to treat with the greatest reserve the famous angelology of Thomas. Its character is too unequivocal not to demand an equally unequivocal attitude. It is interesting as the classical opposite of the only procedure which we can regard as theologically meaningful. This work of probably the greatest angelogue of all Church history unfortunately has nothing whatever to do with the knowledge of the *veritas catholicae fidei*[EN78], or with attention and fidelity to the biblical witness to revelation. Far from accepting the inspiration which might have been received from Dionysius, it has made a principle of all the more doubtful features of earlier angelology, reducing them *ad absurdum*[EN79] by its very exactitude. In its misguidedness we can compare it only with the foolish explanations which many modern theologians have given for their complete scepticism or indifference to the whole problem. And we must add that the negations of the moderns are explicable if not excusable against the background of the assertions of the ancients as classically codified and systematised by Thomas. Even the angelological views of Protestant orthodoxy have nothing to offer in the last resort except Thomas weakened and modified. But on this basis no one could or can be brought face to face with the real question.

[392]

In proof of this judgment I will cite as an example the way in which Thomas gives his basic

---

[EN73] Whether there is any creature that is altogether spiritual and utterly incorporeal?
[EN74] That there are some substances which are intellectual and not joined to bodies
[EN75] angels
[EN76] mission of angels to human beings
[EN77] distinct substances
[EN78] truth of the Catholic faith
[EN79] to absurdity

demonstration of the existence of these *substantiae separatae*[EN80] in *S. c. gent.* (II, *cap.* 91). He knows and develops no less than 8 grounds for maintaining their existence. 1. From the survival of the human soul on the dissolution of the body it follows that there is a non-corporeal existence of intellectual substances. This existence is proper to the human soul only *per accidens*[EN81]. But what in this case can accrue to the intellectual substance only *per accidens*[EN82] must first, in a higher form than the human soul, belong to it *per se*[EN83]. Thus there are intellectual substances higher in character than the human soul to which it belongs to exist as such and therefore apart from the body. 2. It does not belong to the species of the human soul, but to the genus of intellectual substance to which the human soul belongs, to exist independently and not in conjunction with a body. From the fact that the human soul, which exists in conjunction with a body, belongs as a species to this genus, it follows that there is in the same genus another species of beings which do not exist in this conjunction, i.e., intellectual substances without bodies. 3. On its lowest level, as *anima intellectiva*[EN84], which is the purest form of the human soul, higher, i.e., intellectual nature finds itself in contact with the highest stage of lower, i.e., physical nature. But if the *anima intellectiva*[EN85] in its relationship to a body is the lowest form of intellectual substances generally, there must be higher forms which do not have this relationship and which are therefore non-corporeal substances. 4. Being in the form of matter is imperfect. But being in a body is a being in the form of matter. Thus being in a body, even though it be that of a *substantia intellectualis*[EN86], is imperfect. But where there is the species of something imperfect in a genus, there must also be the species of something perfect, and therefore in the genus *substantia intellectualis*[EN87] there must be the species of a *substantia separata a corpore*[EN88]. 5. A corporeal substance has quantity. But it does not belong to the essence of every substance to have quantity. There can thus be substances which are without quantity and therefore non-corporeal. God Himself is an example. But the universe created by Him would be incomplete if it lacked any possible substance. Since it was created perfect, it cannot actually lack substances which are without quantity and therefore non-corporeal. Hence there are substances of this kind. 6. In the case of something composite, there is an autonomy of the individual components. Man is a being composed of intellectual and bodily substances. It is recognised that bodily substance can and does exist independently. If this is true of the lower substance, how much more is it true of the higher! Hence there are intellectual, non-corporeal substances. 7. The distinctive activity (*operatio*) of intellectual substance consists in cognition (*intelligere*). Conjoined with a body, it can exercise this activity only as it apprehends objects (*intelligibilia*) in sensual form. But this is an imperfect form of cognition. The perfect consists in knowing objects in their own nature. If there are intellectual beings with a capacity of imperfect cognition, there must also be such as are capable of perfect cognition and are not therefore conjoined with a body. 8. Where there is a regular, continuous and unceasing movement (*motus*), according to Aristotle there must also be an unmoved mover (*motor*), and where there are many such movements there must be many such movers. "Astrological" knowledge proves that there are actually many such movements, and therefore there must be many movers. But a bodily mover, or one which is conjoined with a body,

---

[EN80] distinct substances
[EN81] accidentally
[EN82] accidentally
[EN83] in itself
[EN84] intellective soul
[EN85] intellective soul
[EN86] intellectual substance
[EN87] intellectual substance
[EN88] substance distinct from a body

[393]   cannot be an unmoved mover. There must thus be many movers which are neither bodies nor conjoined with bodies. This, then, is the eight-fold demonstration with which Thomas believes that he has not only proved the existence of his *substantiae separatae*[EN89], but also refuted the Sadducees who according to Acts 23[8] questioned the existence of spirits and angels, the scientists of antiquity who would accept as substance only that which was corporeal, the doctrine of Origen who would concede non-corporeality only to the triune Godhead, and all the fathers who wished to ascribe some slight measure of corporeality to angels.

It cannot be contested that in a specific sphere and on a specific assumption proof is here given of the existence of a specific object interesting to the one who conducts the proof. It might be asked whether this sphere is real, and if so accessible, and if so able to be marked off in this way and approached with this assumption. It might be asked whether the proof furnished on this assumption and in this sphere is really conclusive and convincing either in detail or as a whole. But if we assume that everything is in order in this respect, and that Thomas has legitimately proved what he really could prove, there can be no doubt that with this assumption (or with the criticism or partial or total rejection of his demonstration) we are merely making philosophical and not theological decisions. Whether there are intellectual substances without bodies, and whether their existence can be proved in this or some other way, may be a question which is interesting and important in the sphere of philosophy. It may be one which can be discussed and even decided in this sphere. It may even be one which is decisive. But it is purely philosophical. On the basis of the Word of God attested in Holy Scripture we are not asked whether there are or are not substances of this kind, nor are we required to prove their existence in some way. If there are, and if their existence can be proved, this does not lead us to angels in the biblical sense of the term. And if there are not, and their existence cannot be proved, this is no argument against angels in the Christian sense. What are called angels in the Bible are not even envisaged in Thomas' proof of the existence of these *substantiae separatae*, let alone is anything said for or against their existence, or anything meaningful stated about them at all, with the eight proofs. And what Thomas later constructed upon the demonstrated existence of these *substantiae separatae* is very different from a doctrine of angels in the Christian sense of the term. In his demonstration Thomas has given us philosophy and not theology, and he has done so far more exclusively than Dionysius. He does occasionally refer to Holy Scripture, and therefore it may be asked whether he does not incidentally and in some sense contrary to his own intention make some contribution to theological knowledge. But fundamentally and as a whole he simply offers us a classical example of how not to proceed in this matter.

Yet his doctrine of angels is so classical a statement that we cannot refrain from a brief glance at the most notable features in its extensive treatment. For this purpose we shall confine ourselves to the *S. theol.*

The first part (I, *qu.* 50–64) stands in the context and (as distinct from the *S. c. gent.*) at the beginning of his doctrine of created being. Its main point is as follows. Angels are non-corporeal and non-material, and therefore incorruptible (50, 5). But in execution of their functions among us they can assume bodies from the air which they condense in the power of God, and in these bodies they can be really and not merely apparently seen by men (51, 2), having something similar to the corresponding vital operations (e.g., eating, moving and speaking), although not really fulfilling the activities themselves (51, 3). The number of angels is greater than that of all material beings put together (50, 3). And none of them is a mere specimen, but each has his own individual nature (50, 4). They are always at a particular point, although not limited by it (52, 1 f.). Yet only one angel can be at the one point at

---

[EN89] distinct substances

one and the same time (52, 3). In accordance with this, they really move from one place to another, and claim a span of time (53, 1 f.). Unlike that of God, their cognition is not identical with their essence; it is an activity (54, 1 f.). It is also distinguished from that of God [394] by the fact that for knowledge angels have need of certain images (55, 1 f.). Yet their cognition differs from ours in the fact that these images are not received from things, but are given them with their nature as the essential images of all things in the Word of God (55, 2), the degree to which they enjoy them varying with their status in the angelic world (55, 3). This is how they know themselves, incompletely in respect of their creation by God, which is inconceivable to them (56, 1). This is also how they know one another as naturally related (56, 2). This is how they know God, not the divine essence, for no created image is adequate to represent this, but—*quia imago Dei in ipsa natura angeli impressa*[EN90]—in this image which is directly given to them as opposed to us (56, 3). And this is how they know material things in their individuality (57, 1 f.), although not knowing the future or the inward thoughts of the human heart as God does (57. 3f.), and having to be instructed by the special revelation of God, and actually being instructed (to some extent from the very first), concerning the mysteries of divine grace and particularly the incarnation (57, 5). Thomas takes up the doctrine of Augustine that the cognition of angels is both *a priori* and *a posteriori*. To the extent that they know all things in the Word of God and therefore *a priori, cognitione matutina*[EN91], the knowledge of angels is an actual and simple knowledge embracing all things at once and altogether (58, 1–4). To the extent that they know all things in their own created being and therefore *a posteriori, cognitione vespertina*[EN92] (58, 6 f.), their knowledge is potential, discursive and syllogistic as ours is (58, 1–4). But it is never mistaken or false (58, 5). Since they are perfectly disposed by nature to good, we must ascribe to angels a volition distinct from their knowledge and carrying with it the capacity to choose (*liberum arbitrium*, 59, 1–3), but in this respect there can be no question of any strife of different passions (49, 4). Both by nature and on the basis of their free choice and decision their volition is distinct inclination (*inclinatio*), a love (60, 1 f.), in which they first love themselves (like men according to Thomas), then other angels as themselves (60, 3 f.), and finally more than themselves God as the *universale bonum*[EN93] to be loved for His own sake (60, 5). Now that the question of the nature of angels is answered (*qu.* 50–60), the next question to arise is that of their creation. That this is not explicitly mentioned in Genesis Thomas ascribes to the fact that Moses was speaking to an uncultured people which was unable to comprehend *incorporea natura*[EN94] (61, 1). But this does not mean that they existed from all eternity. They, too, are created out of nothing, and (for the sake of the necessary co-ordination of the universe) at the same time as the physical creation (61, 2 f.). The place of their creation is in the highest of all spheres, the *coelum empyreum*[EN95] or whatever else we may call it, but not the *coelum sanctae Trinilatis*[EN96] (61, 4). Concerning the standing of angels in grace, and therefore their participation in beatitude and the glory of God, the following points are made. A first and natural beatitude belongs to angels by creation, but not the final and supernatural beatitude to which they too must attain by their activity (62, 1). To do this they too need sanctifying grace, *gratia gratum faciens*[EN97] (62, 2). In fact, however, they were created in this state of grace (63, 3). Yet this does not exclude the fact that they must merit supernatural beatitude

---

[EN90] because the image of God is stamped on the very nature of an angel
[EN91] unconditional "morning knowledge"
[EN92] conditional "evening knowledge"
[EN93] universal good
[EN94] incorporeal nature
[EN95] empyrean heaven
[EN96] heaven of the Holy Trinity
[EN97] grace that makes one acceptable

as empowered by this grace (62, 4). But as non-corporeal beings they attain it at once and definitively with the first of their acts of volition (62, 5), although with different degrees of fulness according to their grade in the angelic order and the measure of the grace imparted to them (62, 6). The fact that they have attained beatitude does not mean, of course, that the activity corresponding to their nature (their cognition and volition) ceases: *Quamdiu manet natura aliqua, manet operatio eius. Sed beatitudo non tollit naturam, cum sit perfectio eius. Ergo non tollit naturalem cognitionem et dilectionem*[EN98]. (62, 7). Holy angels, those which have their first act of will behind them as an act of appropriate love for God, cannot again fall into sin. They still maintain a freedom of choice, but without the imperfection of a freedom which carries with it the choice of deviation. They lie in the perfect freedom in which free choice and volition is as such that of the good (62, 8). And the definitiveness of their beatitude also means that this cannot be increased by any further merits, but may consist in pure joy at the reward already received (62, 9). Concerning the exceptional fall of a number of angels we learn the following. Angels could sin in virtue of their natural freedom of choice (63, 1). According to their nature, their sin could only be spiritual, but for this reason it was all the more serious, consisting in pride and envy against God (63, 2). This was the terrible sin committed by the devil and a number of other angels. What was it that the devil wanted in committing this sin? He was like an ass wanting to be a horse. That is to say, he was not content with his own stage of being, but wanted to be like God. But what does it mean to want to be like God? He sought as the highest goal of bliss (as only God can do) that which he could himself attain in virtue of his nature, instead of striving as a creature on his own level of being for the supernatural beatitude which derives only from the grace of God (63, 3). Like bad men, he and the other wicked angels neither were nor are bad by nature, but if their sin took place at the moment of their creation it did so contrary to their nature and the grace imparted to them in an act of free choice. But in this way there took place once and for all, immediately after their creation, the division of angels into good and bad (63, 4–6). Thomas believes that the chief of the fallen was a cherub, whereas the rest belonged to the lower angelic orders (63, 7) and were seduced by him (63, 8). Concerning the numerical proportion of good angels and bad it can be stated in the light of 2 Kings 6[16] that the good are more numerous (63, 9). Finally, it may be said of the status of bad angels after the fall that their natural knowledge as angels remains intact, but that their knowledge of divine things is diminished and they are completely deprived of the knowledge from which love for God proceeds and which is essential to true wisdom (64, 1). And as good angels persisted and will always persist as such in perfect freedom after that first act, so the bad are committed to wickedness by that definitive choice. Thomas believed that a contrary opinion would necessarily jeopardise the beatitude of the holy angels and men, and was therefore quite intolerable. Once he has made his choice, the will of an angel is immutably fixed on that which is chosen. Thus evil angels are as such finally incapable of repentance, and cannot be reached or liberated by the divine mercy (64, 2). They can only suffer eternal torment, kicking at that which is for them but not for them (64, 3). As to their location, we are told that in expiation of their guilt they are in hell but for the testing of man in the *caliginosus aer*[EN99], in the clouds (64, 4). This is what we learn from Thomas concerning the inner drama of the angelic cosmos (*qu.* 61–64).

In the context of his doctrine of divine providence Thomas returns to the subject (I, *qu.* 106–114) and speaks of the activity corresponding to their nature, i.e., of what we might

[395]

[EN98] So long as a given nature exists, its specific form of activity exists. But blessedness does not destroy nature, but is its perfection. Therefore it does not destroy the nature's mode of knowing and loving

[EN99] misty air

1. The Limits of Angelology

almost call their historical existence. What is it that the good angels do? The higher angels enlighten the lower, and, since the light which illuminates them all is God this can only mean that they strengthen them (not unlike human *doctores*^{EN100} their pupils) by passing on, distinguishing and giving concrete form to the truth as it is better known to themselves (106, 1). Thus one angel can incite the will of another (*inclinare eam ad amabile quoddam*^{EN101}) but not move it—which only God can do (106, 2). And there can be no question of the enlightenment of the angels of a higher degree by those of a lower. For the *ordo qui convenit spiritualibus substantiis nunquam a Deo praetermittitur*^{EN102}. By their very nature the higher angels are nearer to God, and therefore they can pass on the knowledge directly received in this closer proximity but cannot receive knowledge from the member of a lower order as in the hierarchy of the Church (106, 3). Instead the lower angels receive from the higher a full impartation of the very light which the latter have received, of all that they know. The only thing is that they cannot grasp it with the perfection with which it is mediated, so that the distinction of degree remains (106, 4). The speech of angels is then investigated. Angels speak with one another in the simple form of definite acts of will in virtue of which what they carry within themselves as *verbum intemum*^{EN103} can be revealed at once to other angels (107, 1). In this process one or more angels can be addressed to the exclusion of others (107, 5). In this sense the lower angels can speak to the higher (107, 2). And in this sense the angels can speak with God, for although they have nothing to tell Him which He does not know already they speak in order to receive from Him, or to seek His advice, or to give expression to their admiration of His inconceivable majesty (107, 3). And because this speech of the angels is a purely intellectual occurrence, it cannot be hampered by distance in space or time (107, 4). In the eight articles of *qu.* 108 Thomas takes up the question of hierarchy in the angelic world, and it is here that we can see how he adopts and understands and amplifies what is said by Dionysius. In general, he is clearly not interested by the heavenly hierarchy as a whole, but by the hierarchies (as he calls the triads of Dionysius), and within these by the *ordines*^{EN104} (as he calls his choirs). Again, these hierachies and *ordines*^{EN105} do not interest him as the moments of a heavenly movement and history, but as the elements of a stable heavenly system. Finally, they do not interest him decisively as the heavenly *prius*^{EN106} of an earthly order of salvation, but in their relationship to the world-order, to the *ratio* of created being in general and as such. The distinction of three triads or hierachies, with three choirs in each, is to be kept, for illumination, even of angels, is from the threefold standpoint of the divine origin of things, their relation to *causae creatae universales*^{EN107} and their contingent individuality (108, 1), and even in earthly states there are the *optimates*^{EN108}, the *vilis populus*^{EN109}, and between the two the *populus honorabilis*^{EN110} (108, 2). It is interesting that for Thomas this collective distinction of the angelic *ordines* cannot be the last word. On a closer knowledge of these beings than we are given we should have to recognise that there are as many angelic *officia*^{EN111} and therefore *ordines*^{EN112} as there are angels (108, 3).

[396]

---

^{EN100} teachers
^{EN101} incline it to something desirable
^{EN102} order which is appropriate to spiritual substances is never violated by God
^{EN103} internal word
^{EN104} orders
^{EN105} orders
^{EN106} precondition
^{EN107} universal created causes
^{EN108} aristocracy
^{EN109} common people
^{EN110} gentlefolk
^{EN111} offices
^{EN112} orders

Undoubtedly it is both ordained by grace and also in keeping with their nature that angels should exist in these gradations (108, 4), continuing to do so even after the last judgment (108, 7). The explanation of the individual choirs and their relationships from their names is adopted by Thomas with the modification that fundamentally all angels participate in all angelic perfections, the angels of the higher choirs with a greater portion in the higher of these and the lower a less, so that the giving of specific names to specific *ordines*[EN113] is always to be understood *a parte potiori*[EN114] (108, 5–6). Finally Thomas thinks that he can show that men who attain to blessedness by the grace of God, without losing their distinctive nature, will be "as the angels of God" (Mt. 22[30]), and therefore ranged with the angelic *ordines*[EN115] according to their merits, departed saints being already active among us in fulfilment of angelic functions (108, 8). We also have to reckon with a corresponding order in the kingdom of demons. For all their perversity they have not lost their angelic nature and therefore their character as ordered beings which are either superior or subordinate. In this sphere, too, there is ruling and obeying (109, 1–3). But the order of good angels is superior and victorious in face of this opposing sphere (109, 4). Particular attention is now paid to the operation of angels *ad extra*[EN116], to and in the rest of the created world. Even if only indirectly, angels control all bodily things: *Et hoc non solum a sanctis doctoribus ponitur, sed etiam ab omnibus philosophis, qui incorporeas substantias posuerunt*[EN117]. (110, 1 f.). That they control them means that they set them in movement from place to place (110, 3). The only restriction is, of course, that they cannot perform miracles (110, 4). Again, they illuminate men, according to their capacity, by mediation of the truth in the form of sensual images and by the strengthening of their subjective power of reception (111, 1). They can stir up but they cannot move the will of man. The latter, like the performance of miracle, is a matter for God

[397] alone (111, 2). But both bad and good angels can set in motion the imaginative power of man, and thus determine the character of his outward experiences (111, 3–4).

Finally in *qu.* 112, under the title *De missione angelorum*, Thomas comes to the theme which in the light of the Bible ought surely to have been the controlling if not the exclusive theme. But we do not gather that Thomas was even remotely aware of this. The question of this real sending of angels does not interest him except as one of their possibilities of action in relation to corporeal things and men as treated in the two preceding questions, and he is more interested in the question of the existence and action of guardian angels to which he will come later. Indeed, even in respect of this *missio*[EN118] his concern is with purely formal questions, questions of competence as it were. Thus some angels are actually sent by God as *particularia agentia*[EN119] for specific tasks. That is, they are transferred from their own sphere to that of man. God Himself is always the *principium*[EN120] and *finis*[EN121] of their action. They themselves are His *instrumenta intelligentia*[EN122]. And since their action remains purely intellectual as distinct from ours, their contemplation of the divine wisdom as the true and proper activity corresponding to their nature cannot be disturbed by this action *ad extra*[EN123]

[EN113] orders
[EN114] to refer to their particular strengths
[EN115] orders
[EN116] outside of the heavenly sphere
[EN117] And this is maintained not only by the holy fathers, but also by all philosophers who posit the existence of incorporeal substances
[EN118] mission
[EN119] special agents
[EN120] beginning
[EN121] end
[EN122] intelligent instruments
[EN123] outside (of heaven)

but is conducted through it (112, 1). Not all angels, however, are sent in this way. The higher angels do not take part in this work (112, 2), but only the lower *ordines*[EN124]; and Thomas thinks that he can know and prove in even greater detail that it is undertaken only by the five lower and not the four higher of these *ordines*[EN125], a distinction which does not really seem to tally with that of the three hierarchies (112, 4). Conversely, not all angels stand in the immediate presence of God, for they are not all capable of what this involves, i.e., of grasping the depth of the divine mystery with the immediate clarity of the present divine essence. This can belong only to the higher angels, as in the entourage of an earthly monarch there are both constant *assistentes*[EN126] and *administrates*[EN127] who come and go. By the higher angels preferred in this way Thomas means specifically the highest hierarchy (112, 3). But what about the first *ordo*[EN128] of the middle hierarchy, which also has no part in the *missio*[EN129]? However that may be, this is all that Thomas actually has to say on the point.

For in *qu.* 113 we are already dealing with guardian angels. Is it that Thomas thought of the particular activity of angels *ad extra*[EN130] mainly or even exclusively in these terms? At any rate, it is only here that he comes to speak of any concrete activity of angels *ad extra*[EN131]. Does man need a guardian angel? Can he not protect himself? Ought he not to do so? Is not the protection of God sufficient? Does not the fact of the daily sin of many suggest that they have no guardian angels, if the latter are not to come under the accusation of negligence? In spite of all these difficulties, Thomas assures us that as the providence of God moves all corporeal things by spiritual substances and all the lower among them by the higher, and as in our thinking we must be guided by immutable principles, so men with their fallible insights and emotions must be assisted by angels by whom they can be directed and inclined to the good. For this purpose it is not enough that man has freedom of choice and a knowledge of the natural law. And although the immediate protection of God works itself out in the form of the general direction of man to the good through infused grace and virtue, it does not have the form of special instruction concerning the concrete paths which he has to tread. For the latter purpose, he is given a guardian angel. If he still sins, this is not due to the negligence of the angel but to his own wickedness (113, 1). As there are different angels for the different types of corruptible things, so there are for the higher and lower human collectives and even for individual men (since each individual is a *creatura incorruptibilis*[EN132]), and higher or lower angels according to the higher or lower determination given to each individual (113, 2). By "higher" angels, in so far as we are referring to men, Thomas does not mean those from the higher hierarchies, which have nothing whatever to do with this ministry, but higher angels within the lowest hierarchy, through whom the powers of the higher can be mediated to man (113, 3). Does every individual really have his own particular angel? Yes, says Thomas, in the *status viae*[EN133] and *quamdiu viator est*[EN134]. In the eternal kingdom he will not have an *angelus custos*[EN135] but an *angelus conregnans*[EN136]. Even those appointed to perdition, even unbelievers, if only to protect them from some of the harm

[398]

[EN124] orders
[EN125] orders
[EN126] attendants
[EN127] administrators
[EN128] order
[EN129] mission
[EN130] outside (of heaven)
[EN131] outside (of heaven)
[EN132] incorruptible creature
[EN133] condition of earthly life
[EN134] so long as he is a pilgrim
[EN135] guardian angel
[EN136] angel who reigns with him

they might do to themselves and others, have a guardian angel. Even Antichrist will have his guardian angel. This angel is just as indispensable as the assistance of natural reason. Adam had his guardian angel even in the state of innocence. As the sequel showed, he was under serious enough threat from without, if not from within. The only exception to this rule is the man Jesus in virtue of His direct relationship to the Word of God. The angels who attended Him could not be *angeli custodes*[EN137] but only *angeli ministri*[EN138] (113, 4). Is the guardian angel assigned to man at birth or at baptism? The answer is that he is assigned at birth, for he is one of the gifts of the providence directed to man as *natura rationalis*. If prior to baptism he cannot help man to eternal salvation, if he cannot instruct an infant in divine truth, he can ward off demons and preserve it from spiritual and physical harm. How about the child in the womb? The answer is that since at this stage it still belongs to the person of the mother we may assume that prior to birth it stands under the protection of the guardian angel of the latter (113, 5). Can a guardian angel abandon the man allotted to his care? The answer is that he cannot do so strictly and totally, for nothing can escape the providence of God. There can only be a temporary and local abandonment, and even then the angel still keeps his ward in view from heaven, and the efficacy of his protection is not impaired (113, 6). Can angels bewail the evil which their wards commit and bring upon themselves? The surprising but logical answer is in the negative. They can certainly rejoice over them, e.g., over the sinner repenting. But sorrow and pain are alien to the angels in perfect bliss. Sorrow and pain can be felt by a being only when his will is crossed. But the will of the angels is at one with that of the divine righteousness without the operation or permission of which nothing can take place, not even the sin and punishment of man. Hence the latter cannot be contrary to the will of the angels. Hence it cannot be an object of their sorrow and pain. Hence angels cannot bewail the evil which their wards commit and bring upon themselves (113, 7). The final question is whether there can be disunity and strife amongst the angels. The answer is again surprising, for this time it is in the affirmative. For Thomas does not accept the view of Jerome that the "prince" of the kingdom of Persia, of whom we read in Daniel 10[13] that he withstood for 21 days the angel sent to Daniel, was really a demon, but he agrees with Gregory the Great that he must be regarded as a good angel, as one of the collective guardian angels, and his exposition is then as follows. All angels obviously agree that the will of God should be done. But there are relative contradictions within created things and relationships as such, and therefore between the *merita*[EN139] and *demerita*[EN140] of individual men and kingdoms. For the resolving of these contradictions even the angels must be instructed by divine revelation. In their functions as guardian angels they may, therefore, be involved in temporary disunity and even conflict, i.e., in a different reading and seeking of the one will of God. In the less drastic language of a modern Thomist (Franz Diekamp, *Kath. Dogm.*⁶, Vol. II, 1930, 70), "the independence with which guardian angels have to fulfil their commission explains why there can be differences of opinion and opposing movements among them as indicated in Daniel 10. This passage also shows that their measures, although always proceeding from the holiest intention, may sometimes be objectively unsuitable."

To the work of guardian angels there corresponds *in pejorem partem*[EN141] the *impugnatio daemonum*[EN142], the devilish assaulting of man. Thomas' doctrine of angels closes with his consideration of this sinister theme. What is the source of temptation? It derives wholly from

---

EN137 guardian angels
EN138 ministering angels
EN139 merits
EN140 demerits
EN141 in a worse sense
EN142 attack of demons

the malice of demons. But while it has this origin, it is ordered by God and takes place [399] according to the measure of His ordering. To the extent that it is temptation to sin, it is only permitted by Him. To the extent that it serves as a chastisement, it is expressly sent. But either way His righteousness is its basis and aim. Is God unjust to expose weak man to a conflict which is so unequal in view of the power of demons? He is not unjust because He provides for man in His grace a force which is more than adequate compensation. Are not the assaults of the flesh and the world enough to test man? They do not satisfy the demons in their malice, and under the superior *ordinatio divina*^{EN143} this additional temptation can serve only to the glorifying of the elect (114, 1). In its truest and purest sense, demonic assault consists in temptation as an inducement to sin. God Himself "tempts" man, not to corrupt him, but to reveal to him and to others what He Himself knows concerning him. But the devil, using the flesh and the world and its good or ill fortunes, tempts to sin. Taking upon himself something which is the prerogative of God alone, i.e., to search and reveal the inner secrets of man, he wills the corruption of man, and he tries to accomplish this by influencing his will, which he cannot control, through the lower impulses of his nature, thus guiding him to that which is evil (114, 2).

Is all sin to be traced back to temptation by the devil? Indirectly yes, in the sense that the burning of pieces of wood can be traced back to the one who sets them aside for this purpose. To this extent the one who led the first man into sin is the seducer of all sinners. But not all sin can be attributed directly to the devil. Much sin has its direct cause only in the free will of man and the corruption of his nature, the flesh. To be sure, man is capable of good and meritorious action only with divine assistance and through the ministry of angels. But this does not mean that all his evil acts are to be explained directly by demonic action (114, 3). Can demons perform miracles to serve their evil ends. The answer is that they cannot do so in the strict and proper sense of the term. They cannot do anything *quod fit praeter ordinem totius naturae*^{EN144}. No creature, no angel and therefore no demon can perform miracles in this sense, but only God. There are, however, miracles in a relative and improper sense, i.e., happenings which are beyond the capacity and understanding of man. Demons no less than angels are capable of these, just as some men can evoke the astonishment of others by doing things which the latter can neither do nor understand. These miracles have their own distinctive reality and effect and are not to be dismissed as mere *phantasmata*^{EN145}, although in the case of those which are demonic we also have a determination of the human imagination and even the senses so that under this influence things seem to be very different from what they really are. Yet there is more to it than this. As Thomas sees it, demons like angels have access to the *semina quae in elementis mundi inveniuntur*^{EN146} by which natural forces, although they cannot be destroyed or altered, can be moved in a particular direction. And as they themselves, like the angels, can assume definite shape and form from the air, they can invest other things (objectively) with bodily shapes in which they can be seen by man. What they produce—we remember the signs of Pharaoh's magicians—are *signa mendacii*^{EN147}, but they are *vera prodigia*^{EN148} by which man can be really deceived. *Diverso fine et iure*^{EN149} their operations are technically the same as those of the saints and good angels. They do for their own glory and in pursuit of their private ends that which the latter do for the glory of God: *publica*

---

^{EN143} divine ordaining
^{EN144} which takes place outside the order of nature as a whole
^{EN145} illusions
^{EN146} constitutive principles that are found in the world's constituent elements
^{EN147} signs of falsehood
^{EN148} genuine wonders
^{EN149} Though different with respect to their aim and the right by which they are done

administratione et iussu Dei[EN150] (114, 4). The last question is whether demons can renew their attack on a man when it has been repulsed. The answer is given by Luke 4[13]: "And when the devil had ended all the temptation, he departed from him for a season." Victory over a demon gives a certain security against him, but it does not give an unlimited security. Does not the unclean spirit cast out of a man (Mt. 12[43f.]) say when he has wandered through desert places and not found the rest which he seeks: *revertar in domum meam, unde exivi*[EN151] (114, 3)? With this not very consoling prospect Thomas closes his final round of questions and his whole doctrine of angels.

[400]   No less than 118 individual questions are raised and answered by Thomas on this theme. It was probably because of this series, prominent both for quantity and material interest, that Thomas earned the particular title in the Middle Ages of the *Doctor angelicus*. We gladly accept this style. The only thing is that in all his 118 enquiries we do not find an answer to the question on which the theological relevance and serviceability of his doctrine of angels depends. As Evangelical theologians, committed to the witness of the Bible, we are ill-advised to treat the subject on the ground which he was not the first to select but which he did so with a radicalness that can hardly be surpassed. And because we cannot do this, we cannot follow him in the detailed questions which he poses or answers which he gives.

Let us take a retrospective glance. In his "*Die Engel und Wir*" (*Kirchenbl. f. d. ref. Schweiz*, 1937, No. 18–19)—to my mind the most useful modern contribution to the subject—Gerhard Spinner has given us an excellent appraisal of the results of Aquinas' investigations which we can accept apart from a final reservation. His assessment is as follows: "The angelic world of Thomas functions to some extent as a powerful co-ordinated system by which the place of man is determined in the universe. The scholastic system resembles a gigantic ladder set up to heaven, on which the heavenly messengers do not ascend and descend, but all have their appointed places with the rigidity of the utmost objectivity. Catholic man needs this objectivity of forces reaching up to the supreme point of the universe if he is not to hang in the unknown or plunge into the abyss. The much admired objectivity of the Catholic Church in its doctrine and cultus rests finally on the objective cosmos of supra-sensual power as depicted in the scholastic doctrine of angels which has so prominent a place in the whole system of Thomas .... Thomas' assertion that beings which are intellectual and supernatural greatly surpass in number those which are bound to matter serves to shift the whole emphasis onto the heavenly cosmos, to which the world of the visible, and man within it, cannot be regarded as more than an almost insignificant annexe. The man who knows that he is in this coordinated system can hardly be in danger of thinking of himself and his fellows as the central point in the universe and thus adopting an anthropocentric and egocentric view of the world or mode of life .... Angels as understood in Scholasticism perform the service of again setting man under the heavenly cosmos, and therefore in his true place before God, humbled and redeemed." With regard to this final statement, it is to be noted that it is not the angels as understood in Scholasticism which really do us this service. What is needed to-day is not that "behind the high peaks of the Reformation the ice-cold summits of Scholasticism should again enlighten us as summits of our Church." Angels as understood in Scholasticism are those *essentiae spirituales*[EN152], those *substantiae separatae*[EN153], and the objectivity of the heavenly cosmos in the scholastic sense is only that of an artificially and arbitrarily separated, i.e., abstracted and hypostatised, intellectual being as opposed to a material and to our own intellectual conjoined with matter, which Thomas like Plato and

---

[EN150] by the general disposition and the command of God
[EN151] I will return to my house from which I came
[EN152] spiritual essences
[EN153] distinct substances

1. *The Limits of Angelology*

Aristotle regarded as relatively less perfect and essentially earthly. Armed with this criterion, Thomas could certainly disclose ice-cold summits of objectivity. But this objectivity of the spiritual or intellectual is much too equivocal for us to want it to shine again in our Church. If another age, armed with a different criterion, were to set up another system, orientated less by spirit and more by the matter which is here despised, it might easily be exchanged for another and no less icecold objectivity. And was the scholastic view really so free from anthropocentricity and egocentricity that it could effectively oppose an exchange of this kind? When the new age came, it did not actually do so. Is it really so certain that on this view man has any genuine knowledge of the heavenly cosmos? May not the converse be true? May it not be that the second part of the Thomistic doctrine of angels is only the attempt at a gigantic self-projection of the *anthropos*[EN154] or the ego into an objectivity in which it thinks [401] to find in the angel its desired and in the demon its dreaded superior *alter ego*, i.e., itself supremely magnified? Only one of the lowest angels has to do directly with man, says Thomas, not on any biblical ground but with notable humility, and he affirms that above this there are higher and supreme angels which are far too exalted to be directly concerned about man. Yet directly or indirectly is not man the goal of the whole of the heavenly cosmos? At any rate, it is he who has sketched and devised it as a titanic counterpart of his own social and individual existence. With his knowledge and recognition of this higher cosmos, has he really done anything but magnify the intellectual side of his own nature? And has he not crowned this by seeing in God Himself, beyond this objective world of the spirit and spirits, a purely intellectual being which is merely self-grounded, self-resting and self-motivating in contrast to all creatures, himself being far below this God and all angels, and yet the product of this God and on this side divine by nature? No, to build on the rock of this system is as little advisable as to construct a materialistic or for that matter any system at all. All systems, and therefore this too, have a tendency to tip over and turn into their opposite. To God and therefore to angels as understood in Scholasticism there cannot be denied an objectivity which is remarkable in its own way. But we have no real cause to admire the objectivity of the Catholic Church and its doctrine and cultus to the extent that it rests on the objectivity of the scholastic doctrine of angels. For this is not the objectivity with which we have to do in Christian faith when it speaks of God and the angels. Real humility and redemption are not to be expected from these ice-cold summits. Christian theology asks concerning another God, and therefore concerning other and less equivocal angels.

But with his praise of Thomas, Gerhard Spinner had something very true in mind, as the continuation of his work reveals. An open-minded reader of Thomas cannot escape the impression that—no matter how—we are here pointed with imperative urgency in a direction in which Christian theology has genuine cause to look, i.e., to the heavenly cosmos above our earthly, and to its participation in the history which is enacted between God and man, this creature of the earthly cosmos. If Thomas missed the mark when he thought that this heavenly cosmos should be described as specifically spiritual, and if his whole doctrine of angels necessarily became in consequence the depiction of an unreal heaven and unreal angels, yet by treating the matter as he understood it in a way which is quantitatively so prominent and also so concentrated and meticulous, he set up a sign and bore a witness for which we must always be grateful to him. The same is true of the angelology of the fathers. The same is true of Pseudo-Dionysius. But it is particularly true of Thomas in view of the monumental form which the matter took in his case. The problem must be differently posed and treated from the way in which he posed and treated it. But he was and is the man who so handled it that we either do not know him or we are complete philistines if we think that there is nothing in this subject which moved him so strangely, and that we can thus ignore it

---

[EN154] human being

113

altogether. In this sense the angels as understood in Scholasticism can render us a genuine service, and we cannot refuse to their great interpreter the title of *Doctor angelicus*.

4. We return to the *Credo ut intelligam.* We have so far applied it to our present subject in two ways: 1. that by the *credo*[EN155], i.e., by the witness of Scripture to which faith refers, there is given us in this question of angels, too, a task of knowledge; and 2. that this task must be taken up and pursued only on the basis of the *credo*[EN156], i.e., of the witness of Holy Scripture. Our next statement is the sharper and more emphatic one that we must view the task exclusively in this light, confining ourselves to the *intelligere*[EN157] which it offers, and not [402] turning back or aside to other grounds, motives or concerns alien to the *credo*[EN158] or the witness of Holy Scripture, to freely selected constructions which might also cause us to put this remarkable question concerning angels and suggest this or that answer to it. We have considered and illustrated the great possibility that the term angels might lead us quickly to forget or push into the background the preceding *credo*[EN159], and in the task of knowing angels generally to move off in a different direction—in the direction of a view or concept concerning which we are convinced from some other source than the Bible that it stands for something true and valid and describes approximately or even precisely what an angel is. On the whole the angelology of the primitive and mediaeval Church gives us an example of this possibility. But there is also another possibility. We may seriously ask concerning the angels of Holy Scripture, and really receive the instruction of Holy Scripture concerning them. In theology orientated by the Reformation it is inevitable that the Scripture-principle should be basically and theoretically accepted in this matter too. And yet, even though we may recognise this principle and go out from Egypt, we may still long after its flesh-pots. We may in fact proceed with one eye on the angels of the Bible and the other on a real or invented complex which we assume to be identical with these angels.

We may do this in all innocence and for no precise reasons. Why should not angels exist otherwise than in the contexts and sense of the biblical witness? And why should they not be seen and known in this other form? Are not two threads stronger than one? Must we not deal with God in such a way that, although we know how important the *credo*[EN160] is, we set beside it a little *intelligo*[EN161] in order to press on the more surely in respect of the intended and decisive *ut intelligam*[EN162]? But usually those who adopt this course have good reasons for doing so. Perhaps in this little *intelligo*[EN163] set alongside the

---

[EN155] I believe
[EN156] I believe
[EN157] understanding
[EN158] I believe
[EN159] I believe
[EN160] I believe
[EN161] I understand
[EN162] in order to understand
[EN163] I understand

*credo*EN164 it is a matter of persuading oneself that the latter cannot be understood except with the help of the former. The Bible is consulted, but if it is not to be consulted in vain a hermeneutical principle must first be sought. The biblical ciphers concerning angels are so obscure. They must be solved if they are to be understood. For this purpose a key is needed. To secure and use this key one has to look both to the Bible and also elsewhere where information can be gleaned which, if it is not so authentic, is at any rate clearer and more accessible and direct, and therefore helpful in this whole question of biblical angels. Or again, the looking aside might be more for the sake of apologetics than hermeneutics. That small *intelligo*EN165 is set beside the *credo*EN166 because there is no assurance that full confidence can be placed in the Bible in this matter. At any rate, the witness of the Bible is surely more powerful if it can be shown to be confirmed by the witness of other observations, considerations and deliberations, and to have at least a degree of probability. Indeed, the [403] confirmation of these witnesses is perhaps regarded as essential if credence is to be given to that of the Bible. Or more sharply still, the witness of the Bible cannot be accepted at all without this confirmation.

Well, these are all processes of thought which here as elsewhere we must rule out in dogmatics. Neither at this nor at any other point can we trifle with the *credo*EN167. At this point, too, we can attain to an *intelligere*EN168 worthy of the name only if we give to the *credere* our full and exclusive attention and confidence. *Credere* is to believe. But we cannot believe and yet at the same time not believe but want to know. This is not to believe at all. In dogmatics as in life, and at this point in dogmatics no less than any other, the comfort of faith is linked with the fact that it is the only comfort, and that as such it is accepted with the appropriate joy. And faith relates to the witness of Holy Scripture. It is the willingness and readiness to be taught from this source, referring all the concern for *intelligere* to what is said there, because there we have to do with the origin and object of faith. Faith is the confidence that what we are told there will be intelligible in terms of itself, i.e., of the context in which it is said. Or negatively, it is radical mistrust in face of the supposed understanding of what we are told there in terms of insights and criteria acquired elsewhere. And faith is the confidence that what we are told there is grounded in itself, i.e., in the matter attested. Or negatively, it is radical mistrust in face of the supposed grounding of what we are told there on that which is not identical with the substance of the biblical witness. Faith is thus free from any anxiety lest the biblical witness should not be intelligible in itself; and it is certainly free from any anxiety lest it should lack any basis or certainty without external confirmation. Faith has only one anxiety, namely, lest it should cease to be this

---

EN164 I believe
EN165 I understand
EN166 I believe
EN167 I believe
EN168 understanding

free faith. It does not therefore try to find any other comfort or clarity or certainty than that which it abundantly receives at this source, from this object, and by the biblical attestation of this object. Faith is confident that it will not be left in the lurch either hermeneutically or apologetically if it confines itself to this witness. It also knows that every supposed enrichment by another hermeneutics or apologetics can only mean impoverishment, any assurance of this kind uncertainty, and any extension in this direction the jeopardising and loss of the one thing needful. Faith dares to trust the Holy Spirit. But even in this matter of angels we must dare to trust the Holy Spirit, and for good or evil we must dare to trust Him alone. Here too, then, we must rule out all those processes of thought.

[404] The consequences of a failure to do so are almost always fatal. To look in two directions is not to see straight in either. In the matter of angels it is better to look resolutely and exclusively in a different direction than to try to look at the Bible and other sources of knowledge at one and the same tune. In so doing, as may be seen from the example of Thomas, we shall at least find something orderly. But if we try to find angels both in the Bible and elsewhere, we shall only see hazy pictures. Our philosophy will spoil our theology, and our theology our philosophy. Our present concern is with the first point. The knowledge which does not dare to be wholly and exclusively theological and therefore in faith and therefore based on the witness of Holy Scripture will as such be a pale and uncertain knowledge and erroneous at the decisive point. As theological knowledge it could be free. Bound to other concepts, even though only incidentally for hermeneutical or apologetic reasons, it is unfree, and therefore an unfaithful half-knowledge estranged from itself and its object. A key is found to the dark ciphers of Scripture, but the results are either artifical or platitudinous. And the statements of Scripture may seem to be well-grounded, but what they say is robbed of any relevance or significance by the fact that they are grounded elsewhere. Yet this threat can only be of secondary importance at this point. If we do not accept the promise of the Holy Spirit, and on this promise dare to look with both eyes at Holy Scripture and not to look aside with either, we shall not even realise how fatal is the threat to which we expose ourselves. There are many theologians who have succumbed to this threat and never even noticed the consequences for their theology. But if we dare to be content with Scripture alone, it can only be because the promise of the Holy Spirit has itself been given us by Scripture. The risk is not then a real risk, but simply the obedience required of us. If we are to have the freedom and to be compelled to see this limit, like all the limits of a Christian angelology it must be drawn by a higher hand. It is perhaps as well to be clear at this point that in angelology too the theological question is a spiritual one. And it is at this point that we must realise it because the promise of the Holy Spirit is the only force between heaven and earth which has the power to direct us wholly and exclusively in a particular direction, enforcing the prohibition of

deviation to the right hand or the left which is primarily at issue under this fourth head.

Some historical illustrations will show clearly what I have in mind.

As we have seen, the patristic and mediaeval angelology inevitably made frequent allusion to the Bible, either adducing passages to support the theses adopted, or accepting the questions and limits posed by it. But the example of Thomas makes it quite clear that these references belong only to the apparatus of scholarship and not to the matter itself. The Bible is a particularly important element in the guidance offered by antiquity. But it is introduced formally in the same sense and with the same diligence as the fathers, Pseudo-Dionysius, and above all Aristotle, the supreme *philosophus*EN169. In this respect an appalling ignorance is revealed. With disarming innocence it is decided to work out one's own view of angels, but nothing is seen against, and much in favour of, accepting the stimulus and control, the compulsion and restraint, of the Bible as of many other books of recognised authority. [405]

Evil vacillation or aberration is not yet a problem in the early and mediaeval period, but it is the great problem in the post-Reformation epoch with its conscious awareness that the Bible is not merely one respectable text-book among others but the witness of the concrete divine revelation which constitutes the Church and therefore the text to which Christian doctrine has to keep, on the content of which it must base its thinking, and to which it is always responsible. In Protestantism there was posed for the first time the question of belief or unbelief in respect of the sufficiency of this revelation and its attestation, and there has to be a clear decision between the venture, the act of obedience, in which theology is ready to be free as it is bound to Scripture, between the well-known command and the transgression of this command, the looking past Scripture, the drawing on other sources of knowledge.

We have already seen with what distinctness Calvin saw and drew the limit of angelology in this direction, and how Quenstedt spoke of the *apodicticum argumentum scripturae*EN170 in contrast to every other. But if Calvin's doctrine of angels (*Instit.*, I, 13, 3–19) is in fact an attempt along these lines which must be taken seriously, and if even in J. Gerhard (*Loci*, 1610 f., V, *cap.* 4) we have the impression that not without a certain measure of success he was engaged in resistance to the penetration of alien standpoints, Quenstedt no less than other orthodox Protestant divines did in fact make unthinking use of a non-biblical knowledge of angels derived from Scholasticism. And in the great work of J. W. Baier (*Comp. Theol. pos.*, I, 3, 3) which appeared a year after that of Quenstedt we can see clearly the beginning of even a theoretical cleavage in theological consciousness. Scripture shows us *disertissime*EN171 that angels exist as a species of creatures (*species creaturarum*) different from men and all others by their nature as *spiritus completi*EN172, as *substantiae simplices, spirituales, incorporeae*EN173. That this is the case cannot be clearly proved *lumine naturae, quamvis suaderi possit rationibus probabilibus*EN174. It is worth noting that a diligent search has now begun for these *rationes probabiles*EN175.

In the supranaturalist F. Volkmar Reinhard (*Vorl. üb. d. Dogm.*, 1812, § 50) we read the following. Observation and physics teach that species of creatures are "uncommonly varied and numerous" on our earth. "Since, then, the heavenly bodies, whose number and size are

---

EN169 philosopher
EN170 Scripture's apodictic argument
EN171 most explicitly
EN172 perfect spirits
EN173 substances that are simple, spiritual and incorporeal
EN174 by the light of nature, so far as one can be persuaded by probable arguments
EN175 probable arguments

almost immeasurable, cannot possibly have been left untenanted by God, but are incontestably filled with creatures appropriate to their nature, we are freely justified in assuming a host and variety of creatures infinitely surpassing all human conception." And if we are taught by natural science that there is an ascending series of earthly classes of creatures, in which the human race is commonly accepted to be the last and final link, it is "easily seen that we may not be the most perfect creature, but that the series may well reach up to infinity through higher and more excellent natures." The divine wisdom, power and goodness, and the immeasurable span of creation, make this so probable to reason that it may take it as proved and perfectly clear. But it is not evidently confirmed by Scripture. Yet this undoubtedly speaks of angels. "Hence it is necessary that we should gather what the Bible says on this theme, and complete from this source what reason only suspects, as we shall now proceed to do ...."

In the rationalist K. G. Bretschneider (*Hand. d. Dogm. d. ev.-luth. Kirche*, Vol. I, 1838, § 104) we find an excellent expansion of this proof from reason into a conception of angels which serves as a canon for the understanding of Scripture. It is established by a series of postulates. To the arguments of Reinhard, Bretschneider adds that the perfection of God makes it probable that apart from the soul of man there are other kinds of rational creatures, spirit and reason and virtue being called into being by God in every possible form in spiritual and [406] moral individuals. Moreover, the doctrine of "immortality" leads unavoidably to the thought that the men who lived centuries ago must now constitute a much more exalted class of rational beings than we are. Again, as our earth and solar system "stand in the closest physical relationship" to the universe, so it is to be expected that the invisible kingdom of reason throughout the universe should stand in a moral relationship of which we can have a fuller conception only when we die. Nor can reason regard it as unlikely that God uses these higher rational creatures to mediate certain effects, "thus exercising their gifts and perfecting them." Bretschneider, too, thinks that he can maintain all this with a "moral probability tantamount to certainty." The resultant conception of angels is then compared with "the form of the doctrine of angels as present two thousand years ago," i.e., that of the Bible, the latter being regarded as a form, temporally conditioned and associated with a defective world-view, of this intrinsically valid and important conception. It is hardly necessary to state in detail how much or how little he is ready and able to appropriate of this biblical form.

Further on in the 19th century, within the framework of later Idealism, Richard Rothe (*Dogm.* Pt. I, 1870, 205 f.) declares that speculative (for him scientific) theology not only does not take offence at the idea of an angelic world but is necessarily led to it (p. 244). There can be no doubt that it is biblical, and the scriptural foundation of the older dogmatic concept is to be recognised in its main features. But quite apart from this Rothe reckons on the existence of a "higher world of spirits." What are good angels? They are personal creatures which have been perfected, i.e., which have become pure spirit. That these exist is proved by the fact that there are perfect worlds. According to Rothe, this earthly and imperfect creation of ours cannot be the first or the last. Hence there are earlier spheres of creation, or worlds, which are already perfect, and to which there belong personal creatures which are already perfect. And these are our angels, concerning which Rothe thinks that he may say: "Even angels have had to serve in the ranks and make their way up from below. From material or sensually personal creatures they have become by way of moral development perfected and purely spiritual persons, i.e., angels" (p. 232). To these perfected beings of earlier spheres of creation there are continually added the perfected human individuals of our own. Yet the fact that all these beings have become perfected spirits does not mean that they are absolutely non-corporeal. At this point Rothe has gone back behind the customary doctrine and even Thomas, and adopted the view of Origen and the other Greek fathers, teaching that each of these perfected persons is the absolute unity of a personal I and a natural organism, a spiritual body, distinctively belonging to this I. Unrestricted by space and time as they are, the universe is opened up to them without limitation, and we can only assume that they exercise a specific influence on our as yet imperfect sphere and particularly on its imperfect personal creatures. In this sense, then, the good angels have a part in the divine rule. Indeed, they are the specific organs to mediate it. As each sphere is produced and determined by God through the mediation of those which precede, "these individual worlds organically proceed from one another as mediated by one another" (p. 245). Thus the mutual relationship of these higher beings is necessarily that of a completed organisation. And this organisation is held together by the "absolute, creaturely-spiritual, central individual of the universe, which must be thought of as a collective individual, namely, as the absolute, personal unity of the spiritual individuals which are the sources and centres of the individual spheres of creation—the endlessly increasing axis of the whole world of spirits. Quite uncapriciously, therefore, we agree with the doctrine of Holy Scripture that Christ (in His completion) is the Head of the whole world of good angels." Uncapriciously indeed! And in the same uncapricious way Rothe agrees with the teaching of the Bible concerning the devil and demons. It is worth noting that J. C. Blumhardt (*Schriftauslegung*, ed. 1947, 160) refers not unsympathetically to this angelology, obviously thinking of Rothe's presentation, though not mentioning him by name. [407]

With less certain tread J. A. Dorner (*Syst. d. chr. Gl. lehre*[2], Vol. I, 534 f.) moves in the same direction as Rothe. We shall return to an instructive hint to be found in his doctrine of angels. His exposition as a whole is as follows. The concept of the angelic world not only contains no contradiction, but angels can actually be described as a necessary class of creatures. Their existence or recognition in the form of a doctrine of angels constitutes a safeguard against a false this-worldliness, namely, on the one side against an exaggeration of the earth and the earthly spirit, and on the other side against a depreciation of the infinite significance of the spirit in face of the apparent preponderance of material quantities. The doctrine of angels sets our mind in a great perspective, calling it back from restriction to our planets, widening our consciousness of the world by the consideration of a higher and infinitely rich world of spirits, and assuring to the consciousness of God a powerful point of contact for the religious consideration of the universe. If on this side it resists the pride and defiance of the human heart, on the other it resists the pusillanimous doubt of the spirit. It forces us to think of other regions as filled in a manifold ascending series by rational creatures. As a doctrine of the participation of higher spirits in our history it contains an indication of the fact that in the world of the spirit nothing is isolated, but that what takes place on this earthly body, this drop in the bucket, has a significance for the totality of spirits. Beyond this, following traces already known to us, Dorner thinks that he can give to the doctrine of angels the following positive significance. If our earth and history are not eternal, but the thought of a temporal beginning of the divine work is impossible, the doctrine of angels gives us the possibility, as a "necessary postulate," of reckoning with circles of creation which, in relative independence but mutually intersecting, precede our own. Even the beginnings of the human race "seem to need the doctrine of angels." The spiritual in man required for its development spiritual stimulation by a more powerful spirit outside. As this could not be mediated through men, "the beginning of human development points to the fact that our race is not a self-enclosed and self-sufficient totality, but remains a place where the ring of our species expects to be penetrated by that of another." In this other we recognise the biblical angels, who in many different ways serve the divine impartation to the world. Dorner tried to represent angels, if not as non-corporeal, at least as unrestricted by space and unburdened by matter. And he thought that the doctrine of angels brings before us "the wealth of the spirit in the most manifold forms," the possibility of unsitiful development and a cheerful fulfilment of the divine will, and finally the already present reality of the Church triumphant.

The matter took a more original and bolder turn, with some instructive points, in Dorner's Danish friend, Hans Lassen Martenseu (*Chr. Dogm.*, 1856, 118 f.). As he saw it, the angels are one of the presuppositions of human existence. They are pure spirits, not bound to bodies or the conditions of space, but also not subject to space. "An angel cannot become old." It cannot have a history in the sense of development, progress and maturity. The home of angels is the intelligible heaven, and from here they come into the world of men, as spirits of light working for the furtherance of the kingdom of God on earth. And now Martensen ventures the astonishing statement—a genuine Columbus' egg, far more tempting than anything which has preceded—that when we think of the world of angels we cannot avoid thinking of that of ideas. Does not the description of angels in the Bible and Church doctrine tally fairly exactly with these mediatorial beings between God and the real world, these bearers of light, which bring to man the message of God? Angels are ideas, not as they appear to abstract thought, but "as they are seen as living powers and active spirits." That is why they are called by Paul "principalities and powers," "forces which rule in certain circles of the [408] divine providence, dominions to which different regions of creation are subject." Furthermore, "when we think of angels under this aspect, we have to think of what mythology calls gods. What philosophy calls ideas and mythology gods, revelation calls angels," namely, to the extent that they are active for the kingdom of God. Martensen favours the LXX text of Deut. 32^8 (as in the Zurich Bible): "When the most High divided to the nations their inheritance, when he separated the sons of Adam, he set the bounds of the people according to the number of the angels. But the Lord's portion is his people; Jacob is the lot of his inheritance." Thus in distinction from Israel with whom He came to dwell in person, God set angels, finite mediators, subordinate deities, over the nations of the Gentiles. It was His goodness. His revelation, that even the Gentiles should not be left destitute of ideas, even though they did not know the one to whom the world of ideas belongs. Their mythical deities are in truth the ministering spirits of providence, the angels of God. Confused with God, and turning man away from the true God, they are of course idols or demons. But at all events they are powers or forces—whether as angels or demons depends on their attitude to the kingdom of God. And even in paganism we always have to do with both. Have angels as understood in this way personalities? No unequivocal answer can be given to this question. There are impersonal, semi-personal and personal spirits of this kind, and according to Martensen this is what is meant when the older doctrine maintains that there are different grades and classes of angels. In the winds and flames of fire which execute the will of the Lord according to Ps. 104^4, and in the angel which according to Jn. 5^4 stirred the water in the pool of Bethesda, we obviously have to recognise "personified forces of nature." The national spirits and mythical deities are to be construed as "beings half-way between personification and personality." In addition there is a third class of cosmic powers which constitute a free and personal kingdom of spirits. In relation to men angels have both advantages and disadvantages. Their chief advantage is that they are more powerful spirits. But men are richer. "The angel in all his power expresses only one side of what man in the inwardness of his soul and wealth of his individuality is to comprehend in microcosmic totality." Angels are spirits, but they are not souls; they are not points of unity between spirit and nature. They can participate only in the majesty of God. They cannot be genuinely united with God as man can—Jesus in the incarnation and Christians in the sacrament. "This superiority of men to angels is expressed by Scripture in the fact that the Son of God did not become an angel but a man." Do we still have to reckon with the reality of angels to-day? Certainly, for angels continue to be active throughout history. And if belief in angels is muffled in these days, in current ideas about "powers of cosmic life" we have a point of contact for this faith. It is only a matter of understanding these ideas "in a sacred sense." Once they are stated in the light of the Christian doctrine of providence, "we enter the sphere of belief in angels." Have not "national angels been active in the introduction of Christianity"? Are not the ideas under whose dominion the nations are naturally set the natural points of transition for holy things, and have they not conditioned and determined the distinctive appropriation of Christianity by these nations?

And now the remarkable fact may be noted that in the extra-biblical demonstration of angels two well-known modern theologians are met who are very different from each other and whom one would hardly expect to come across in this field. Yet there is nothing fundamentally new or clearer in what they say.

The first is none other than Adolf Schlatter (*Das chr. Dogma²*, 1923, 85 f.), whose view has also been adopted by Paul Althaus (*Die christliche Wahrheit²*, 1949, Vol. II, 69). We seem to be back in the world of Reinhard and Bretschneider when he tells us that for those who speak to us in Scripture man did not stand at the head of creation, "but that they saw above him a multiple kingdom of spirits. Confirmation is to be found in the fact that a sober self evalu- [409] ation forbids us to think of ourselves as the supreme and final product of God's creative activity." There are many things below us. "Then we come with the narrow limitation of our spirituality—and surely it cannot be that there is nothing above us." It cannot be said that in our world-view with its infinite space filled with the elements and forces of nature there is no room for anything beyond us. "In truth our natural view makes the thought of angels even more indispensable. Can it be that in this infinity of spaces and powers there is no other life but that of beasts and men, or that the power of the world-basis which fashions persons is exhausted in the formation of the intellect which we have?" Since God has created space and localised all things in it, since He has thus a positive relationship to space, why should there not be for angels too a positive relationship to space? "Our incapacity to think of any other relationship to space than that which we men have is subjectively grounded; it arises through the limitation of our thinking by our being."

Pointing unmistakeably in the same direction, but more enigmatically and in the style of the postulates of an angelology of the beginning of the 19th century, Ernst Troeltsch (*Glaubenslehre*, 1925, 255 f.) asked whether the cosmic purpose of salvation or ethical communion with God which is accepted by faith can be regarded as the only cosmic purpose. That this is "absolutely impossible for the lower spiritual" creation has become all the more certain with the extension of our knowledge of the greatness of the universe. And on the same basis it has become continually more impossible to maintain that man and his salvation are the centre of faith in the divine government of the world. What then? A first point is that there must be a purpose of the lower spiritual creation in the revelation of divine power and the outliving of its vital impulse which can be conjoined with the supreme purpose of spirit only as its preliminary stage and presupposition. And a second is that "there must be a plurality of spiritual realms beside man." There must—this is the view which we meet in almost all these angelologies. Yet it was a more respectable and better founded "must" that we found in Richard Rothe. Rothe did at least know what he was saying and could explain what he meant when he spoke of his kingdoms of spirits, whereas Troeltsch simply tossed off the term and was quite unable to say what he understood by it. Rothe did at least consult the Bible and early Church doctrine before he proceeded to his really Gnostic speculation, whereas Troeltsch does not give a moment's thought to either. At this point the dogmatics of Troeltsch is formally the nadir of the Neo-Protestant development which commenced at the beginning of the 18th century.

Everywhere, in Troeltsch no less than a serious theologian like A. Schlatter, we meet that "must." What is it that "must" be? The angels as inhabitants of the other heavenly bodies

(Reinhard). The angels as moral and spiritual individuals in the invisible kingdom of reason within the universe (Bretschneider). The angels as the spirits of preceding spheres of creation perfected after undergoing a kind of angelic course (Rothe). The angels as stimulators of spiritual life at the beginning of the human race (Dorner). The angels as identical with intellectual forces and mythical deities (Martensen). The angels as supreme and final products of the creative activity of God (Schlatter). And finally, if the unexplained reference is really to angels, the angels as the members of a "plurality of spiritual realms" (Troeltsch). In each case everything depends upon the great assertion that there must be such things. *Quamvis suaderi potest rationibus probabilibus*[EN176], maintained J. W. Baier in 1685. And here in the bright light of the 18th, the 19th and even the 20th centuries we are given *rationes probabiles*[EN177] for the existence of angels which do not derive from Holy Scripture. Do I need to prove that it was all a mere groping in the dark, and that only the hazy pictures of a scattered and uncertain knowledge, only artificialities and platitudes, can result when the attempt is made, as in the case of angels, to learn from other sources as well as from the Bible? Everything leads into the void, and by comparison the doctrine of angels taught by Thomas appears respectable. Is it not plain that at this point philosophy has been corrupted by theology, not to speak of the corruption of theology by philosophy? But this brings us already to the fifth and final point in our introduction.

[410]

5. We have only to add that if we keep to the rule stated and emphasised in 3 and 4 we need not be anxious concerning the knowledge required in 2, whether in respect of the possibility or the correctness and importance of a theological knowledge of the reality of angels. Theology has only to be theology at this point too. It has only to be on its guard against unwittingly becoming philosophy. It has only to accept the discipline of being wholly and exclusively theology. It has only to refrain from seeking *rationes probabiles*[EN178], from also trying to be a little philosophy, whether on hermeneutical or apologetic grounds. If it does this, it cannot be lacking in a concrete objectivity of theme. And in some degree, and in a way which is basically worthy, it will do justice to it. And the theme itself will be sufficiently important to claim it seriously and profitably. Holy Scripture gives us quite enough to think of regarding angels. And it is something positive. We have only to consider what it says in its distinctiveness, and to try to assess it without pre-judgment. Nor does it do so in such a way that we can quickly leave the problem on the pretext that it is merely peripheral. If we wholeheartedly accept angels in the position and role assigned to them in the Bible, in their own place and way they make themselves so important that we can no longer ignore them when we consider the centre and substance of the biblical message. Again, the Bible is not so obscure in respect of angels that we cannot responsibly draw out certain notions and concepts which are quite adequate for a Christian understanding. All that is required is a firm resolve that the Bible should be allowed both to speak for itself in this matter, i.e., in the course of its message, as a witness of what it

---

[EN176] So far as one can be persuaded by probable arguments
[EN177] probable arguments
[EN178] probable arguments

understands by the revelation and work of God, and also to be very impressively, and in its own way very eloquently, silent.

For example, we must not take offence or stop short at the fact, as already indicated, that there are undoubtedly passages introducing angels which are saga or legend or poetry. On the contrary, we have to see and understand that this is of a piece with the matter, with the nature of angels in the biblical sense of the term.

Again, we need not be surprised that in a whole series of points which arouse particular interest, and in which it has been promptly and fully augmented, the biblical doctrine of angels gives us no information whatever. It tells us nothing, for example, about the much ventilated question of the "nature" of angels, whether they are persons, or what is their relationship to the physical world and to space, their number and order, their creation, their original unity, their ensuing division into angels and demons, and many other things which later there was both the desire and a supposed ability to know. Is it not [411] supremely instructive to start from the fact as from a very eloquent circumstance that in the Bible itself nothing is to be known about these matters? Is not positive light shed by the fact that certain questions in respect of the existence and history of angels which may seem very pressing to us are not to be put if angels are rightly understood?

Again, we must not be misled by the fact that in the Bible, as there is no independent doctrine of God or man, so there is no independent doctrine, i.e., no independent definition, depiction or account of angels, and that this is particularly true in the case of angels because in the sense in which they are introduced in the Bible it is obviously essential to them to be only in the movement from God to man, i.e., only in the history between these two factors which are not dogmatically rigid, existing as it were incidentally beside them, or rather in their common history, the history of the divine covenant of grace. Hence they cannot be regarded as independent objects, nor constitute an independent theme. That this is the case does not mean that we cannot have any true knowledge of them, but that we know that in a sense yet to be determined they exist in this way, in this relation, and in this way are to be apprehended as an object of knowledge and teaching. The angels cannot conduct themselves in accordance with what may be desired of them for the purpose of an orderly angelology, but to be genuinely orderly an angelology must keep to the angels as they encounter us in the Bible, whether they fit in easily with our theories or not.

Again, when we have grasped the fact that in the Bible the angels exist only incidentally with God and man in the history between them attested by Scripture, the further question arises what we are to make of them, what significance they have for us, whether, and in what sense for our understanding of the Word of God as it comes to us and for our faith, they have a bearing on our world and our view of the world, and may thus be a practical, significant and determinative factor in relation to our existence and the greater and lesser happenings in our age and environment. On this point it is to be noted that the history between God and man as attested in the Bible is the Word of God here and to-day in our world and time and environment; that the point at issue in Christian faith is that we should have a part and in some sense find ourselves caught up into this history; and that what counts in Christian preaching is that this history is the centre, mystery and meaning of all that happens on earth. If, then, the angels belong incidentally but genuinely to this history; if they are not really general elements in the world; if they cannot be separated from the concrete event of Christ as attested in the Bible; if for all that they are inciden-

[412] tal they are elements which cannot be overlooked in this happening, the decisive point of which we have to take account in our doctrine of angels is that the Word of God by which we take part in this happening also speaks to us concerning the existence and work of angels. Thus the real question is not what we can make of angels. It is whether in our supposed Christian faith and proclamation we really have to do with the Word of God attested in the Bible if we can easily ignore angels and regard them as superfluous, or cheerfully and confidently ask what we are to make of them. In other words, there may well be given here a *testimonium paupertatis*[EN179] in respect of our Christianity and churchmanship. We may be forced to note that we have not really noted the Word of God as it is really given. We may have to affirm that we have cause to regard not the angels, but ourselves with our obviously precarious understanding of the Word of God, as superfluous and in need of correction. If the existence of angels stands indeed in a once-for-all relationship with the once-for-all event attested in the Bible, and if we believe that this once-for-all event has some reference to us, this can only cause us the more seriously to consider the angels in their distinctive once-for-allness. Angelology will then have to build not only on the once-for-allness of God in Jesus Christ but also on the related once-for-allness of angels, and in this way to prove its truth and relevance.

But all this depends upon whether the condition proposed in 3 and sharpened in 4 is really fulfilled and not allowed to drop. The Scripture-principle must obtain in all its exclusiveness. Angelology cannot be confused with a philosophy of angels, nor what the Bible says about angels interpreted in terms of such a philosophy. Otherwise we cannot reach the *intelligere*[EN180] demanded in 2. Instead, everything becomes uncertain, equivocal, suspect and superfluous. Imagination is used, and a bad conscience is created by the fact that the resultant product is undisciplined, ill-defined and basically unnecessary. Questions are accepted, and answered with notions, which may be very illuminating for the horizon and taste of one age but which will arouse the scorn of the next at its sophistries and metaphysical obscurity. We are then lost in impossible hypotheses with whose conceptual construction we only advance the more surely our own scepticism and that of others, the more reflectively and sol-

---

EN179 confession of poverty
EN180 understanding

emnly we conduct ourselves. We only further the question what is the point of it all and what is to be made of it, if we do not begin with a genuinely necessary "must," with the vitally important material offered by the Word of God, but begin instead with the "must" of an arbitrary postulate, and then look for reasons to show that this postulate—assuming a corresponding reality—is vitally important. What can be built by hands can be destroyed by hands. Behind this kind of "must" there lurks near or far the "must not" which at some point and in some way will revolt against it. If angelology ignores the conditions of 3 and 4 it hastens to the point where one day it will become the [413] angelology of the weary shrug of the shoulders. If in this matter we desire or do anything but the one thing demanded in theology, sooner or later we shall prefer not to desire anything more, not to put any more questions or to desire any more answers, and therefore to abandon the task of *intelligere*[EN181] with a tired sigh. We may do this. Indeed we must. But if we do we must not imagine that it corresponds to or is required by the matter. It simply rests upon the fact that we have not allowed ourselves to be warned and kept to the matter itself.

We may fitly conclude this introduction with a little warning picture of this angelology of the shrug of the shoulders.

"Heaven may be left to angels and sparrows," was how Heinrich Heine once put it. Theologians may have something similar in view, but they do not usually express themselves so crudely. Yet D. F. Strauss (*Die chr. Glaubenslehre*, Vol. I, 1840, 670 f.) is almost as frank. When humanity "freed itself from the Middle Ages, and laid hold of the principle of the modern world in its different relationships, the notion of angels which had flourished on very different soil was bound to wither on this alien territory." We now trace back occurrence as a whole and not its individual parts to the divine causality, and have thus no further use for a particular activity of angels in the world. "The Copernican view of the world has robbed us of the place which Jewish and Christian antiquity thought of as the throne of God surrounded by the angels. For us the supra-sensual world is not beyond and above but in the sensual. We immediately treat that which is not yet explained on the assumption that it will yield to explanation by natural causes. Hence we not only cannot accept the possibility of such beings as angels, but we cannot even leave the question undecided. If the modern idea of God and conception of the world are right, there cannot possibly be beings of this kind." And "these basic notions of the modern age as fashioned by our increasing knowledge of nature undoubtedly rest on better grounds than the Church's belief in angels, the primary source of which is simply popular thinking and saga which Jesus and the men of the New Testament undoubtedly shared in all seriousness and which we must leave to them, but by which we must not be bound, as they themselves never thought of taking our views from us." This is clear speaking. It has all the clarity of a man who thinks with axiomatic certainty upon the basis of what he takes to be the only possible picture of the world and who can speak for believers in this view (his "we") with genuinely apostolic authority, but who finds it impossible to give an unprejudiced account of the meaning and importance of the biblical message, and in this context of the biblical meaning of this particular matter. We have only to compare D. F. Strauss with Thomas or R. Rothe to see the common source which in his case could give rise to such an expressive shrug of the shoulders.

[EN181] understanding

Other theologians were more reserved. This is especially true of Schleiermacher, whose famous two theses concerning angels (*D. chr. Glaube* § 42 and 43) are very typical. The first of these is as follows: "Since this conception native to the Old Testament has passed over into the New, and on the one side neither contains anything impossible nor contradicts the basis of all God-fearing consciousness, but on the other is never brought into the circle of true Christian doctrine, it can be present in the language of Christianity without imposing any necessary affirmations concerning its reality." And the second: "The only thing which can be represented as a doctrine of angels is that whether angels exist can have no influence on our conduct, and that no further revelations of their being are to be expected." G. Spinner (*op. cit.*, p. 276) has summed this up in the formula: "The reality of angels is questionable; their influence none; their revelations to us none." And he adds: "We shudder at the empty spaces which open up at this point." For Schleiermacher himself these empty spaces were filled by a reference to the private and liturgical use which we still accord to the idea. On this point he made the following statement in the first edition of his work (Vol. I, p. 218): "The private use is limited in the first instance to a materialising of the divine protection in circumstances where there is no scope for dutiful activity and concern. The liturgical—which each can of course make his own in the free place of his religious impulses—consists supremely in the fact that God is to be represented as surrounded by pure and infinite spirits."

[414]

There were many who followed Schleiermacher in the view that the doctrine is neither established nor relevant. We may refer to W. M. L. de Wette (*Lehrb. der chr. Dogm.*, Part II, 1821, 89): "This doctrine, which derives from pious yearnings and symbolic imaginations, is enriched by an alien mythological metaphysics and has been falsely introduced into the sphere of Christian dogmatics, has only doubtful value as a subject of conviction," while "the doctrine of bad angels is to be totally rejected, since the idea of a purely bad spirit is quite impossible."

We may refer to R. A. Lipsius (*Lehrb. d. ev, prot, Dog.*[2], 1879, 418 f.): "The notions of angels and devils are quite impossible for scientific thought, but may be used in the symbolic speech of religion so long as we take care to see that they are of no practical significance for the religious relationship itself, and are thus never invested with dogmatic importance." To ban them even from the speech of religion Lipsius regards as misplaced pedantry in view of the symbolic nature of this speech. "The only thing is that they are to be used in this field in keeping with a purified dogmatics, as transparent symbols and not as metaphysical truths."

We may refer to Julius Kaftan (*Dogm.*[3–4], 1901, 268): "Angels are not an object of faith, for this is true only of God in His revelation. Consequently they are not an object of the know-ledge and doctrine of faith." But does the postulation of angels help to make more conceiv-able the divine providence ruling in the world? Even this is not the case: "The secret of the divine rule is not lessened by such a doctrine. And for this reason dogmatics has nothing to say concerning angels." This is not meant as a denial of the existence of angels. "On the basis of Scripture it will still be a pious opinion that there are such creatures as angels. And there is nothing to disprove this." Kaftan has no objection to the postulation of spiritual beings on a level above that of man, but a doctrine of angels cannot be built upon this assumption. "This mention of the topic is quite enough in dogmatics, so long as we make it clear that our relationship with God is not in any case mediated by angels, and that the doctrine of angels becomes a dangerous error if deductions of this kind are drawn from it."

We may refer to Otto Kirn (*Grundr. d. ev. Dogm.*[8], 1930, 72). He sees no possibility of giving to the idea of angels the certainty and clarity which can be guaranteed only by a connexion with the central Christian experience of salvation. This connexion cannot be ascribed to the "notion of superhuman servants of God." This notion does not belong to the essential con-tent of the revelation of salvation itself. But Kirn does not want it excluded from the speech of religious contemplation. Its use is to be left to religious taste, particular care being taken "that it never encroaches on the direct relationship between God and man."

We may refer to T. Haering (*Der chr. Glaube*, 1906, 261 f.) Angels are not an object of pious experience like sin and grace. Angelic manifestations are not necessary to the Christian. The belief of Jesus in angels is not bound up with the innermost core of His self-consciousness, His filial belief. Have we then to recognise the authority of Jesus in matters which are not indissolubly connected with the heart of the Gospel? We cannot use the belief in angels as a necessary element in saving faith, or regard it as the measure of a particularly strong faith. Yet some value may with a good conscience be ascribed to it as a living representation of [415] inexpressible truths which are in themselves independent of it, and particularly as a representation of divine help through means as yet unknown to us.

We may refer to F. A. B. Nitzsch (*Lehrb. d. ev. Dogm.*, 1889, ed. Horst Stephan, 1912, 443 f.). What Scripture tells us concerning angels does not constitute an adequate basis for a connected doctrine. If it cannot be said that the reality of angels is impossible, there can be no proof of it. There are no historically demonstrable facts to compel belief in the existence of angelic beings. The idea of angels may well have been no more than a passing notion of Judaism and early Christianity. Nor is the suggestion to be dismissed that Jesus linked the proclamation of the infallible truth which belongs to His calling with national concepts which do not themselves form any part of objective truth. Still, the doctrine of angels can be highly estimated, whether in its connexion with the idea of the glory of God or as a means of stimulating faith in divine providence. "The idea of angels maintains this significance even when no real existence can be ascribed to them. For even a poem can serve to embody and present objective truths."

We may refer to Reinhold Seeberg (for forty years the head of the modern positive school, *Christl. Dogm.* Vol. II, 1925, 91). The idea of angels comes from the Israelite view of things, and is taken over by the men of the New Testament. But since they have no significance beyond the divine rule, they do not belong to Christian dogmatics. On the other hand, the notion is not in any sense dangerous for Christian piety if understood in its biblical sense. Thus there is no reason to contest it. "But a doctrine of angels cannot possibly be regarded as one of the tasks of dogmatics."

And we may refer to Horst Stephan, who echoes the same views in his *Glaubenslehre*, 1928, 125 f. The idea of angels is inherited from pre-Christian religion. If the older dogmatics developed a doctrine of angels, "in so doing it did not obey its knowledge of faith but its external biblicism. For this reason it may be left out of account." This is not meant to be a verdict on the existence of angels. But Christian piety has no need of the idea. "The proximity of God is so vital through Jesus and the community, and the modern picture of the universe with its infinity and severity has so transcended all geo- and anthropocentrism, that pre-Christian means are no longer necessary to represent it."

The consensus of all these modern dogmaticians, both among themselves and with their master Schleiermacher, is overwhelming. But in theology there can be agreement even in aberration. And this is what has happened in the present instance. For in what consists the general consensus of opinion at this point?

First, it obviously consists in a definite negation. These modern thinkers are not prepared to take angels seriously. It does not give them the slightest joy to think of them. They are plainly rather peevish and impatient at having to handle the subject. And if we are told in Hebrews 13[2] not to be neglectful of hospitality, since some have entertained angels unawares, these theologians are almost anxiously concerned to refuse the angels a lodging in their dogmatics, and think that all things considered they should warn others against extending hospitality to them. They are obviously of the opinion that they have never had any dealings with angels. At any rate, they show themselves quite determined to direct the attention of Christianity as far as possible away from them.

What is the reason for this negative attitude? Here, too, they are agreed. Angels are dispensable and superfluous for the religious relationship, for faith, i.e., saving faith. The Christian has to do with God alone, with the will and presence of God. What, then, is the point of angels? We cannot believe in them as we do in God. They cannot even be an object of our pious experience, nor can it be maintained that they stand in any necessary connexion with this. Indeed, it is to be feared that if their existence is accepted they will be venerated and even worshipped, and that they will prejudice the immediate relationship to God in other respects as well. It is for this reason that they cannot be "invested with dogmatic importance." In a serious undertaking like a doctrine of faith, they are unworthy of any positive consideration, discussion and presentation. Thus the door is shut against them, and they remain without.

[416]

But no, the door is not completely shut. With common consent, something else is said. All these dogmaticians agree in some sense that they are not denying the existence of angels. Nor do they ever speak of them with the negativity of Strauss or the mockery of Heine. There is no reason to contest their existence (Seeberg). Even the formulation of de Wette is regarded by some as rather too severe. Angels are not desired in dogmatics. But a kind of internment camp (or is it a nursery?) is opened for them in which they are tolerated. They are allowed to stay for the present as objects of pious opinion, as elements in the symbolic speech of religion, as symbolic representations. On the assumption that tact will be exercised by those who receive them, they are accepted as visitors if not as residents. Not without some shaking of the head, a certain value is ascribed to them, just as Schleiermacher himself had given them free scope in the sphere of private and liturgical usage.

The fact that there is this consistent unity is striking and gives rise to questions. If these dogmaticians were putting the question of truth; if in their own way, by the analysis of the religious consciousness or faith, they came to the conclusion that angels are not to be accepted and that there is no serious place for them; if they were sure of themselves, why did they not, as responsible teachers of the Church, maintain that even pious opinions and the symbolic speech of religion should not cling to the assertion of angels, but that this superfluous element ought to be banished even from liturgies and hymn-books and the quiet chamber of the private religious life? This is what the Reformation did in relation to Mary and the saints and purgatory once it was seen that these were elements which were not true according to the Word of God and were thus necessarily alien to faith established upon this Word. When the length is reached of seeing that something is erroneous, in no serious period in the Church's history has it then been described as valuable and left to religious taste; it has been called an error and rejected and no longer practised even as a transparent symbol. Following his own critical canon, i.e., the modern view of the universe, D. F. Strauss drew this conclusion in respect of angels. Why, then, did not modern Liberals and Ritschlians draw it? Why did they not simply deny the existence of angels, and declare all further references to them to be unlawful superstitions? Why were they not purists in this matter?

It would be excellent if we could explain it as follows. They were prevented by a serious theological reason, by their relationship to the source and norm of all theological knowledge. The Bible always stood in their way. They had not been able to dismiss it. They could not follow its own interpretation of angels. They could not deduce from it with certainty how it stands with angels. They could not see from the Bible what angels really have to do with God's revelation and faith in it. And therefore, in order not to say what they could not say responsibly, they preferred to be silent concerning them, and to leave undiscussed the *locus*

De angelis[EN182]. But again they were not so sure of their knowledge in this respect as to be able to say with a good conscience that the Bible leads us to a negative decision, that there is nothing in the matter at all. They were not so sure as to feel capable of a direct denial and a general cleansing of the temple. Hence they did not deny the existence of angels like Strauss because they did not find in the Bible a final negative. And they were so reserved and patient in respect of the private and liturgical use of the idea of angels because they did not wish to forestall a final positive which might be reached on the basis of the Bible. It would be excellent if we could interpret in this way the restraint and mildness which we see exercised by   [417] these theologians in contrast to their basic attitude.

But unfortunately this interpretation is not possible. They are quite clear as to the negative result of their conception of the biblical testimony. They are all agreed that the biblical doctrine of angels belongs to the Old Testament or more generally to pre-Christian religion. They are all agreed that it is an idea of the time which stands on or beyond the margin of the biblical witness to revelation. From their understanding of the Bible they can understand its doctrine of angels only as a representation, historically transparent to us, of truths in respect of the divine providence etc. which are quite independent of the existence and work of angels. What they find in the Bible is once and for all the revelation with which angels have basically nothing to do and the faith for which angels are strictly superfluous. Hence Haering is quite certain that belief in angels does not belong to the inner core of the self-consciousness of Jesus. None of these thinkers is really prevented from dismissing angels just as energetically as Strauss did on his basis, and from drawing the practical deductions from this dismissal. Indeed, they really ought to have done so on the basis of their understanding of the Bible.

But the revolution which they underwent was not so deep, nor the question of truth so urgent, as to force them to do so. The power of the negation was not by a long way so great as that of the Reformation in relation to Mary, the saints and purgatory. It was great enough only to make them very definitely refuse to invest the idea of angels with dogmatic importance. Yet the fact that it was not greater has nothing whatever to do with their understanding of the Bible, the question of truth raised by it, the *docta ignorantia*[EN183] possibly imposed, or openness to a final word still to be spoken. The painful thing about the position of these modern theologians is that in each of them one can fairly easily lay one's finger on the point where there was restraint from a very different quarter, and consideration was given to the possibilities of a non-biblical and speculative demonstration of faith in a spirit-world as more or less impressively exploited by Bretschneider, Rothe and Dorner, Schlatter and Troeltsch. The thinkers to whom we refer could not accept ideas and constructions of this kind. They did not find them convincing. Yet the fact remains that they were illumined by these conceptions, even to the point of a certain coquetry with them on the part of more than one of those mentioned. If the spirit-world could not be proved; if it could not be seen what significance it might have for the religious relationship and faith; if nothing could be erected on such hypotheses any more than on the biblical doctrine of angels, their possibility could not be flatly denied. *Hinc illae lacrymae*—hence the mildness and restraint! There was no doubt as to the understanding of the Bible. On this side the verdict was negative. The decision did not rest on the authority of the Word of God and it was not therefore so categorical as to involve an absolutely unconditional No, but it had at any rate been taken. There could thus be no restraint from this angle. In respect of the general possibility, however, the matter was not quite, so simple. Perhaps from this standpoint there was something in it after all. Who could tell? Who could really deny it? This is what constituted the barrier. They were not

---

[EN182] place of the angels
[EN183] learned ignorance

prepared for exclusion on this side. They had no confidence in the possibility and did not use it, but they could not reject it altogether as a possibility. And it was this possibility which dictated the ultimate ambivalence. It was this which separated them from Heine and Strauss, with whom they ought to have been at one in substance if not in basis and tone. Their understanding of the Bible would never have prevented this agreement, but it was prevented by the consideration that a philosophical demonstration of the doctrine of angels was not perhaps wholly out of the question.

[418] The painfulness of the whole situation is obvious. We might have had confidence in the theological seriousness of these dogmaticians if their understanding of Scripture had led them either to a strict and full rejection of the doctrine of angels, or if it had led them to an acknowledgment not merely of their inability to make anything of the doctrine but also of their inability to oppose to it a simple negation in theory and practice. A *Non liquet* of this kind might well have been a theological decision which is formally at least in order. And I do not wish to be so unjust as to question that this was perhaps the true opinion of at least some of those mentioned. But what in fact they all did in concert is quite impossible. If they were as sure as they made themselves out to be of their understanding of Scripture in the matter, they ought not to have been prevented from carrying through to the last the full negation which they obviously had in view. Or, on the other hand, they ought not to have refrained from showing from Scripture why they could not do this and restraint and mildness were demanded. Yet even as and although they appealed to Scripture, they allowed themselves to be halted, not by Scripture, but on the ground of the consideration that there might be something about this spirit-world which others if not they themselves thought they knew quite apart from Scripture. It was this possibility which arrested them. Hence the fact of the matter is that the poor angels, excluded from dogmatics yet not contested, denied or abolished, owe their shadowy existence, like that of the dead in Hades, to the circumstance that these dogmaticians will not close if they do not open the door to a philosophy of angels, but out of a final respect for this possibility (not for the Bible) try to leave it on the latch. We hardly dare contemplate what they themselves think of these dealings with them in the studies of theologians. No, this *Non liquet*[EN184] was and is profoundly unsatisfactory.

This, then, is the angelology of the shrug of the shoulders, the weary sigh, which is the necessary consequence when an attempt is made in this matter to do something other than that which is alone possible in theology. Now that we have tasted this cup, and considered this limit of angelology, we can turn to the matter itself.

2. THE KINGDOM OF HEAVEN

The dialectic of the concepts God and man, or rather the real dialectic of the factors denoted by these concepts, has in the thought and speech of the biblical witnesses to revelation its exact correspondence in the dialectic of the concepts, or again in the real dialectic of the circles of being denoted by the concepts, of heaven and earth. What the biblical witness says concerning angels, and what the angels are and signify in the context of the work and revelation of God, can be understood only if we are open, and remain open, to this twofold dialectic. If we insist that theology is exclusively and abstractly a matter of God and man, or, in other theological schemes, of God alone or man

---

EN184 it is not clear

alone, then obviously there will be no place for, or understanding of, angels. But obviously, too, we shall not be dealing with the work and revelation of God as attested in the Bible, with Jesus Christ, and therefore with God and man in the form in which they are normative for the Christian Church and its faith and proclamation. For where it is a matter of God and man in this normative form, in the sense of the biblical concepts of these two factors, it is always a matter of heaven and earth. And the converse is also true—that where it is a matter of heaven and earth, it is also, and decisively, a matter of God and man. [419] But this follows from the former truth. Its validity is secondary. Hence it does not need to be emphasised in the present context. The first truth is what calls for emphasis. To say God in the biblical sense and therefore with a responsible Christian understanding is also to say heaven; and to say man in the same sense and with the same understanding is also to say earth. Hence if we are to speak of God and man in this sense and with this understanding, if we are to say something theologically relevant, we must remember that explicitly or implicitly we have also to speak of heaven and earth. If we think in this twofold dialectic, we are necessarily led to the concept of angels appropriate to the context of the biblical witness and therefore true in the Christian sense. For in the relationship first between God and heaven, then between heaven and earth, and then and decisively between God and man, the angels have their specific place. In the history of angelology many devious and erroneous paths, much confusing play with alien presuppositions, much wasted effort in blind alleys, and above all the angelology of the shrug of the shoulders, might well have been avoided if there had been a fundamental realisation of this fact and further thinking had been based upon it.

It is self-evident, but we must begin with the assertion that in this twofold dialectic—it is a genuine dialectic which cannot be resolved—we are not dealing with two equal terms. Our present interest in this assertion is that God and heaven are naturally not identical or of equal essence. The same cannot be said of man and earth. Jesus Christ is in His own person identical and of one essence with God, but this is not true of anything or anyone apart from Him, not even of heaven. Heaven with earth—and in this sense it is not different from earth—is the creature of God, posited by Him, called into being from nothing by His Word, needing to be sustained by Him, and absolutely subject to His rule. As this is to be said of heaven, it is implicitly said of the angels too. And the decisive negative and positive determination of their existence and being is that they are not God and not divine, but creatures. Heaven is not, therefore, under God as earth is under heaven, but it is under God as earth is under Him. We shall have to speak of a difference between heaven and earth, of a precedence of heaven over earth in their relationship to God. But this difference and precedence are within the radical equality in which they are both the creatures of God. As the bracket which encloses everything else, this must also be said of the angels. There is a correspondence, a similarity, of the relationship between heaven and earth to that between the Creator and the creature. We shall have to speak of this. It gives to heaven and the angels a dignity in relation to earth and to man who is of the earth and on the earth. But this dignity is not to be confused with that of the Creator in relation to the [420] creature. Compared with this it is littleness. And the supreme glory and true honour of the Creator are displayed in the fact that in Jesus Christ He has not taken to Himself heaven and the angels in their majesty but man and the earth. The secret of this glory is so great that in the unity between Him and man in the person of Jesus Christ, and in the promise which this One is for all men, the distinction is not merely removed, but man who is of the earth and on the earth is exalted, not only to heaven and to fellowship with the angels, but above these to fellowship with his Creator. The free, electing grace in which this is the case is the majesty and glory with which God is exalted even above heaven. We must make use of this decisive key of Christian knowledge from the very outset. For we should be merely speculating without rhyme or reason if we tried to measure the majesty of God above heaven and the angels, or the depth of heaven and the angels under God, by anything but the mercy of God which is in Jesus Christ.

The Old Testament does not use the term "world" to denote the sum of the reality distinct from God and posited by Him. It speaks of "heaven and earth," and in this way it describes the world within that twofold dialectic, in the differentiation in which it reflects the distinction between God and man. When the New Testament was written the word "cosmos" had long since come into current usage, but for the most part it follows the Old Testament in speaking of heaven and earth. Thus the Bible as a whole understands the world in the light of its meaning and purpose. Its meaning and purpose is the relationship of God and man. Jesus Christ, in whom both are one, is its goal and its basic order. This basic order is reflected in the fact that it is "heaven and earth." But it is only reflected. Heaven is not God. Heaven did not create earth. But "in the beginning God created the heaven and the earth."

The Old Testament lays emphasis on the fact that Yahweh created heaven too (Ps. 96⁵). "By the word of the Lord were the heavens made; and all the host of them by the breath of his mouth" (Ps. 33⁶). They are the work of His hands (Ps. 102²⁵) or fingers (Ps. 8³). Thus the perfection of the Almighty is not only deeper than the underworld but higher than the heavens (Job 11⁸). God is exalted above the heavens (Ps. 57⁵). Jesus Christ has ascended above all heavens (Eph. 4¹⁰). Heaven and the heaven of heavens cannot contain God (1 K. 8²⁷). Even the heavens are not pure in His eyes (Job 15¹⁵). Heaven itself is shaken when He acts (Joel 2¹⁰). "The pillars of heaven tremble and are astonished at his reproof" (Job 26¹¹). One day "the host of heaven shall be dissolved, and the heavens shall be rolled together as a scroll: and all their host shall fall down, as the leaf falleth off from the vine, and as a falling fig from the fig tree" (Is. 34⁴). Yes, "the heavens shall vanish away like smoke" (Is. 51⁶). Heaven no less than earth will flee from the presence of God, "and there was found no place for them" (Rev. 20¹¹). It will perish with the earth as it came into being with it (Mk. 13³¹, Rev. 21¹), and God will create both a new earth and a new heaven (Is. 65¹⁷, Rev. 21¹). For this reason it is forbidden to worship it (Deut. 4¹⁹). Even in heaven the pious man can find no consolation but in God Himself (Ps. 73²⁵).

All this refers implicitly and explicitly to the angels too. They are unquestionably

2. The Kingdom of Heaven

κτίσις EN185 (Rom. 8³⁹). The θρόνοι, κυριότητες, ἀρχαί EN186 and ἐξουσίαι EN187 are all created in and by and to Jesus Christ, so that He is before them all and they all consist by Him (Col. 1¹⁵ᶠ·). They are the Old Testament host of heaven to worship which can only mean apostasy and abomination (Deut. 17³, 2 K. 17¹⁶ and *passim*). Hence the scene in Rev. 22⁸ᶠ· between the seer and the heavenly interpreter: "And when I had heard and seen, I fell down [421] to worship before the feet of the angel which shewed me these things. Then said he unto me, See thou do it not: for I am thy fellowservant, and of thy brethren the prophets, and of them which keep the sayings of this book: worship God." Hence the scene in Rev. 4⁹ᶠ·, where the four and twenty πρεσβύτεροι EN188 fall down before Him that sits on the throne, and worship Him who lives to all eternity, and cast their crowns before the throne and say: "Thou art worthy, our Lord and God, to receive glory and honour and power: for thou hast created all things, and for thy pleasure they are and were created." Hence the warning in Col. 2¹⁸ against the θρησκεία τῶν ἀγγέλων EN189 introduced by those early Gnostic errorists. What are angels before God? "Behold, he put no trust in his servants; and his angels he charged with folly" (Job 4¹⁸ cf. 15¹⁵). And in accordance with what we are told concerning heaven, there is no heavenly ἀρχή EN190 or ἐξουσία EN191 or δύναμις EN192 which will not some day be removed and as it were dismissed from service (1 Cor. 15²⁴). Any anxiety lest the existence and study of angels might entail injury to the direct relationship between God and man and man and God, or a jeopardising of the knowledge of the uniqueness of God and respect for it, is quite unfounded. Indeed, it is the very thing which is made impossible by what emerges from the very outset in the witness of Holy Scripture to angels. When we have to do with heaven and therefore with angels, we are wholly within the sphere of the creature.

But what is to be seen and learned concerning heaven and the angels cannot really be reduced with a good conscience to this necessary reservation. If the distinction between heaven and earth is not identical and cannot be equated or confused with the distinction between Creator and creature, or the decisive distinction between God and man, it cannot be seen and understood in abstraction from the latter. Biblical thinking knows also this dimension of heaven and earth. Only as we follow it into this dimension do we come up against the reality to which it refers. And the first point which we have to notice in this connexion is that the created world in its totality (and therefore heaven and earth) corresponds to that for which it was created; to the encounter, history and fellowship between God and man. In its twofold form it is the home, and recognisable as such, which God chose and willed and posited for this purpose because we were to be called His children. In what does the correspondence consist? In the fact that here too and already there is an above and below, an earlier and later, a more and less. For the sake of precision, we must add that this is not an absolute antithesis, of which there can be no question. It lies within the relativity appropriate to an intracosmic relationship. But

EN185 creation
EN186 thrones, dominions, principalities
EN187 authorities
EN188 elders
EN189 worship of angels
EN190 principality
EN191 authority
EN192 power

there is a real distinction, and indeed a fundamental and essential distinction, and it consists in the fact that there is in the one cosmos an above and a below, and to that extent an upper and a lower cosmos. And these are heaven and earth. They only reflect, but they do reflect, the true and proper and strict above and below of Creator and creature, of God and man. They attest the manner of this confrontation and conjunction; the relationship which is at issue in that encounter, history and fellowship and therefore in Jesus Christ; the relationship in view and for the sake of which the one whole cosmos is created. They only reflect and attest, but this they do. The heavenly above can no more be effaced than the earthly below. They are both creatures, but they cannot be interchanged or confused. The world would not be the world without this above and below, this earlier and later, this more and less of heaven and earth. This dialectic steadily accompanies that of Creator and creature, of God and man. We do not experience or know the second and decisive dialectic—which is that of the history of the covenant and salvation—apart from the first dialectic grounded in the nature and constitution of the created world. Indeed, the latter is the form in which, noetically and ontically, we participate in the former and decisive. Man is on earth under heaven. In no way and on no pretext can we abstract from the fact that we have the earth to which we belong beneath us and the heaven which is not as such our place above us. That which did and does and will take place between God and man is an event which, willed and accomplished by God and relating to us, is both heavenly and earthly. In this way alone is it an event of revelation and salvation, of which God is the basis and in which we participate. Only in this correspondence does it speak. Only in this mirror can it be apprehended. Only in this witness is it manifest. Only in this likeness does it come from God and apply to us. We cannot try to go behind this likeness to a true reality which can be detached from it. We cannot treat this likeness as a cipher which can be dispensed with once it has been solved. To dismiss the reality of this likeness is to dismiss the reality of the event, its divine origin and human goal. It is the event between heaven and earth, or it is not the event between God and man, the event of Christ. To exclude oneself from the former is to exclude oneself from the latter. And all that is left is a little morality and mysticism, a little psychology or existential philosophy. This can be avoided only if we have an active concern for the realism of Holy Scripture with its basic law that we should give the serious attention which it deserves to the subordinate but indispensable dialectic of the antithesis between heaven and earth in its relationship to that between God and man.

To take up first this question of understanding, why is it that we are compelled to think of heaven as an above and earlier and more, and earth as a below and later and less? The answer which the Bible gives to this question is simply that within the one cosmos God is nearer to one of the spheres, i.e., heaven, than He is to the other, i.e., earth. It is better not to say that heaven is nearer to God than earth, although this inversion may seem to be both possible and necessary. In the greater nearness of heaven and the lesser nearness of earth it is not a question of qualities proper to heaven and earth as such, but of an action and attitude of God in which He draws and is nearer to heaven [423] than earth. We are thus dealing with a qualification of the two spheres in which they are posited in this distinct relationship to Him and the corresponding relationship to one another. It is for this reason that heaven is superior to earth. It is for this reason that heaven is the upper cosmos and earth the lower; that heaven is before and more than earth. It is not these things in itself and as the creature of God. But it is made these things by the divine action.

It is always an abstraction to think of God apart from the fact that, as the One from and by whom the creature is, He is also its Lord, Preserver and Ruler, and above all, as the meaning of His lordship, preservation and rule, its Saviour, the God of grace and the covenant. It is in the light of this that we have to understand His action and attitude to the world and therefore to heaven and earth. But if for the sake of conceptual clarity we momentarily allow ourselves this abstraction and therefore do not take into account the history of the Creator with the creature, we can only say that God has not created heaven and earth in this superiority and subordination; that He has not made heaven the upper and earth the lower cosmos; that He has not created both creaturely spheres in this qualification and mutual relationship. It is not, therefore, proper to them by nature. It does not belong to their creaturely constitution.

Yet they receive and have it as and because there begins with their creation. the history of God with them, the history of His grace and covenant, and therefore the history of His cosmic rule. As this takes place, they receive and have and maintain this qualification. In the biblical view of things, heaven is in every respect the upper cosmos and hierarchically superior to earth as the presupposition of the biblical witness to the revelation and work of God. A theology based on this witness cannot evade the concept of this intracosmic hierarchy. But we have to realise that in accepting this concept we are already thinking in terms of the grace and revelation and work of God. Hence we must not be surprised if thinking which is not cast in these terms stumbles at this concept. And the fact that we are continually inclined to stumble at it makes it clear that it is not at all self-evident that in our own thinking we should really think in these terms. The action and attitude of God to the creature are the basis of this hierarchy. From what is to be said concerning heaven and earth in themselves and as such there does not follow the superiority of heaven to earth as a likeness of that of God to man. If it is this likeness, it is not on the basis and in the power of the nature which it is given at creation. We can say only that in this nature it is destined to become this likeness. But it does become or receive it only on the basis and in the power of the divine action to and in and with the creaturely world.

Concerning heaven itself and its nature a first cautious statement which we [424] can make is that, as earth exists as the sphere of man, heaven also exists, thus constituting the inalienable counterpart of earth. What exists and takes place in our sphere exists and takes place in the presence and with the participation of this other sphere, this counterpart, heaven. It belongs to earth as our sphere to be open to the other. And it belongs to happenings in our sphere to be set against that other sphere and thus to take place in relationship from and to it.

To the outlook of man in the Old and New Testament there belongs the consciousness of existing as an earthly creature in the presence and with the participation of this other sphere. Even apart from his relationship to God this man is not alone. With his cosmos which he can see and in which he is at home he is not alone even apart from God. Another cosmic sphere has also been created by God and is also present in addition to his own. There are celestial as well as terrestrial σώματα EN193, even though the glory of the celestial is one and that of the terrestrial another (1 Cor. 15^{40}). There are knees which can bow in heaven as well as on earth (Phil. 2^{10}). There is a binding and loosing in heaven corresponding to what takes place on earth (Mt. 16^{19} and 18^{18}). There is a connexion, a relationship, a common tie. The prodigal son does not sin only before his father but also against heaven, and he sins against heaven first and only then before his father (Lk. 15^{18}). Similarly in 2 Chron. 28^9 we read of a transgression which cries aloud to heaven. As the earth can mourn, heaven too can wrap itself in darkness (Jer. 4^{28}). And heaven no less than earth can rejoice and be glad (Ps. 96^{11}, Is. 49^{13}, Rev. 12^{12} and *passim*). Together heaven and earth grow old and are renewed. And if in Eph. 1^{10} the end of the ways of God is described as the process in which heavenly and earthly reality come to have their Head (ἀνακεφαλαίωσις) in Christ, this is to be understood as a confirmation of their mutual relationship and confrontation as grounded in their creation (Col. 1^{16}).

A second thing which we may cautiously maintain concerning the nature of heaven is that as this counterpart of earth it is the sum of all that which in creation is unfathomable, distant, alien and mysterious in creation. Earth is the sphere of man; the sphere of his vision and comprehension; the sphere of his access and capacity. But this is not true of heaven. Heaven is the boundary which is clearly and distinctly marked off for man. It exists. But in distinction from earth it exists as invisible creaturely reality. It is invisible and therefore incomprehensible and inaccessible, outside the limits of human capacity. If man reaches this frontier even in his own sphere; if the really invisible or the invisibly real meets him even on earth, this is of a piece with the fact that earth is under heaven, having its counterpart in heaven, and standing in this relationship to it. To the extent that it encounters man on earth, heaven is not to be equated, of course, with the heights and depths and other mysteries of the earthly sphere which have not yet been fathomed but are not basically unfathomable. Obscure, i.e., unexplored parts of the earth are not on this account heaven. The unknown is not as such the unknowable. But the unknowable waits at the limits of the knowable. The definitive and essential mystery of all creaturely being waits at the limits of the provisional. Again there must be no false equation. Even this final mystery is not the mystery of God. But it is the mystery of heaven as the sum of that which is really invisible or invisibly real.

[425]

EN193 bodies

The frontier which separates God and creation is thus higher. It embraces both heaven and earth, both the visible and the invisible. But across that which is outside God and has its reality from God there also runs the frontier between the visible and the invisible. And we exist before this frontier as well as that of creation. It is not merely God who is incomprehensible; the same can also be said of heaven within the creaturely world.

In saying this I have followed in the first instance the Nicene definition (A.D. 325). On the basis of Col. 1¹⁶ this brings together earth and heaven under the phrase πάντα ὁρατά τε καὶ ἀόρατα (*omnia visibilia et invisibilia*EN194), Almighty God being the ποιητής EN195 (*factor*) of both. It may well be said that in effect this is in agreement with the biblical definition of their relationship. For biblical man, too, heaven is not merely the supreme but the proper notion of what he does not see and understand; of the sphere of creation which is basically inaccessible and outside his control, yet not identical with God even in its incommensurability, but created by Him and therefore distinct from Him, even though it represents and reveals the mystery of creation to man as a creature of earth. The only point is that the biblical view is more naive and radical in the sense that when it speaks of heaven it first thinks of the visible (atmospheric or astronomical) heaven, being led from what it sees in these far heights and distances to the reality of the invisible. It is also more naive and radical in the sense that it finds the same invisible and incommensurable no less on earth than in heaven. If heaven above cannot be measured, the same is true of the foundations of the earth (Jer. 31³⁷). "Who hath measured the waters in the hollow of his hand, and meted out heaven with the span?" But then the verse goes on: "And comprehended the dust of the earth in a measure, and weighed the mountains in scales, and the hills in a balance?" (Is. 40¹²). And if it is asked in Job 38³¹ᶠ·: "Canst thou bind the sweet influences of Pleiades, or loose the bands of Orion? Canst thou bring forth Mazzaroth in his season? or canst thou guide Arcturus with his sons? Knowest thou the ordinances of heaven? canst thou set the dominion thereof in the earth?", these questions belong to a whole series of similar challenges in respect of the earth and sea and underworld, and later of a list of puzzling animals from the lion and goat to such semi-mythical figures as Behemoth and Leviathan. To climb up or journey to heaven is one impossible venture, and to break through into hell and dwell there another (Deut. 30¹³, Amos 9², Ps. 139⁸). Thus the frontier between the visible and the invisible is not co-extensive in the Bible with the frontier between heaven and earth. For in heaven there is also that which is visible, the sun and moon and stars, the wind and the clouds, and it is in face of these visible things that we are set before the invisible. Similarly, even on earth in the direct sphere of man there are many things which cannot be seen or measured or counted or weighed or reckoned or brought under human apprehension, so that apart from the mystery of God man is continually occupied with that of creation. Yet we cannot fail to see that for the Bible heaven is in this respect, even perhaps as *pars pro toto*EN196, a particular factor in virtue of its particular nature, and stands with its own mystery in some sense at the head of all mysteries. Quite apart from the special relationship of God to heaven, there are passages, constantly recurring from Gen. 1¹ onwards, in which the correlation and distinction of heaven and earth can mean only that the sphere of man is accompanied and preceded by another sphere which is not in any sense his. The folly of men which leads to their dispersal and the confusion of their languages is typically expressed in the fact that according to Gen. 11⁴ they tried to build a tower whose top should reach to heaven. That the [426]

EN194 all things visible and invisible
EN195 Maker
EN196 part for the whole

excellency of the godless mounts to heaven and his head touches the clouds (Job 20[6]); that Babylon mounts up to heaven and fortifies the height of her strength (Jer. 51[53]); that in a dream Nebuchadnezzar sees himself as a tree high in the midst of the earth and growing and becoming strong until its height reaches heaven (Dan. 4[7f.]); that the little horn waxes great even to the host of heaven (Dan. 8[10]); that the sins of men reach to heaven (Rev. 18[5])—these are all the extreme limits of pride rising to a supreme height before it falls. In the same way the fact that the godless and corrupt speak loftily is one of the signs that God has set them in slippery places (Ps. 73[8, 18]). Heaven is the epitome of the limit set for man. And the height of heaven above earth is obviously calculated as such to serve as a likeness of the height of the ways and thoughts of God over those of man (Is. 55[9]), or of the incomprehensibility of His goodness and faithfulness (Ps. 36[5]) or of His grace to those who fear Him (Ps. 103[11]). Heaven thus seems to be the norm of that which is inconceivable to man.

This is what is to be said concerning the nature and essence of heaven as such, and therefore concerning its ordination to be this likeness. But it can be stated only with great reserve. It is no accident that though the witness of Scripture in respect of the character of heaven as the counterpart of earth, and as the world of the mystery which encounters us, is not obscure or ambiguous, it is certainly sparing. The fact is plain to see that the men of the Bible have no intention of instructing us concerning the nature of heaven, and that they are as little occupied with heaven as such as they are with earth as such. Indeed, it is only in the context of the witness to the divine Word and attitude that heaven emerges with decisive clarity either as that counterpart or as the world of mystery. And in all that we have said on this topic we have been guided from the very first by the fact that the nature of heaven as we have attempted to indicate it can be seen only in the light of the divine action and attitude. This reveals it for what it is, i.e., the mysterious counterpart. That the divine creation is actual in this form, with this duality and crossed through by this frontier, is something which man has to be told by the Creator Himself and His work and revelation. He can recognise it in creation only as he is first told it in this way.

And this is particularly true of the subject of our investigation: of the hierarchy in the relationship of heaven and earth; of the superiority of the former to the latter; of the characterisation of heaven as the upper and earth as the lower cosmos. Even if we could assume (as we cannot) that we have behind us a kind of demonstration of the nature of heaven in relation to earth, this would not mean that heaven is above earth or earth below heaven. This involves something more than an assertion of the nature of heaven. It involves a judgment; the recognition of a dignity, function and significance of heaven in relation to earth. It tells us that God is nearer to heaven than earth. It makes [427] heaven in its relation to earth a likeness of God in His relation to man. It gives it a specific precedence in the history of God's dealings in and with and to the world created by Him. It compels us to bring at once into our thought of God the thought of heaven, and to connect at once the thought of God with that of heaven. But no presentation of the nature of heaven, of that counterpart and mystery, can compel us to do this. The knowledge of the nature of heaven does not include that of its superiority. According to the description of its nature as here attempted, heaven could only be the partner, a duplicate as it were, of earth. There might well be another or many spheres alongside our own, different yet corresponding and interconnected, and yet we are not forced to speak of a hierarchy in which our sphere is necessarily below and the other or others necessarily above. And the limit which has been drawn, the radical separation of that which can be measured and controlled from that which cannot, might well be a very real one, and yet not signify more than that we must quietly venerate what is incommensurable but without being compelled to add to this veneration genuine awe and humility and adoration because in this limit we have a greater proximity to God and in the mystery of creation a likeness to His mystery. Even if the question of superiority and subordination necessarily arises, why should not the converse be true that earth is the first and upper and true cosmos and heaven only a monstrous shadow or reflection of earth, that counterpart and limit being perhaps a determination and the supreme work of the human spirit, an unavoidable idea or a superfluous fiction? No concept of the nature of heaven can exclude this. None can place us under the compelling judgment that in heaven we have to do in a serious and definitive sense with an upper cosmos and in our own sphere with a lower. It would thus be an impossible act of caprice if we were to assume that in our deliberations thus far we have already answered the question before us, demonstrating the hierarchy in which heaven is more than earth.

It may well be that the two statements which we have cautiously advanced with regard to the nature of heaven can receive illumination, concretion and enrichment from certain aspects of the cosmic picture of modern physics on the one side and from an impartial historical appraisal of the so-called magical view of antiquity, the Middle Ages and the early Renaissance on the other. But it would still be the case that the decisive foundation for these statements can only be the theological, and that in themselves these statements do not provide what is needed to make heaven a magnitude which is theologically relevant.

If in this question of the superiority of heaven to earth we are to emerge from obscurity to light, and if we are to set on solid ground that which we have provisionally stated concerning its nature, we must abandon this attempt to consider and define and describe it abstractly, and press on resolutely to survey it in the position and function which it is specifically allotted in the context of the activity of God as the God of grace and the covenant. We took up the [428] attempt only to bring into focus as such the problem of the heavenly, i.e., of that counterpart to our creaturely sphere, of the limit which is set for us by the existence of another creaturely sphere. And we had to do this in order to make it clear that it is not the nature of heaven, so far as we may speak of this, which makes it theologically relevant and gives it that distinctive superiority to our own sphere of existence. To know the latter, we must now speak of what we have already called the qualification which it is given by God. It is this alone which gives heaven the character in virtue of which it is above and before and more than the earth. And it is this alone which unequivocally reveals its nature and makes it the counterpart and limit of the earthly sphere.

We are now at the end and goal and climax of the whole doctrine of creation, and here if anywhere it ought to be evident that the first article of the creed can be understood and explained only in the light of the second, which speaks of the turning of God in His free mercy to the world created by Him; of the faithfulness of the love in which, when He had created the world, He did not abandon it, but, in accordance with the fact that it is His, willed to be its God and Saviour and as such its Lord; of His kingdom, the kingdom of His almighty Word and living Spirit, which He causes to come and break into the creaturely world, which He establishes within it, and as the King of which He comes in person to be its Ruler, Helper and Deliverer. It is in this setting that we must understand creation, the Creator and the creature, or we cannot understand at all this whole tract of dogmatics. It is here and here alone that the different views and concepts of this sphere acquire relief and colour and contour. For here it is a matter of the sense in which God is called the Almighty and the Father in the creed. But the same holds good in a very particular way of our enquiry concerning heaven and the angels. By means of certain biblical references or even without them—for God is the Creator of heaven and earth—we can have some idea of what is meant by heaven. We can give the kind of answer already attempted. But we cannot really know at all why the formula and its biblical patterns always speak of heaven and earth rather than earth and heaven. Nor perhaps can we be certain why there is this mention of another sphere than that of earth, or what is involved in this sphere. This is possible only when we see how heaven and earth, in this hierarchical order and in their particularity and differentiation, are implicated in that great movement of God, in His turning in free mercy to the world, in the work of His faithfulness, in the coming of His kingdom, and, as we must also say, in the history of His covenant of grace, which secretly from the very first and publicly in its consummation bears the name of Jesus Christ. If this happening is seen,
[429] even in its recapitulation in the second article of the creed, there may be seen in this happening not only creation and the Creator but also the creature and man as God created him (although rather strangely there is no reference to him in the first article of the creed). There may be seen heaven and earth, which in the first article comprehend the whole, in their differentiation, their reality and their obviously irreversible order; and in and with heaven the angels of heaven. If we are to see all this, we must not fall back into the other and in some sense naturalistic mode of contemplation. Otherwise all that is to be seen in the sphere of the first article will lose its clarity and credibility. We must continue steadily to see everything—the Creator and His work, the creature in general and man in particular, and therefore heaven and earth, and in and with heaven the angels—in this movement and history. When we do this, we can know this whole sphere theologically. In respect of the problems which are our particular concern we shall thus have no need to resort either to philo-

sophy or to mythology, but with a genuine necessity and propriety we may reach certain dogmatic conclusions.

We shall first consider in its most general form the happening between God and the creature which transcends the act of creation. In it we have to do with a movement which has its origin in God and its target and goal in the creature. We may think of it in terms of the content of the second or even the third article of the creed, or more explicitly of the whole history which is partly reported and partly announced in the Bible. We may think in terms of what is envisaged in divine service, in preaching, baptism and the Lord's Supper, as the objective content, as the divine response confirming what is done by man. In the same sense, i.e., in relation to what is done on God's side, we may think in terms of the personal dealings of each individual Christian with God, or of the divine guidance of the Church both as a whole and in detail, or finally of the cosmic rule of God in its most comprehensive sense. But always we have to do with a movement in which God Himself is the *terminus a quo*[EN197] and the creature the *terminus ad quem*[EN198]. God speaks and is heard; He reveals Himself and is known; He comes and is present; He goes and comes again; He acts and effects; He gives and takes; He hastens and waits. Christian witness must and will be conscious that, because God Himself is the Subject, the reality behind all these statements, and the many other statements which give them their fulness and content, far surpasses any ideas or concepts which we might link with the terms used. But it must either be silent or become a denial if it refuses to speak in such statements; if it will not venture affirmations of this kind; or if it does so otherwise than with reference to the movement really executed by God. The God who did not really execute this movement would not be the living God of Christian witness. And to take up towards this movement an attitude of silence or denial is to do the same to the living God Himself. In this movement we have to do with a divine will and a divine way. We have to do with a divine intervention and a divine execution. We have to do with something begun and something accomplished. We have to do with a Whence and a Whither. Nor is the movement only in one direction. As God turns to the creature, there is also a turning of the creature to Him, not in its own strength, but in virtue of what God does in and with and to it. Thus, when it reaches its goal, the divine movement returns to its origin. The *resurrexit*[EN199] follows the *conceptus*[EN200] and *natus*[EN201], the *mortuus*[EN202] and *sepultus*[EN203]. An *ascendit*[EN204] follows the whole *descendit*[EN205]. The faith,

[430]

[EN197] starting point
[EN198] ending point
[EN199] He rose again
[EN200] conceived
[EN201] born
[EN202] dead
[EN203] buried
[EN204] He ascended
[EN205] He descended

obedience and prayer of the Church and of Christians follow the outpouring of the Holy Spirit. The only thing is that the cycle does not end as it were; the last word again becomes a first: *unde venturus est*[EN206]. Remission of sins, the resurrection of the flesh, eternal life, everything which can only be ascribed and given to the creature, which can only come upon it—all this comes as God Himself comes to the creature, speaking and acting, saving and resurrecting, in exclusive omnipotence and glory. The content of Christian witness is this movement. Otherwise it is not Christian witness.

But as the creature, man, is the goal and object of this movement, it is characterised as a movement executed within the creaturely world. God Himself is its Subject and Author. But this could also be said of the movement of intra-divine life of which we have to speak in the doctrine of God's triunity. That God the Father begets the Son and sends the Holy Ghost; that the Son is begotten of the Father and with Him sends the Holy Ghost; that the Holy Ghost proceeds from the Father and the Son—this is how we describe the inner life of God, the *opera Dei ad intra*[EN207], in which the movement to which we now refer has its basis and model. But this movement is an *opus Dei ad extra*[EN208]. It is a work in which God does not remain alone, in which He is not alive and active merely in Himself, but in which, as the One He is and will be to all eternity, He enters space and time, and the structure and conditions, and even the perceptibility and conceptuality of the created cosmos distinct from Himself. In His free mercy the One who made us has elected to be our God, God for us and with us. And in the execution of this decision He enters our world and makes its form His own. How else could He be our God, God for us and with us? How else could that movement of His concern us? How else could it reach and profit us? How else could we take part in it? How else could we be called by it and made responsible, humbled and exalted, judged and blessed? How else could it be the theme of Christian and therefore a human and creaturely witness? If it is a reality for us, then irrespective of the fact that God is its Subject and Author it really takes place where we really are, and therefore in our world, in the world created by God. It is here that it has its origin and goal.

[431] It is here that there takes place that *descendit*[EN209] and *ascendit*[EN210], that divine intervention and execution. It is here that the Holy Spirit is outpoured and returns to its origin in the form of the faith, obedience and prayer of the Church and of Christians. The height and depth of the free grace of God is that He has chosen Himself and the created world for the fact that He should be wholly alive and active within it, that He should wholly rule and initiate and fulfil His will within it, that He should speak and cause Himself to be heard within it, that He should promise and perform and plan and execute within it.

[EN206] whence He will come
[EN207] internal works of God
[EN208] external work of God
[EN209] He descended
[EN210] He ascended

As He causes His honour to dwell in the world created by Him, this becomes the theatre of His glory. We cannot ignore, deny or restrict this. If we did, we should violate the reality of the movement, its basis in God's free grace, and the living God Himself who is so gracious and who in His grace has such genuine dealings with His creature.

But if we see all this, and therefore see the divine history of the covenant and salvation, the event of Christ, and this as God's action in and with and to us, and therefore as His dealings in our creaturely world, with many other things we also see how the two great cosmic spheres of heaven and earth emerge distinctly and confront one another and then come together again in a genuine hierarchical order. And we see this with a clarity which obviously could not be imparted by even the most profound or exalted knowledge of the nature of the two spheres. It is from God's gracious action in the world, from this movement within it of His turning and faithfulness and kingdom, that we receive this clarity.

We shall take a first glance at earth. What is earth as seen in this historical context? Our starting-point is that it is the place of the man to whom this divine action refers, and therefore the goal and end of this action. Even though there is a return to its origin, the fact is not abolished but confirmed that earth is first and last the *terminus ad quem*EN211 of the divine action. The promise of God refers to man and must be fulfilled in him. The command of God refers to man and must be observed by him. But man is a creature of earth. Therefore it is for the earth's sake that God fulfils the movement to the world created by Him. It is on earth that His faithfulness is to be demonstrated and His kingdom established. For God wills to be for us and with us. We are the target of His whole movement to the creature. And we are of earth and on earth. Hence the divine qualification or distinction of earth consists in the very fact that it is the depth below to which God condescends in free grace; our sphere to which the God who reigns in the world stoops and comes down— and all this is in order that the secret will of God which was from the very first should have open and effective consequences in what He does here. In this context, therefore, there can be nothing derogatory or disgraceful in the fact that earth is below. It is not thereby disqualified. Its glory as this particular [432] sphere of God's creation is not contested. It is no less glorious than other real or possible spheres may be in different ways. It is below because the man to whom the free mercy of God is addressed is below. It is below in the light of the majesty of the God who is active for and to man in the world. Since this is what is at issue in the universe, or rather in the divine activity in the universe, what else could it be but the lower cosmos? It is to this sphere that the Word of the Most High is given. It is to this sphere that the Son of God humbles Himself, being born and obedient and dying on earth, accepting solidarity and unity with the creature of this sphere in order to exalt it in His own person beyond

---

EN211 ending point

this sphere, drawing all men after Himself. It is in this sphere that the Holy Spirit is outpoured, in order to return to His origin in the form of the faith, obedience and prayer of the Church and Christians. Is it not really a distinction for the earth to be the lower cosmos in this sense and context? It has at least the advantage over every other created sphere of being the goal of the free grace of God and therefore below.

But our present concern is with heaven. In that historical context, our first statement concerning it is simply that it is the place in the world from which God acts to and for and with man. If the great movement of the living God which is at issue is a movement within the created world, then a place within the world must be allotted to its *terminus a quo*[EN212], its origin, no less than to its goal and end. As the One who is at work in the world, God, who is the only Subject and Author of this movement, does not work above the world, but in the world, even in the sense that in fulfilment of His earthward action He occupies another place from which He may really come to man and have real dealings with him. Without this special place of God, and the distance therewith posited between Himself and man in his own place, there could obviously be no genuine intercourse between them. There could be no dialogue, but only a monologue on the part of God (or perhaps of man). There could be no drama, but either God or man could only live in isolation with no relationships to others or significance for them. If this is not the case; if the theme of Christian witness is neither the life of an isolated God nor isolated man, but the history enacted between them of isolation, estrangement, reconciliation and fellowship; and if this history is really enacted in our world, then this means that God as well as man has a distinctive sphere in this real world of ours. This distinctive sphere of God is heaven. Self-evidently this does not exclude but includes the fact that as the Creator and Lord of heaven and earth He can also enter and occupy particular spheres on earth which give to that movement its concrete—or, in the narrower sense, historical—forms. But heaven is primarily, originally and properly that which all God's particular spheres on earth become in virtue of the fact that God comes from it to speak and act on earth. Heaven is the Whence, the starting-point, the gate from which He sallies with all the demonstrations and revelations and words and works of His action on earth. And this is what distinguishes it from earth. This is what makes it genuinely and validly and definitively the upper cosmos in relation to earth. This is what gives it its own distinct and higher nature. God in the omnipotence of His grace is first in heaven to come down from heaven to man and earth. It is from heaven that He speaks and works. It is from heaven that His majesty encounters us. It is from heaven that His mystery limits us. Hence this place, heaven, is before earth and more and higher than earth. The mere fact that it is heaven does not bring this about, making it so superior to earth, and constituting it an exalted mystery for us who are on earth. No, this is due to the fact that it is

[433]

[EN212] starting point

from heaven that the kingdom of God comes to us, so that as such the coming kingdom of God is also the kingdom of heaven.

We adopt at this point an expression which is dominant in St. Matthew's Gospel and which characterises his theology. Outside the First Gospel there is only one reference (2 Tim. 4^{18}) to the βασιλεία ἐπουράνιος EN213 of the Lord. In the New Testament the word βασιλεία EN214 does not denote the institution or state or sphere but the act and exercise of kingly rule by the being and activity of a royal person. If in Matthew the phrase ἡ βασιλεία τοῦ θεοῦ EN215 is usually replaced by ἡ βασιλεία τῶν οὐρανῶν EN216, this certainly does not mean that the existence, action and dignity of God as this royal person are pushed into the background, let alone denied. In Mt. 12^{28}, and 21^{31}, 43 there are express references to the kingdom of God, which is also called the kingdom of the Father in Mt. 13^{43} and 26^{29}. "Thy kingdom come," is also the prayer of Mt. 6^{10}. In Matthew, therefore, heaven does not take the place of God. But in the distinctive language of the First Gospel the divine rule is described as a heavenly, so that we are continually invited by these passages to consider that where God rules heaven is also involved. It is to be noted that the Hebraic plural οὐρανοί EN217 is always used in this connexion.

In the LXX and the New Testament (I say this on the authority of E. Lohmeyer, *Das Unservater*, 1947, 78), the word "heaven" is always in the singular when it is explicitly or implicitly conjoined with earth to describe the totality of creation, whereas the plural is consistently used where it is linked with βασιλεία EN218 to denote the sphere and world of God, the reference being to heaven "in the form in which it is dissociated from everything earthly and related to God." If, then, in Mt. 6^9 (as distinct from Lk. 11^2) God is addressed as "Our Father in the heavens," and if in many other passages in Matthew He bears this name (Mt. 5^{16} and *passim*) or the adjectival alternative "heavenly Father" (Mt. 6^{14} and *passim*), this serves to emphasise that, apart from His own being as God and Father, God has in the relationship to us men indicated by the word "Father" (as my, our or your Father) the particular nature and essence of heaven. Or rather, His own divine and fatherly essence encounters us men—as though to be both near and distant, both knowable and unsearchable. He had invested Himself with an alien but not inappropriate or unworthy cloak—in the nature and essence of heaven.

In this sense His kingdom, and therefore His action as Ruler in the world which He has created and the covenant which He has instituted, can and must also be called the "kingdom of heaven." The fact that His kingdom has drawn near (Mt. 3^2, 4^{17}, 10^7), i.e., that it has come to earth, to the sphere of men, to us, includes within itself (as it is called the kingdom of heaven) the fact that in and with the being and speech and activity of God on earth, the reality of which is the content of the New Testament kerygma, there have also appeared and are active on earth the created but decidedly supraterrestrial possibilities and illuminations and powers of heaven. The μυστήρια EN219 of the kingdom of heaven (Mt. 13^{11}) are naturally the mysteries of God, i.e., the divine orders executed on earth and revealed to some but concealed from others. But how can these be seen by man at all? The answer is that although they are divine, they are also decidedly supraterrestrial and therefore heavenly, and now that the kingdom of God as the kingdom of heaven is nigh, they are reflected in the natural

[434]

EN213 heavenly kingdom
EN214 kingdom
EN215 the kingdom of God
EN216 the kingdom of heaven
EN217 Heavens
EN218 Kingdom
EN219 mysteries

relationships and processes of earth. Hence the kingdom of God as the kingdom of heaven can be likened to (ὁμοιώθη) or like (ὁμοία) good seed (Mt. 13²⁴), or a grain of mustard seed (Mt. 13³¹), or leaven (Mt. 13³³), or the king (Mt. 18²³), or the more than dubious οἰκοδεσπότης EN220 (Mt. 20¹), etc., and in this ὁμοιουσία EN221 it can be known by those to whom it is given and missed by those to whom it is not, but either way it is in the circle of human vision. As the kingdom of God is known or missed in these parables, heaven is also known or missed. But the converse is also true. As heaven is known or missed, necessarily and *per se* EN222 God is also known or missed. To be a scribe instructed in matters of the kingdom of heaven (Mt. 13⁵²), to enter the kingdom of heaven (Mt. 5²⁰ and *passim*), to have a share in the kingdom of heaven ("Yours is ...," Mt. 5³, ¹⁰, 19¹⁴), to sit down to meat in the kingdom of heaven with Abraham, Isaac and Jacob (Mt. 8¹¹), to be the least (Mt. 5¹⁹) or great (Mt. 18¹) in the kingdom of heaven, to do violence to the kingdom of heaven (Mt. 11¹²) or to close it *per nefas* EN223 to men (Mt. 23¹³)—all these are expressions in Matthew which have certainly to be understood as metaphors and comparisons, but as such they are to be regarded as of supreme reality, for here the kingdom of God is also called the kingdom of heaven, so that although it is a supraterrestrial it is not a supracosmic but a cosmic kingdom. God Himself undertakes to speak and act and give His help on earth, to be God for and with the man who lives on earth. But in so doing He steps down from the heaven created by Him, and as He does so heaven becomes a plurality of heavens, and He moves from these heavens in the direction of earth. Thus, when His kingdom comes to us, to earth, in this way, as its circumference and in its service, as the cosmic attestation of His distance in our proximity, or of His proximity as the One who is so radically distant from man on earth, there also comes to earth, if not all heaven, at least its essence, something of heaven, something of its cosmic possibilities and illuminations and powers; and His kingdom on earth acquires the character of the kingdom of heaven. In other words, when this Gospel uses the term "kingdom of heaven" it describes the kingdom of God as a kingdom which, because it is real in the divine, is also real in the cosmic sense, and has really entered the circle of human vision.

It may be responsibly affirmed that in this usage of the First Gospel we already have to do in principle and *in nuce* EN224 with the biblical view and doctrine of angels. In this sense the title and theme of this basic sub-section can and must be "The Kingdom of Heaven." But if we are to advance with any degree of certainty, we must examine this initial concept in rather greater detail. We have understood it in the light of the divine action in the world. And conversely we have understood the divine action and therefore the kingdom of God as the kingdom of heaven. Yet the linguistic usage of St. Matthew's Gospel might not seem to afford a sufficient scriptural basis for this interpretation. It is confirmed in substance, however, by the proposition that the royal measures of God as the Lord of earthly history are frequently described in the Old and New Testament as events which proceed from heaven and move earthward with the participation of heaven.

[435]   This is first true of all the external and spiritual benefits which God confers on man. A general biblical view and insight is formulated in Jas. 1¹⁷: "Every good gift and every perfect gift is from above, and cometh down from the Father of lights." The same truth is negatively stated in the saying of John the Baptist in Jn. 3²⁷: "A man can receive nothing, except it be given him from heaven." The pious man of later Old Testament days knows that "God hears him from his holy heaven" (Ps. 20⁶). He thus prays that God will send His goodness and

---

EN220 householder
EN221 likeness
EN222 in itself
EN223 wrongly
EN224 in a nutshell

truth from heaven to save him "from the reproach of him that would swallow him up" (Ps. 57³). A plastic representation of this divine help which comes right down from heaven to human need and folly is to be found in the narrative of Ex. 16²ᶠ, where God answers the murmuring of the people in the wilderness, and its ridiculous hankering for the fleshpots of Egypt, by causing the bread called "manna" to fall from heaven. It is no accident that this passage is so solemnly taken up and given a new meaning in Jn. 6³⁰ᶠ. Similarly, in Deut. 28¹² heaven is the rich chamber opened up by the Lord "to give the rain unto thy land in his season, and to bless all the work of thine hand." The fact that the divine benefits are already fixed and ready as it were in heaven, and have only to come down to the recipient, is also a distinctive New Testament conception, the meaning being that although the men have to receive the divine benefit they are already its lawful possessors and have already tasted the heavenly gift (Heb. 6⁴). It is not the end but the beginning of the apostolic proclamation that God has already blessed us with all spiritual blessings (Eph. 1³) and even set us (Eph. 2⁶) ἐν τοῖς ἐπουρανίοις EN225. Disciples who are despised and persecuted and calumniated on earth have in heaven the reward in which they may genuinely rejoice already (Mt. 5¹¹ᶠ). They are to heap up to themselves treasures in heaven, in contrast to the ephemeral treasures of earth (Mt. 6²⁰). Their names are already written in heaven (Lk. 10²⁰, Heb. 12²³). Their reward is reserved and secure for them in heaven (1 Pet. 1⁴). When our earthly tent perishes, we have a building prepared by God in heaven, an eternal house not made with hands (2 Cor. 5¹), the better country to which men of God have always been on the way in faith (Heb. 11¹⁶). There in heaven is our Jerusalem: the free woman which is the mother of us all (Gal. 4²⁶, Heb. 12²²); the πόλις EN226 which will come down from thence "prepared as a bride adorned for her husband" (Rev. 3¹², 21², ¹⁰); the heavenly πολίτευμα EN227 in relation to which our present status is that of colonists who live in this world but are lawful members of that which is above (Phil. 3²⁰).

There is also a heavenly dimension and scope, however, in the fact that to the divine measures there also belong judicial warnings and punishments. Heaven can remain closed and refuse the expected rain (1 K. 8²⁵, Deut. 11¹⁷). It can be as iron (Lev. 26¹⁹) or brass (Deut. 28²³) over man. The wrath of God can be "revealed from heaven against all ungodliness and unrighteousness of men" (Rom. 1¹⁸). In Is. 34⁵ we find the astonishing expression that the sword of the Lord has become drunk in heaven. "Behold, it shall come down upon Idumaea, and upon the people of my curse, to judgment." Or again, the windows of heaven can be opened (Gen. 7¹¹), and it is no longer a treasure-house but the firmament of waters (Gen. 1⁷), which come plunging down in a flood, as they also arise from the deeps, to destroy all life on the earth. Or again, it is from heaven that fire and brimstone are rained on Sodom and Gomorrah (Gen. 19²⁴ cf. 2 K. 1¹⁰ᶠ), as also hail-stones upon the routed Amorites (Josh. 10¹¹).

But all these divine benefits and judgments are only the epiphenomena of what comes primarily and centrally from heaven to earth, namely, the Word which the God who is gracious in His holiness and holy in His grace addresses to man as the Lord of the covenant; the Son in whose person He Himself becomes man and therefore earthly for our salvation. The earlier and later Hebrew traditions in this matter are probably not so different as often supposed when the statutes which according to the former are given to the people by the God who dwells and encounters Moses in the darkness of Sinai (Ex. 20²², Deut. 4³⁶, Neh. 9¹³) are said by the latter to have been spoken from heaven. In accordance with the later view the prophet of the exile (Ez. 1¹) ascribes his visions to the fact that "the heavens were   [436]

EN225 in heavenly places
EN226 city
EN227 commonwealth

147

opened." Similarly, the series of visions in the New Testament Apocalypse begins with the fact (Rev. 4^1) that a door is opened in heaven through which the seer can perceive everything which follows. What we have here is not merely a development in the history of religion, but at the same time, and as the material basis of this movement, a development in the history of revelation. The intensity, clarity and concreteness of the voice and Word of God are not lessened as heaven is increasingly described as their origin and they are increasingly separated from everything which might encounter man from within his own sphere and claim him with earthly authority and power. And as the voice of God is regarded as a heavenly voice, it is not idealised but genuinely seen in its reality. It is obviously envisaged as a final word regarding both the majesty and the urgent proximity of the directly divine mission and appearance of Jesus when the evangelical tradition (Mk. 1^{10} and par.) says of the beginning of His Messianic way in the baptism in Jordan that heaven was opened and the Spirit lighted upon Him like a dove and there came a voice—again from heaven—proclaiming: "Thou art my beloved Son, in whom I am well pleased." To this there corresponds the saying of Jesus (Jn. 1^{51}): "Verily, verily, I say unto you, Hereafter ye shall see heaven open, and the angels of God ascending and descending upon the Son of God." Not merely the majesty of God, but the reality with which He finally became man and earthly, seems to make necessary so emphatic a stress on the participation of heaven in the events of earth. For these sayings are not to the effect that an earthly man is approved and applauded from heaven, but that One has come from God and therefore from heaven, and has become man and earthly. The Jesus who receives Stephen when he too sees heaven opened (Ac. 7^{56}) is the Son of Man standing at the right hand of God. As we see from the vision of Daniel $7^{13f.}$, even the latest parts of the Old Testament know something more than the man over whom heaven opens. Now that the preceding beast-empires have been overcome, this man who comes on the clouds of heaven and therefore from heaven is One "like the Son of man" to whom as such there is granted power and glory and an indestructible kingdom. Again, in Rev. $12^{1f.}$ the birth and youth of the boy who is threatened by the dragon that appears at the same time, but who is "to rule all nations with a rod of iron," are described as "a great wonder in heaven"—not on earth. Again, in Acts 26^{19} Paul describes as a heavenly ὀπτασία [EN228] the appearance of Christ which came to him on the Damascus road. Again, he tells us in 1 Cor. 15^{47} that Christ is the second man who is from heaven. The Fourth Gospel also tells us that Jesus is from above (8^{23}), that He comes from above (3^{31}), or that He has come from above (3^{13}). He is "the true bread from heaven. For the bread of God is he which cometh down from heaven, and giveth life unto the world .... I am the bread of life" (Jn. $6^{32f.}$). And as He has come from heaven, and in confirmation of the fact that this is so. He ascends into (Ac. 1^{11}) and is received by heaven (Ac. 3^{21}), entering into heaven "to appear in the presence of God for us" (Heb. 9^{24}), and traversing the heavens (Heb. 4^{14}). It is from heaven that He has poured out His Spirit upon the community (Ac. 2^2, 1 Pet. 1^{12}). It is from there that He now speaks with it (Heb. 12^{25}). It is from there that it now expects Him (1 Thess. 1^{10}). And it is from there that He will come again, conclusively revealing Himself as the Lord (2 Thess. 1^7), appearing "in the clouds of heaven with power and great glory"(Mt. 24^{30}, 26^{64}, Mk. 14^{62}). In Him we are already blessed with all spiritual blessings in heaven (Eph. 1^3). In Him we are already set in heaven (Eph. 2^6). And if even Christian exhortation can sometimes take on a cosmic character, so that James $3^{15f.}$ can oppose to an earthly wisdom which is described as earthly and even demonic, a σοφία ἄνωθεν κατερχομένη [EN229] which is not contentious but peaceable, and Col. 3^2 can apparently sum up all Christian ethics in the antithesis: τὰ ἄνω

[EN228] vision
[EN229] wisdom descending from above

φρονεῖτε μὴ τὰ ἐπὶ τῆς γῆς EN230, the context of the latter passage makes it clear that there   [437]
is no question here of the establishment of ethics upon something cosmically higher, but
rather of its establishment upon the higher One who, as and because He is God coming in
Him to men, does in fact confront men as One who is cosmically higher, so that *per se*EN231
the establishment of man upon Him necessarily implies a cosmic *Sursum corda*EN232.

This then, or this One, is the substance of what according to the biblical witness comes
down (with blessing and punishment in its train) from heaven to earth because from God to
man. It is He who bears the movement of God to the cosmos. In Him there is fulfilled that
turning of God. He is the faithfulness of God in person. He is the kingdom of God and
therefore the kingdom of heaven. For this is what it is only in relationship to Him. Thus
heaven is decisively the place where and from and to which He is. For this reason we have
still to receive conclusive instruction concerning it from Scripture.

We have not so far considered all the biblical statements from which it emerges that the
Old and New Testaments see heaven as a cosmic reality constituted and consolidated by the
fact that, as there is an operation of God from heaven, so there is a being of God in heaven. It
is obvious that if we are speaking of the living God of the biblical witness the distinction is
only provisional. For this God is as He works and works as He is. But even in this context we
cannot dissolve or ignore the second statement that He is as He works. It is to safeguard this
that we make the provisional distinction. God will not be dissolved into a relationship in
which we find ourselves. Otherwise He is no longer God, and the relationship itself is dissolved into the mere idea of it. To the real Whence of the divine activity there necessarily
corresponds a real Where of its origin, a real place of God as its Subject and Author. This real
place of God as the Lord acting in the world is heaven. Even heaven would not be a cosmic
reality in the biblical sense if it were only the Whence of the divine activity and not as such
also the Where, the place of its Subject and Author. The former itself would not be true
without the latter. Heaven is a place: the place of God in view of which we have to say that
God is not only transcendent in relation to the world but also immanent and present within
it; the place of God from which His dealings with us, the history of the covenant, can take
place in the most concrete sense, and His majesty, loftiness and remoteness can acquire the
most concrete form, where otherwise they would simply be a product of human fantasy. As
the place of God heaven is, of course, a place which is inconceivable to us. It cannot be
compared with any other real or imaginary place. It is inaccessible. It cannot be explored or
described or even indicated. All that can be affirmed concerning it is that it is a created place
like earth itself and the accessible reality of earth which we can explore and describe or at
least indicate; and that it is the place of God. The final point is the decisive one. And for
good reasons the Old and New Testaments do not hesitate to speak of the fact that God is in
heaven and heaven is the place of God.

We cannot pray the Lord's Prayer without saying at once: "Our Father ὁ ἐν τοῖς
οὐρανοῖς EN233 (Mt. 6⁹), and this is continually emphasised: "Flesh and blood hath not
revealed it unto thee, but my Father which is in heaven" (Mt. 16¹⁷). "If two of you shall agree
on earth as touching any thing that they shall ask, it shall be done for them of my Father
which is in heaven" (Mt. 18¹⁹). "Love your enemies ... that ye may be the children of your
Father which is in heaven" (Mt. 5⁴⁴ᶠ). If we take seriously the words "Father" and "my" and
"our" and "your" in these verses, surely we must do the same with the phrase "in heaven." But
if we do we are forced to say that God is in heaven as His place. And there is also the witness

---

EN230 set your affection on things above, not on things on the earth
EN231 in itself
EN232 Lift up your hearts
EN233 which art in heaven

of the Old Testament at any rate in the later books. If we ask where God is, we seek in vain for the banal answer that He is everywhere. The omnipresence of God in the biblical sense (cf. Ps. 139⁸ᶠ·) really means something more spiritual and dynamic than this "everywhere." What we are told is that "God is in the heavens" and therefore that "he hath done whatsoever he hath pleased" (Ps. 115³). He is "above," "on high" (Job 31²), "in the height of heaven" (Job 22¹²), and in this sense ἐν ὑψίστοις ᴱᴺ²³⁴ (Lk. 2¹⁴). "God is in heaven, and thou upon earth," we are told in Eccles. 5² in an intentionally sharp antithesis. He is thus called the" Lord of heaven" (Ps. 136²⁶, Jon. 1⁹, Dan. 2¹⁹). Heaven is His holy and glorious habitation (Is. 63¹⁵). Perhaps in the saying in Jn.14² about the Father's house in which there are many mansions we have also to think of heaven. It can also be called the upper storey (Amos 9⁶) from which He beholds everything that is done on earth (Ps. 14², Job 28²⁴ and *passim*), so that the tempted man may boast: "And now, behold, my witness is in heaven, and one who knows on high" (Job 16¹⁹).

The decisive view, however, is the one according to which heaven itself is the throne of God (Ps. 2⁴, Ez. 10¹, Is. 66¹ and *passim*). Hence to swear by heaven is to swear by this throne and the One who sits on it (Mt. 5³⁴, 23²²). Yet this throne is not a place of rest. It is rather the official seat of God. The sense emerges clearly in Ps. 103¹⁹: "The Lord hath prepared his throne in the heavens; and his kingdom ruleth over all." From the fact that God is enthroned in heaven (Ps. 33¹⁴, 123¹) we learn that He is not merely present or looks down from there, but that He reigns there, exercising authority and rule. The sovereignty with which He does so is drastically stated in Ps. 2⁴; "He that sitteth in the heavens shall laugh: the Lord shall have them in derision," i.e., He shall mock the raging of the nations, the futile imaginations of the peoples, the pretensions of earthly rulers and the counsels of the rulers. This divine laughter is not to be thought of merely as the amused laughter of a disinterested spectator. But when God sees and laughs, there takes place something corresponding on earth. In the idea of God seated on His heavenly throne the being and work of God in and from heaven merge into each other and are one. There is no suggestion that He is there in a kind of frozen immobility. The One who is enthroned in heaven can also be called the One "that rideth upon the heaven of heavens, which were of old" (Ps. 68³³). And how He can come from thence to be mightily near to His own—we shall hear more about this later—is very powerfully described in Ps. 18⁶⁻¹⁸ and especially in v. 13: "The Lord also thundered in the heavens, and the Highest gave his voice," or v. 9: "He bowed the heavens also, and came down: and darkness was under his feet," or v. 16 f.: "He sent from above, he took me, he drew me out of many waters. He delivered me from the strong enemy."

The New Testament gives fulness and precision to this view by describing Jesus Christ not merely as the One who has come from heaven, has ascended to heaven, and is to be expected from heaven as the definitive revelation of God, but also as the One who is in heaven. These points are all gathered up in the remarkable saying in Jn. 3¹³: "No man hath ascended up to heaven, but he that came down from heaven, even the Son of man which is in heaven." In view of this the saying in Col. 3¹ may well be regarded as the normative biblical definition of heaven: Εἰ οὖν συνηγέρθητε τῷ Χριστῷ, τὰ ἄνω ζητεῖτε οὗ ὁ Χριστός ἐστιν ἐν δεξιᾷ τοῦ θεοῦ καθήμενος ᴱᴺ²³⁵. Where is this whole strange "above" from which we are told (not without the accompanying warnings) that all good gifts come, where our names are already written, our house or city or country awaits us, our reward or treasure or inheritance is already prepared, and we ourselves are secretly present? Where is this heaven? The answer is that it is where Christ is. But Christ sits at the right hand of God. We cannot

---

ᴱᴺ²³⁴ in the highest
ᴱᴺ²³⁵ If ye then be risen with Christ, seek those things which are above, where Christ is seated on the right hand of God

explain the ἐστίν EN236 without at once considering this καθήμενος EN237, which leads us at once *in media res sc. gestas et gerendas* EN238. For the session and therefore the right hand of God are explained by the fact that a consideration of the Christ who is in heaven brings us again and this time fully into the historical context of the divine activity. To "sit" is to be enthroned and therefore to enjoy and exercise power, to rule or reign. And the idea of the right hand of God points in the same direction. If Christ is seated at the right hand of God, this does not mean that He has a mere place of honour as a spectator, and that He is now indolent. In point of detail, of course, the interpretation is rather more difficult. [439]

According to the linguistic usage of the Old Testament what is signified by the right hand is His right arm and therefore God Himself active in His omnipotent righteousness and goodness as Judge, victorious Helper, Liberator and Protector; in short, in the exercise of His kingly might. If, then, it is said of Jesus in Acts 2³³ and 5³¹ that He has been exalted by the right hand of God (in His resurrection from the dead), it seems first as though He is wholly the object of this divine activity, the One to whom God has acted in this way and who is therefore exalted. But in Acts 5³¹ we are told that He has been exalted by the right hand of God to be an ἀρχηγὸς καὶ σωτήρ EN239, and therefore that as the object of this divine action He has been made its Subject. Thus His exaltation consists in His institution to the exercise of the royal power of God to which He owes this exaltation.

But the right hand of God can also mean His right side, and in this case we have to think of the throne of God and a place at its right side. This seems to be the meaning in Heb. 8¹ and 12², where it is expressly said that Christ is seated at the right hand of the throne of God. The reference in Mt. 26⁶⁴ is to the right hand of δύναμις EN240, and in Heb. 1³ and 8¹ to the right hand of μεγαλοσύνη EN241. In this case to be at God's right hand is to be in His direct proximity and to have a direct share in His action. It is obvious that the two meanings are materially the same. But problems obviously arise which we cannot leave unsolved in our present investigation. We must therefore try to clear up the difficulties involved.

We may confidently assume that the place taken by Christ at the right side of God is definitely not that of a privileged spectator of the divine activity. On the ancient oriental view, the one who sits or stands (Ac. 7⁵⁶) or simply is (Rom. 8³⁴, 1 Pet. 3²²) at the right hand of a ruler is the one who in his person represents that of the ruler, acting for him in his name and with his authority. In the first instance, therefore, the fact that Christ is at the right hand of God means metaphorically that in His relationship to God He is this agent or grand vizier of God, His first official act being to pour out upon His community the Holy Spirit whom He for His part has received from the Father (Ac. 2³³).

But again, in the place which He has taken at the right side of God Christ does not have only a partial share in the royal might of God, but He has assumed it wholly and altogether. "All power is given unto me in heaven and in earth" (Mt. 28¹⁸). When God set Him at His right hand, He set Him "far above all principality, and power, and might, and dominion, and every name that is named, not only in this aeon, but also in that which is to come: and he hath put all things under his feet" (Eph. 1²⁰ᶠ·). The notion of the place of Christ beside the throne of God, and the picture of the grand vizier, should not therefore be pressed. They are limited by the fact that in Rev. 3²¹ Jesus Himself can say to the community of Laodicaea: "I also overcame, and am set down with my Father in his throne," and by the reference in Rev. 7¹⁷ to "the Lamb which is in the midst of the throne" and in Rev. 22³ to "the throne of God

---

EN236 is
EN237 seated
EN238 into the middle of things, namely, of things that have been and must be done
EN239 prince and saviour
EN240 power
EN241 majesty

and of the Lamb." It is not the case, then, that we have to take into account another domin-ion side by side with and limiting that of Christ. On the contrary, it is obvious that the idea of rivalry between the authority of Jesus Christ and a higher divine authority is ruled out by the conception of His session at the right hand of God. The power and majesty exercised by Christ are the whole might and majesty of the One at whose right hand He sits. They have all the authority of God.

But again, this does not mean that God has abdicated and is indolent. This is excluded by the opening verses of Psalm no, which are frequently adduced by the New Testament in this

[440] connexion (Mt. 22[41f.], Ac. 2[34f.], Heb. 1[13] and *passim*): "Sit thou at my right hand, until I make thine enemies thy footstool. The Lord shall send the rod of thy strength out of Zion." Only on this presupposition can the Psalm continue: "Rule thou in the midst of thine enemies." When Christ sits at His right hand in that plenitude of power, God does not cease to be the living and omnipotent God. He is God in supreme activity in the fact that He gives Christ this sovereignty and institutes Him into this fulness of kingly rule. And the kingly rule of Christ is simply His own, and its exercise His own action. When He gives Him all things. He does not deprive Himself of anything. Nothing is taken from Him. But in this way He comes fully into His own—His glory and right and the goal of His will. Being wholly in Christ (2 Cor. 5[19]), and putting all things under Him (Ps. 110). He is no less the Most High. In Christ, indeed, He is it in full force and majesty. He rules as Jesus Christ rules as King. The relationship between Him and Christ is that which the Fourth Gospel and Paul in his commentary on Ps. 110 (1 Cor. 15[24f.]) expressly describe as that of Father and Son. But this Father can as little be limited, rivalled or even effaced by the Son as He for His part can limit, rival or efface the Son. It is only when the Son works that He really works. They are not two persons in our sense of the term, i.e., two different subjects which will and work independently, so that their activities might cut across and restrict one another, and necessarily give rise to a conflict of priority and authority. But as the ancient doctrine of the Trinity had it, they are two modes of being (τρόποι ὑπάρξεως) of the one divine Subject, two times the one God, the one omnipotent will, the one eternal righteousness, goodness and mercy. What, then, is the difference? God the Father is the one true God in so far as He is this and only this, and as such is in heaven. The Son is the same true God in so far as He became and was and is also as such true man to all eternity, having come on earth to be born and to suffer and to die. And the exaltation of the Son to the right hand of the Father is that in heaven as on earth the one true God will and can be no other than the One who is also true man and was born and suffered and died on earth. He wills to be this in heaven and in the whole cosmos. The fulfilment and revelation of this will of the one true God is the resurrection of Jesus Christ from the dead, which forms the explicit or implicit presupposition in all the passages in the New Testament which speak of the elevation of Jesus Christ to the right hand of the Father. For in His resurrection, completed in the ascension, it took place that as true God and true man He was taken from earth and set in heaven. And it is simply this one event seen from different standpoints—now as the act of the one true God who is the Father, and now as that of the one true God who is the Son—if the Easter-event is sometimes described as His resur-rection in the power of the Father and sometimes as the resurrection which He Himself has accomplished; if in Ac. 2[33] and 5[31] and Eph. 1[20] we are told that He was exalted by God or by the right hand of God, and in Heb. 1[3], 10[12] and 12[2] we read that He seated Himself at the right hand of God. Again, it is only a question of standpoint if in Heb. 10[12] (with reference to Dan. 7[14]) we learn that Christ seated Himself for ever (εἰς τὸ διηνεκές) at the right hand of God, and in Eph. 1[20f.] that His kingdom will last into the future aeon as well as the present, whereas in 1 Cor. 15[24f.] Paul takes the beginning of Ps. 110 to mean that when everything is subject to the Son He will hand over His completed and manifested kingdom to the Father who has subjected everything to Him and is thus excepted from this subjection, so that when

it is accomplished "the Son also himself will be subject unto him that put all things under him." And this leads us to the well-known conclusion at the end of v. 28: ἵνα ᾖ ὁ θεὸς πάντα ἐν πᾶσιν EN242 If our former deliberations are correct, it would be foolish to relate this saying merely to the last link in Paul's exposition, and therefore to the subjection of the Son. On the contrary, it sums up the whole passage. God is all in all in His subjecting of all things to the Son. And He is again all in all in the Son's subjecting of Himself to the Father. In both cases, in the action of Father and Son alike, it is a matter of all things in heaven and earth, in [441] the heights and depths of the created universe, in the whole history of all created spheres and individuals. And in both cases, in the action of Father and Son alike, the one true God Himself is all in all: the beginning, middle and end; the origin and goal; the fulfilment and limit; the power and the effect. This then, the glory of the one true God, constitutes the relationship between Father and Son, between Him that sits on the throne and Him that sits at His right hand.

But to return to our previous question, where is this above? Where is heaven? The answer of Col. 3¹ has now been filled out. "Where Christ sitteth on the right hand of God," there is the glory of the one true God who is not merely this, not merely the Father, but who as the Son also became true man, and who even as this Son, and therefore as true God and true man, was not only once on earth, but is also with the Father in heaven, ἐν ὑψηλοῖς EN243 (Heb. 1³).

It is this one true God who dwells and is enthroned and rules in heaven, who looks down from this upper storey on the children of men, who laughs at His enemy, and who is not merely the Witness but the Judge and Helper and Deliverer of His own. How concrete everything which is said by the Old Testament along these lines becomes when we are told by the New Testament that it is this God who is in heaven, and works there, and thence also on earth; that it is this God who is the θεὸς ἐν ὑψίστοις EN244 (Lk. 2¹⁴)!

At this point we might quote the solemn words of *Qu.* 49 of the *Heidelberg Catechism.* "Of what value to us is the ascension of Christ? First, that He is our Advocate in heaven in the presence of His Father. Second, that we have our flesh in heaven as a sure pledge that He as the Head will take us to Himself as the members. Third, that He sends us His Spirit as an earnest by the power of which we seek those things which are above, where Christ is seated at the right hand of the Father, and not those things which are on earth." What is said here concerning the ascension is also the final word concerning heaven itself. For it is the fact that He, the Son, the one true God who became one with our poor flesh, the omnipotent mercy of this one true God, is there for us above in heaven, which confirms this above, which makes heaven higher than earth, which distinguishes it as the upper cosmos, and yet which also sets it in indissoluble union with earth. Is He only in heaven? Of course not ! For the *inde venturus* EN245 is also true; and the end and goal of all earthly history is the definitive revelation of His glory and therefore that of the Father, the one glory of the one true God; and already by His Holy Spirit He is not remote from His community on earth in the present course of earthly history, but by His Word (*kerygma*, baptism and the Lord's Supper), He is genuinely present as very God and very man. Again, He is not only in heaven because in His exaltation He has traversed the heavens (Heb. 4¹⁴), ascending up "far above all heavens" (Eph. 4¹⁰), and becoming ὑψηλότερος τῶν οὐρανῶν EN246 (Heb. 7²⁶). God Himself and His right hand or side are not merely in heaven. The heaven of heavens cannot contain Him.

EN242 that God may be all in all
EN243 on high
EN244 God in the highest
EN245 thence He will come
EN246 higher than the heavens

And Jesus Christ shares fully in this transcendence of God over heaven which is merely His throne. But neither this nor His presence on earth alters in the very slightest the fact that even as the Giver of His Spirit and in His presence on earth He is still for us in heaven, in this created above, and therefore truly in our world, and in this world truly above us. And the fact that He is there, that His work from there is effective for us, that He, this One, the Son in His unity with the Father, is for us the one true God, constitutes and consolidates heaven as the counterpart of earth, as the mystery, the upper cosmos, which limits but is for this reason near to us as creatures of earth. He rules, and He rules in the kingdom of heaven.

[442] God rules in the kingdom of heaven. This means that His work, His speech and action, the whole execution of His omnipotent mercy, commences in heaven, and then comes down from heaven to us on earth in a form which is partly determined by its commencement in heaven. By the fact that it comes to us in this way, in a form which is partly determined by its heavenly commencement, we are invited to consider first this heavenly commencement, and with the required reservations to say what is necessary and possible concerning it.

Reserve is demanded because, although heaven as the place of God is known as a place, as another created place, as a higher cosmic sphere confronting our own, beyond these delimiting definitions it is unknown and inconceivable, and therefore a mystery. Even the revelation of God does not give us any further information. This means that as we direct our attention to this heavenly commencement of the Word and work of God we cannot expect and we shall not try to amass data concerning heaven as such or the relationship of heaven and earth. In any such attempt we should be building on sand, missing what we could attain, and failing to attain what we cannot. How much or little we shall know of heaven in itself and heaven and earth as such when we come into the presence of God and look on the new heaven made earthly and the new earth made heavenly, remains to be seen. But here and now—and surely there and then too—it is wisely arranged that we cannot know what we do not need to know and for our own good ought not to try. Because it is the place of the God who is and works there, the nature of the upper cosmos can be known to us only to the extent that it is illumined for us by the heavenly commencement of His Word and work with reference to us. For the rest, i.e., in itself and as such, it is a mystery, and here and now at least will always be so. In the further step which we have now to take we shall have to respect this mystery. Respect for this belongs essentially to the knowledge which is possible, salutary and necessary at this point. Any attempt at an independent ontology of heaven would at once estrange us from this knowledge and lead us into the realm of an impossible, dangerous and forbidden desire for knowledge. We must keep strictly to the fact that we have only to see and know of heaven what may be seen and known as it is illuminated by the kingdom which comes from heaven. Hence we have not really been led to the threshold of an ontology of heaven by our deliberations thus far.

On the other hand, they have set us the task of giving methodical consideration to the heavenly commencement of the kingdom of God which comes on earth, and therefore to the kingdom of heaven in the original and strictest sense of the concept, i.e., in so far as it is first in heaven and only then on earth. To the extent that it subsequently comes to us on earth, we can and must say that by the revelation of God which consists in the coming to us of His kingdom we are taught concerning the commencement of this kingdom, and therefore empowered and summoned to give it this consideration. Our reserve cannot, therefore, go to the point of evading this consideration or refusing the necessary and accessible thoughts on what can be seen and   [443] known in this connexion. There is indeed a visible and perceptible illumination of the upper cosmos as the Word and work of God which refer to us find their commencement there. And if it is impossible, dangerous and forbidden to try to know more of this upper cosmos than is visible and perceptible in this illumination, in another sense it is also impossible, dangerous and forbidden not to see what is to be seen or know what is to be known. At this point, again, we must err neither *in excessu*EN247 nor *in defectu*EN248, i.e., neither in the direction of misplaced speculation nor in that of an equally misplaced scepticism. The objection that the heavenly commencement of the divine Word and work, and that which is to be seen and known in the light of heaven, is not a proper object of faith and cannot therefore be a true theme of dogmatics, is without substance. The theme of faith and dogmatics is the proclamation of the Christian Church. But the theme of this proclamation is the kingdom of God come on earth. If this kingdom of God is in fact the kingdom of heaven, i.e., the royal speech and action of God which commences in heaven and come from heaven to us, the heavenly commencement, and therefore that which is to be seen and known of heaven in the light of this happening, certainly belongs to the theme of faith and therefore of dogmatics. If we refuse to know anything of what is to be seen and known at this point, it might be tragically the case that we refuse to know anything of the kingdom of God which really comes to us. For this reason, we are genuinely invited, summoned and empowered to attain even in this respect the clarity which is both necessary and possible.

We may begin by affirming that heaven, the above where Christ sits at the right hand of God, the whence of the kingdom which comes to us, is certainly not a vacuum, however inconceivable it may be to us. It is not nothing. It is inaccessible and unknown, but it is a real context of being. In its own very different way it is just as real as the earth which is ontically and noetically our sphere. The place where God is as He turns to the world created by Him itself belongs to this world of His creatures. It has, therefore, a creaturely and as such a true being; a being under very different presuppositions and conditions from our own, but a true being. And in this true being it is heaven under God, at His disposal, and therefore obedient to Him. In the first instance, this is true in the general sense in which it is true of all creatures. Like all creatures

---

EN247 by saying too much
EN248 by saying too little

heaven was created good, i.e., according to His own purpose and for His own ends. He gave it the form and constitution which adapt it to serve Him and to be perfect in this service. But there is also a special sense in which this is true. Heaven is under God and at His disposal in the sense that it has a particular place and function in the historical context, in the plan and execution, of the divine purpose of salvation and grace for man. The being of heaven is concretely determined by the fact that Christ is seated there at the right hand of God. It is the creaturely place of that unity of the Father and the Son; of the one true God in His might and majesty as such; and of the same one true God who is also true man. That it is the creaturely place of this unity, and the creaturely whence of occurrence on earth, is grounded in this unity and will find fulfilment in it; and this is the peculiarity of its being which we may and can and must know for all the incomprehensibility with which it otherwise confronts us. Heaven cannot remain unaffected but is supremely impelled and determined and fashioned by the fact that it is this place, this whence. In face and as the witness of this presence of God, this commencement of His Word and work, it cannot be neutral, let alone inimical or antithetical to this Word and work. Whatever may be the manner in which heaven was created good, as God is over and in it in fulfilment of His purpose of grace and salvation, it cannot express and actualise itself except in acts and attitudes which acknowledge the right and necessity, the supreme glory, the true wisdom and beauty, of that which commences in its presence, in proof of its willingness and readiness for helpful participation in this commencement. Whatever the manner of heaven, its being is an obedient being.

Thus our first point is that something is done in heaven, so surely is it the place of God, and so surely is something done on earth as subsequently and from heaven it too becomes the place of God. And as this occurrence on earth in correspondence with what God does is creaturely, so that which takes place in heaven in accordance with the divine action is creaturely. And we may go on to say that this heavenly happening is not neutral, independent, opposed or arbitrary in relation to the divine will and action. It is the fulfilment of the will of God. That is, it is a happening in which the creature, the heavenly creature, whatever its manner and kind, is obedient to and actually serves the will of God. The presence of God in heaven, the origin and commencement there of His action in the world, makes it necessary that He should find there the obedience of His creature; that His creature in heaven should do His will. This corresponds exactly to the fact that the coming of God from heaven to earth, if His action in the world is to attain its goal and end in man (thus involving for man a new origin and commencement), makes it necessary that God should find on earth the obedience of His creature; that His will should be done on earth too; and that here too it should be done in definite acts and attitudes on the part of His creatures.

In saying this, we have brought ourselves into tacit relationship with a verse which cannot but be regarded as of central importance, namely, the third petition of the Lord's Prayer: "Thy will be done in earth, as it is in heaven" (Mt. 6¹⁰). In codex D and some old Latin manuscripts, which omit the ὡς EN249, this is made into a prayer that the will of God should be done both in heaven and on earth. It thus becomes a petition for the triumph of the will of God throughout the universe, opposition being presumed in heaven as well. Now although the New Testament nowhere suggests that heaven itself can have anything to do with opposition to the will of God, it does refer to opposition which takes place in heaven too. This interpretation cannot, therefore, be described as materially impossible. On the other hand, the ὡς EN250 in Matt. 6¹⁰ is so overwhelmingly supported that we must accept the common rendering, i.e., that the will of God should be done on earth as the end and goal of the divine purpose and activity as it is done in heaven as its origin and commencement; that it should be done on earth to-day and to-morrow as it was always done in heaven; that it should be done on earth by the obedience of the earthly creature as it is done in heaven by the obedience of the heavenly; that it should be done on earth with the same self-evident necessity as it is done in heaven. Lohmeyer (*op. cit.*, p. 87) seems to leave it an open question whether the meaning is that earth should be raised to heaven or heaven should descend to earth. In the light of the second petition the latter seems to be more obvious, i.e., that from heaven God should cause His will to be done on earth as in heaven. Lohmeyer is certainly right when he says that the petition presupposes that heaven and earth are still divided or at least distinct, and asks therefore that this differentiation should cease in the day of consummation. But its material presupposition is that the will of God is done in heaven. Heaven is the sphere of the created world where God has always found the obedience which he has still to find in our sphere, so that we in our sphere, where it is not found, have to orientate ourselves by that in which it is, and we can thus know what we ask when with Jesus (who had no need of such orientation) we pray: "Thy will be done." Hence we can and should think of heaven as the creaturely sphere in which the will of God, which we pray should be done on earth, takes place already, and has always done so. Not incorrectly, Chrysostom (quoted from Lohmeyer, p. 88) has given us the following paraphrase :"O Lord, let us be so zealous for the heavenly kingdom that we may will as it does."

[445]

The idea of heavenly occurrence is not unknown in other parts of the Bible, especially the Old Testament. And in the relevant texts it is always a happening which is initiated by God in His gracious and judicial action as the Lord of the covenant with Israel, and must therefore serve Him, but which also has its correspondence in an earthly history which runs parallel with it or follows it. It is part of the description of the coming terrible day of the Lord in later prophecy that God causes heaven as well as earth to be shaken and to tremble. In Is. 13¹³, for example, this is one of the many signs of the divine judgment executed on Babylon; in Joel 3¹⁶ the voice of God which goes out from Jerusalem brings this and many similar things to pass in the great moment when worldwide judgment and the beginning of a new age of salvation for Judah and Jerusalem are to take place in the valley of Jehoshaphat, in the valley of decision; and in Hag. 2⁶ ²¹ it forms part of the promise of a new and more splendid temple as this is given to Zerubbabel, Joshua and the whole people. The remoteness and height ascribed to heaven in the language and thinking of the Old Testament must be remembered if we are to assess what is involved when we are told that it cannot remain intact or neutral in the day of judgment and salvation, but must undergo with men and beasts and land and sea and sun and moon and stars the great convulsion which this day means not only for the history of the nations but for the whole earth and therefore, and especially, for heaven. It is no accident if we find this view of the eschatological shaking of heaven expressly adopted in

---

EN249 as
EN250 as

certain passages of the New Testament (Mt. 24^{29}, Ac. 2^{19}, Heb. 12^{26}). And even more forceful than this view of the shaking of heaven with the consummation which dawns on earth is the tumultuous cry of Is. 64$^{1f.}$: "Oh that thou wouldest rend the heavens, that thou wouldest come down, that the mountains might flow down at thy presence, as when the melting fire burneth, the fire causeth the waters to boil, to make thy name known to thine adversaries, that the nations may tremble at thy presence! When thou didst terrible things which we looked not for, thou camest down, the mountains flowed down at thy presence. For since the beginnings of the world men have not heard, nor perceived by the ear, neither hath the eye seen, O God, beside thee, what he hath prepared for him that waiteth for him."

[446]

The fiery apocalyptic of these passages must not blind us to others which speak of a cosmic occurrence, a shaking of heaven and earth, of a very different character, namely, those passages in the Psalms in which heaven and earth are summoned to praise the Lord as though they were a choir or orchestra (Ps. 69^{34}, 148^4), or in which it is said of them that like chroniclers or court poets they recount the glory of God, and like messengers proclaim His handiwork (Ps. 19$^{1f.}$). or declare His righteousness, since "God is judge himself" (Ps. 50^6), or praise His wonders (Ps. 89^5). In this praise of God which is sung or played by the heavens we are not to think of the sounding of a cosmic organ like the Greek harmony of the spheres, outside time and unrelated to anything or related to all things. The One whom the heavens praise is the God of Israel who led His people through the Red Sea; the God of Abraham, Moses, David and the Son of David. It is His glory which they tell and His wonders and righteousness which they declare. They themselves are the work of His hands. It is incontestable that in these passages creaturely nature, in its supreme form of heaven, is summoned to be the witness of God. But it is highly contestable whether these passages, like others in the Psalms and Job which refer to the rest of creation, represent or reveal an abstract natural theology. There are no "nature-psalms" in the pure sense in the Old Testament. As the contexts show, what these Psalms tell us is that the cosmos, and therefore the upper cosmos, attests the God who called the fathers, and revealed Himself to His people at Sinai, and gave it an inheritance in Canaan. And the wider setting in which we have to see it is naturally the poor praise on earth which, even as the heavens extol Him, is offered to God, or still withheld from Him, by this people of His. Hence in the praise and declaration of heaven referred to in these Psalms we are not so far removed from the shaking and rending of the heavens on the day of the Lord as attested by the prophets. They, too, speak of an obedient being of heaven, and particularly of a participation of heaven in the history of the great acts of God on earth. The attempt to harmonise them in detail with the prophets is, of course, both hopeless and irrelevant. All these passages speak of the heaven which, because God dwells in it, is as incomprehensible to us as God Himself. Their contradictions cannot and do not need to be resolved. It is enough that in their different ways they say that which is succinctly summarised in Mt. 6^{10}, namely, that there is done in heaven the will of God which, in fulfilment of what God has resolved and commenced in heaven, is to be done on earth.

What Luke tells us concerning the entry of Jesus into Jerusalem (19$^{37f.}$) is a solemn acknowledgment and welcoming of this heavenly fulfilment by the earth which is affected by it: "And when he was come nigh, even now at the descent of the mount of Olives, the whole multitude of his disciples began to rejoice and praise God with a loud voice for all the mighty works that they had seen; saying, Blessed be the King that cometh in the name of the Lord: peace in heaven, and glory in the highest." All the details in this description are significant. What is at issue is an entry—the entry of the King into the royal city which belongs to but is estranged from Him. This entry takes the form of a descent (κατάβασις). There are verbal reminiscences of the manifestation of the angels in Lk. 2$^{13f.}$, the angelic host being now replaced by a multitude of disciples singing the same praises of God. By the inversion of the phrases the song of the disciples becomes genuinely antiphonal to that of the angels. What is done on earth, the fulness of the acts of power which have now taken place, is crowned and confirmed in the Messianic entry. And behind all these things in the fore ground there are [447] seen the heavenly presuppositions in the background. The man of the divine εὐδοκία EN251 has become the one King manifesting Himself with the divine εὐλογία EN252. The peace of God, which has come on earth according to Lk. 2¹⁴, is now magnified as the peace which rules in heaven. The glory to God in the highest, in general correspondence to the change of place, is no longer the first phrase but the last, and therefore the horizon of the whole. It would be hard to imagine a finer commentary on Mt. 6¹⁰ than Lk. 19³⁷ᶠ· taken in conjunction with Lk. 2¹³ᶠ·, especially when we compare these passages with those in the Old Testament which speak of the movement of heaven in relationship to that of earth.

God rules in heaven as in a creaturely sphere. We have thus to reckon with a happening which takes place in this sphere. But this heavenly happening is determined by the fact that the goal of the lordship of God by which it has to orientate itself is a happening in our sphere, on earth. If we can assume this, we can venture the next step—not forgetting the high incomprehensibility of the whole subject—and say that this heavenly happening is one which is ordered, harmonious and integrated, but also differentiated. If its nature is unknown, we are not wholly ignorant of its purpose, function and direction. It takes place under the lordship of God, and therefore, because the lordship of God is that of the One at whose right hand Christ is seated, under the determination that it should find its continuation and correspondence in a happening on earth. It serves this continuation and correspondence in advance. It precedes it, as it were, in heaven. For this reason, it is unitary but not formless, collective but not without individuation, total but not uniform or monotonous. This conclusion might be based on the wealth of the essence of God, which surely finds no less expression in His being and work in heaven than on earth. But possibly this smacks of a mere hypothesis. And weight is given to it only by the fact that the lordship of God as that of the Father and the Son has as its goal man and the multiplicity and mobility of his history and existence, or of earthly history and existence generally. It is the lordship of His omnipotent grace, which is concerned with the order, harmony, integration and differentiation, the reorganisation of our earthly history and existence according to the model and plan of His wisdom and goodness. Because as heavenly occurrence it is determined by this model and plan, it cannot lack form, individuation and multiplicity, but is already ordered, harmonious, integrated and differentiated in its unitariness, collectiveness and totality. If we do not know what might be called the sub-stratum of this happening; if we do not know as such either heavenly being or its qualities, this does not mean—for God Himself stands before us as its Creator and Lord, and the goal of His will is perceived—that the obedience which He finds in this heavenly occurrence is not the obedience of a subject which can be understood as a single subject but also in its singleness as a multiple, and as a single in its multiplicity. And it is thus

---

EN251 good pleasure
EN252 blessing

[448]   that the kingdom of God comes to earth as the kingdom of heaven, not at a single stroke, on a single note, or in a single shade or form, but in a concentrated multiplicity of revelations and declarations, of events and relationships, of individuals and societies, which have their constitutive centre in God Himself, namely, in Jesus Christ as very God and very man, but which all the same, or for this very reason and in this very way—otherwise grace would not be grace—form this concentrated multiplicity addressed to the history and existence of the creature. But since the kingdom of God comes from heaven to earth in this way, this is tantamount to saying that in heaven and in its commencement there it has and is itself this concentrated multiplicity—an organisation.

In this respect our first reference is to the fact that according to the usage of the Old Testament heaven is a plural term. To this there corresponds the notion discernible in 2 Cor. 12^2 of three heavens one upon the other: the firmament above the stars; the heavenly ocean; and heaven in the true sense, in or above which is the throne of God. We have already noted that the plural is always used in the New Testament where the reference is to the sphere and world of God.

But the Bible leads us a decisive stage further when in the Old Testament it gives to God the title of Yahweh (or less frequently Elohim) Sabaoth, the Lord of hosts, which entails the corresponding notion of a host of Yahweh or of heaven. The title does not occur in the Hexateuch, Judges or Ezekiel, but it is found in the Books of Samuel and Kings, comparatively infrequently in Psalms, more often in Amos and Jeremiah, and predominantly in Isaiah and Zechariah. In the first instance, it excludes any idea of a lonely God sitting on His heavenly throne in an empty or formless heaven. By this name Yahweh is described as the Sovereign of a multitude, and of a multitude constituted as a host, and of a heavenly multitude constituted in this way. So surely as He is in or above heaven as His throne, and rules there or thence, so surely is He surrounded by the multitude of this heavenly host of servants. The saying of the prophet Micaiah in 1 K. 22^{19} and 2 Chron. 18^{18} is particularly illuminating in this respect: "I saw the Lord sitting on his throne, and all the host of heaven standing by him on his right hand and on his left"—an armed and disciplined force standing at His disposal for instant use. Instead of a host of God Ps. 82^1 speaks of a congregation, and Ps. 89^7 of an assembly of the saints. It is obvious that we have here what we described as the organisation, order, integration but also differentiation of what is done in heaven; and that this is the master-concept under which the Old Testament groups the beings which in their decisive function bear the name of angels. We must keep strictly to the fact that our concern is with that organisation and differentiation of heavenly being and occurrence—we know of no other—which are grounded in the fact that it is from heaven and therefore in the character of the kingdom of heaven that the kingdom of God comes to us men and therefore to earth. This is finely expressed in Rev. 19^{11-16} in the description of the sallying forth of the Rider on the white horse whose name is "Faithful and True" (v. 11) and "The Word of God" (v. 13), who is clothed with a vesture dipped in blood, from whose mouth there goes a sharp sword, and who bears inscribed on His thigh the further name: "King of kings, and Lord of lords" (v. 16). What we have here is a description of the parousia of Christ. But we are also told in v. 14: "And the armies which were in heaven (τὰ στρατεύματα τὰ ἐν τῷ οὐρανῷ) followed him upon white horses, clothed in fine linen, white and clean." They obviously have and reveal their true being as the host of heaven in the Word of God whom they follow

[449]   and accompany as He comes from heaven to earth. Similarly, the picture in Rev. 4—the great heavenly doxology offered by the four and twenty elders, the seven spirits and the four living

creatures gathered round the throne of God—is only as it were made actual and concrete, or at any rate explained, by that of Rev. 5, in which the Lamb slain (v. 6), the Lion of the tribe of Judah, the Root of David (v. 5), comes forward and takes the book with the seven seals (v. 8), and a corresponding doxology is offered to Him by that assembly, accompanied this time by ten thousand times ten thousand angels, and thousands of thousands (v. 11). It is also of a piece with this that there is only one passage in the Bible, namely, in the account of the nativity (Lk. 2^{13}), which speaks of a manifestation and function of the πλῆθος EN253, i.e., of the fulness or totality of the heavenly hosts on earth.

This connexion of the existence of the heavenly host with the event of salvation of earth gives to this master-concept, especially in the Old Testament, an ambivalence which is at first sight confusing. This host does not always have the direct meaning of the heavenly host, and even when it does it does not always mean the host of truly angelic beings around the throne, the organisation and differentiation of the upper cosmos. In Gen. 2^1 for example ("Thus the heavens and the earth were finished, and all the host of them"), the most that we can say is that it includes this reference, and the same is true of Neh. 9^6. It is true, of course, that a particular creation of the heavenly host might be envisaged in Ps. 33^6: "By the word of the Lord were the heavens made; and all the host of them by the breath of his mouth"; and also in Is. 45^{12}: "I, even my hands, have stretched out the heavens, and all their host have I commanded." But in some of the passages which warn against worshipping the host of heaven instead of God (Deut. 4^{19}, 17^3) it is expressly stated, and in others of like content it may be inferred, that the sun and moon and stars are meant by this host. This is certainly the reference in Is. 40^{26} where man is challenged to "lift up your eyes on high, and behold who hath created these things, that bringeth out their host by number: he calleth them all by names ...." And on the other hand it has to be taken into account that in 1 Sam. 17^{45} the divine name "Lord of hosts" is equated with "the God of the armies of Israel," and that even in Is. 13^4 the army mustered by the Lord of hosts seems to be an army of men. On this point it is to be noted that the heavenly assembly of elders, spirits and beasts in Rev. 4–5 has at least an affinity to human gatherings on earth, although it is only with great caution that we must see in it a direct prefiguration even of the Church. We shall meet the same ambivalence when we come to deal with the concept of the individual heavenly beings within these hosts, and especially of the angels which exist and work on earth.

Yet there can be no doubt that this concept of a host is more than a description of the stars or a term for the armies of Israel or any other human array. In 1 K. 22^{19} the heavenly host on the right hand and the left cannot possibly be the stars or human warriors. And there is a clear distinction in Ps. 148. After the general call: "Praise the Lord from the heavens; praise him in the heights," we have the specific summons: "Praise ye him, all his angels: praise ye him, all his hosts," then again specifically: "Praise ye him, sun and moon: praise him, all ye stars of light," and yet again specifically: "Praise him, ye heavens of heavens, and ye waters that be above the heavens." Similarly, the host of God in Gen. $32^{1f.}$ cannot have any direct connexion with a Hebrew or any other army. Indirectly the different applications of the notion are naturally inter-related, and in such a way that the idea of God's host or assembly as the direct *entourage* of His throne forms the basic concept reflected in that of the stars and then of the armies of God's earthly people, but with all kinds of cross-references as in the Song of Deborah in Jud. 5^{20}: "They fought from heaven; the stars in their courses fought against Sisera." If only we keep to the fact that, as in our general view of the heavenly world, so in our consideration of its discipline, order and integration, we have to do with a movement under the lordship of God from above to below, to earth and to human history, we shall not regard as in any way strange this peculiar interchange of meanings in virtue of

[450]

EN253 multitude

which we are at one moment really above with God, then in the sphere of a very earthly heaven, and finally on earth itself, where the heavenly hosts are very definitely earthly. These hosts exist at all only as they follow the Word of God (Rev. 19^{14}) in His movement to this goal in earthly existence and history. This is true already of the organisation, the concentrated multiplicity of heavenly being and existence, which is the immediate point at issue.

We must now venture a further step. If the kingdom which as the lordship of God comes from heaven to earth, and therefore commences and is first in heaven, is an order, then it embraces certain elements ordered within it and adjusted to its order. If there is integration, there must be members. If there is concentrated multiplicity, there must be simplicity and individuality. If there is a collective, there must be individuals. If heaven, known to us as the kingdom of heaven, is a creaturely sphere, it must embrace creatures. And however strongly we must emphasise their unity and fellowship, the plurality of these creatures cannot be submerged in identity. An army is made up of soldiers, an assembly of participants. This is no less true of the host or assembly around the throne of God.

We must remember the incomprehensibility of the heavenly sphere of being, and therefore exercise the greatest caution, if we dare to draw these conclusions in relation to the biblical view. As the Bible sees it, these elements or members or units or individuals or different creatures of heavenly being and occurrence appear only (1) in the course and context of the history which commences in heaven and aims at earth, and therefore only in this movement, and their distinctive functions within it; (2) in clear relationship to the order, the collective, the fellowship and unity which they enjoy with others of their kind; and (3) with the unmistakeable stamp of elements, members, units or individuals which are heavenly by nature. But this constitutes a threefold warning against any attempt to define these creatures on the assumption that we are in a position to consider them in their abstract essence and to make pronouncements concerning them on the basis of this consideration.

This is where the fathers go astray, and the scholastics, and all angelology which—whether its answer is positive, or negative, or critical—puts the question as if it were a matter of understanding the existence and manner of certain beings which can be known apart from their function in that history, their membership of that collective and therefore their mutual unity and fellowship, and finally the fact that they are heavenly beings and cannot be grasped in earthly terms. We cannot ignore these things. To maintain the existence of angels and describe their nature as the ancients did is to try to limit the sea with a handful of sand. And to deny them, or reduce them to a comical state of immobility, like the moderns, is to tilt against windmills. To be sure, these beings are distinct creatures, different from the other creatures of earth known to us, and also distinct both in numbers and nature among themselves. But it is a mistake to range them schematically with other creatures as the older dogmatics usually do with the sequence *De homine* and then *De angelis* (or *vice versa*), for we cannot know how these beings are different as creatures from the earthly creatures known to us, nor how they exist, nor what is their particular nature, nor how they are inter-related in unity and plurality. We cannot know these things because as they appear in the Bible they can be known to us as elements, members, units or individuals of the kingdom of heaven only in the movement of the coming of this kingdom to earth, only in their adherence to an

[451]

order which we cannot survey, and only as heavenly and therefore incomprehensible beings. In consequence, we can only regard it as a mistake for which we have no warrant in the Bible to concern ourselves with the famous question of their creation, and to adopt one or other of the answers given to this question.

They are known to us not in their abstract but in their concrete nature as the heavenly *entourage* of the God who acts from heaven to earth, and therefore not as an abstractly existent heavenly collective of abstractly existent heavenly individual beings but as the concretely operative heavenly collective of concretely operative heavenly individual beings. At this point, of course, the caution demanded of us reaches its limit. In this form they are indeed known to us, for God's coming kingdom on earth is the kingdom of heaven and is revealed to us as such. If the kingdom of heaven were not a collective, and if it did not consist of individuals, it would not be the kingdom of God coming on earth and bursting into earthly nature and human history with all its universality and particularities. Our present emphasis is upon the latter. If it comes to us, it does not come only in universality, but also in particularity; it does not come only as a totality, but also as a multiplicity. And if as God's kingdom it comes into this world and therefore from heaven, as the kingdom of heaven, it is itself characterised by both universality and particularity, totality and multiplicity, collectivity and individuality. Hence when we consider it we have not to think only of heaven and its heavenly essence, or globally of the heavenly host and assembly, but also of the heavenly being and therefore of the angels who are comprehended in this unity.

We knew nothing of their essential being and its particular nature. We know nothing of the mode of their mutal relationship and distinction. We know nothing of the way in which they are a totality and yet distinct. But we do know that even in the mystery of their being they exist in and with the kingdom of God coming and revealed to us. And we do know that they are both interrelated and distinct, both a totality and individuals.

They are in and from heaven in the service in which they precede, accompany, surround and follow the coming kingdom. This is all that we know concerning them. But we can and must define them in these terms. And the definition can be explicated as follows. They are in the service of God. It is their existence and nature to observe the will of God and stand at His disposal. [452] Their heavenly glory consists solely in this determination. Moreover, they are in the service of the merciful God, for whom there are no problems, and in the strict sense nothing to will and do, where He is with them in heaven, but who is confronted on earth by the illimitable need of an existence of the creature which is not only threatened but assaulted, disturbed and destroyed by the forces of negation, so that He has resolved and is willing and ready to take up its cause and be its Saviour. This is the will which they observe. This is the God at whose disposal they stand. It is in the service of this mercy of His that they are glorious. Moreover, they stand for this reason and to this extent in the service of the earthly creature, not to give it help in things in which it might very well help itself or receive help from its fellows, but as the heavenly witnesses and messengers of the Saviour God, i.e., as the special heralds of His mystery as of the necessary form of His revelation and work. This will be our express theme in the next sub-section. Moreover, they fulfil this service perfectly. They stand before the throne of God. They are at the place where the speech and action of God commence in the created world. They are its direct *entourage* and original witnesses. They follow the Word of God as riders on white horses. They have no part in the confusion and contradiction and opposition of the earthly sphere which they enter with God Himself and as His following. Their only *raison d'être*[EN254] as heavenly beings is to render this service. They have no neutral place in view of which they might be something other than God's servants. Finally, whatever this may mean for their mutual inter-relationship, they are something distinctive in this service. In correspondence with the concreteness of the saving will and work of God, and notwithstanding their integration and subordination under the one God, but in this subordination, their service is not one and the same, but a service in fulfilment of different commissions and therefore of varying character. They are not therefore one, but in distinction from God, yet corresponding to what He wills and establishes on earth, they are many, the plurality of angels which has its necessary basis in the universality of heavenly being as this is concretely related and fashioned. This is what may be legitimately said in general definition of these beings.

In Heb. 1^{14} we are given what is virtually a definition of the nature of angels, and one which might almost be called the *locus classicus*[EN255] for the biblical view: οὐχὶ πάντες εἰσὶν λειτουργικὰ πνεύματα εἰς διακονίαν ἀποστελλόμενα διὰ τοὺς μέλλοντας κληρονομεῖν σωτηρίαν[EN256]. The question is formulated with the intention of bringing out the transcendence of Jesus Christ over these beings. No matter from what height they come, what functions they exercise, or what dignity they may enjoy, when they are compared with Him they cannot be described as anything more than the λειτουργικὰ πνεύματα[EN257] of this verse. But it may well be that the positive thing which has to be said concerning them cannot be better said than by extolling against them the more excellent name of Jesus Christ (Heb. 1^4). To be sure, we must exercise care in our reading of the decisive statement. The main point is not that angels are πνεύματα[EN258], but that as such they receive from the adjective λειτουργικὰ[EN259] and the participle ἀποστελλόμενα[EN260] a distinctive character and activity which differentiate them from Jesus Christ but also set them in a positive relationship to Him. It was the exegetical error of Thomas Aquinas to show far too lively an interest in the equation of ἄγγελοι[EN261] and πνεύματα[EN262], and the results were catastrophic when with

[453]

EN254 reason for existence
EN255 classic reference
EN256 Are they not all ministering spirits, sent forth to minister for them who shall be heirs of salvation?
EN257 ministering spirits
EN258 spirits
EN259 ministering
EN260 sent forth
EN261 angels
EN262 spirits

the help of a concept of spirit alien to Old and New Testament alike he tried to find in these πνεύματα [EN263] his *substantiae spirituales separatae* [EN264].

The same mistake was later responsible for leading J. C. K. Hofmann (*Der Schriftbeweis* Vol. I, 1852, 274 f.) to the brilliant but impossible and finally quite intolerable doctrine that there is a plurality in the unity of the concept God (*Elohim*); that since God is a Spirit this is a plurality of spirits; that the one essence of God, the supracosmic Creator, resolves itself into multiplicity in terms of the presence which He exercises in the world by His Spirit; and conversely that the world of spirits, to the extent that in it the one essence of God resolves itself into the multiplicity of His qualities exercised in the world, is enclosed in the Spirit of God and gathered up in its self-multiplying unity (cf. esp. p. 354 f.). In this exposition far too much weight is laid on the term πνεύματα [EN265] in Heb. 1¹⁴, and the decisive statement in the verse is completely neglected. It is true that when God is described as the Father of spirits in Heb. 12⁹ the reference is probably to the angels, and that the seven spirits of the Apocalypse (3¹, 4⁵, 5⁶), and also the four and twenty elders and the four living creatures, are to be understood as angelic forms. But in the Apocalypse not all angels are called πνεύματα [EN266] as they are here. Indeed, the fact that it is here an ἅπαξ λεγόμενον [EN267] ought to restrain us. The context does not give us any compelling reason for calling angels πνεύματα [EN268]. And the description is only a negative characterisation, telling us that the angels are not beings which can be conceived or grasped or controlled by us, but that like demons, which are often called πνεύματα [EN269] in the New Testament, they can be understood in their movements and impulsion only from a very different standpoint. It is thus better to leave this definition rather colourless. The essential determination of πνεύματα [EN270] is not the fact that they are πνεύματα [EN271], but the fact that they are λειτουργικὰ πνεύματα [EN272], i.e., incomprehensible beings which have a sacred office. And as the bearers of this office they are εἰς διακονίαν ἀποστελλόμενα [EN273], i.e., despatched to fulfil this office. It is the twofold fact that they have this office and this mission which makes these incomprehensible beings ἄγγελοι [EN274] in the sense of this passage. Their relationship to Jesus Christ in their sphere is like that of the apostles in the human sphere. This is both their greatness and their limitation.

In this connexion we may recall the interesting exposition of this verse by Erich Schick (*Die Botschaft der Engel*, 30 f., *Vom Dienst der Engel*, 18 f.). His rendering of λειτουργικὰ πνεύματα [EN275] is "liturgical spirits." By liturgy he means "standing in adoration before the presence of God," and by διακονία [EN276] "service in the world and to men." He thus gathers from the verse that in time, inner meaning, rank and essential significance there is a twofold ministry of angels, liturgy and diaconate, in which both are bound together in an indissoluble unity, but of which it may be said that for the angels (and Schick obviously thinks for us too) there can be liturgy without diaconate, but not diaconate without liturgy. Yet I am not

---

[EN263] spirits
[EN264] distinct spiritual substances
[EN265] spirits
[EN266] spirits
[EN267] form of words that appears only once in Scripture
[EN268] spirits
[EN269] spirits
[EN270] spirits
[EN271] spirits
[EN272] ministering spirits
[EN273] sent forth to minister
[EN274] angels
[EN275] ministering spirits
[EN276] service

convinced that this is the real meaning of Heb. 1¹⁴. That the sacred office which is integral to the essence of angels includes their being as λειτουργικὰ πνεύματα EN277 in the sense of standing in adoration before the presence of God is certainly to be gathered from the express statement of the angel Gabriel in Lk. 1¹⁹ and from the general context of Rev. 4–5. But is this to be regarded as a first ministry of angels from which their διακονία EN278 can be

[454] distinguished and even divided as a second? Is it really possible to think of a purely liturgical being and action of angels (or men) addressed only to God, of a pure being and action in sacred office which is not as such a being and action in the corresponding service, but can take place quite apart from this service? Can any created being do God a service which does not at once take the form of a service in the world and to man? Schick is prepared to maintain that there is no service in the world or to man which does not proceed from service to God, i.e., that there is no diaconate without liturgy. But can he really contend for a liturgy without diaconate? What kind of a God would it be—surely it could not really be the God of grace and the covenant, God in Jesus Christ—to whom heavenly or earthly beings might turn even momentarily in such abstraction, without *eo ipso* EN279 becoming His messengers and going forth as such? In Heb. 1¹⁴ does not the very transition from the adjective (λειτουργικά EN280) to the participle (ἀποστελλόμενα EN281) exclude even linguistically any such separation of ministry? Does not the accent of the statement plainly rest on the fact that in practice angels have their sacred office, and stand before the presence of God, in the fact that they are sent to the ministry corresponding to this office? Is not the emphasis on this side strengthened by the fact that this ministry is expressly stated to be "for them who shall be heirs of salvation," whereas we look in vain for a similar explanation of what Schick supposes to be a distinct and primary "liturgical" ministry. In view of these doubts, I prefer to take it that this passage describes all angels unequivocally as ἄγγελοι EN282, as the host of those who are appointed and commissioned to the service of God, and therefore to service in the lower cosmos. It describes them by speaking of the sacred office which they are given and of their commission in execution of this office. It thus describes the movement in which they exist and have their distinctive being. The fact that in origin and execution this movement is one of service distinguishes them from the One who in this matter, in what is to take place "for them who shall be heirs of salvation," is Lord and King.

It is within this framework that the other general names, definitions and descriptions of angels, and such other statements as are made concerning them in the Bible, are to be correlated and become relatively intelligible.

In the context of our whole exposition we can see at once why in Zech. 14⁵ and Ps. 29¹ they are called "the heavenly ones," and in Phil. 2¹⁰ the ἐπουράνιοι EN283 in contrast to the ἐπίγειοι EN284 and καταχθόνιοι EN285. They are given this title as the individual members of the kingdom of heaven and its order, of the occurrence which commences in heaven and aims at earth, and in which they have a part with their ministry. On account of its connexion with the kingdom of heaven we might well be tempted to make this designation both exegetically and dogmatically a leading concept. We often enough read of the coming down of an angel from heaven (e.g., Dan. 4¹⁰), or more briefly of an angel from heaven (e.g., Gal.

EN277 ministering spirits
EN278 service
EN279 in itself
EN280 ministering
EN281 sent forth
EN282 angels
EN283 things in heaven
EN284 things in earth
EN285 things under the earth

1^8), or of the angels in heaven (e.g., Mk. 12^{25}). But to make this the leading concept might well involve an undesirable emphasising of the ontological side of the matter. It is wiser, perhaps, not to adopt any main concept, but to treat the usual word "angel" as a *tabula rasa*^{EN286} to which to relate the many other things which are said of them, including the fact that they are "heavenlies." This is the more advisable because the word "angel" will also prove to have the fullest content at the decisive point.

In Ps. 89$^{5\ 7}$ and Job 5^1 and 15^{15} (and perhaps also in 2 Thess. 1^{10}) they are called the saints. In accordance with the general usage of the Bible this means that they are selected, ordained and separated by God for the ministry. What we called the discipline of heavenly occurrence is expressed in this designation of the individual figures. And if in Dan. 4$^{13\ 17\ 23}$ these saints are equated with watchers, we can see in this an indication that their holiness is not merely related passively to what they are on the basis of the divine order, but also to their active function in the history of salvation. They guard the frontiers, as in their opposition to the pretensions of Nebuchadnezzar in Dan. 4.

In a third series of passages (Ps. 89^6, Job 1^6, 2^1 and 38^7), they are called the sons of God, [455] and even "gods" in Ps. 82^1. (The difficult passage in Gen. 6, which speaks of the sons of God in v. 2 and v. 4, is a special case which probably does not belong to this series and cannot therefore be adduced in this connexion.) It would be foolish to allow these passages to tempt us on to the thin ice of Martensen's theory, which would have it that the angels are identical with the pagan deities, or of that of Hofmann, which treats them almost as self-emanations of God. There can be no question of angels being sons of God in the sense in which this is said of the Son of God in the New Testament, just as no rivalry with Christ is entailed if in the New Testament Christians are also called the υἱοὶ θεοῦ^{EN287}. Men are also addressed as "gods" or "sons of the Most High" (Ps. 82^6, cf. Jn. 10^{34}). Both terms have a sense in which they can also be applied to creatures. Like "saints," they tell us that these creatures belong and are pledged and committed to God in a special sense. This is what is said of angels when they are called the sons of God or "gods." As the individuals of heavenly being and occurrence and its order they are impressed into God's service, and are thus made these individuals and members of the heavenly family.

In an isolated but important passage (Is. 6$^{1f.}$) we hear tell of seraphim, and it seems as though this term denotes the totality of the heavenly *entourage* of God. There is more frequent mentions of cherubim. In Gen. 3^{24} we are reminded of Daniel's description of the angels as the watchers of Paradise, or of the way to the tree of life, but for the most part the reference is to God enthroned (1 Sam. 4^4 and *passim*) or riding upon them (2 Sam. 22^{11}). In this function they figure prominently in the ornamentation of the ark. The linguistic sense of the two terms is so disputed by the experts that it is better for a mere layman to ignore this question, and the same is true of their material role and significance. In respect of the seraphim it is plain that their activity (the threefold *Sanctus*^{EN288} by which the foundations of the temple are shaken, and their purification of the lips of the prophet) points in the direction of "saints" in the active as well as the passive sense. And Gen. 3^{24} indicates that the same is true of cherubim, while we learn from the other references to them that they are thought of partly as representatives of the subordination of even the heavenly world to God, and partly as accompanying elements in the comprehensive movement executed by God from heaven.

In some passages individual angels are given specific names. Dan. 10^{13}, 12^1, Jud. 9, and Rev. 12^7 speak of Michael, Dan. 8^{16}, 9^{21} and Lk. 1$^{19, 26}$ of Gabriel, and the Book of Tobit of

---

^{EN286} blank slate
^{EN287} sons of God
^{EN288} Holy

Raphael. Michael means "Who is like God?", Gabriel "the man of God," and Raphael "God heals." With a whole series of other phenomena of angelic manifestation in the Bible, these names show us that the host or assembly of God in heaven, the heavenly ones or saints or sons of God, and therefore the seraphim and cherubim, must not be thought of merely as a collective but also as individuals. As we shall see, they do not appear and act only *in corpore*[EN289], but also as individuals; they do not speak only in concert, but personally. But we do violence both to the historical character of the texts and to the matter itself if we try to press ontologically what is said more or less clearly concerning angels in this respect. For all the vitality with which it speaks, the biblical doctrine of angels is more sober in this respect than what was later fashioned from it. Heavenly individuals are no more earthly than the heavenly collective. But as the πνεύματα[EN290] exist only in virtue of the predicates λειτουργικά[EN291] and ἀποστελλόμενα εἰς διακονίαν[EN292], as the heavenly host exists only as it is assembled around the throne of God and sent out from it, so individual figures, to the extent that their names and speech and action are mentioned, exist only as they are specific-ally summoned and separated from the rest with a specific commission and in a specific relationship to the earthly history of salvation, disappearing again into the general body as [456] soon as their work is accomplished. Hence it is futile to ask what Gabriel did or was between the role ascribed to him in Daniel and his part in the events of the nativity. All that we are told concerning the individual existence of angels is that they are there as the mighty ones "that do his commandments ... ministers of his, that do his pleasure" (Ps. 103[20f.]), and we do well, therefore, to picture their individual existence, if at all, only in the actuality with which it is presented in this Psalm. The more strictly we do this, the more the angels lose the character of a curious gallery of legendary figures, the more clearly we see their practical significance, and the more clearly above all we see their existence in direct relationship to the reality and will of the living God. The specific names of specific angels are themselves a clear challenge to think along these lines. They are eloquent in the very fact that they slip between our fingers, what they say individually being merely a declaration about angels gen-erally and their relationship to God, and in this way about the nature of angels. The name Michael: "Who is like God?", is particularly interesting in this connexion. It may be com-pared with Ps. 89[6, 8]: "For who in the heaven can be compared unto the Lord? who among the sons of God can be likened unto the Lord? ... O Lord God of hosts, who is a strong God like unto thee?" Thus what is said of Michael in particular is to be said of all angels generally. They all can and must be called Michael, and by this name they propose the question to which the only answer is that even in heaven there is none like God.

This brings us to the problem whether and how far there is an inner order of the angelic world on the biblical view. We have seen what the theology of the primitive and mediaeval Church thought it knew concerning a ranking and therefore a hierarchy of angels. Is this a tenable idea from the biblical standpoint?

It results from the notion of the heavenly host or assembly only if we believe that what is true of human and earthly phenomena of this kind may be postulated of the heavenly real-ity. But the passages which speak of the numbers of angels are a warning in this connexion: "Thousand thousands ministered unto him, and ten thousand times ten thousand stood before him" (Dan. 7[10], Rev. 5[11]). These are not statistical but hyperbolical statements. They simply tell us that numbers fail. But how can there be any ranking without numbers?

Allusion has been made to Job 33[23], where after the reference to other ways and means by

---

[EN289] as a body
[EN290] spirits
[EN291] ministering
[EN292] sent forth to minister

which God can speak to man we are told that "if there be a messenger with him, an inter-preter, one among a thousand," who can both explain to man the chastisement which has fallen upon him and also pity him and make intercession for him, it may well be that "twice and thrice" (v. 29) he will be helped and enlightened with the light of life. But why should this one among a thousand be higher than the other nine hundred and ninety-nine ? That he is separated from them is obvious. But it is equally obvious that this is only on the ground and in the sense of the special commission which he is given in relation to this man, and not of a higher rank proper to him *in se*[EN293].

More illuminating perhaps in this connexion, although not wholly clear in context or preserved in wording, is the passage Joshua 5^{13-15}, where outside Jericho a man with a drawn sword meets Joshua, and when Joshua asks him: "Art thou for us, or for our adversaries?", he answers: "Nay, but as captain (*sar*[EN294]) of the host of the Lord am I now come." The only thing is that, as so often in the Old Testament, this angelophany shows itself to be really a theophany: "And Joshua fell on his face to the earth, and did worship, and said unto him, What saith my lord unto his servant? And the captain of the Lord's host said unto Joshua, Loose thy shoe from off thy foot; for the place whereon thou standest is holy. And Joshua did so." It was obviously to characterise the angelophany as an occasion of the first order, to declare the power of the host of Yahweh and in and with it of its true Lord, and to show that the angelophany was a theophany, that the heavenly being made itself known to Joshua under this title. But the passage hardly gives us to understand that there are *sarim*[EN295] by birth or commission in the host of Yahweh. [457]

The same is true of the two passages in Daniel which are often quoted in this respect: Dan. 10^{13}, in which Michael is called one of the chief *sarim*[EN296]; and Dan. 12^1, in which he is called the great *sar*[EN297]. We have already stated that the specific name of this particular angel is against a view which would give him any inherent distinction as compared with others. If he is here called a *sar*[EN298], and one of the chief, the obvious context of the chapter shows that the reference is to his function. He is the angel who, in the fulfilment of the earthly events of salvation history, is associated with the people of Daniel, i.e., the elect people (as a heavenly *sar*[EN299] is also active in relation to Persia, $10^{13\ 21}$, and another in relation to Greece, 10^{21}). According to the clear statement of Dan. 12^1 Michael is "the great *sar*[EN300] which standeth for the children of thy people"; and according to Dan. 10^{21} he is "your *sar*[EN301]." It is in honour of his commission as distinguished by the divine election of grace in history, and not in relation to any inherent rank of his in the angelic hierarchy, that these emphatic statements are made. Here as in Joshua 5 the term *sar*[EN302] is not to be taken as a *nomen numeri*[EN303] but as a *nomen officii*[EN304]. Nor is a higher rank ascribed to Michael in Jude 9 when he is called Μιχαὴλ ὁ ἀρχάγγελος[EN305]. An archangel is not like an arch-bishop or an archduke—not even the archangel whose voice will be heard at the return of

---

[EN293] in himself
[EN294] captain
[EN295] captains
[EN296] captains
[EN297] captain
[EN298] captain
[EN299] captain
[EN300] captain
[EN301] captain
[EN302] captain
[EN303] name of a type
[EN304] name of an office
[EN305] Michael the archangel

Jesus Christ (1 Thess. 4^{16})! The term ἀρχάγγελος^{EN306} obviously derives from the Septuagint version of Daniel which has εἷς τῶν ἀρχοντῶν^{EN307} for *achad hasarim*^{EN308} (10^{13}), ὁ ἄρχων ὑμῶν^{EN309} for *sarekem*^{EN310} (10^{21}) and ὁ ἄρχων ὁ μέγας^{EN311} for *hasar hagadol*^{EN312} (12^{1}). The Vulgate uses *princeps*^{EN313} in all three passages. An ἄρχων^{EN314} or *princeps*^{EN315} is one who exercises power, and therefore an angel which is called ἄρχων^{EN316} is one to whom a specific authority is given in history, as in the case of Michael in relation to Israel (Dan. 10 and 12). He is the bearer and representative, not of any power and least of all of his own, but of the power of God over this people. It is this power which is proclaimed by the ἀρχάγγελος^{EN317} of 1 Thess. 4, and an inherent dignity is as little ascribed to him by the fact of this office as is a higher rank to the accompanying trumpet in relation to other trumpets. The distinction of both angel and trumpet is to be found in what they say and blow, not in what they are. Hence we cannot speak of a higher dignity of Michael, or of a general hierarchy of heaven, merely on the basis of the term ἀρχάγγελος^{EN318}.

In the light of all that has been said we obviously cannot agree with the militarists that when Rev. 12^{7} speaks of Michael and his angels making war against the dragon which has invaded heaven we are to think of the ἄγγελοι αὐτοῦ^{EN319} as a force commanded by Michael and Michael himself as the officer at their head. They are called "his" angels because now, in contrast to the Book of Daniel and perhaps in view of the accession of the ἔθνη^{EN320}^{EN321} to Israel, they share his commission and are responsible with him for its execution.

What is true of Michael is no less true of Gabriel. His name "Man of God" might well be that of any other angel and does not give him any pre-eminence. According to Dan. 8^{16} and 9^{21} his commission and service are to explain the vision which Daniel has seen. In Luke 1 it is he who announces to Zacharias the birth of John (1$^{11f.}$) and to Mary the birth of Jesus (1$^{26f.}$). From the fact that he is called ὁ παρεστηκὼς ἐνώπιον τοῦ θεοῦ^{EN322} (v. 19) we are ill-advised to deduce that there is ascribed to him "a higher, extraordinary rank" within the angelic hosts (E. Schick, *op. cit.*, p. 30), for according to Rev. 4$^{3f.}$ κυκλόθεν^{EN323} or ἐνώπιον τοῦ θεοῦ^{EN324} seems to be used of all angels (and according to Rev. 7^{15}) of all the perfected saints), and in Rev. 8^{2} the seven angels with trumpets are described as οἱ ἐνώπιον τοῦ θεοῦ^{EN325}. It is hard to see, therefore, why any ontic dignity should be ascribed to Gabriel on the basis of this expression. His honour is great enough if understood in the light of his commission in Luke 1.

---

^{EN306} Archangel
^{EN307} one of the Chiefs
^{EN308} one of the princes
^{EN309} your chief
^{EN310} prince
^{EN311} the great chief
^{EN312} the great prince
^{EN313} prince
^{EN314} chief
^{EN315} prince
^{EN316} chief
^{EN317} archangel
^{EN318} archangel
^{EN319} his angels
^{EN320} Gentiles
^{EN321} heathen
^{EN322} one who stands in the presence of God
^{EN323} round about
^{EN324} before God
^{EN325} which [stood] before God

2. *The Kingdom of Heaven*

And now finally in this connexion we must consider the terms or realities in the Pauline [458] Epistles especially which once claimed the interest of Pseudo-Dionysius and contributed so largely to the construction of his hierarchy: the ἀρχαί[EN326] and ἐξουσίαι[EN327] (1 Cor. 15²⁴; Col. 1¹⁶, 2¹⁰; Eph. 1²¹, 3¹⁰, 6¹²; Titus 3¹); the δυνάμεις[EN328] (1 Cor. 15²⁴; 1 Pet. 3²²); the κυριότητες[EN329] (Col. 1¹⁶, Eph. 6¹²); the θρόνοι[EN330] (Col. 1¹⁶); the κοσμοκράτορες[EN331] (Eph. 6¹²); and θάνατος, ζωή, ἐνεστῶτα, μέλλοντα, ὕψωμα[EN332] and βάθος[EN333] (Rom. 8³⁸). The term ἀρχαί[EN334] is used in all these passages with the exception of 1 Pet. 3²². Mention might also be made of the ἄρχοντες τοῦ αἰῶνος τούτου[EN335] (1 Cor. 2⁶ᶠ). The term ἐξουσία[EN336] is present in each case except Rom. 8³⁸ᶠ, and in Romans it seems instead to be given a particular application in 13¹ᶠ It is obvious that all the terms are used to denote power. In view of the context ("Who shall separate us from the love of Christ?", Rom. 8³⁵) this is true even of the extended list in Rom. 8³⁸ᶠ. In the other passages the terms have a ring and scope which are political in the widest sense. They speak of the powers which control and fashion human history. Three meanings intersect in these passages and must be given greater or lesser prominence in their exegesis. (1) In Rom. 13¹ and Tit. 3¹ (cf. Lk. 12¹¹ and Jn. 19¹⁰ᶠ) the reference is plainly to the powers of state instituted by God but exercised by men. Indeed, 1 Pet. 2¹³ speaks expressly of an ἀνθρωπίνη κτίσις[EN337]. (2) In Col. 1¹⁶ and 2¹⁰, Eph. 1²¹ and 3¹⁰ and 1 Pet. 3²², where the same words are used, it is a matter of the heavenly powers created and established for the sake of Christ and in His service (δι᾽ αὐτοῦ καὶ εἰς αὐτόν[EN338]) and therefore controlled by Him—powers whose function and service will attain their goal with His coming again, and will thus be "put down" by Him. (3) In the other passages, the same terms refer to the illegitimate and perverse demonic powers which imitate and rival the heavenly and of which it is said that they have already been taken prisoner by Christ and will be marched in His triumphant procession (Col. 2¹⁵), so that although we have still to fight (Eph. 6¹²) we do not need to fear them (Rom. 8³⁸ᶠ). Our present concern is with the second interpretation, and there can be no doubt that the words ἀρχαί, ἐξουσίαι, θρόνοι, κυριότητες[EN339] and δυνάμεις[EN340] do also denote the heavenly powers which are subject to Christ and have in Him their Head (1 Pet. 3²², Col. 2¹⁰). It is plain that in this connexion we are basically on the same territory as that of the heavenly *sarim*[EN341] of the Old Testament. If for the time being we ignore the existence of demonic powers of the same name, these heavenly powers, directly determined from heaven by the action of God, stand over against the earthly formations, and especially the powers of state, instituted by God but fashioned by men. They are not identical with them, yet they are also related to them as their divinely marked originals. If we can say of earthly powers that they

---

[EN326] principalities
[EN327] authorities
[EN328] powers
[EN329] dominions
[EN330] thrones
[EN331] world ruler
[EN332] death, life, things present, things to come, height
[EN333] depth
[EN334] principalities
[EN335] the princes of this world
[EN336] authority
[EN337] human ordinance
[EN338] through Him and to Him
[EN339] principalities, authorities, thrones, dominions
[EN340] powers
[EN341] captains

are ὑπὸ θεοῦ τεταγμέναι EN342 (Rom. 13¹), we owe this to the fact that they correspond on earth to these powers in heaven. As God speaks His Word from heaven, He reveals and exercises His power to make peace on earth. The heavenly ἀρχαί EN343 and ἐξουσίαι EN344 are this revelation and exercise of His power to make peace on earth, and they find their counterpart in the earthly powers of state as forces for the maintenance of a relative peace. The fact that the same terms are used for both the heavenly originals and their earthly counterparts shows us (as we may gather from the political terminology) that the former first and properly, because determined by the divine action in respect of the covenant and salvation, are powers of order, and that they are not merely obscure *potentiae* EN345 but definite *potestates* EN346, salutary forces for the establishment of a relative peace, the relative aversion of chaos and therefore in this sense the furtherance of the kingdom of God. Whether they are called ἀρχαί, ἐξουσίαι EN347, or anything else, they have in Christ their Head, and, in the phrase which J. C. Blumhardt used of the angels, they represent the power of order in the covenant and grace. As and because there are these representations of the divine power of order from heaven, earthly history can never be given up wholly to chaos, but there can always be within it, as poor but genuine replicas, real forces of peace and order; and it is by [459] these powers, and as their imitation, that the forces of disorder live—the demonic powers with their specific human replicas. Yet because in the case of all these terms we have to do with the representation, revelation and expression in human history of the one divine power of order differentiated in form and action by time, place and circumstance, we are completely wide of the mark if we try to conclude from the different terms or descriptions an inner gradation in these forces, various sections or departments of the kingdom of heaven, and therefore the existence of a heavenly hierarchy. The exegesis of these terms by Pseudo-Dionysius reached the very limit of arbitrariness and futility. There is absolutely nothing to authorise or compel us to regard the ἀρχαί EN348 as higher than the ἐξουσίαι EN349, the δυνάμεις EN350 as lower than the θρόνοι EN351, etc. All these terms denote in their own place the one whole power of the kingdom of heaven. There can be no question of any ranking of the realities indicated by them because the power which they represent, reveal and express is in each instance the power of the one God, and because Christ is the Head of them all, and they would not be powers apart from the power of this Head. To be sure, their distinction, and their integration in this distinction, are also real. But as the kingdom of heaven as a whole is a historical reality, so it is with its integration and with each of the powers which these terms show to be different from others. Their difference is to be understood from the sequence and differentiation of the divine Word and act coming down from the heavenly sphere to the earthly. It is to be understood as the outworking of the πολυποίκιλος σοφία τοῦ θεοῦ EN352 from the knowledge of which, as it attains its goal and is revealed in the existence of the community, even the angels in heaven have something new to learn (Eph. 3¹⁰). If there is order in heaven, it is not the order of rank, but of function and service. And with this conclusion we may bring this excursus to a close. As we have seen, it is not impos-

---

EN342 ordained of God
EN343 principalities
EN344 authorities
EN345 forces
EN346 powers
EN347 principalities, authorities
EN348 principalities
EN349 authorities
EN350 powers
EN351 thrones
EN352 the manifold wisdom of God

sible to understand Pseudo-Dionysius in this sense, or at least in this direction. He has not made it easy for the Church to understand him meaningfully. But his concept of the heavenly hierarchy is sufficiently dynamic not to exclude the possibility that for all his mistakes in detail he should be understood as a whole as a man who unfortunately spoke of an order of rank but perhaps had in mind an order of service.

And now within the framework of this general survey of our subject we may venture a final question and answer. What is the order to which heavenly occurrence is subject both as a whole and in detail, and by which it is both differentiated and integrated? What is it that commences above and then comes down to earth with the kingdom of God? What is the purpose in which these heavenly hosts have their being, i.e., stand in their ministry? In what does the service of angels consist? Here, too, we must be on our guard against thinking that we know too much, but also against the stupidity which refuses to know what is to be known. As we have stated, it is a question of the service of God, of the merciful God, and therefore of the earthly creature to whom He has turned; of a perfect and a highly specific service. If we gather up these various threads, the answer to the question in what this service consists is so obvious that no speculation is needed to see it, for only wilful blindness can fail to receive it. If we have rightly described the ministry of angels as their vital function in relation to Christ their Head, or more expressly as the perfect and highly specific assistance which they give to God as the Lord of the covenant and grace in His relationship to the earthly creature, it is evident in what their [460] ministry can alone consist materially, and does in fact consist.

But first a brief mention must be made of that in which it naturally cannot consist. It cannot consist in their doing what God alone can do. It has no basis here. Angels cannot, then, speak words which as their own are the words of God. They cannot do works which as their own are divine works. They cannot save, redeem or liberate the earthly creature. They cannot forgive even the smallest sin, or remove even the slightest pain. They can do nothing to bring about the reconciliation of the world with God. Nor are they judges of the world. They did not create it. They can neither be wrathful nor gracious toward it. They did not establish the covenant between God and man, and they cannot fulfil, maintain, renew or confirm it. They do not overcome death. They do not rule the history of salvation, or universal history, or any history. Otherwise they would not be the angels of God. They would have nothing whatever to do with the kingdom of heaven coming on earth; they would deny their own nature; they would be apes of themselves, demons, if they did anything along these lines, or rather if they tried to do (for these are things which no creature can do), if on the pretext and with the appearance of being helpers, saviours, comforters, prophets, priests and kings, they assisted the earthly creature with their own word and work, directed its attention, adoration and gratitude to themselves, and approached it as lords in their own right and with an autonomous claim. And how terribly they would be misunderstood by the creature if they were seen in this role, and on the basis of any consideration or presumed experience, or in any form, independent expectations, hopes, appeals and thankgivings were addressed to them! We really do not know what we are about if we treat them in this way. For we confuse them with their express opponents. We do not really have to do with them at all, or with the kingdom of heaven, but with their express opponents and with the kingdom of falsehood and darkness. The heavenly beings, the saints, the sons of God, the seraphim, Michael and Gabriel, neither are nor do these things that they are falsely assumed to be and do. They are heavenly creatures, but they are creatures no less strictly than all earthly creatures. If they speak the Word of God and do the work of God, it is never as their own. If they have power to do so (as they have); if they themselves are heavenly powers, it is as representatives, in the revelation and exercise of the one power of God Himself. They never take the central position, but always leave it open for the One who alone can occupy it. They merely come and go again, having maintained this freedom of God. They never catch the eye. They always look away from themselves, and they invite and command others to look away from every creature, themselves included, to the One who alone is worthy that the eye of every creature should rest on Him, and from whom alone they can really see themselves and their fellow-creatures. How could their ministry be genuine ministry if things were otherwise, if it were in any sense their own rule or partial rule? How could it then be the service of God? Or what God would they then serve? It would certainly not be the merciful God. Nor would they serve the earthly creature whom the merciful God wills to adopt and has already done so. And far from being perfect their being and action would always be total and desperate rebellion, and all its particularity would resolve itself into a wild anarchy in which the individual would be lost instead of honoured. In no circumstances, therefore, can the ministry of angels consist in this usurpation of the position and function of God. And it is obvious that any presumed dealings with angels or discussion of their reality cannot avoid the test whether it keeps within or has long since crossed the fine but very definite limit beyond which we enter at once the sphere of a mythology which is not harmless but savage and destructive. Here as elsewhere, for example, Christian art has almost always rendered poor service, demonic rather than angelic, to the cause of Christian truth.

[461]

The true service of angels, like that of all other creatures to God, is that of witnesses. Whether heavenly or earthly, the creature can render assistance in relation to God and its fellows by being the witness of God. That is to say, it can exist in such a way that in its existence, while it cannot usurp His functions or take His place, it gives an appropriate response to His existence, Word and work. In their existence they can render and be a response which corresponds to Him as their Creator and Lord. In this correspondence they can declare Him, and their declaration can have the character of thanksgiving in relation to Himself and proclamation in relation to their fellow-creatures: the more powerful as proclamation the more radically it is thanksgiving; and the more sincerely as thanksgiving the more seriously as proclamation. The creature may praise God. It cannot do this on its own initiative, but solely at His behest and in obedience. It cannot do it in well-meant disclosures, but only as it corresponds to His Word and work. It praises the Lord as it obeys this behest and is this correspondence. And praising Him in this way, it is His witness. This is the one thing required of it. When it does this, it does not trangress its limits but respects them, doing within them that which is possible to it, for which it is free, and which is required of it as it has this freedom. When it does this, it serves God, and as and because it serves God it also serves its fellow-creature. This is what is required of it. God expects the praise of His creature, for He does not will to remain alone in His Word and work, but, as He speaks and acts, to be together with the creature, and in this way, in this covenant with it, to be its God. This expectation of God makes the praise of God necessary. But all creation waits to hear the praise of God and to be summoned to take part in it. It needs to do this to achieve its true nature and thus to be itself a correspond- [462] ence of the Word and work of God. And in so doing it does not will to be alone. It cannot strike up the praise of God—no creature can do this—but only join in the praise of God as it hears it already in the existence of other creatures and is thereby summoned to it. Thus the expectation of the fellow-creature also makes the praise of God necessary. And where God is praised, He is served and has His witnesses.

All this is true equally and primarily of angels. That "He rules in the kingdom of heaven" is a phrase which we have already used at the appropriate point, and we may now continue the quotation: "Ye strong angels, discharge His praise, and magnify the great Lord, and set forth His holy Word." Nor should we omit the conclusion: "My soul, increase His praise in every place." The ministry of angels is the supreme ministry of witness, to the increase of which our praise of God and ministry, and all service of God, can be added only as a secondary ministry attaching itself to it. The will of God is first done in heaven, and then on earth. We can paraphrase this to the effect that it first takes place in heaven and then on earth that God is praised by the creature, finding His creaturely correspondence and witnesses. He has found these in heaven before He finds a single one on earth. They exist in plenitude and perfection there even when there seems to be or are only a few on earth, and these are all extremely feeble witnesses. And because His kingdom comes from heaven to earth, this means that in those who come with Him He will always have many trustworthy witnesses on earth, namely, in the existence of His strong angels who are always present and active in full numbers, willingness and readiness even where the earthly creature seems to be sadly lacking with its praise both in quantity and quality, and in view of whom we can never find completely intolerable and hopeless the apparently or genuinely troubled state of things on earth. The heavenly witnesses to God's rule of the Church and the world, these witnesses of the first rank, are always and everywhere present. And when we have the insight into the protocols of ecclesiastical and universal history which is denied to even the most perspicacious of ordinary historians and students of human affairs, we shall probably find the most unexpected traces of the way in which the angels have been present and effectively spoken and acted, not as demigods or fabled creatures, but simply in the heavenly power of their witness and praise.

We must insist that their ministry is a ministry of witness. God alone rules. God alone is holy and gracious, sovereign and merciful, kind, omnipotent and glorious. Jesus Christ alone is the Lord of all things. Creatures, including the angels, can only praise Him and be His witnesses. But in the course of the divine speech, action and rule the angels as heavenly creatures are His pri- [463] mary, authentic, constant, inflexible and infallible witnesses. Their praise of God is pure praise. Their existence corresponds perfectly to His Word and work. The service which, in praising Him, they render both to Him and to their fellow-creatures is always an authentic, a fully authentic service. It is this because it is quite free from any personal desires for power or lordship. What is represented and present in the angels is always the whole secret of God. And it is the genuine secret of God, poles apart from any mystagogy or pseudo-mystery, and finally consisting only in the simple, but in its simplicity inaccessible and unfathomable reality that He, God, is with us and for us: He, the Lord, who alone can command but does command; He, the Lord over every difficulty, and always in some way the Lord who leads us out of every difficulty; He, the Lord of life and death; He, the Lord who imputes and does not impute sins; He, the Lord who in all things is to be feared and loved; He, the Lord even of nature and history; He alone, but He totally and infallibly. This is the great and genuine mystery of God. What do we know already of this mystery? How stupid even the best of us are in face of this simple "He"! What are all our theology and liturgy, preaching and piety, when we realise that they must deal with this total and genuine mystery of God? And what is the praise of our soul and existence, what are we ourselves, when we measure ourselves by the fact that we are to correspond to this mystery? But the angels know and praise and attest Him in this mystery. As those who do, they are present when heaven comes down to earth, and He speaks and acts and rules on earth. They observe and sanctify this mystery, declaring it in all its glory, as first in heaven, then between heaven and earth, and finally on earth they form its accompaniment and circumference. They are not blind or deaf or without feeling for this mystery. They exist in contemplation of it, from afar but steadily and openly. And for this reason they are not dumb or indolent. They exist as they declare it, and therefore as they are faithful in relation to God and their fellow-creatures. Their existence is thus exemplary. This is not because they are heavenly creatures, but because as heavenly creatures they are ordained and summoned by God Himself to exist in this way. They do so in obedience to this calling. This is, in general terms, the service of angels. The fact that they are real servants in this sense, that they are nothing but servants, is what makes then: existence exemplary in a way in which this cannot be said of any saint, let alone of any of the other great men in the earthly sphere.

2. *The Kingdom of Heaven*

We can best illustrate the biblical presuppositions of what is said from the main themes of Revelation 4 and 5, where we have an authentic general depiction of the ministry of angels. The two chapters exercise a retarding function in the context of the apocalyptic narration (E. Peterson, *op. cit.*, p. 19). In 4^1 the seer is told: "I will shew thee things which must be hereafter." But in the first instance he is not shown these things. Through the open door of heaven he first sees (*c.* 4) the throne of God, then—in highly characteristic movement—its immediate *entourage*, then (*c.* 5) in the midst of the throne and those around it the Lamb to whom there is given the book with seven seals in which these future events are inscribed, and finally the renewed movement of the whole *entourage*, which is now inimitably extended. "The invisible background of world history is disclosed" (J. T. Beck, *Erkl. d. Off. Joh.*, 1884, 92). It is from this that the eschatological events later revealed to the seer acquire their true relevance. Our interest must now be particularly focused on this background to the extent that to it there also belongs the heavenly *entourage* of God and the Lamb, and its distinctive movement.

The controlling centre of what the seer is shown is the throne with its lightnings, thunders and voices (4^5) and He who sits on it (vv. 2–3). But He who sits on it is not named. He does not need to be named. There is only One who can sit on it. And what He is, is indicated by the radiance which streams from Him and which is compared with that of particularly bright diamonds and the rainbow. We are reminded of 1 Jn. 1^5: "God is light, and in him is no darkness at all." He is the Holy One who reveals Himself, to whom everything is revealed, and who reveals all things in what He does. There then follows the description of His immediate *entourage* in vv. 4–8.

It begins with the 24 $\pi\rho\epsilon\sigma\beta\acute{u}\tau\epsilon\rho o\iota$[EN353] sitting on thrones, clothed in white robes and bearing crowns. Irrespective of any questions of superiority or subordination, these obviously form the outer circle around the throne of God. They are not glorified men, and therefore they cannot be identified with ecclesiastics, whether Roman cardinals, Lutheran pastors or Presbyterian elders. According to the place, speech and action ascribed to them, they are undoubtedly angels, so that the seer can address one of them as $\kappa\acute{u}\rho\iota o\varsigma$[EN354] in 7^{14}. Already in Is. 24^{23} the term "ancients" seems to be used for angels. But the fact that they are given this designation does not mean that they are to be thought of either as old men or as counsellors. It has often been suggested that the heavenly assembly is a kind of privy council around the throne of God, but this rests on a conception which here as elsewhere is quite alien to biblical angelology. There is not a single trace of any such function in their conduct in Rev. 4–5. And Is. 40^{13} (and possibly Rom. 11^{34}) is quite conclusive in this respect: "Who hath directed the Spirit of the Lord, or being his counsellor hath taught him?" We cannot deduce from their name more than that they are exalted and authoritative beings, as suggested by the fact that they sit on thrones and bear crowns. A sober but possibly the best translation is "representatives," which brings us at once into proximity to the terms used by Paul to denote the heavenly beings. Of these we are particularly reminded of $\theta\rho\acute{o}\nu o\iota$[EN355]. It would be a mistake, of course, to think of them as representing the earthly community, or a perfected community translated into heaven. If they represent anything or anyone, then, in accordance with their general function, it is God in His relationship to a specific earthly sphere of reality. To which sphere is decided by the interpretation of the number 24. Is this the number of the tribes of Israel doubled with the accession of the Gentiles? Does it represent the 12 patriarchs together with the 12 apostles? Are we to think of the 24 priestly classes

---

[EN353] Elders
[EN354] Lord
[EN355] thrones

and their "princes" in 1 Chron. 24⁴ᶠ.? If these suggestions are correct, the 24 are the representatives of God in relation to the fellowship of the old and new people of God. In other words, they are in plurality what in the Book of Daniel Michael is said to be in particular. Or are they the 24 hours of the day as determined by the movement of the firmament, thus representing on a Pythagorean interpretation the totality of the astronomical heaven? This suggestion has the advantage of establishing a clear relationship between the 24 elders and the 4 living creatures, which are obviously the representatives of God in relation to the sublunary or earthly sphere. But in the text itself there is no direct indication that the 24 have

[465] this astral character. Possibly the text itself ought not to be read in such a way as to entail a clear decision between these alternatives, but something of all of them ought to be found in the number 24. The important thing, however, is that they are clothed in white garments. We remember that in Rev. 19¹⁴ the heavenly hosts who follow the Word of God are also clothed in white and ride on white horses. Again, the head and hair of the Son of Man—and this has nothing to do with old age—are said to be "white like wool, as white as snow" (Rev. 1¹⁴). Again, we are told that at the transfiguration the raiment of Jesus "became shining, exceeding white as snow; so as no fuller on earth can white them" (Mk. 9³), or "white as the light" (Mt. 17²). This whiteness is the appropriate response of the creature to the multi-coloured radiance of God (v. 3). The fact that the 24 elders wear white clothes means that they reflect this δόξα EN356 of God. They do not owe these clothes to their own nature, or to the fact that they are heavenly beings. These are not the robes of earthly kings or priests, but the festal garments with which they are invested in virtue of the fact that God has sat on this throne among them. It is He alone who makes heaven and its creatures bright.

The question arises whether we are to take it that the "seven lamps of fires burning before the throne, which are the seven Spirits of God" (v. 5), are angelic beings. They are not mentioned again. And it cannot be denied that the context in which the phrase is introduced in Rev. 1⁴ supports the view that this is perhaps a distinctive designation of the Holy Spirit Himself. Rev. 5⁶ points in the same direction with its reference to the seven eyes of the Lamb "which are the seven Spirits of God." But the images and terms used by the writer are so elusive that we cannot rule out the possibility that in this case, where it fits the context better, the seven spirits are not the divine Spirit in His activity and manifoldness, but heavenly creatures, described as λαμπάδες πυρὸς καιόμεναι EN357 in correspondence to the radiance of God and in analogy to the white clothes of the elders, and certainly to be understood as representatives of the divine lordship in process of establishment over the whole cosmos.

Finally—beyond the crystal sea, in which we have probably to see the heavenly ocean of Gen. 1⁷ now made transparent and robbed of its terrors—there are the four living creatures of v. 6f., in whose depiction we seem to have a combination of the seraphim of Is. 6 and the four similarly described creatures of Ez. 1, the first like a lion, the second like a calf, the third with a face as a man, the fourth like a flying eagle, and all with six wings and full of eyes within. In the fact that we have here a wild beast, a domestic animal, a man and a bird, there is a clear reference not only to the earthly but to the sub-lunary sphere. It would be even clearer if we were to relate their number to the four parts of the day, or the four seasons of the year, or the four quarters of heaven, or to all these things in conjunction. And it is remarkable, and to be noted in our exposition, that these earthly beings in the narrowest sense stand in an innermost circle around God almost like an immediate bodyguard, just as later they will have a most important part to play. On the other hand, it must be pointed out that their description bursts the limits of all observation or even conception of earthly crea-

---

EN356 glory
EN357 lamps of fire burning

tures. They are not earthly creatures. We cannot, then, regard them, as I was once tempted to do, as the "representation and concentration of creaturely life in the world in the original form of paradisal perfection" (W. Hadorn, *Die Offb. d. Joh.*, 1928, 72). Certainly the reference is to creaturely nature on earth, but what we have here is the representation and relationship of God to it, of the representation of His lordship even in this sphere. The four living creatures are creatures; but they are not earthly creatures. They are quite definitely heavenly beings.

The point is now reached where the whole picture comes to life, or where it is shown to the seer to be already caught up in a secret movement. For while the 24 elders continue to sit on the thrones, and the lamps only burn, it is said of these creatures in the innermost circle that "they rest not day nor night." It is as though they were the perpetual motion by which   [466] the earthly sphere in the narrowest sense, the sub-lunary world, but latently too the astral and even the heavenly, is constantly kept in unrest, or tension, or expectation of things to come. It is as though the whole historical drama in which all heaven is later engaged were initiated at this point by what the four creatures, as the heralds of the eternal vitality of God Himself, have always done and will obviously do up to a certain moment in the process of that general movement, when they are themselves caught up in it (5^8). At any rate, we can see in them first what is meant by the ministry of angels: the praise which is offered to God but in this way is also proclaimed to the whole earthly and heavenly cosmos; the praise of God in His absolute uniqueness, superiority and lordship in relation to all His creatures. In other words, they strike up the well-known, threefold *Sanctus* of Is. 6^3. They confirm and express the fact that the angels are holy ones by looking away from themselves and again and again praising God as the Holy One. They are characterised as heavenly beings by the fact that they can and self-evidently do do this, not being a people of unclean lips as the prophet confesses in Is. 6^5, but a people of clean lips.

We must go on at once to comment on v. 9 if we are to understand this *Sanctus*-cry. The concept of a heavenly cultus-act continued in all kinds of corresponding earthly actions is surely far too narrow to describe what is here represented as the heavenly liturgy commencing with the call of the four creatures. They "give" glory and honour and thanks to Him who sits on the throne and lives from aeon to aeon. This means that they render or ascribe to Him that which belongs to Him. They acknowledge that all these things are His, and cannot belong to any other. They acknowledge Him as God. Hence they do not do anything which is strange, but that which is natural and self-evident to their nature as creatures. They do not do anything which is particularly solemn or festal, but that which is supremely everyday. They do that which is proper to them and to all creatures from the very first. They do not know any other creaturely act but that which they fulfil with the threefold *Sanctus*. To be sure, this is a liturgy, but it is the kind of liturgy which can find a true correspondence on earth only when earthly creatures join the heavenly with the same self-evident totality as is actually described in 5^{13}. For this reason we should bring it into indirect and not into direct relation (like Peterson) with the liturgy of the Church in its isolation and separation from the natural and everyday events of life. The thought expressed in Rev. 4^8 by the term ὁ παντοκράτωρ [EN358] is found already in Is. 6^3: "The whole earth is full of his glory." Not the earthly Church, or a monastic or congregational choir, but the earthly cosmos as such and in its totality is the true and proper participant in the heavenly song of praise initiated by the four living creatures. What the earthly Church can do in this respect will surely be done the more joyfully and solemnly and festally the more consciously it is done with the incumbent modesty.

[EN358] the Almighty

A further point to be noted in the *Sanctus* of the four living creatures is that the call of the seraphim in Is. 6³ is visibly expanded in v. 8. The doxologies of Rev. 4 have often been brought into specific relationship to the first article of the creed: *Credo in unum Deum* (W. Hadorn, p. 68, 73). There is a grain of truth in this. Only in Rev. 5 do we see the Lamb in the midst of the throne. But it must not be overlooked that the God whose uniqueness, superiority and lordship are first confessed by the four living creatures is He who "was, and is, and is to come." The ontological sequence of praise is obviously broken in the third link where instead of the expected "who will be" we have "who is to come" (Peterson, p. 24). God is the Creator, but He is not only the One who as such always will be, as He always has been and now is, the Lord of the creature. He is also the One who has set off and is in process of coming as such. The fact that in the answering chorus of the 24 elders He is expressly praised as the Creator (4¹¹) must certainly be taken to mean that He, this One who comes, who does not abandon the creature but is on the way to it as Judge and Saviour, is the Creator of the universe by whose will it was created. He is thus worthy that all δόξα, τιμή EN359 and δύναμις EN360 should be ascribed to Him. The song struck up in 5⁹ is, of course, a new song in the sense that it explicitly proclaims this coming of the Lord, or rather the fact that He has already come in what the Lamb has done on earth. But even so it only confirms what is implicitly declared and proclaimed to the heavenly and earthly world by the four living creatures. Did not their praise of God in v. 9 expressly add to δόξα EN361 and τιμή EN362 the εὐχαριστία EN363 which goes beyond anything we meet with in Is. 6³? Is not their song already a true *Benedictus qui venit in nomine Domini* EN364, and to that extent an anticipation of that new song?

If this were not the case, the 24 elders could not do what they twice do later (5⁶, ¹⁴). They could not fall down and worship (προσκυνεῖν) before the Lamb, thus repeating exactly the action which is their present answer to the praise of the 4 living creatures (4¹⁰). This, then, is the action with which they too are set in motion. It is plainly presupposed, although not explicitly stated, that they come down from their thrones. They then prostrate themselves before the One who sits on the throne, worshipping the One who lives for ever, and casting their crowns before the throne.

It is to be noted especially that according to the plain sense of vv. 9–10 it is the praise of the 4 living creatures which sets the 24 elders in motion. The former precede and the latter follow. Yet according to the whole depiction the former are angelic beings in which the lordship of God over the depths of earth is particularly represented, so that as compared with the 24 crowned heads on their thrones we might well regard them as lower angels. We have already seen, however, that the whole conception of higher and lower angels is quite untenable. And how we should be thrown into confusion in this passage if we tried to apply it, and thus regarded the 4 as inferior and the 24 as superior, but then suddenly found that the 4 came first and the 24 only second and for the moment last ! But it would be equally false to reverse the classification. All that we can and must say is that the 4 precede the 24 because they are angelic beings which stand in particular relation to the depths of earth. As they look into these depths with their countless eyes, they see something which evokes their *Sanctus*-cry. In anticipation of what will be expressly said in the hymn of 5⁹ we might well expand this from Eph. 3¹⁰. In these depths they see the ἐκκλησία EN365, and there is thus

[467]

EN359 glory, honour
EN360 power
EN361 glory
EN362 honour
EN363 thanksgiving
EN364 Blessed is the one who comes in the name of the Lord.
EN365 Church

revealed to them the πολυποίκιλος σοφία τοῦ θεοῦ[EN366]. At all events, in His relation to this sphere in the depths they recognise Him who sits on the throne as the Holy One, as the παντοκράτωρ[EN367], as Him who was, and is, and comes. We can and must hazard the statement that what the 4 living creatures proclaim is the evident mercy of God in relation to this lower sphere. And in this respect the 24 elders, the crowned heads on their 24 thrones, which seem to be superior in their significance for salvation history or their astral character, can only follow them. It is as they hear this proclamation that they too are summoned and set in motion.

It is also to be noted that in the first instance their movement takes the form of a silent action and only later finds expression in the corresponding word or song. They first perform a simple act of humility. We are not told that the 4 living creatures performed a similar act, perhaps because their particular nature and position made such an act superfluous, whereas it was natural for the 24 in authority to express their supremacy by placing their powers so dramatically at the disposal of God. But quite apart from the meaning of this action it is worth noting that here (and again in 5^8, ^{14}) there is such explicit reference not merely to the speech or singing of angels but also to their action. This is of a piece with the fact that in 5^7 there is brief reference to something which takes place between the Lamb and Him who sits on the throne. One might have supposed that the two chapters would have consisted only of a description of the encounter between God and the heavenly world and an accout of the doxologies pronounced or sung by the angels. How easily heaven might then have been regarded as a kingdom of spiritual truths and eternal ideas, as a static background to world history! Yet this is not the case. For it is in heaven that the occurrence originates which then takes earthly form as cosmic and eschatological occurrence. The angels in heaven do already what will also be done on earth by earthly creatures. [468]

Their action consists, however, in the fact that they leave their thrones and worship and cast their crowns before the throne, unequivocally acknowledging before God and all other heavenly creatures and even earthly creation in the person of the seer that there can be no question of any rivalry between their being and majesty and greatness and distinction and rule, and the being, activity and rule of God Himself. They let it be known that they cannot occupy or claim the position of viceroys or regents in their relationship to God. If we can say this of a happening within heaven itself, they go down into the depths. The movement which they execute is an act of solidarity with the rest of creation. They first associate themselves with the four living creatures, and then indirectly with the host of earthly creatures to whom these have addressed themselves from heaven. We are reminded of Lk. 1^{51f}: "He hath shewed strength with his arm; he hath scattered the proud in the imagination of their hearts. He hath put down the mighty from their seats." But in this case there are no tyrants to be deposed nor is there any pride to be broken. The proud become humble and the great small in the glorious liberty of the children of God. There is an imitation of God Himself, whose majesty is proclaimed in the song of the 4 living creatures as a majesty of His mercy and condescension. The prostration of the 24 conforms to this pattern. It is this that they praise when they cast their crowns before the throne of God.

It is in this sense, too, that we are to understand the hymn of the 24 as recorded in v. 11. We can hardly agree with Peterson (p. 26) in describing it as "acclamation," for this suggests that formally at least they were engaged in passing a resolution (like an ancient crowd at a public election or the like). But this is not the case. The ἄξιος εἶ[EN368] with which the hymn

---

[EN366] manifold wisdom of God
[EN367] Almighty
[EN368] Thou art worthy

opens has the following significance—that it is intrinsically proper, that it belongs or corresponds to Thee, to … Hence that which is stated of God in what follows is not a predicate ascribed to Him, nor a title conferred by others. It is to be understood analytically as the recognition of what He is originally and essentially in Himself before any other being can resolve or approve or confer it, and of what He would still be if no other being attributed it to Him. The λαβεῖν EN369 is to be understood along similar lines. It corresponds to the δώσουσιν EN370 of v. 9. What can be given to Him who sits on the throne? What has He still to receive? This hymn, as in v. 9, tells us that δόξα, τιμή EN371 and δύναμις EN372 belong to Him, and to Him alone, and to Him in fulness from all eternity. If the heavenly creation here says that He is worthy to receive these things, this does not mean that He needs to receive them from it, but that it is its own honour and greatness to be able to "give" them to Him, i.e., to acknowledge Him as the One to whom they belong. Doing this, it actualises and increases its own glory and honour and power. It has this in the acknowledgment that what it is and has— this is the explination of the descent from the thrones and casting of the golden crowns before His throne—is His. He has created all things, including the heavenly creation. All things, and therefore this creation too, are and were created by His will. As it recognises this, it exists in its own particularity. And we remember what impelled it to this recognition, and therefore what aroused the 24 to their action, thus causing them to expand and to find their true being in what they do and say and sing. They heard the voices of the 24 living creatures; their *Sanctus*-cry *e profundis* EN373. They accepted the statement that εὐχαριστία EN374 as well as δόξα EN375 and τιμή EN376 belong to Him who sits on the throne. They recognised His

[469]

mercy, and in this they saw His majesty and His glory as the Creator. This is what brought them into motion, summoning them down from their thrones and opening their mouths in this hymn. This is what integrates them into the ministry of angels. Indeed, this is what makes them angels. What they were before, or would be in themselves, and apart from this, it is difficult to see. But at least they would not exist in their particularity as angels if they merely sat on their thrones and bore their crowns and in the heights gazed dumbly at the even greater height of God, or merely looked straight in front of them, not entering into solidarity with all other creatures or participating in their own way in the service and praise of God. The fact that they fulfil this act of humility and offer their hymn is the climax of Rev. 4 from the standpoint of the *entourage* of God which is our present concern.

If our view of Rev. 4 is correct, the following chapter is not to be regarded as the description of another event but as a deeper and more specific consideration of the event already recorded in *c*. 4. What is implicit in the earlier chapter is now made explicit. But for this purpose a new picture is introduced and a new song has to be sung.

Something already before the seer, but not yet noted or named by him, now claims his attention (v. 1). In the right hand of Him who sits on the throne there is the roll of a book. That it is written on both sides is an indication of the fulness of what is designated in it. It is hardly a happy description to call it the "book of destiny" (K. L. Schmidt, *Aus der Joh. Apok.*, 1944, 8). The fact that it is sealed with seven seals characterises it as a will, or at least as a document which has to be executed as well as noted. Thus the opening of the book means that what is written in it takes place in history. This is what will be shown to the seer in Rev.

EN369 taking
EN370 they will give
EN371 glory, honour
EN372 power
EN373 out of the depths
EN374 thanksgiving
EN375 glory
EN376 honour

6–7. But we have not yet reached this point. How will the book come to be opened and these events set in train? The book is in God's hand. It obviously contains His will and counsel, which will be executed when it is opened. And vv. 2–3 make it plain that it is in the hand of God alone. Who is worthy to open it? Who can and may and will be in a position to open it? This is the question of a "strong angel" which rings out through heaven and down to earth and to the depths under the earth. It is a task genuinely worthy of an angel to put questions like this. But even in heaven there is no answer. No one can or may or will execute what God has resolved. No one can even know it. No one can even look into the book in His hand. No creature can do this, not even the strong angel who addresses the question to his fellow-creatures. God is always sovereign. He alone decides and effects, and He alone knows the things which must be hereafter (4^1). "And I wept much," says the seer (v. 4), namely, because this is how matters stand between the Creator and the creature. The creature is implicated in what God proposes and will execute. It is a matter of itself and its future, of His judgment on it, of its salvation or perdition. Surely, then, it ought to have some say, or at least to know something about it. But this is denied to it. No one can open the book (v. 3). No one is found worthy to do so (v. 4). This is a startling thought for at least the earthly creation represented by the divine who here sees and hears what goes on in heaven. It is startled to think that its future is so wholly in the hands of God. It is startled that it is so completely abandoned to that which comes and which it can neither influence nor foresee. It is startled to think of events which it cannot control or even foreknow. And human creatures which have sinned against God have every cause to be terrified on these counts. But possibly the text is merely suggesting that quite apart from any fear or weeping there is dreadful suspense even in heaven in relation to this closed book. For heaven, too, belongs to the cosmos. It thus participates in what God causes to take place on earth, in the sphere of man, and in the expectation of these coming things. But it, too, is quite unable to open the book or even to look into it.

What follows in v. 5 is in the first instance a word of comfort addressed by one of the [470] heavenly beings—one of the 24—to the terrified human seer, but it is also an announcement which is new and important not only to him and the earthly creation represented by him, but to all the heavenly creatures gathered round the throne of God, both ending the weeping of man and preparing the angelic world for a resolving of the tension which oppresses it. The announcement is to the following effect: "Behold, the Lion of the tribe of Judah, the Root of David, hath prevailed to open the book, and to loose the seals thereof." This news of the victory of the Lion of Judah and Root of David is obviously the Easter message of the resurrection of Jesus Christ from the dead, in which it has been revealed at a specific time and place in the earthly sphere that God Himself has closed the gap between Himself and the creatures in the person of this Jewish man, and that He has exalted this Jewish man to participation in His lordship over all creation. It is a victory of God, and for this reason and in this way of man too; a victory from above, and therefore from below. It is God who has raised this Jewish man from the dead, and it is therefore this Jewish man who has passed through and over the abyss of death. It is God who has placed this man at His side, and it is therefore this man who has become equal to God. What is the reason for all this? It is in order that He, the human Victor in the grace and power and glory of God, or the divine Victor in the grace and power and glory of this man, should open the book, and thus set in train the future events still concealed from all creatures. It is in order that He should stand at the beginning of these events as their Lord. It is in order that He should resolve and know the things which must be hereafter. And because this is true the seer need not weep and the heavenly creation may rejoice at that which will come to pass.

It is to be noted that the saying of the elder in v. 5 only contains this announcement as such. The declared Victor is not yet seen. The book is still closed and in the hand of God. Hence the seer has every reason to continue weeping. That which holds the heavenly world in tension has not yet been objectively removed. There has been no perception of the revelation of God and of that Victor, the Lion of Judah. The elder himself is not God, nor is he the Lion of Judah, but only his creaturely witness and herald. So far only the witness is to hand. The seer can only be comforted, and the solution of the tension which causes the upper cosmos to hold its breath prepared. This is the provisional accomplishment of the elder with his announcement. He cannot do more. Having done this, he will take his place with the rest and have no further claim to special attention. What we see him fulfil is the typical ministry of angel and witness, in all its greatness and with all its limitations.

The new and decisive vision and occurrence are to be found in vv. 6–7. "And I beheld," we are told in v. 6. But according to v. 8 the whole of heaven beheld, and it then struck up a new song from which we gather that it had seen something new and decisive (v. 9). The author of the early Christian hymn quoted in 1 Tim. 3^{16} had perhaps something of the same picture in mind as that described here when he said: ὤφθη ἀγγέλοις EN377. No angel has a part in what is seen by the divine and all angels. There takes place that which is announced in v. 5: the revelation of the Lion of Judah, the Root of David, as the One who will receive and open the sealed book; His revelation before all the creatures of heaven, with whom there is associated the earthly creature as a dumb and distant participant. But the surprise is twofold. The Lion was indicated, but what is revealed—"in the midst of the throne and of the four beasts, and in the midst of the elders," as we are forced to translate—is the Lamb. The Lamb is the Lion, the divine and human Victor, who has crossed the abyss between God and man and made the unprecedented step from man to God. The earlier reference to the Lion had the Lamb in view. And it is the self-revelation of the Lamb which declares and confirms that the Lamb is the Lion. We are in heaven and not on earth. The description of the Lamb is thus beyond

[471]   normal apprehension. It is "as it had been slain," which means that it is a sacrificial animal still bearing the marks of its immolation. But in Rev. 1^{18} we are told concerning the One who is here called the Lamb: "I was dead; and, behold, I am alive for evermore." Seven horns are the marks of His power, and seven eyes of His manifold knowledge proceeding from Him in countless ways. Although He is only a Lamb, and "as it had been slain," He is well equipped to undertake and execute what is later committed to Him. It is clear that the reference is to Jesus Christ: to Jesus Christ Himself and not merely to the witness who declares Him; to Jesus Christ, not as resurrected, but as suffering, crucified, dead and buried for the sin of human creatures; to Jesus Christ in His humiliation and sacrifice, in the event of Golgotha. But humiliated and sacrificed, He was the victorious Lion announced in v. 5. As such He accomplished that which is revealed in the event of Easter and attested in the Easter message. As the Humiliated and Sacrificed He declares and confirms this witness. The offering of the Lamb is the triumph of the Lion, the victory of God and man, the closing of the gap between them, the elevation of man to the side of God. This is how the divine sees Him. This is how the heavenly creatures see Him. But they see more. They see how this Lamb "came and took (ἦλθεν καὶ εἴληφεν) the book out of the right hand of him that sat upon the throne." He came—this is His enthronement. He took—this is His seizure of power. For what He received and took is obviously the closed book. As yet there is no word of the opening of the book, but the Lamb takes up the position in which this will follow. The closed book is now in His hands. He will break its seven seals one after the other. The execution of all God's secret counsel will be His affair. Is God dead? Or has He gone into retirement? Far from it! The Lamb is not a second and different God. He is the one God. He will not change the counsel of the one God but execute it faithfully. What is revealed in His enthronement and seizure of power is that from all eternity the secret counsel of God, whatever may be its content in detail, has had the meaning which finds form and reality in the fact that this Lamb is the

---

EN377 seen of angels

Lion, the all-powerful and all-wise Executor of His will and plan. The majesty of God as His mercy was the outline and shadow of the divine mystery as indicated already in Rev. 4. And now at the climax of Rev. 5 we are confronted by the form and reality of the same mystery.

But for creation this entails a basic alteration of the picture. And first the angelic world is set in new and decisive and comprehensive motion at the sight of the Lamb (v. 8f.). In 4^8 it was angels who set other angels in motion. But this time these and all angels are stirred to action by the revelation from the throne itself. Only when the secret of God is present as the Lamb which is the Lion can the majesty of God even over the heavenly creation be unequivocally seen, i.e., that He does not merely receive its praise but evokes it; that it can be only the answer to His Word; that the word and ministry of angels can be only a witness to Him which He Himself commissions and empowers. The divine summons is the enthronement of the Lamb and His seizure of power.

Its first effect in v. 8 is the common prostration of the four beasts and the four and twenty elders, self-evidently before the throne of God, but specifically before the Lamb as the Executor of the will of God and therefore as the divine King in whom the substance of the will of God is seen. And something new is now said concerning them. It is not quite clear whether it is said of the 4 beasts too, or only of the 24 elders. I prefer the former view. But at any rate we are told that they all ($\H{\epsilon}\kappa\alpha\sigma\tau\sigma\varsigma$) have "harps, and golden vials full of incense." The harps are to be particularly noted, for in spite of Rev. 15^2 as well as this passage, Peterson (p. 62), obsessed by his monastic choirs, is rash enough to say that there is only vocal music in heaven. Nor should we ignore what we are told concerning the vials—that they are the "prayers of saints" (cf. Ps. 141^2). The "saints" (cf. Rev. 8^3 and *passim*) are members of the Christian community on earth to which there is an immediate and most important reference in the new song of v. 9f. That their $\pi\rho\sigma\epsilon\upsilon\chi\alpha\acute{\iota}$[EN378] penetrate to the throne of God only [472] through the mediation of angels is a thought which is quite alien to this context and to the whole biblical doctrine both of prayer and of angels. According to Rom. 8^{27} it is the Spirit who intercedes for the saints according to the will of God. And the biblical angels do not work from below upwards, but from above downwards. Yet what encounters them from below, the prayers of the Christian community, may well serve to adorn and distinguish and demonstrate their downward operation as its fruit and result. To that extent we can say with Hadorn (p. 79) that there is at least an indirect reference at this point to a uniting of the community of God on earth with the adoration of the creatures of heaven. Where there is a praying community on earth, the angels are also present (cf. 1 Cor. 11^{10}). And where the angels are present, as they are orientated on earth, there are also present—hence the golden vials in their hands—the prayers of the saints. And there too, also evoked by the angels, are the voices of the rest of the lower cosmos which can neither sing, pray, nor even speak, but which yet has voices which in something analogous to the prayer of saints, in longing and gratitude, in pain and joy, can come to the angels and to God Himself, sounding before Him and being heard by Him. Peterson is quite wrong to speak so unkindly of mechanical instruments of music. Surely the playing of musical instruments is a more or less conscious, skilful and intelligent human attempt to articulate before God this sound of a cosmos which is otherwise dumb. Surely the perfect musician is the one who, particularly stirred by the angels, is best able to hear not merely the voice of his own heart but what all creation is trying to say, and can then in great humility and with great objectivity cause it to be heard by God and other men. Hence the harps in the hands of these angels. As they cast themselves down before the Lamb in the midst of the throne, they are adorned not merely by the prayers of saints but by the general sighing of creation articulated in the instruments invented and played by man. We are well advised not to draw hasty conclusions from this fact

---

[EN378] prayers

as to the form of divine service (e.g., the use of organs). The praying community and the sounding cosmos are two very different things. So, too, are divine service and a concert. If the angels may have harps and vials, this does not mean that it is legitimate for us. But the fact remains that it does seem to be right for the angels to have both, to offer divine service in the form both of worship and of the concert, and thus to fall down before God with this twofold adornment.

And now we come to their new song in v. 9f. It is a new song because it is addressed to the form and reality of the One whom they have previously hymned only in outline and shadow (Rev. 4). Hadorn has justly observed (p. 79) that "in days of small things no new songs emerge, but we have to make do with the old." And it might be added that we usually display an understandable but anxious concern for the oldest possible songs and liturgies etc. The concept of the new song seems to refer even in the Old Testament (Ps. 96^1, 149^1; Is. 42^{10}) to the coming and crucial time of the Messiah. But here it is a matter of the incomparable new song. Again we hear the ἄξιος εἶ[EN379]. Again, and here particularly, the idea of a popular assembly with its advice or resolutions or acclamation is quite out of place. What is ascribed to the Lamb is only the subsequent assertion and recognition of what has not merely been resolved by God from all eternity but has actually taken place on earth. The Lamb has taken the closed book. He will open this book and set in train the events resolved by God. It is now only a matter of time and of His own free decision. And the event which makes Him worthy to do so, because in it the majesty of God has taken concrete form and reality in the work of His mercy, and the Lion is the genuinely victorious Lion as the Lamb, is an event which has already taken place. "Thou wast slain." It is an ἐφ' ἅπαξ[EN380] which can never be reversed and which needs no acclamation. It can only be affirmed and acknowledged and attested, first in heaven, and then on earth. And this is the service of the angels in their new song. As [473] they fulfil it, they look at the Lamb in the midst of the throne. But we have to realise that what they really see is the event which took place on earth. It was on Golgotha, before the gates of Jerusalem, in the reign of Tiberius Caesar, that this Lamb was slain. But it is decisively important that for all its finality and uniqueness this earthly event did not take place in isolation. This point is the middle of a circle. For when this Lamb was slain He did something particular on earth. He created a particular situation. He thus initiated a specific chain of corresponding events. By His blood (by giving His life) He redeemed for God. This sentence has no object. We are simply told, and this shows us unmistakeably that we are involved in the affairs of earth, that He redeemed "out of every kindred, and tongue, and people, and nation." This obviously means men from all these different spheres. And since they are redeemed, it means men who were imprisoned and enslaved. And since they are redeemed for God, it means men who in their imprisonment and slavery were estranged from God. The slaying of the Lamb has put an end to this state of affairs. They are liberated by this event. They are now free for God and for His service. This is the first thing which takes place in and with the slaying of the Lamb, and like this slaying it takes place on earth. The second is an act of creation. It is again the Lamb who accomplishes it. He has made these prisoners who have now been redeemed and set in the service of God "a kingdom and priesthood unto our God," so that they "shall reign on the earth." This is the positive aspect of what has taken place on earth in the light of Golgotha and around this central point. It might properly have been expected that in correspondence with the centre the reference would have been to the community despised, persecuted and suffering for the sake of Jesus Christ. A choir of mystics, ethicists and aesthetes could then have sung much the same song. And the earthly view of this earthly reality would correspond to it. But it is the angels who are

---

[EN379] Thou art worthy
[EN380] once for all

singing, and they see and assess the community as it is in heaven and in truth. The little collection of the baptised, scattered among the nations, has hardly escaped the intoxication and stupidity, the blasphemies and blunders, of its heathen past. It is exposed on all sides to oppression and menace. As Paul says in Rom. 8³⁶: "For thy sake we are killed all the day long; we are accounted as sheep for the slaughter"—and the quotation seems to be particularly apt. Yet this harassed flock is the kingdom of God and its members are His elect priests. They and not the *senatus populusque*EN381, or Caesar and his representatives, shall reign on the earth. For it is to be noted that we are not told that they for their part shall one day reign in heaven, but that—in correspondence with what is real in heaven—they shall reign on earth. We must not miss the correspondence. As they are seen from above, and therefore as they are in reality, they are there below what the Lamb is here above, the risen Christ seated at the right hand of God. According to Col. 3¹ they are not only dead with Christ but also raised with Him. And what is called in Col. 3³ their hidden life with Christ in God is here described as a concrete, earthly reality, concealed from earthly beings but revealed to heavenly, and no less a compact reality than the lordship of their risen Lord at the right hand of the Father. This, then, is what the angels have seen according to their new song. They have seen that centre, but they have also seen this circumference. They have seen the Lord, but they have also seen His people. They have seen the glory of Jesus Christ in heaven, but they have also seen it streaming back from earth where He did this for God (note the twofold τῷ θεῷ EN382), redeeming this people for God by His blood and refashioning them as God's incontestable possession. Again, and this time unmistakeably, the depths of earth have the advantage over heaven that it was here below that the decisive event took place, that the Lamb gained the victory as the Lion which He is now seen to be in heaven, that the will of the divine majesty attained its goal in the mercy with which God took earth to Himself. It is for this reason that the angels can and must sing that the Lamb is worthy to take the book and open the seals. It is for this reason that they can and must see and praise Jesus Christ [474] (*vere Deus vere homo*EN383) as the One who stands in the power and wisdom of God at the beginning of all cosmic occurrence and who will initiate and control all cosmic occurrence. It is for this reason that according to the new song the tension is broken with which even angels considered the closed book and contemplated things to come. It is for this reason that even man, the divine, who sees and hears things in the opened heavens, who may see with heavenly eyes what the angels saw, can no longer weep. That He has wiped away and will wipe away all tears from their eyes (Rev. 21⁴) is something which has already taken place, and taken place perfectly and irrevocably, in that which is here seen by the angels and man.

And now we read in v. 11f. that this man saw and heard the heavenly horizon and the heavenly choir extend into infinity. Many angels—we are reminded of the πλῆθος στρατιᾶς οὐρανίου EN384 of Lk. 2¹³—are revealed to the seer, in numbers which defy all calculation, as the outer circle of the heavenly assembly, joining "with a loud voice" in the ἄξιος εἶEN385. That their hymn, too, is addressed to the Lamb slain shows that they have all seen what has taken place on earth and then been revealed in heaven and attested first by the acts and words of the two angelic choirs in the immediate proximity of the throne. They too, the many angels, are witnesses of this happening. There is no angel who does not have and even receive his particularity in the service of witness to this event. But there is no more explicit reference, either here or in the final verses of the chapter, to the particular theme of the

---

EN381 [Roman] senate and the people
EN382 for God
EN383 truly God and truly a human being
EN384 multitude of the heavenly host
EN385 Thou art worthy

previous hymn, the taking of the book by the Lamb and His commissioning to open it. This is not forgotten, but it is caught up in the adoration of the Lamb as the Bearer of all the divine predicates of power and lordship (in a way reminiscent of the praise of Him that sits on the throne in 4^9, ^{11}). In the light of this it is surely imperative that Rev. 4 should be understood as we have tried to expound it. And if the same predicates of power and lordship are there ascribed to the one God and Creator, it is evident, now that Jesus Christ appears as their Bearer, that in Him we do not have to do with another but with one and the same God. The only difference is that not without cause a greater number of predicates is now mentioned. And it is no accident that the number is seven, but this indicates the perfection of the One to whom they are ascribed. And they seem to mount as it were to a climax. All the same, it is a little artificial to try to see in the seven predicates, as J. T. Beck does (p. 98), the seven means in the divine economy placed at the disposal of the Lamb for the opening of the seven seals, the four first serving to prepare and the three last to consummate the universal lordship committed to Him. The decisive point is not the difference or peculiarity of these predicates, but their character as moments and designations of the divine essence, and of the divine as the royal essence, superior to all created power and uniting in itself the plenitude of all power. It is this royal essence of God which all angels ascribe to Jesus Christ the Crucified and Resurrected and find united in Him. We remember the report which in the 2nd century the astonished Pliny sent to the emperor Trajan concerning Christians: *carmen Christo quasi Deo dicere*EN386. According to the text, this was first done by the hosts of heaven.

And now the circle opens again in v. 13. The divine does not see other creatures, but he certainly hears them. So far the reference has been only to the heavenly κτίσμα EN387 and its movement and witness. But now, unseen but heard by the divine, the κτίσμα EN388 on earth, under the earth, in the sea and within all these lower spheres, stands at the side of the heavenly creation. *Πᾶν κτίσμα* EN389, both heavenly beings and earthly now unite in a final song of praise.

It is worth adding with Hadorn (p. 80), however, that man is excluded. Man's praise of God forms a separate chapter and is not included here. Man is the target of the witness of all creation. If and to the extent that he takes part in its action, he is not simply one with all [475] other κτίσματα EN390. Thus it is not without reason that he is not mentioned here. He is all ears and eyes, but he does not take part. It is a little surprising, perhaps, that there is no reference at least to the earthly community of the saints, who are clearly mentioned in v. 8 and especially v. 10. According to the thesis of Peterson that there is a cultus in heaven in which the Church participates (p. 37). it ought to have appeared at this point. For here at the very latest it ought to have emerged that what is described in these chapters up to 5^{12} as the ministry of angels has its response and continuation in specific cultic actions of the earthly Church. The fact that there is no glimpse of this even in v. 13 shows how hollow is the thesis. Those in whom we find this response and continuation as participants in the heavenly cultus are the dwellers of earth and air and sea, the earthly cosmos as such and in its totality. What we are told is that in its own way, which differs from that of angels and men, it has a voice and language formally to join in the ministry of angels in a great cultic act. To be sure, the fact that there is no mention either of man generally or of the earthly Church in particular does not mean that they cannot sometimes join in the ministry of angels in the form of

---

EN386 they sing to Christ as God
EN387 creature
EN388 creature
EN389 every creature
EN390 creatures

such acts. Yet it does not seem likely, indeed there is not the slightest indication, that the participation of man and the Church in the ministry of angels is either exhausted or consists essentially in the kind of action which is here described as the participation of the earthly cosmos in this ministry. In other words, there is not the slightest indication that the fulfilment of such acts is the decisive action required of man and especially of the earthly Church on the model of what takes place in heaven. Man, and therefore the earthly Church, is certainly the target of the witness of heavenly beings and of all creation. But this does not mean—at any rate primarily and essentially, let alone exclusively—that man and the Church are required to join with the heavenly and earthly creation, to take part in their harmony and to conform to their action. What it does mean is that they are summoned by this ministry to enter the service of God in a way corresponding to their own nature. This is not ensured merely by their joining other earthly creatures in the heavenly cultus and thus participating in the harmony of the universe, no matter how faithfully they may reproduce the heavenly in their earthly cultus. For the ministry of angels is addressed to the God who did not become an angel but man, and who took man to Himself. This means that the service of God to which the angels summon man and the Church is one which is proper to them and different from their own. Imitation of angels is not what is demanded of man and the Church by the ministry of angels. Thus the earthly Church will never see its decisive task in copying the cultus of heaven. May it always be restrained from doing so! It must never cease to hear the ironical warning of Amos $5^{21f.}$: "I hate, I despise your feast days, and I will not smell in your solemn assemblies .... Take thou away from me the noise of thy songs; for I will not hear the melody of thy viols. But let judgment run down as waters, and righteousness as a mighty stream." When the witness of heavenly beings and all creation really reaches the ear of man, and is taken seriously by the earthly Church, it will be realised that from the Church there is demanded a service which is perhaps more strict and stringent but also more full of promise, and certainly its own and not just a replica of what is done by others. This is the point which we have to make in relation to the striking silence of v. 13 concerning man and the Church, and in opposition to the thesis of Peterson.

But now we must emphasise the positive truth that there is an important conjunction of the lower with the upper cosmos in the same praise of God. It is addressed in common "unto him that sitteth upon the throne, and unto the Lamb." There is a confluence of the two apparently separate streams of the doxologies of *cc.* 4 and 5. With the conjunction of the earthly and heavenly choirs there is this conjunction in the theme of their praise of God. But the converse is also to be seen and stated that it is because there is already this conjunction in theme in the hymns struck up in v. 9f. and v. 12 that the earthly choirs can and must join the [476] heavenly, and all those of whom it was said in v. 3f. that they could not open the book can and must rejoice together. We can hardly regard this conjunction of earthly creatures as spontaneous like that of the many angels in v. 11, as though beings on the earth and under the earth and in the sea had seen of themselves what was seen by the angels and the man associated with them in his vision. The knowledge that Christ is risen, that the Lamb is the victorious Lion, that the closed book of the divine counsel has been given to Him to open, that all power is given to Him in heaven and earth, is not a knowledge which originates on earth and can be attained by the human earthly creature of itself. It is a heavenly knowledge which comes down to earth from heaven. And we are told in v. 13 that it has actually come down to earth from heaven, that with the sole exception of man, who is a special case, the lower cosmos in its totality, in all its heights and depths, has heard as a message the preceding praise of the angels. Nor has it remained silent in face of this message, but it has taken up the song and made it its own. Indeed, it could not remain silent. It found and used its own voice and language. It was not referred to, nor could it be content with, that which man could do for it in this respect, as in v. 8. Whether its song was taken up by man or not, whether it was given musical articulation or not, it joined *de profundis*[EN391] in the hymn of praise struck up by the angels *in excelsis*[EN392]. The praise of God thus rang out *una voce*[EN393] from both heaven and earth, and not merely general praise of God, but praise of God and the Lamb who in their unity are the true and genuine God. The divine did not see this. The inversion at this point is remarkable. He saw the heavenly choirs, but not the earthly. He only heard the latter. But he did hear them. And it was necessary that he should hear them. For this is what distinguishes his vision from mere hallucination. What distinguishes the heavenly beings themselves from mere ideas or spirits or figments of the imagination is that their praise of God should prove effective on earth; that it should not return empty; that it should not awaken merely the ominous echo of a contradiction; that it should not find the response of an arbitrarily different confession; but that the whole cosmos, stirred by the praise of the angels, should express itself in harmony.

In v. 14, however, the circle which has been constantly extending is suddenly narrowed again in a most impressive way. Only the immediate *entourage* of the throne can be seen and heard. The four beasts—note that they again take the initiative—pronounce the Amen, and the 24 elders, following the sign given by them, make a final act of adoration. There is something sobering in the thought, and it warns us plainly against any systematisation of the preceding climax, that the harmony of the universe in the praise of God and the Lamb is not the last word. This harmony refuses to be equated with the wild shout of joy in the 9th symphony of Beethoven. The last word is the short anticlimax with which we are brought back to the beginning to the extent that the narrowest sphere of heaven is all that is seen. The Amen and the final act of adoration are the last thing which the divine sees and hears of the ministry of angels at the conclusion of this great introduction to the ensuing opening of the book.

A final observation may be made. At one time θεολογία[EN394] was thought of as knowledge of the kind of matters which have occupied us here. Rev. 4–5 was thus regarded as a typical specimen, and it was for this reason that the author was called John ὁ θεόλογος[EN395]. He would have been most surprised, and the 4 living creatures, the 24 elders and the many angels in heaven, must surely have been surprised, at most of the things which have since been given the name of theology.

[477]　　　　3. THE AMBASSADORS OF GOD AND THEIR OPPONENTS

The kingdom of God coming to us on earth is the kingdom of heaven. And when the will of God is done on earth as in heaven, this is not merely a divine happening, established, controlled and brought to its goal by God, but also a heavenly happening, executed on earth in the presence and power and with the co-operation and accompanying revelation of heaven. We may state at once that it is primarily, substantially and centrally a divine happening, and only secondarily, accidentally and peripherally a heavenly. Thus the fact that it is both divine and heavenly does not mean that it is twofold, that there takes place an autonomous heavenly happening side by side with the divine, and

---

[EN391] out of the depths
[EN392] in the highest
[EN393] with one voice
[EN394] theology
[EN395] the theologian

that this claims independent consideration and appraisal. The fact that it is both divine and heavenly means rather that the one divine happening has also as such the character, the (self-evidently) creaturely form and vesture, of a heavenly. But in this sense it is genuinely heavenly, and the visitation of the earthly creation by God its Creator means its visitation by its heavenly fellow-creation, and its encounter with God—whether it is aware of it or not—its encounter with angels. Where God is—the God who acts and reveals Himself in the world created by Him—heaven and the angels are also present.

The last and best sentence in the rather short and dubious doctrine of angels advanced by A. Schlatter (*Das chr. Dogma²*, 1923, 87) is clear and pointed: "The mystery is near to us." Correctly understood, this statement tells us all there is to be said concerning the reality and significance of angels in the earthly sphere and concerning their relationship to the presence and act and revelation of God. Perhaps Calvin had something similar in mind when he said of angels: *quod in suo ministerio, velut in specula, divinitatem aliqua ex parte nobis repraesentant*[EN396] (*Instit.*, I, 14, 5). The mystery would not be near but distant if the divine happening were not also a heavenly. And the appropriate representation of deity would be lacking if it were not given us *velut in speculo*[EN397] by the ministry of angels. And the lack would probably be much more than one of mere beauty. At bottom a piety or theology in which there is no mystery, which lacks the mirror of self-representing deity, and in which there are therefore no angels, will surely prove to be a godless theology. To quote Calvin again: *Quia Dominus, pro immensa sua dementia et facilitate vult huic nostro vitio subvenire, non est, cur tantum eius beneficium negligamus*[EN398] (*ib.*, 14, 11).

We must leave aside the foolish question whether and how there is or may be a special experience of angels. It is a foolish question because it is wrongly put. There can be no question of any special, autonomous or abstract experience of angels in and for themselves. The subjects of this kind of experience could not be the angels of God, but only ideas or ghosts or figments of the imagination or even demons and therefore the opponents of the genuine angels. It is best not to speak of any experience of angels at all. For the point at issue in the [478] Bible is always an experience of God and of Jesus Christ, and not an independent experience of angels. The real question is whether and how far there can be any experience of God and His Christ, any encounter and co-existence with Him, which does not take place in supreme truth and reality—whether we are aware of it or not—in the presence and with the participation of His angels. Is God really present and does He really work and speak, help and save, awaken and nourish and consummate our faith and obedience, rule the Church and the world both as a whole and in detail, if in all these things His angels are not present and at work in His service? What would we earthly creatures be before Him, and how could we be before Him and with Him, if He were to visit and encounter us only in divine and not also in creaturely form, in the heavenly

---

[EN396] that in their ministry, as in a mirror, they in some respect represent divinity to us
[EN397] as in a mirror
[EN398] Because the Lord, in His immense mercy and kindness wishes to cancel this fault of ours, there is no reason why we should neglect this great benefit of His.

vesture which as such is the representation of His mystery and deity, and therefore in angelic mode?

What is the meaning of the presence and operation of angels in the doing of the will of God on earth? It certainly does not mean that there is any competition with the presence and operation of God Himself. But it is not for this reason without any significance at all. It means the presence and operation of God Himself in the heavenly-creaturely form which, because it is heavenly, is appropriate to God and able to represent and attest Him, and, because it is creaturely, appropriate to man and the earthly creation generally and able to make God accessible and His representation and attestation apprehensible. Thus to say that where God is present we shall also find His angels is to say that where God is engaged in the work and revelation of His mercy, there—in order to be genuinely God to the earthly creation, but to be genuinely *its* God—He is surrounded and accompanied and served and attested by the heavenly creation which as heavenly belongs radically to Him and as creation belongs radically to the earthly creation. Where the God who acts and speaks in His grace is present, it is in this mediation. It is not that in this mediation He has beside Him a second acting and speaking subject, or a plurality of such, but that He always acts and speaks Himself in this mediation. In this mediation, by the ministry of the heavenly creation, He is great and powerful and holy but also gracious and merciful and patient on earth. In this mediation the doing of His will on earth is His work, the work of the living God, and therefore wholly divine, but as such it is addressed quite concretely to our creaturely sphere. That His will should be done on earth as in heaven necessarily implies that it should be done on earth in a heavenly way, in this heavenly mediation. God would not be Himself in the granting of this request, nor would the answer correspond to the request, if His will were not done in this mediation.

[479] This then, is, what we must say generally concerning the being and action of angels on earth and therefore in what we call the history of salvation and the Church, in world history, in the histories of individual lives, and in all earthly occurrence. It carries with it two delimitations. We avoid both the overestimation of angels on the one side and their under-estimation on the other. We contend for the sole lordship and glory of God, but we contend for the lordship and glory of God through the ministry of angels.

Cautiously laying one stone upon the other, we shall now try to understand in detail the second and undoubtedly more difficult but also more practically important aspect of the matter. But where are we to begin? We certainly cannot begin with a definition of angels in their relationship to the earthly creation with which they undoubtedly come into contact as God takes this to Himself and as they are present where God is. If they were definable like earthly creatures they would not be angels, heavenly creatures. Even to have any prospect of success in venturing to explain the name or concept "angel" as "ambassador," we first make the necessary presupposition. But this consists in an answer to the question in what the service properly consists in which alone angels can have their essence and existence on earth as in heaven, and to which they owe their name. Only then can we consider when and where they are present on earth, and what opposition they have to encounter. The worst possible blunder that we could commit would be to try to understand them in terms of this opposition, and therefore to begin by describing them as the enemies of the devil and demons. There can be only one starting-point for our discussion of all these problems, namely, to consider more precisely something which self-evidently impressed itself upon us as the main problem in our short introduction, namely, what is the nature and manner of angels in their relationship to God.

We may begin with a simple assertion which is not likely to fail for lack of adequate support. This is that in all the biblical passages which instruct us most precisely concerning the relationship of angels to God and therefore concerning their own essence and existence the word "angel" does not stand alone but is linked with God or Christ either by a genitive or by a possessive pronoun.

A few illustrations may be given. In Ps. 34[7] we read: "The angel of the Lord encampeth round about them that fear him, and delivereth them"; in Gen. 28[12]: "And he dreamed, and behold a ladder set up on the earth, and the top of it reached to heaven: and behold the angels of God ascending and descending on it"; in Gen. 24[7]: "The Lord God of heaven ... shall send his angel before thee"; and in Mt. 16[27]: "For the Son of man shall come in the glory of his Father with his holy angels; and then he shall reward every man according to his works." And we might also add the unforgettable conclusion of the evening blessing in Luther's *Smaller Catechism*: "Thy holy angel be with me, that the evil foe have no power over me! Amen. And then quickly and happily to sleep." It might almost be said of this sentence that it contains the whole doctrine of angels *in nuce*[EN399], and decisively so on account of the address: "Thy holy angel."

Each angel stands in relationship to God, and is an angel, and has his being [480] and is present as such, in the fact that he is God's holy angel. The only thing is that no possessive pronoun or genitive of human speech has the force adequately to express the relationship, the distinction and the connexion which call for expression at this point. The angels are not emanations of God. They are creatures. But as heavenly creatures they are in an exemplary and perfect way that which constitutes the essence of all creatures and characterises earthly creatures as their origin and goal. That is to say, they belong to God, as belong to Him strictly. They are, only as He is and they are His. But He, God, is in His omnipotent mercy. He is as from heaven He speaks and acts on earth. They are His, and therefore are, as He takes them with Him on His way from heaven to earth as His precursors, companions and followers, giving them a share in His own speech and action on earth. They are, as they are given this share. What makes heaven heaven, and heavenly beings heavenly,

---

[EN399] a nutshell

giving heaven precedence over earth and heavenly creatures a greater dignity than earthly, is the fact that God is in heaven and not on earth, that He has His dwelling and throne among them and not among us, that His way does not lead from here to there, but from there to here. He thus gives to the There, and to those who are there, a share in Himself which earth and those who are on it do not and cannot have. To this particular participation there corresponds, of course, the fact that, unlike earthly creatures, they have no standing of their own in relation to Him. As the recipients of this incomparable and non-transferable participation, but with no standing of their own, taken by God in this strictly heavenly mode, they come with Him to earth, genuinely distinguished above all the creatures of earth, but only in this way, without any different being or existing differently. Their high advantage in relation to the earthly creation is also their disadvantage. They have no definable being in relation to it. They do not exist and act independently or autonomously. They have no history or aims or achievements of their own. They have no profile or character, no mind or will of their own. They have all these things, yet not as their own possession, but wholly and exclusively as God is so rich in relation to them. They are themselves only a possession, His possession. The lowliest creature of earth has an advantage over even the highest of angels to the extent that while it belongs to God it may also belong to itself. But conversely even the least of the heavenly hosts is more than the most perfect of earthly creatures to the extent that it belongs so fully to God and in no sense to itself.

Where an angel appears and is and speaks and works, God Himself appears and is and speaks and works. The angel derives no benefit at all from being a creature and different from God, although he is is this, and is indeed an exemplary and perfect creature in the fact that he belongs so fully and exclusively to [481] God. He would be a lying spirit, a demon, a being which deceives both itself and others in respect of its heavenly character, if he were to try to profit from his nature and position, deriving any personal benefit, cutting an individual figure, playing an independent role, pursuing his own ends and achieving his own results. A true and orderly angel does not do this. He has his honour, dignity and joy, and all that earthly creation has in its autonomy, in the fact that he has these things only in dependence, that he only stands before God and is at His disposal, that he is only an element in the creaturely sphere of being in which God has His dwelling and His throne, that he has himself only as he participates in Him, and exists for himself as he is there for Him. He triumphs and exults in this absolute humility before God.

And wherever the being and action of an angel are perceived, there the Word of God is heard, the doing of His will is contemplated, and gratitude, faith and obedience to Him are awakened or confirmed or rekindled. The part of the angel, then, has merely been to serve, to give his witness, to help. Although he is a creature, and an exemplary and perfect creature, his task as such has simply been to come and then to go again, to pass by. He would again be a lying spirit, a demon, if he were to tarry, directing attention and love and honour and even perhaps adoration to himself, causing even momentary pre-occupation with himself and enticing man to enter into dealings and fellow-ship with Himself instead of through him into dealings and fellowship with God. Again it must be said that a true and orderly angel does not do this. The truth in which he is perceived will always be the truth of God. The work which he accomplishes will always consist in the fact that the majesty and mercy of God are better, more seriously and more gladly seen and acknowledged by man. He is accepted and glorified exclusively as God is accepted and glorified. He can himself be honoured only as he causes man to look away from himself to God.

We again recall the ἄξιος εἶ λαβεῖν EN400 of the doxologies of Rev. 4–5, the prostrations, the casting of the crowns before the throne of God, the remarkable "giving" ascribed to heavenly creatures, the thoroughgoing ascription of all δόξα and τιμή and δύναμις and πλοῦτος, of all σοφία and ἰσχύς, of all εὐλογία and εὐχαριστία EN401 to Him that sits on the throne and to the Lamb. This ascription which looks away from self, this witness that every-thing belongs to God alone and not to them, is the ministry of angels not only in heaven but also on earth. And it is because there are not and cannot be such pure witnesses of God among earthly creatures independent even in their relationship to God—for earth is not heaven—that when the will of God is done not only in heaven but also on earth He does not come to us alone but with His holy angels. It is for this reason that where He is they too are present, and as He causes Himself to be perceived and is perceived, there is also a perception of the angels who serve Him.

In this connexion we must make a last incidental reference to the work of E. Peterson, and especially to the dreadful third part (p. 83f.) in which he brings the being and activity of angels in their relationship with God into connexion with that of the mystic Gnostic (or *vice versa*). If we could adopt to his historical presentation of the relationship between the heav-enly cultus and that of the Church a rather distant attitude, and to his supposed scriptural proof from Rev. 4–5 an attitude of gentle repudiation, a very definite protest is now demanded. His doctrine of the quasi-angelic mystic is a refined heresy. It is refined because, presupposing a partially correct view of the being and activity of angels in their relationship with God, it does the very worst thing which can possibly be done in a doctrine of angels, causing these angels who are in some sense rightly perceived and understood to direct the attention and concern of man to themselves instead of to God. According to this teaching, the angels which exist only in relationship to God and for Him do not summon and invite man to give to God the service appropriate to him as an earthly creature but rather to imi-tate the angels as heavenly creatures. And according to this doctrine, the point of the being and activity of angels is not that we should see and know and express ourselves as creatures in the incarnate Word of God but in a higher, angelic creatureliness, in the being and essence of angels.

As Peterson sees it, the real mystic Gnostic reaches out above purely conceptual know-ledge to the metaphysically higher form of being attained only by *apatheia* EN402—to being in the order of being which as that of the angels is above that of man. This elevation of man takes place in the cultus when the number of angelic choirs is swelled, not by those of all the

[482]

EN400 Thou are worthy to receive
EN401 glory and honour and power and riches, of all wisdom and strength, of all blessing and thanskgiving to him …
EN402 apathy

lower cosmos as in Rev. 5^{13}, but by those of quasi-angelic priests and monks (p. 84). For mystic Gnostics participating as esoterics in the cultus of the Church, namely, in the mass, this participation has the metaphysical significance (rather than that of faith) that the archetypal import of the being and life of angels—not of all angels, for there are some which "leave them cold," but of the supreme angels, the cherubim and seraphim—is made actual for them. "The man of angelic likeness desires to be taken up into their ranks, and so in gnosis he begins to rise above the world, flying above everything visible and invisible in heaven and earth to a world which bears no more relationship to the perceptible cosmos but is orientated solely on God," to the fellowship of beings which are what they are as they "pour forth" in praise of God (p. 87 f.). His desire is to participate in their being directly orientated on God, and therefore in their praise of God; and this is something which he can actually attain. But can man really draw near to the angels in this way? He can do it no less surely than the angels can draw near to him, and have actually done so in the birth and temptation and resurrection and ascension of Christ. As Christ was above all angels prior to His abasement, and was again exalted above them with His elevation, so the quasi-angelic man stoops down from his being with the cherubim and seraphim to the orders of earth, to priest and people, to the earthly *ecclesia*, to the theological virtues of faith and love and hope which are a model for him too, only to rise again continually to the fellowship of these heavenly beings (p. 90 f.). Their being signifies "a possibility of our being, an enhancement and intensification of our being" (p. 93); the possibility of "man's constant rise, not in a moral but in a metaphysical sense, until he becomes the companion of angels and archangels, and attains the frontier where the cherubim and seraphim stand. And there, where even they are halted, he begins to make music with the spheres and to sing with the archangels" (p. 94)—a song which "breaks forth from his innermost being" and in which his coming to himself is completed as he is present with the angels and archangels, and is poured out before God, only as a song (p. 95), so that with the very lowest and the very highest of creatures he expresses his own lowliness, and "can say only that he is absolutely nothing" (p. 96). The grace of the Crucified has awakened the last depth of his creatureliness, "so that he does not merely stand there as the sinner who has experienced mercy, but also as this poor creature, related to the ass, which has no other possibility but to pour forth in praise of God" (p. 97).

[483]   Peterson is right in two respects: first, in describing the being of angels as one which is directly orientated on God; and second, in calling it a pouring forth before God, namely, in His praise. But he is wrong already—although we can leave this point aside—when he limits this description to a supposedly higher class of angels. It is, of course, this class which interests his mystic Gnostic, who takes the liberty of saying that other angels "leave him cold." And this brings us to the basic error of Peterson, for, as he sees it, these supposedly higher angels whom the Gnostic desires and is able to resemble are directly orientated on God in the sense that they and their praise of God have nothing whatever to do with the service of God on earth. They turn to God in such a way that they turn their backs on the earth and man. The saying of Heb. 1^{14} that all angels are ἀποστελλόμενα seems not to apply to them. That God's will is to be done on earth as in heaven seems not to concern them. Their outpouring in praise of God seems to have another and in some way more excellent meaning. The will of God to which they are supposedly obedient seems to be a majestic will which is not that of His mercy. What gladdens Peterson in these angels, what his mystic Gnostics hope to attain and actually do attain, is something which is wholly alien to the φιλανθρωπία, to the resolve and act in which God has taken man to Himself and Himself become man. In their orientation on God and outpouring before Him these angels have a metaphysically higher form of being. In this they are "archetypal." For this the esoteric yearns when he takes part in the mass of the earthly Church and condescends to concern himself with the theological virtues. In this he thinks he has found a possibility: that of the enhancement and intensification of

his own being; that of fulfilling the being of the creaturely to its utmost limit. In its own way the angel does this, and in its very different way the ass. But man—the man who is mystically called and endowed—finds that even though he is still related to the ass he is summoned and equipped to rise constantly like the angel, sharing his metaphysical form of being and thus coming to himself and attaining true creatureliness before God. Yet it is surely a false coming to himself when he becomes more lowly even than the sinner who has experienced mercy. It is surely a false ascent. Let those who value their eternal and temporal welfare steer clear of it! For it raises us past the God who in His Son came down to us men, and will come again. It raises us past His holy angels, who are directly orientated on Him and have their whole being in outpouring before Him, not in the fact that they say that they are nothing, but in the fact that they come down with Him to us as the servants of His mercy. In this kind of ascent we merely disturb the angels by making the humility in which they exist only for God and therefore for us into a creaturely honour, a goal of human yearning. And whether we think to fulfil the being of the creaturely in relationship with the angel or with the ass, we fail to make use of the possibility which is given to man as man by the grace of God and the ministry of angels, i.e., that of being serviceable to God in our own human metaphysical form of being (which is neither that of the angel nor that of the ass), as the angels are serviceable to Him in theirs. What is said in Col. 2^{18} about the angelic piety and theology of the false teachers who had arisen in Colossae is too scanty and obscure to give us any clear picture of the point at issue. But we are not malicious if we affirm that the little which is said might well be applied in detail to Peterson's mystics competing with the angels. And after consulting this doctrine of angels it is certainly refreshing to read the exposition of the third petition in the *Heidelberg Catechism* (*Qu.* 124): "Thy will be done on earth, as it is in heaven, that is to say. Grant that we and all men may renounce our own will and obey without contradiction Thy will which alone is good, each of us fulfilling his office and calling as willingly and faithfully as the angels in heaven."

We now turn to the positive fact that the angels are God's pure witnesses, [484] beside whom there is none to compare on earth, who are therefore needed on earth, and who by the goodness of God are given to us in their reality. They are pure witnesses because they are heavenly beings. They are heaven itself coming with God to earth and invading the earthly world. The essence of heaven consists in the fact that within the created world it is the dwelling-place and throne of God from which He comes to us. Heavenly beings are distinguished by the fact that they are in and from heaven. They lack the autonomy of earthly creatures. Instead, they see the face of the Father—of the Father of Jesus Christ—in heaven (Mt. 18^{10}); the face which cannot be seen by any earthly creature. They can thus give pure witness of God. Pure has the positive meaning of absolutely genuine and authentic witness as compared with the earthly witness which can have its full truth only in that which it attests and not in itself. And it also has the negative meaning of unalloyed with alien elements of its own, which are always to be found in even the best and most sincere and fitting earthly witness, which are always heard in it and must always be expressly or tacitly discounted by the hearers. It will be seen that the very thing which makes the angels seem essentially weak and feeble as compared with earthly creatures, the fact that they are what they are so exclusively in their relationship with God and in that outpouring, is also the thing which elevates them above earthly creatures and makes them pure witnesses whose service is indispensable. When an angel is present, although he is not God, it is *eo ipso* the case that God is present. When an angel says anything, although he is not God, it is God who speaks. When an angel acts, for all the infinite difference between God and heaven or God and the angel, it is God who acts. To the apparent ontological weakness of the angel there corresponds the fulness, the authority, the incontestability, the divine glory of his functional reality. The angel is not merely an emissary; he is a plenipotentiary. He is the kind of emissary which no man can ever be, even though he be a prophet or apostle. The witness of the latter is also genuine witness. And in its own place, as the witness of man to man, it is, of course, absolutely indispensable. But like all earthly witness to God, it draws its strength directly or indirectly, consciously or unconsciously, explicitly or implicitly, from the fact that before, above and beside it there is the pure witness to God which it can never be even as the best of earthly witness.

All genuine witness to God lives by the witness and therefore the ministry of angels. For by this it becomes in a sense technically possible and real that God is genuinely present and may be genuinely known as God in the earthly sphere, that He genuinely and recognisably speaks and acts, and that He is genuinely honoured and loved and feared. In their so utterly selfless and undemanding and purely subservient passing, in their eloquently quiet pointing to God which is always a pointing away from themselves, heaven comes to earth. And this means that even here there is a real above, a real distance, a real whence of God. It means that even here the dimension is opened and perceptible in which God exists and in which alone He can be known and feared and loved as God. In the being and work of angels, whether notable and noted as such or not, there lies the basis of the fact that the mystery of God can have a place on earth. If God cannot be confused with any static or dynamic, spiritual or material circumstance of the created cosmos; if above all man cannot equate Him with himself, this is something which is unfortunately not guaranteed by any theological or philosophical art, nor by any internal power and purity of faith, nor by any desperate or apparently promising extreme situation in which man may find himself; but it is very definitely guaranteed by the ministry of angels, by the heavenly-creaturely essence by which God is surrounded when He comes to us. To be sure, it is God Himself and He alone who guarantees it, His almighty Word and Holy Spirit. And it is obvious that in His divine work as such angels no more than men can replace or even represent Him or support Him or contribute to His action in such a way that they stand beside Him or take His place as the acting and speaking subject, as though they had the Word and were the moving spirit. Self-evidently even angels can only be the witnesses of God. But where the revelation and work of God take place, it is a cosmic occurrence. Thus heaven dawns on earth. The witness of angels is given. There is established as pure witness that which no man can establish for himself or others, namely, that on earth and in its internal or

[485]

external situations there is disclosed and perceptible the real above, the real distance, the real whence, the real mystery of God, in a word the dimension and category of the divine. Without the angels God Himself would not be revealed and perceptible. Without them He would be hopelessly confused with some earthly circumstance, whether in the form of a sublime idea or a golden calf. But by means of His holy angels He sees to it that this dimension is always open and perceptible. And we have to realise that if we do not perceive it we are not merely abandoned by God but by all good spirits and angels, being entangled not merely in a spiritual but a cosmic disorder and catastrophe, for which God and the angels certainly cannot be blamed. But above all we have to realise that if we have the grace to perceive it we do not owe this in the slightest to our work, but all our theology and philosophy and seriousness and depth and soul-shattering experience can only serve at very best to confirm and illuminate the heavenly as the token of the divine, the mystery in which God alone is God, thus providing us with earthly marks by which to recall it when we are in danger of forgetting it and making God an idol. Within cosmic reality, and therefore apart from God Himself, there are always the angels to prevent this and to see to it that we do not lose contact with the living [486] God. They alone are God's pure witnesses.

As such, although creatures as we are, they stand over against us at the side of God. The very thing which they lack in comparison with us includes within itself their infinite advantage over us. In face of God they have no cause of their own in the espousing of which they have to submit to His will. They do not exist in any reciprocal relationships which have to be conformed to the divine model. They do not sing any hymn of praise which well or badly they have to strike up. They are themselves an eternal hymn of praise. And theirexistence is not tedious, as tedious theologians usually imagine, because as the *entourage* accompanying God they have their hands full with what He wills and does and therefore with us. Their liturgy is their service to Him and therefore to us. But in this service they stand over against us at the side of God. They exist in His glory, speak in His truth and work with His power. We cannot rely on them as we do on God. But we must not forget that when we rely on God we can rely on them. We can as little dispute with them as with God; we can as little deny them as we can deny God. In faith in a God of theory or ethics or aesthetics we may well deny the angels, because in the company of this kind of God it makes no odds whether there are angels or not. But in faith in the heavenly Father of Jesus Christ, whose majesty is operative and revealed in His mercy; in faith in the God of Abraham, Isaac and Jacob, the case is very different. To deny the angels is to deny God Himself. For it is an implication of His greatness and condescension that He comes to us in His angels. Although in the smallest no less than the greatest matters He keeps the reins in His own hands, the angels represent Him to us with the plenary authority appropriate to them as pure witnesses.

This is perhaps the point to consider one of the most difficult concepts in biblical angelology, that of the *maleak Yahweh*[EN403]. We do so within the limits of what is important and necessary for our present purpose (cf. for what follows. Walter Baumgartner, "*Zum Problem des Jahwe-Engels*," *Schweit. Theol. Umschau*, 1944, 92 f.). In brief, we are confronted with a figure which is not unusual in the world of the Old Testament, but this time it is called *the* angel rather than merely *an* angel of the Lord, thus seeming to unite and represent in itself the essence of angels generally and their essential functions, and therefore to merit the title of ἄγγελος κατ᾽ ἐξοχήν[EN404]. Our question concerning the relationship between God and angels and angels and God is more insistently posed in the passages in which there is brief and simple or more extended and complicated reference to this angel.

The exposition of the Early Church succumbs to the obvious but very real temptation of seeing in this angel simply the pre-existent Logos, the second hypostasis of the Godhead. Even F. Deliztsch (*Komm. über d. Genesis*[4], 1872, 290 f.) was prepared to understand him as at least a prefiguration of the future incarnation of God, a real angel but as such made by Yahweh an extraordinary organ and phenomenon, i.e., an angel in human shape. H. Cremer (*R.E., Art. Engel*, Vol. 5, 367f.) advanced an even more attenuated version of the same view when he maintained that a replacement of the presence of God by the ministry of angels, and a mediation of His revelation through them, are just as essential to the period of the old covenant as His revelation and presence in Christ and the Holy Spirit to the essence of the new. In all this, however, no real justice is done to the incomparable and irreplaceable nature of the speech and action of the covenant God of the Old Testament and later of the Word incarnate in Jesus Christ, nor indeed to the specific features of the ministry of angels. Because they are so intimately related, these ought not to have been identified; nor should the latter have been brought into relationship with the former even as a prefiguration or a temporary substitute. Christ is far more than can be embraced merely by the concept of ἄγγελος κατ᾽ ἐξοχήν. He is more than a pure witness of God. Like the covenant God of the Old Testament (and as His reality concealed in the Old Testament but proclaimed in the form of pure promise), He is the Godhead Himself speaking and acting on earth. He is the Son of God and Son of Man with whom as such no heavenly being, which is neither God nor man, is identical, who cannot be prefigured by any such being or set alongside it as a fulfilment. And quite apart from these basic considerations, we are closer to the meaning and text of these Old Testament passages if we accept purely as an angel this one angel of God which is given such prominence, learning from it the supreme relevance of the existence and ministry of angels in their connexion with the incomparable and irreplaceable Word and work of God.

The suggestion of G. v. Rad (*ThWBzNT*, I, 75f.) seems worth considering that we start with the passages of what he calls folk-lore in which the *maleak Yahweh*[EN405] is simply an "organ of the particular relationship of grace to Israel," the personification of God's assistance of this people. According to Ex. 14[19f.] he stands protectively between the host of Israel and the pursuing army of the Egyptians. According to Num. 22[22] he is an adversary to Balaam in the way when the latter intends to curse Israel. According to Jud. 6[11f.] he salutes Gideon: "The lord is with thee, thou mighty man of valour," and according to Jud. 13[2f.] he announces to Manoah and his wife the birth of Samson. According to 1 K. 19[5] he restores the weary Elijah. According to 2 K. 19[35] he smites the 185,000 men in the camp of the Assyrians. According to Zech. 1[12] and 3[1f.] he appears before God as the advocate for Israel and the opponent of Satan. It is true that in 2 Sam. 24[16f.] he can appear as the destroying angel, standing between

[487]

[EN403] angel of the Lord
[EN404] angel par excellence
[EN405] angel of the Lord

heaven and earth with his sword drawn and stretched out against Israel (1 Chron. 21¹⁵ᶠ·). But this is the exception which proves the rule, for, from the standpoint of salvation history, this does not take place against Israel but for it. In all this it is natural to think of the position and role of Michael in Dan. 10¹³, ²¹ and 12¹. *The* angel of God is very obviously the angel of God for Israel, the heavenly form in which God turns to this people of His. He is called *the* angel of God because Israel is His chosen people.

In the Acts of the Apostles, too, there seem to be reference to *the* angel in the frequently mentioned ἄγγελος τοῦ θεοῦ or τοῦ κυρίου ᴱᴺ⁴⁰⁶ (without the article). At any rate, the position and function of this angel in relation to the New Testament community seem to be not dissimilar to those of the *maleak Yahweh*ᴱᴺ⁴⁰⁷ in relation to the covenant people of the Old Testament. He opens the prison for the apostles in 5¹⁹ᶠ· and for Peter in 12⁷ᶠ·. He orders Philip to the place where he will meet the Ethiopian eunuch (8²⁶), and tells Cornelius to get into touch with Peter (10³ᶠ·). He comforts Paul in the storm (27²³), and smites Herod, the enemy of the community, at the very moment when the people say of him that his voice is that of a god and not of a man (12²³). And even here it seems to be the case that he owes his singular position and designation to the singular task ascribed to him. The well-known passage in Mal. 3¹ is particularly helpful in relation to both Old and New Testaments to the extent that it refers to the coming to the temple of a preceding messenger, of the Lord Himself, and of the angel of the covenant (*maleak berith*ᴱᴺ⁴⁰⁸). If the latter, too, is "a functionary of Yahwek's particular relationship of grace" (v. Rad), it cannot very well be otherwise than that he is identical with the angel who elsewhere is called the angel of Yahweh and who in Jud. 2¹ is expressly said to be concerned with the covenant of Yahweh with Israel. We can thus see how the whole conception came to be taken up by the authors of the New Testament. We are surely dealing with the same angel, for example, in the ἄγγελος κυρίου ᴱᴺ⁴⁰⁹ of Lk. 2⁹ who proclaims the nativity. *The* angel is *the* witness of God. With his appearance, words and acts he attests the work of God as such in the history of salvation and therefore in primal and eschatological history. He attests the election of Israel, the election of the Church, the election of the covenanted community. Hence it is no accident that the name of this angel does not proclaim anything specific but only that which denotes the essential nature of all angels. What angel could be anything other, anything more or less, than an angel of God?

[488]

But now in relation to these simpler passages which treat of the angel of God we must consider that what is ascribed to him in the way of word and act and achievement might just as well—we are almost tempted to say, better—be said of Yahweh Himself, as similar things are actually ascribed to Him in other passages. Indeed, similar and even the same things, as, for example, all that takes place in connexion with the Exodus and the wilderness wandering, are more frequently described and honoured as Yahweh's own words and acts without any mention of the angel of Yahweh. There can, of course, be no question of any rivalry between God and His angel. A pure and transparent witness is one who when he acts does not in any sense introduce himself but only the one whom he attests. It is not for nothing, then, that in the passages mentioned the presence of the angel means that of the Lord. Even the exposition of the Old Testament in terms of religious history, which is particularly honest in such matters, has never, so far as I am aware, found any indications that in Israel any particular sphere of operation was allotted, or any cult dedicated, to the angel of the Lord side by side with that of Yahweh. Where he appears, he is absorbed, as it were, by his speech

---

ᴱᴺ⁴⁰⁶ angel of God or of the Lord
ᴱᴺ⁴⁰⁷ angel of the Lord
ᴱᴺ⁴⁰⁸ angel of the Lord
ᴱᴺ⁴⁰⁹ angel of the Lord

and action, which are none other than those of Yahweh Himself. The story in Jud. $13^{2f.}$ is particularly instructive in this respect. "I asked him not whence he was, neither told he me his name," says the woman to her husband (v. 6). And when the man later asks the angel: "What is thy name?", he is given the answer: "Why askest thou me thus after my name, seeing it is wonderful?" (v. 18). And when the man detains him to offer a burnt offering, the angel refuses: "If thou wilt offer a burnt offering, thou must offer it unto the Lord" (v. 15 f.). And when the man offers it to the Lord who does wondrously, "the angel of the Lord ascended in the flame of the altar. And Manoah and his wife looked on, and fell on their faces to the ground. But the angel of the Lord did no more appear to Manoah and to his wife. Then Manoah knew that he was the angel of the Lord. And Manoah said unto his wife, We shall surely die, because we have seen God. But his wife said unto him, If the Lord were pleased to kill us, he would not have received a burnt offering and a meat offering at our hands, neither would he have shewed us all these things, nor would as at this time have told us such things as these" (v. 19 f.). This is what happens when this angel appears. He obviously appears only to efface himself in favour of the One on whose behalf he appears to man. But how effectively and impressively he does so! It is understandable that in the Old Testament world he is not a constant, regularly occurring or systematically comprehensible figure; that he can appear, but can equally well not appear, and often does not do so. We have to see and understand that it is in this very form that he is so important and indispensable. We have only to imagine that he were always present where there is mention of the appearance and Word and work of God, and the impression would be unavoidable that he is an intrinsically

[489]   important being or principle side by side with God. On the other hand, we have only to imagine that there were no references to his appearance, but obvious mention were made only of God and not of His angel, and the prosaic reader and theologian would be spared a great deal of trouble, but the mystery of God would also be lost. For it is the mystery of God which is concretely revealed and set before the reader in these constantly recurring references to the angel of God. It is the unmistakeable fact that the presence of the God of grace and mercy is very different from that of a harmless supreme being. In these passages, with their happenings which are so strongly cosmic in form but so absolutely supracosmic in meaning, we can see what is meant whenever there is reference to God and His Word and acts, even though there may be no mention of the angel of the Lord. Where the angel of the Lord appears, the dimension of the divine is disclosed and the category of the divine imposes itself. God can no longer be equated with an intellectual or sentimental or aesthetic epitome. He presents Himself as a divine factor which genuinely occupies space and time even in the earthly sphere. Earthly beings cannot fail to see that God is God, and that only fools can say: There is no God, and that those who take one another for God are even greater fools. Worship and sacrifice are demanded, as in the story of Manoah. Man must die, as Manoah rightly perceives. No, he may live, as he learns from his better instructed wife. Not the angel of the Lord is superfluous, but the man and especially the theologian who crossly strikes out these passages, and misses the fact that in them there sounds the great bell which we ought to hear in other apparently—but only apparently—less striking places. What we are told by the intervention of heaven as God's witness as revealed in these passages is that the covenant of grace, the election and calling of Israel and the Church, the Gospel, are not historical events like others on this earth of ours, and that they do not establish ordinary historical relationships, with well-planned theologies, well-intentioned systems of piety, well-run institutions, well-weighed conclusions of assemblies and commissions under the well-meaning oversight of a wisely invisible supreme God. This is what is declared by the angel of the Lord who is the angel of the covenant, and it is declared in such a way that man can see and hear even though sight and hearing fail.

And now we come to the more complicated passages in which the angel of the Lord appears. We refer to the angel in the story of Hagar (Gen. 16$^{7f.}$, 21$^{17f.}$), to the visit of the three men to Abraham at the terebinth of Mamre (Gen. 18$^{1f.}$), : to the two angels who come to Lot in Sodom (Gen. 19$^{1f.}$), to the angel in the story of the sacrifice of Isaac (Gen. 22$^{11f.}$), to the angel in Jacob's dream before his parting from Laban (Gen. 31$^{11f.}$), to the angel of the burning bush (Ex. 3$^{2f.}$), and to the introduction of the angel as the leader of the people in the wilderness when God is incensed with them (Ex. 33$^{1f.}$). All these passages contain more or less obtrusively the great difficulty, which is brought out rather than removed by source-criticism, that the angel of Yahweh can hardly be distinguished from Yahweh Himself but seems very clearly to be one with Him. The angel appears and speaks and acts, but the appearance and word and action are those of God. Or conversely, God appears, and man has to do with His angel. For example, in Gen. 18$^{1-16}$ we are told that God appears (v. 1). But we then go on to read that Abraham "lift up his eyes and looked, and, lo, three men stood by him" (v. 2). He then greets them: "My Lord, (*adonai*) if now I have found favour in thy sight, pass not away, I pray thee, from thy servant" (v. 3). But the invitation to rest and eat is addressed to "them" (v. 4), and it is they who answer: "So do, as them hast said" (v. 5). We may ignore the additional difficulties that in this case we are dealing with three instead of one, and that this time, unlike the story of Manoah, they (or God Himself) actually eat cakes and a "calf tender and good," and drink butter milk and fresh milk (v. 6 f.). It is "they" again who ask concerning Sarah (v. 9 f.). But then in v. 10 we read: "And he said, I will certainly return unto thee according to the time of life; and, lo, Sarah thy wife shall have a son." Who [490] is this "he"? Is he one of the three men? Obviously not, for in v. 13 we are told expressly: "And the Lord said unto Abraham, Wherefore did Sarah laugh …? Is any thing too hard for the Lord?" And when Sarah denies that she laughed: "I laughed not; for she was afraid," the reply is again in the singular: "And he said, Nay; but thou didst laugh" (v. 15). But then the concluding verse tells us that "the men rose up from thence" (v. 16). The same problems confront us in the other passages mentioned.

The question arises whether they are really so very difficult after all. On the one hand, in Gen. 18 and the other passages we may adopt the explanation of early exegesis that these are not appearances of angels but of the Holy Trinity in which the Logos is obviously the spokes-man. On the other, we may follow v. Rad in seeing and applying a definite system by which Yahweh is referred to when something is said concerning Him apart from His connexion with man, and the angel when He enters the field of human apperception. On the latter view, however, we are forced to assume that a later redactor, concerned for the strict tran-scendence of God, has concealed the original tradition of a sensual appearance of God by interposing the figure of the angel as a form of manifestation. V. Rad himself recognises that this "literary theologisation" is "highly speculative for Old Testament relationships," and no matter how subtly it may be done we can hardly say that it achieves its purpose for subtle readers. The insoluble riddle is also posed why it is done only in these passages and not in the many others in which there is undeniable reference to the appearance, speech and action of God in the sphere of human sense, e.g.. His walking in the garden (Gen. 3^8), His personal closing of the ark behind Noah (Gen. 7^{16}), His smelling of the sweet savour of sacrifice after the Flood (Gen. 8^{21}), or His coming down at the building of the tower of Babel (Gen. 11^7). We can hardly overlook the fact that there is a good deal more material for literary theologisation in the Old Testament, and that many more difficult passages would have been eased by the interposition of the angel of Yahweh. And in any case, if this is really what took place in the present passage, it has increased rather than alleviated the difficulty of interpretation. If we have understood the matter aright in the simpler passages, it surely ought not to be all that obscure in the present instances. May it not be that these texts seem to be more complicated merely because the same matter is for definite reason more palp-able than in the simpler passages?

For what is the matter in question in these texts? As in the earlier series, we have here depictions of the encounter between God and man and man and God; representations which are characterised by the fact that by the introduction of the figure of the angel of the Lord there is underlined and emphasised the urgency of these encounters, the directness and concreteness with which man is claimed by God and for God, not merely in his thoughts, and certainly not merely subjectively, but objectively, with all his senses, as one who hears and sees in the ordinary sphere of life. It may be by a well in the wilderness on the way to Shur (Gen. 16⁷), or by the terebinth in the heat of the day (Gen. 18¹), or at evening in the gate of Sodom (Gen. 19¹), or on Horeb the mount of God (Ex. 3²), but always the man who is confronted with the angel of God, and therefore with God Himself, is man as he is in the normal course of life. What the angel attests in these passages, too, is that God speaks in a way which cannot be missed, that He acts in a way which cannot be resisted, that He is present in a way which is quite incomparable, that He both captures man and frees him, that He takes him into His own hands and therefore places him in His service. The angel has the character and task of a perfect mirror of God, in which He whose face no man has seen is disclosed, and He, the High and Hidden and Eternal, is present. He has this character and task even when he is expressly described as a visionary figure, as in Gen. 31¹¹.

[491] A further point which may be made concerning these particular texts is that they all belong to the period of the patriarchs or the early history of Moses, and therefore to the temporal establishment of the covenant of grace as it takes place in these stories. And it is understandable that in this sphere the narrators should find themselves placed, with respect to the point at issue in angelic appearance, in a state of increased and sharpened attention which has to be divided between the divine theophany as such on the one side and the cosmic or heavenly form in which it is both concealed and revealed on the other, between *God* in His mystery on the one side and God in His *mystery* on the other. We have to consider that we have to do here with the unprecedented beginning of the extraordinary existence of Israel within the history of the nations; with the one thing which constitutes the *raison d'être*, the dignity and the hope of this people. Something very different might have stood at this beginning: perhaps a God without mystery, with no real attestation of His deity; perhaps a mystery without God, a powerful impression and claim which were only accidental or links in an earthly causal series. But in that case it would not be this particular, unprecedented beginning. It would not be the calling of Israel in the eternal election of grace. And what would Israel be then? In the event, however, it was not something different which stood at this beginning. It was the One, *God* in this other, *God* in the mystery, *God* in the angel, *sicut in speculo*. And through this One it was also the other, God in the *mystery*, God in the *angel, sicut in speculo*EN410. The two, God and His angel, do not always have to be spoken of in the Old Testament as they are in these passages. But they can be. And perhaps they have to be in these passages. Perhaps these appearances of God and encounters with Him, on which all the rest depend and by which the whole fellowship of God with Israel is conditioned, have to be depicted in this half-light: now God, now the angel, and now God again; both in the same place and with the same function and as the same subject confronting man. Everything depends on the fact that this is so, that at the calling of Israel God and His angel, His angel and God, are both genuinely present. Everything depends on the recounting of this fact. But if this is so, we need hardly be surprised that the account of the angel of the Lord takes the form it does. The contradiction in the statements is the appropriate form for indicating at least what has to be said. The apparent obscurity of these presentations is the real clarity with which the matter has to be presented. Their complication is merely a reflection of the great simplicity of the narrators in face of the basic phenomenon of Israelite history. And we must

---

EN410 as in a mirror

not forget that this is the basic phenomenon of all Israelite existence, not merely of its origin, but of its continuation and future in the light of its origin. And it is also the basic phenomenon of Christian existence, its beginning, continuation and future. If it does not always have to be presented in the same way, it is the same phenomenon as that which demands this presentation here. And the only real cause for surprise is that it has not demanded this presentation more frequently.

It may be noted concerning this angel of Yahweh that he is mentioned in the singular. He seems to be unique. In this respect, too, he seems to stand in a remarkable correspondence and affinity with God Himself. He seems to represent His uniqueness *sicut in speculo*. There is an exception to this rule, of course, in Gen. 18 and 19, where mention is made of three and then of two angels. But at any rate the angel of Yahweh does not seem to be one of many. His relationship to the hosts of Yahweh is not elucidated. As far as I know, there is only one place where they are mentioned together, and significantly this is in the story of the nativity in Lk. 2¹³: "And suddenly there was with the angel a multitude of the heavenly host praising God, and saying ... " It is only capriciously that we can ascribe to him a hierarchical relationship to the many angels. No mention is made of this in the texts. But because no general or system-atic use is made of this figure we are warned against playing off this angel in his singularity against the rest in their plurality, or interpreting their plurality as a development of his unity. [492] The converse is also untenable. The fact that he is called the ἄγγελος κατ᾽ ἐξοχήν EN411 does not mean that he is merely the epitome of all angels. We cannot number the angels in terms of our arithmetic, or assess them against each other. A wise reader will not remember that there are other angels when he reads of the angel of the Lord, nor will he consider that the one angel can replace all the rest and make them superfluous when he reads of the many. Both are true in their own place, but it is neither possible nor necessary either to compare them or to bring them under a common denominator. It is more fitting that this remarkable relationship should show or remind us that in the being of God Himself unity and plurality, simplicity and wealth, not only do not form any contradiction, but co-inhere and together constitute the ineffable glory of God. This is what the texts palpably bring to our notice concerning the angel of Yahweh. It will not prevent us from proceeding quietly, and with no attempt at harmonisation, to a consideration of angels generally in the light of what is said of *the* angel.

It may also be noted concerning the angel of Yahweh that when we have once read care-fully the texts which treat of him, like those in Judges, or 1 Chron. 21¹⁵ᶠ, or the story of Moses at the bush, or any of the others, we shall lose all desire to understand the notion or doctrine of angels, whether our attitude towards it be positive or negative, either preferably or even essentially in terms of certain playful, trifling, ornamental, or in a word childish conceptions. If I am right, these have obtruded into the matter by way of Christian art, which here as elsewhere is responsible for so much that is inappropriate. There are tolerable and in their way moving and instructive representations of the specifically childlike angel, as, for example, in the famous angelic chorus in Altdorfer's picture of the nativity. But it was obvi-ously out of place when so many painters of his own and a later age surrounded the infant Jesus with a veritable kindergarten of prancing babies amusing themselves in different ways and yet all contriving in some way to look pious. Even more offensive are Raphael's little darlings, which were so much to the taste of even an adult Protestant like Karl Hase. And it is to be noted that it was obviously for the sake of the rhyme that Martin Schelling asked that God's dear little angels (*Engelein*) should carry his soul (*die Seele mein*) to Abraham's bosom, for he found no warrant for any such conception in Lk. 16²². We may certainly think of the

---

EN411 angel par excellence

angels as little to the extent that they are ministering spirits. In this sense they are inconceivably little in relation to God and finally to man. But it would be a good thing if diminutives like the German *Engelein* and the English "cherub," with all the false associations which they evoke, could be banished from current usage. The same holds good of the common conception of angels as charming creatures. We need not agree with R. M. Rilke, who after many changes in outlook finally wrote (in his *Duineser Elegien*): "Every angel is terrifying." This may be true of what Rilke finally understood by an "angel," and it may be far better than what he once thought. But the biblical angel is not always terrifying. Even the angel of Yahweh is not merely terrifying. He can also be sweet and charming. He is this. But again he is more. He can also be terrifying. And he is. The angel is what God orders him to be. And this may mean that he is both small and great, both terrifying and charming. After the sea of sweetness in which angels have been engulfed, especially—be it noted—since the beginning of the modern period in the 16th century, it is a real boon to see them portrayed again as dark and stern and lofty figures, e.g., on the nativity fresco of Fritz Pauli in the Antonierhaus in Berne. But it must be remembered that they are neither great nor small, terrifying nor charming, dark nor radiant, by our conceptions. They are to be respected as the angels of God which attest His holiness and goodness, His majesty and lowliness, His mercy and judgment. We must not overlook the fact that there are some representations especially of the annunciation, like

[493] that of M. Grünewald, in which we seem to see approximations to what must be done and left undone in this respect, and to the transcendent reality which has to be indicated. The same may be said of the great angel on Pauli's fresco. If we could teach all the poets and artists who have taken up the matter the twofold respect required, we could perhaps concede them a good deal of liberty in these matters. But the Christian doctrine of angels must not be influenced by their failures in this regard. And there is no sense in letting ourselves be led astray by their failures in our attempt to work out a sober Christian doctrine of angels. The Old Testament conception of the *maleak Yahweh*[EN412] ought to be an effective reminder in this respect.

What angels do, the manner and meaning of their ministry, is obviously to be understood from what they are in relation to God.

A first and general statement must be to the effect that with the commission and in the name of God they do exactly, neither more nor less nor other than, what God wills with the coming of His kingdom to earth. And in their way they do it exactly as He wills it to be done. What distinguishes their doing of it from that of other obedient creatures is that in it there is no question of creaturely autonomy. The possibility of deviation or omission does not arise. Their obedience does not have to come into being, and it has no limit. Their creaturely freedom is identical with their obedience. Their heavenly nature consists and expresses itself in their perfect willingness and readiness, but also in their capacity to speak and act from and with and for God. We can thus have unlimited confidence that their speech and action is always and in every respect that of God Himself. On the other hand, we cannot expect to find in their speech and action anything specific or new or distinct as compared with that of God, anything extraordinary in this sense, and therefore anything particularly angelic as opposed to divine. The divine action is not exhausted in theirs, but theirs is in the divine. God is not bound to them, but they are to Him. Thus their action

---

[EN412] angel of the Lord

is not a mystery alongside that of God. It is not a magical world between with its own laws and history and outstanding features. The angels are remarkable only in the fact that in distinction from all earthly creatures they stand first and perfectly in the service which forms the determination of all creatures. They see the face of the Father. They come direct from His throne. They are directly involved in His action on earth. They live and move and have their being in preceding and accompanying and following this action. In this sense they come on earth. They enter the sphere of man. They approach him, and he is conscious of them and experiences their existence. Yet in all this they are different and stand apart from him and all earthly creatures. Neither he nor any other earthly creature is or works as they do. They do not confront him as God does. They, too, are creatures. But as God confronts man, the same is true of the heavenly beings which form his *entourage.* And as they confront man with God, God's relationship to man acquires a cosmic contour and concreteness. [494] It becomes a reality for man in the deity of God, in His mystery. This is the general point which must be made concerning the ministry of angels.

In relation to God and man and the earthly creation as a whole, what they do in this ministry can and will be only indirect. In the first instance, this clearly means that it is not they who establish, maintain and direct the covenant of grace. It is not they who rule the course of the world or any of its spheres. It is not their affair to exercise mercy and judgment, and the life and death of the earthly creature, the limitation of its existence and its form between its beginning and end are not in their hands. This must be taken in the strict sense that they do not even co-operate with God in all these things; that not even to the smallest degree are they willing and speaking and acting subjects side by side with Him; that they are not even commissioned as His delegates to do things while He is resting or otherwise engaged, so that these things are not His work but theirs, and are to be ascribed to them. That it is God who reigns is a rule to which there is not the slightest exception even in His relationship to heavenly creatures. What they do in their service does not violate His sovereign right to which they too are subject and which He certainly does not confer on them. What they do can be only the confirmation of His sovereign right. In their action they do not make the divine movement, but as creatures an intracosmic movement which is subordinate and corresponds to the divine. And it is as this movement consists only in a confirmation of the sovereign right of God over man and all earthly creatures that they do that which is specifically angelic, giving to God's relationship to man the contour and concreteness in which it can be perceptible and actual for him as the new creation of God. It is for this that the angels are perfectly willing and ready and fully empowered as heavenly beings, the saints and sons of God. But by doing this they do not add anything new or distinctive or peculiarly their own to the divine action. They show themselves to be creatures of His hand, subjects of His sovereign lordship over all things. In no sense, then, are they lords, or fellow-lords. They are simply servants. In their own way they are wholly what the most modest blade of grass waving on the earth by the will of God is in its very different way. The only thing is that they are not blades of grass; they are heavenly beings. Their movement in accordance with the will of God is thus the movement which He has allotted to them and for which they are determined as such.

Even the frequently heard expression that the ministry of angels consists in mediating between God and earthly creatures is to be used, therefore, only with the greatest caution. God mediates Himself, and does not need a third party for this purpose. He mediates Himself through His own Word and [495] through His own Holy Spirit, and thus needs no assistance either from earthly or even from heavenly creatures. He Himself throws a bridge across the gulf, and secures it on both sides. He Himself speaks, and sees to it that He is heard. He Himself disposes, and sees to it that His will is done. In these things He is quite adequate in Himself, and man is referred to Him alone. This is made clear in the central point of His work on earth: in the incarnation of His Word and in the reconciliation of the world with God accomplished therein; in what took place on Golgotha and was revealed on Easter Day. It is obvious that in these matters even the angels can only note and watch and wonder and adore and praise, unable and unworthy to plan or will or accomplish anything of themselves. It was not they who devised and executed this work. They did not co-operate in it either above or below. They did not contribute anything to it. As the heavenly creatures they are, they were simply present. But what is true at the centre is equally true on the circumference. There are no contiguous spheres in which they have to mediate various things in the sense that these things are even momentarily committed to them and are thus to be expected from them; in the sense, then, that they are agents or middle-men to whom independent attention, gratitude and obligation must be granted as such. We can say that they mediate between God and the earthly creation only to the extent that, as the heavenly creatures they are, and according to the will and command of God, they are actually present in that which He alone does both in the centre and on the circumference when He mediates Himself; and that, since God does not will or command anything in vain, they are not present for nothing but to His glorification. It is exactly the case with the angels as with earthly creatures too, and especially with some men, of whom we can and must say that according to the will and command of God they are present with their action in that which God does, and that they are not present for nothing but to His glorification. But the glorification of God by the ministry of angels consists in the fact that their presence at what God alone does, as the presence of the heavenly creation, gives to the relationship between God and the earthly creation its cosmic character, the concrete form of the divine mystery perceptible on earth.

Understood in this way, the action of angels cannot be valued too highly. Their presence is not in any sense, not even partially, a presence of lordship. It is wholly the creaturely presence of service. But all the same it is a genuinely powerful presence. It is not for nothing that when God speaks and acts they are present at His will and command, and as heavenly creatures. This is something which counts on earth. The glorification of God by their ministry takes place. The relationship between God and the earthly creation acquires and has this character.

God is present on earth even without the angels. How can it be otherwise? [496] But where His presence becomes event, experience and decision for the earthly creature, this is realised in the action of the angels. As He is present Himself, He shows Himself through the angels. They do not make God present to man. Their own presence as such would be meaningless. But as and when God is present for man, it is through their presence that man may and must perceive it. By their presence He makes it impossible that He should be overlooked.

It is God Himself who speaks with man, and not a heavenly voice, however powerful or mysterious, however worthy of respect or attention, trying to cry or whisper something of its own alongside His Word. But when God speaks, when His Word becomes enlightenment, consolation and direction to man, it is by His angels that He makes His voice distinct from all others, giving to His Word the sound and form of the divine direction by which He places man unmistakeably in the unique responsibility which he owes to Him.

It is God Himself and God alone who is the Lord in the covenant of grace and in the community which recognises and proclaims this covenant to be concluded, and therefore the Lord of the cosmic process, the innermost meaning of which is the history of this covenant and this community. But when He exercises this lordship, when He continually evinces His might and power in the execution of His covenant, in the gathering and maintaining and renewing of His community and its service, but also in the process of cosmic and natural occurrence, this demonstration of His lordship takes place in the presence of His angels. It is not that He abdicates in favour of them even for a moment or in a single respect. It is not that any might or power ceases to be directly His own. But as His own these powers are also heavenly powers and in this form cosmic, really active in the world. They are here and now valid orders and precepts, determinations and directions. They are this by the ministry of His angels.

Neither as a whole nor in detail are there any finally true, valid and effective divine acts, preservations, demonstrations, assistances or deliverances in which the angels co-operate with God or act as His vice-gerents. But in all these acts of God the angels are present, and both as a whole and in detail their ministry is that within earthly occurrence they give to them the character of divine acts; that by preceding, accompanying and following them they distinguish them from other events for earthly creatures; that they make them eternally noteworthy. The presence of angels means that these events are distinguished both from the dispositions of fate or chance and from the best works of human self-help or brotherly assistance. The presence of the angels means that even in that which seems to belong only to the nexus of creaturely occurrence, or to be his own or some other creaturely act, man is summoned [497] to see the intervention of God Himself, and therefore an element in His plan and its execution, an element of the salvation history or universal history directed by Him, and within this context an element in his own life-history as controlled by God. It is the angels who impress this stamp as it were on the acts of God. They serve God in this sense. They work with Him in this sense. And in this sense we can and must speak of a mediating ministry of angels between God and earthly creatures.

We now return to our principal thesis that the angels are God's witnesses. In a supreme sense, therefore, they are that which God, when He speaks and acts, wills to make and does actually make certain men and finally all men, and indeed the earthly creation in its totality as He espouses its cause. To restrict ourselves to the narrowest circle, the angels are the originals of the prophets and apostles to whom they often seem to approximate, indeed, with whom they often seem to merge, in the biblical text.

The fact that they are witnesses has on the one side the modest implication that they are actually there when the will of God is executed. They see and hear, and are thus in a position to confirm what they have seen and heard. They are there when the will of God is *executed.* The use of the term "witness" brings us face to face with the limitation that they were not present in the eternal counsel of God, either as advisers, or even as spectators. They are creatures, and therefore they are not eternal. They do not know the Father as the Son knows Him, or the Son as He is known by the Father. They do not know, then, either the ground or the goal of the will of God. Between the beginning and the end they cannot foreknow either as a whole or in detail what God wills or how He will accomplish it. In face of the fact that on the basis of His eternal counsel God speaks and does such and such things, they are no less novices than other creatures. To know His eternal counsel, they are no less referred than other creatures to its continual revelation in what He actually says and does. They have only two advantages over earthly creatures. The first is that as the heavenly *entourage* of God they have primary and original knowledge of what He says and does Because the kingdom of God comes from heaven to earth, they are the first to know the doing of His will, the Word and work in which He reveals it. The Word and work of God are not directed to them. They are directed to earth. Their target is man. But the angels are there, and see and hear, when God comes down from heaven to take man to Himself. They know and revere and praise the Word and work of His mercy before any man can do so. And because they are heavenly creatures they have the second advantage that their seeing and hearing of the divine movement is not only primary but perfect. They are genuine and reliable witnesses—crown-witnesses. It is not really necessary to ascribe to them marvellous qualities. [498] Their being and existence is summed up in this seeing and hearing. All heaven is simply the place from which God comes to man. Hence it is not a meritorious achievement on the part of angels that they are perfect witnesses of this happening. Because their being and existence is really exhausted in this seeing and hearing, and as heavenly creatures they have no room for a deviation or reserve which would mean imperfection, they have no option but to be perfect witnesses of God. I repeat that their freedom consists in their obedience. This is a further reason to extol, not themselves, but the God who made them thus, with this nature. But with this nature they are in this first sense of the term not only the primary but the best witnesses, crown-witnesses, witnesses of the Word and work of God, seeing and hearing spectators of the first and supreme rank.

On the other hand, however, the term "witness" implies the high dignity of angels as those who are ordained, as the primary and perfect spectators they are, to attest or confirm to earthly creatures the Word and work of God, guaranteeing and pledging by their existence that the will of God which commences in heaven is about to be done on earth. They are ordained to do this as the kingdom of God comes from heaven, as it is thus the kingdom of heaven on earth, and as they form the accompanying *entourage* of God on earth. On this side, too, the term "witness" carries with it a limitation. This time it is a limitation in relation to earth. The angelic ministry of witness cannot replace the prophetic and apostolic witness, or the witness of the community. Nor can it replace the witness to which all the lower creation is summoned, and not summoned in vain, by the Word and work of God. The beginning of the doing of the will of God is when it takes place on earth that the Word and work of God are so manifest that even men can see and hear and thus proclaim them, guaranteeing and pledging that His Word is the truth and His work the salvation of the world; so manifest, indeed, that all earthly creation can then join in the praise and proclamation of God. Where and to the extent that this happens, the last time dawns on earth and the consummation comes. That this takes place, that there is this calling and action of earthly creatures, is God's own work, the fruit of His manifestation in the flesh, the fruit of the offering of His Son at Golgotha, the fruit of the Spirit outpoured on all flesh after His resurrection. It is not, then, the work of angels, nor can it be replaced nor anticipated by their work. Their work has its limit in what is finally to be done by men, by earthly creatures generally, as they are moved by God. They can only prepare for this with their witness, as they can only follow and confirm the eternal counsel of God in the light of its execution. In this respect they are below even the least of earthly creatures which God wills to make His witnesses. But when God is on the way to this goal in His Word and work, they mightily precede and accompany and follow Him. They powerfully issue the summons [499] with which He calls earthly creatures and men to be His witnesses. In so doing they serve God and man and the whole earthly creation. It is in this connexion that we speak of their co-operating and mediatorial action. Their witness is not the thing which is finally to take place on earth. In the purpose and end and goal of His action, God is not dealing with them. He is dealing with man, with the earth. All the emphasis falls on the witness of the prophets and apostles and those who are called by and with them, and none at all on the witness of the angels. Yet as heavenly witness, primary and perfect and therefore pure, their witness is important and even indispensable to the extent that it forms the necessary presupposition for the human witness with which the doing of God's will on earth begins. Man cannot of himself cause it to happen that God encounters and may be perceived by him in His deity, that He sees and hears Him, that even cosmically He becomes a reality for him as a cosmic being, and that man as a cosmic being is thus enabled to be His witness in the cosmos. This is something which he must be given, and because he is below he must be given it from above. And in order that he should be given it from above, his great visitation by God does not take place without cosmic form, without the heavenly *entourage* accompanying God, without His crown-witnesses the angels. Their proper office is to be as it were the atmosphere in which there can be a witness of men and earthly creatures, their seeing and hearing and therefore their proclamation of God. That is why there is so much about angels in the Bible. That is why the people of the Bible have so many dealings with them. That is why it is so important for them to affirm that they are not merely in the presence of God but—because in the presence of God, because in His real presence—they are also in the presence of His angels. That is why the biblical authors must continually indicate and mention and frequently record that men are surrounded by angels, experiencing their power, hearing their voices, knowing their protection and guidance. This simply means that, as the earthly creatures they are, they know that they share in a witness to God which they cannot give themselves and which no other earthly beings can give them, but which permits and commands them even as earthly beings to be themselves witnesses of God, hearing and seeing Him, and proclaiming Him in His service. This witness from which the men of the Bible proceed and which the authors of the Bible must take into account is the witness of angels. It is the self-witness of God accompanied by the witness of angels and by this witness confirmed and demonstrated to be divine.

[500]

In our exegesis of Rev. 4–5 we have already considered the powerful and comprehensive picture of the way in which angels as the heavenly *entourage* of God are made witnesses of the will of God as it commences above and is fulfilled below. We can find a similar depiction in the fine saying in Job 38[7], which tells us that at the creation of the earth the morning stars sang together and the sons of God shouted for joy. In the New Testament we may again recall the hymn to Christ in 1 Tim. 3[16], in which the third of the six phrases tells us that He was "seen of angels." This appearance to angels is preceded by the decisive work of God—that He was "manifest in the flesh" and "justified in the Spirit." Hence even the angels are confronted by something new. They, too, need and receive a special revelation. But it is given to them first. Only then do we read that He was "preached unto the Gentiles," "believed on in the world," and finally "received up into glory." But this passive witness of angels has obviously to be augmented, and this takes place. Even when God has appeared in the flesh and in the Spirit, they have much to learn. In Eph. 3[10] we are told, indeed, that the heavenly principalities and powers are instructed concerning the manifold wisdom of God by the existence of the ἐκκλησία EN413 on earth. In this phenomenon, they are again surprised as it were by something new. Again, 1 Pet. 1¹² tells us that the Gospel preached by the apostles on earth is something which the angels desire to look into (παρακύψαι), their knowledge being obviously dependent upon events. Along the same lines we read in Lk. 12⁸ (cf. Rev. 3⁵) that the Son of Man will confess before the angels of God those who confess Him before men, and in Lk. 15⁷, ¹⁰ that there is joy among the angels of God over one sinner who repents. Again, Paul tells us in 1 Cor. 4⁹ that the apostles are made a θέατρον EN414 to the cosmos and angels and men. According to all these passages, what takes place on earth is for the angels a current experience in the course of which they have still to become witnesses. That they are in some way present to see and hear what takes place in the community is shown by 1 Cor. 11¹⁰, where women are called to order by the recollection of the angels, obviously as representatives of the respect due to God, and also by 1 Tim. 5²¹, where Timothy is charged to act prudently in matters of Church discipline "before God, and the Lord Jesus Christ, and the elect angels."

Yet all this is only the presupposition for a consideration of the true and active witness of angels in the service of the saving and cosmic events overruled by God. We shall best proceed if we keep to that which is directly stated in the New Testament concerning the relationship of the action of angels to that of Jesus Christ. It is self-evident that radically and finally all the action of angels attested in both Old and New Testaments can be meaningfully understood only in this context, in its relationship to this centre of the divine action. This is unforgettably expressed in the strong statements in Col. 2¹⁰, Eph. 1²², 1 Pet. 3²² and Heb.1⁶ about the lordship of Christ over heavenly dominions and powers. It is in the relationship to Jesus Christ, in which they are subordinate to Jesus Christ but real in this subordination, that all the things are true which we have said about their presence, their speech, their might, their operations under, before, with and after that of God, their ministering but perfect witness as a movement of the heavenly world consequent upon the divine movement, their greatness and their limitation both above and below. To be sure, angelology is not, like anthropology, a consequence and analogy of Christology. For God did not become an angel in Christ. It is possible that Heb. 1⁵⁻¹⁴ is specifically directed against such a conception. On the other hand, angelology must be understood as an annexe to Christology. For when God passed by the angels and became man in Christ, the angels entered the sphere of man with Him. When He became man among men, and as by His Spirit, concealed instead of revealed. He is still man among men. His presence includes that of the angels. It is a matter for some surprise, perhaps, that in the Bible there are not far more frequent references to angels in connexion with Jesus Christ and in relationship to Him. In fact, however, the number of these references is very limited, and they are to be found only in specific contexts.

We must begin with a surprising negative fact. In none of the four accounts is there any [501] reference to the appearance, speech or action of angels in the centre of the evangelical record of Jesus. Their last appearance at the beginning is the story which is given in such compressed form in Mark (1¹²ᶠ): "And immediately the Spirit driveth him into the wilderness. And he was there in the wilderness forty days, tempted of Satan; and was with the wild beasts; and the angels ministered unto him" (διηκόνουν αὐτῷ). This reference is to be found in Matthew too (4¹¹), but is lacking in Luke, who instead is the only Evangelist to tell us at the end, in the story of Gethsemane (22⁴³), that "there appeared an angel unto him from heaven, strengthening him." In neither case is there any indication of what is meant by "ministering" or "strengthening." Since both passages emphasise the tempted humanity of Jesus, we have to think of a special attestation of the presence of God. In all the middle

---

EN413 church
EN414 spectacle

stretch between these two points, there is no mention of angels in the narratives. Even the angel at the pool of Bethesda in Jn. 5^4 is only a marginal figure which most likely does not belong to the original text at all. And it is only a conjecture of the people that an angel talks with Jesus in Jn. 12^{29}. In this connexion we may also recall the saying of Jesus to Peter at His arrest (Mt. 26^{53}): "Thinkest thou that I cannot now pray to my Father, and he shall presently give me more than twelve legions of angels? But how then shall the scriptures be fulfilled, that thus it must be?" If this verse is compared with others (Mk. 8^{38}; Mt. 16^{27}, 25^{31}; Lk. 9^{26}) which speak of the appearance of angels with the Son of Man at His *parousia*, it is obvious that the great silence in the middle of the records cannot be accidental. The narrators do not intend to give us any stories about angels in this section. We may even say that the marginal references in Mk. $1^{12f.}$ and Lk. 22^{43} have more the character of indications than genuine stories. It is true that in Jn. 1^{51}, in a saying which is clearly reminiscent of the story of Jacob in Gen. 28^{12}, we are told that the disciples are to see heaven opened, and the angels ascending and descending upon the Son of Man. But none of the Evangelists ever records anything of this nature. Why not? The idea that they are not present and do not take part in earthly happenings is too much at variance with the general biblical view of angels, and especially with what we are told concerning their specific relationship to Jesus Christ, to serve as an explanation. Here, if anywhere, they are surely present and have a part. But there is no particular mention of them in this section. They are not distinguished as particular figures as in the Old Testament, or Acts, or the beginning and end of the Gospels. The reason for this is that we have to do here in the strictest sense with the final doing of the will of God on earth in itself and as such. When "the Word was made flesh, and dwelt among us (and we beheld his glory)" (Jn. 1^{14}), it was true on the one side that for a time "he was made a little lower than the angels" (Heb. 2^9), because as opposed to them He became an earthly creature and in relationship to their heavenly being He partook of a lesser and lowlier. But was not this self-humiliation of God in His Son the meaning and goal of the will of His mercy? Could or can the majesty of the God who was in Christ to reconcile the world to Himself (2 Cor. 5^{18}) be more lofty and glorious than in its revelation and expression in the fact that for a time "he was made a little lower than the angels"? Was He ever more genuinely their Head and Lord than in this self-abasement beneath them? Are there not good reasons, then, to forget their manifestations and acts at this point where their ministry, too, was completed with the action of God? This does not mean that we deny them. How could we deny them? But at this point where for a time they stand above Jesus Christ we must think of them as pushed back into purely passive witness, into the function of privileged spectators. Here if anywhere they had simply to look on and watch and learn. Here we have an obvious anticipation of what Paul says concerning them in 1 Cor. 15^{24}, namely, that in the perfect kingdom of God which commences with the general and definitive revelation of Jesus Christ, and in

[502]

which even the work of Christ will be consummated and have no further future, they will not be destroyed, but they will certainly lose their power in the sense that their active function will have attained its goal and will therefore be dismissed as superfluous; although it is to be noted in this connexion that, according to Mk. 8^{38} and par., they themselves will first be revealed again in and with the *parousia* of Jesus Christ, and this time in their full relevance for the earthly occurrence which is concluded. Something of this suppression of the angels is to be seen already in the first *parousia* of Jesus Christ. It is to be noted that even in the stories at the beginning and end of the Gospels they never appear with Jesus Himself, but are introduced only as messengers and witnesses announcing Him as it were from a distance. The holy dependence of angelic existence, which is both their greatness and their limitation, is thus expressed in the fact that there is this eloquent silence concerning them in the middle section of the Gospels. Place is found for them in the Bible where the consummating action of God Himself is not yet or no longer visible to man directly. Where this is visible,

3. *The Ambassadors of God and Their Opponents*

they are not destroyed and therefore they are not denied—how could they be when their whole existence aims at this consummating action of God?—but their particular light is outshone like that of a candle in the noonday sun, and the biblical text honours them by no longer thinking of them, or not yet doing so again. The time and occasion, not of their existence, but of reference to them, are given their limit by the entry of the Lord Himself to whom they witness. This law of the central section of the Gospels might well be described as a law of the whole biblical doctrine of angels. The saying of John the Baptist in Jn. 3³⁰: "He must increase, but I must decrease," is no less true of them. And it is true of them in a far more radical sense than it is of any human witness, because for all the humility in which alone it can succeed when God is present, human witness forms in contrast to theirs the final goal of the action of God on earth. According to the witness of the Bible God came among men and His Word became flesh in order to evoke in earthly creatures praise like the decreasing witness of the Baptist. We cannot say this of the witness of angels. This is not a final goal of the will and work of God. Angels really come only to go again. Hence it is the case in the whole Bible that whereas man thinks he must perish when God causes Himself to be seen and heard by him (cf. Is. 6), but is really constituted a witness by this experience, angels (including the mighty seraphim of Is. 6) help man to see and hear, but when they have discharged this commission they really do withdraw (never recurring, for example, in the biblical account of the activity and prophecy of Isaiah). It is of the very essence of the matter that this should be the case. In the light of this lacuna in the Gospel records we can also understand why it is that although angels are often mentioned they have no constitutive role in the New Testament Epistles. To the extent that the apostolic community has to do with the reality, presence and efficacy of the Spirit in whom the Lord Himself is present in the midst of His community, angels cannot have in the *kerygma, didache*[EN415], or ethical instruction of the apostles even the relatively independent role and significance undoubtedly ascribed to them in New Testament thinking as such and plainly enjoyed by them according to the witness of Acts. They fade away like the stars before the dawn. It is hard to see how Paul could have explained this phenomenon otherwise than by saying that we honour angels by thinking of their Lord, because in so doing we recognise that their service has not been rendered in vain. On the other hand, we dishonour them if we try to ascribe to them independent special functions where the Lord is present in the fulness of His Spirit. In the light of a true understanding of this lacuna, the basic answer to the question why there are not many more references to them in both Old and New Testaments is to the effect that although both Old and New Testaments are the preceding and following annunciation of God's own action they are also the attestation of His present action, of eschatological reality in the relationship between God and man. The more expressly the latter theme is treated in the Bible, the less we can reasonably expect to hear of angels. The ministry of angels is that [503] of the annunciation which precedes and follows. For the most part, then, we meet them in the Bible where there is still or again a certain distance in the reference to God's own action.

It is in this sense that they appear in their relationship to Jesus Christ at the beginning and end of the Gospels. At the beginning, or before the beginning of the true Gospel account of the life and suffering and death of Jesus, the angel of God under the name of Gabriel plays an emphatic role with his twofold message, first to Zacharias (Lk. 1⁵ᶠ·), and then to Mary (Lk. 1²⁶ᶠ·). The general nature of the ministry of angels may be seen very clearly in the angelic figure of this chapter. Yet he comes with a highly specific function, as the herald of what will be decisively accomplished by God. We know from the conclusion of the chapter, and from what follows, the nature of this work. In the first place, there will be born a final and supreme

---

[EN415] proclamation, teaching

215

prophet personifying the whole of the Old Testament and its message of a holy God, its call for conversion to Him, its hope and its threat. But this prophet will be only the precursor preparing the way for Another who is very different and far greater, the Son of God Himself born as man, Israel's Comforter and King, Judge and Redeemer. Thus the promise and the Law will both emerge again in living strength. But this time they will not be present *in abstracto*, or in their own historical form. They will stand in direct relationship to the fulfil-ment which comes down from God in heaven, to the presence of God Himself, not to give further promises or to make further demands, but to make the cause of man His own, taking it personally into His own hands. The ministry of the ἄγγελος κυρίου[EN416] of Lk. 1 is to announce this coming event, which is twofold and yet one, since the first is only the prepar-ation for the second. The angel himself is only the preceding shadow or sound of this event. He is only the herald of the God who will come in person in this event. As in the early accounts of the history of the covenant, there again appears the heaven which comes to earth with God Himself, epitomised in the form of the one angel of the one God. That he is really a heavenly creature may be seen from the first effect of his appearance on both those to whom he comes. Zacharias and Mary are both said to be "troubled" (Lk. $1^{12, \ 29}$). And they are both told not to fear ($1^{13, \ 30}$). It is not the fact that he is a heavenly creature, and there-fore strange to earthly beings, which makes the angel an angel. It is his message, the Word of God which he has to deliver in all his strangeness as a heavenly creature. And for both the persons concerned, and therefore in relation both to the coming precursor and the coming Christ Himself, this message obviously has the character of an annunciation of the covenant of grace which is not merely promised again but is now fulfilled. It is, therefore, a glad message. This is seen in the case of Mary: "Hail, thou that art highly favoured, the Lord is with thee" (v. 28, cf. the salutation in Jud. 6^{12}: "The Lord is with thee, thou mighty man of valour"), and then again: "Thou hast found favour with God" (v. 30). But it is also seen in the saying to Zacharias in v. 14: "Thou shalt have joy and gladness; and many shall rejoice at his birth," and then later when there is given to him, as a punishment for his unbelief, the confirmatory sign which he has requested: "I am sent ... to show thee these glad tidings" (v. 19). And to this there corresponds equally clearly, when the announced event begins to come to pass, and has already done so in part, the unequivocally positive, grateful and joyful tenor of the songs of praise both of Mary (v. 46 f.) and Zacharias (v. 68 f.). These two can-ticles form the climax of the chapter, and if we are rightly to understand the advent-angel of the chapter we do well to begin by considering them. What the ministry of the angel accom-plishes according to this story, and what is obviously therefore the meaning and purpose of his mission, is that the human creation to which he announces the coming of the kingdom, its King and its last and first witness, is thereby caused to break out in praise of the One who has willed this and begun to accomplish it; into praise of His mercy (note that the word occurs in both songs) as it is revealed and operative in this action. But what does it mean to praise God's mercy? The hymns as such are only an expression of the praise, not merely verbal and mental, but existential and actual, to which the earthly creation is stirred by the heavenly. It consists in the fact that men look and move willingly and readily to the One who comes, as earthly creatures who have appropriated what is said to them even though they know that they are in no position for what is said to come to them and actually to happen, it being highly improbable in the case of Zacharias and quite impossible in that of Mary, so that a miracle is involved in both cases. They have appropriated it because it is a matter of the helping and saving presence of God, of the mystery of His grace. The advent-angel announces that the mystery of God's grace will take place in all its improbability and impossi-bility, and this is what the two concerned, Zacharias the priest in the temple and the Virgin

[504]

[EN416] angel of the Lord

3. *The Ambassadors of God and Their Opponents*

Mary in Nazareth, have both actually appropriated in their different ways. They coincide in the fact that they are obedient. The difference is that, although Mary first raises a question (v. 34), she is content with the word of the angel: "Behold the handmaid of the Lord; be it unto me according to thy word" (v. 38), whereas Zacharias asks for a sign, and becomes obedient only when he is given what seems to be a punitive sign. Here then, as in the story of Manoah in Jud. 13²ᶠ·, the man seems to be the less gifted partner of the angel. But the difference is not decisive. The fulfilment of what is announced by the angel is neither retarded by the more sluggish obedience of Zacharias nor initiated by the more spontaneous obedience of Mary. We cannot, therefore, regard Mary as *corredemptrix*[EN417] in virtue of her *Fiat voluntas tua*[EN418]. The angel has actually indicated to both their calling to the service of the One who comes. God Himself has actually brought home His Word to both. They are both obedient to their heavenly calling in accordance with the incitement of the angel. And their two songs confirm the fact that there has taken place, and not in vain, a visitation of the earthly creation not only by God but also by the heavenly creation. What the angel was in relation to both, i.e., the servant of God, one who stands before God and is sent by Him, he is archetypally for what they themselves will be at the end of the story, or rather—for they stand at the head of a great host—for what all those will be after them whom the coming One Himself will call and gather to His community. The ministry of the angel will find its correspondence in their earthly ministry, his heavenly mission in their earthly mission. He cannot be more than the One who announces their calling. It is God Himself who calls Zacharias, Mary and all who will be called after them. But the angel of Lk. 1 is the one who mightily announces this and all divine calling. In relationship and analogy to Lk. 1 we must also understand the appearance of the angel to Joseph in Mt. 1²⁰⁻²⁵, by which he too is in his own way called to the service of the One who comes from God.

There follows in Lk. 2⁹⁻¹⁵ the appearance of the angel in the nativity story itself. It takes place immediately after the event which was announced in Lk. 1 has now taken place. The oneness of the event for all its duplication in Christ and His forerunner, and the true order in the duplication, are confirmed by the fact that the coming of the kingdom announced by the angel is the birth of Jesus Christ which that of John can only precede. Now, when Christ the Lord is born in the city of David, the time is fulfilled, the last time has come, the will of God has begun to be done on earth as it is in heaven, the calling of Zacharias and Mary has found its meaning and content, and these two are shown to be the head of the people of God of the last day. Now—the angelic appearance and message of the nativity story are a retrospective announcement of this Now. It is to be noted that those who are already called and placed in the service of God neither need nor receive it. Hence it does not take place in the vicinity of the cradle at Bethlehem where artists love to depict it. There what has taken place speaks for itself. Where the Son of God Himself is, the presence of heaven is attested in His presence without any particular need to be visible and audible. The angelic appearance and message are to those who are outside, to the shepherds in the fields who are the first to join those who are called and who with them become the first human witnesses of what has taken place. The ἄγγελος κυρίου[EN419] comes no less unexpectedly to the shepherds than to Zacharias, Mary and Joseph. When we are told that the δόξα κυρίου, the radiance of God, the revelation of His glory, majesty and power, shone round about them, this does not merely indicate the cosmic reality and perceptibility of the announcement made to them, nor does it merely denote that they have to do with a heavenly experience and therefore one which is new and strange to them as earthly creatures. It does show this, as appears from the fact that

[505]

[EN417] co-redeemer
[EN418] thy will be done
[EN419] angel of the Lord

they too are afraid, and that the "Fear not" has to be said above all to them. For if with the coming of the angel of the Lord heaven is manifested above the earth, and therefore something strange happens on earth, this is no reason for amazement or terror. For in truth it is the light of God which in this form breaks into the darkness of earth and illumines them. And it is not to blind but to enlighten, not to crush and destroy but to liberate, that the glory, majesty and power of God are revealed to them. Hence the continuation in the message of the angel is again: "Behold, I bring you good tidings of great joy, which shall be to all people" ($\pi\alpha\nu\tau\grave{\iota}\ \tau\hat{\omega}\ \lambda\alpha\hat{\omega}$, to the whole host of those who shall come to know of this happening, to the whole people of the last time already called and sanctified by this happening). Once again, therefore, the angel is clearly and unequivocally an evangelical angel. His word is exclusively of the covenant of grace. But it is of the fulfilled covenant, of what God has now done and accomplished in His mercy: "For unto you is born this day in the city of David the $\sigma\omega\tau\acute{\eta}\rho$ EN420, which is Christ the Lord." At the end of Israel's history there has now come its meaning and goal; at the end of the promise of the Old Testament the promised reality. The radiance of God streams over the dark earth because a child is born. The presence of heaven on earth has the sole purpose of attesting the birth and existence of this child, the redemption accomplished and the lordship of God established in Him. And it is the clear intention of this heavenly witness that men as represented first by the shepherds should not be transfixed by amazement or terror at the revelation imparted to them, as later legends have usually depicted the matter, but that they should be moved to seek and find the child for themselves. The direction with which the angel sends the shepherds away from himself to the child in the manger is the decisive service which he can and must render as an angel. The radiance of God has shone round about them, and the great announcement of the event has been made, only in order that they may run—as they actually do—and see for themselves, thus becoming witnesses on their own account of what has taken place. The ministry of the angel draws their attention, too, to the community, to their own ministry, to the fact that they are also to be witnesses.

And now the text shows in an extraordinary way that it is the ministry of all heaven which is rendered to man with this purpose of pointing them to the event as such, to the child in the manger. For here alone in the Bible we are told that there was with the angel the multitude of the heavenly host, the full complement of the host of Yahweh. All heaven bears witness to $\theta\epsilon\grave{o}\varsigma\ \grave{\epsilon}\nu\ \acute{\upsilon}\psi\acute{\iota}\sigma\tau\omega\iota\varsigma$ EN421, to His majesty, and to the glory proper to Him in this majesty, but to His majesty and glory in view of the fact that He has so inconceivably condescended and humbled Himself. And in view of this true majesty of God, of the secret of the grace of His majestic being, it bears witness to the peace on earth created by Him among the men of His good-pleasure, in the midst of the people of those elected and called by Him, which as such are already taken from the earthly conflict which they still endure and for whom the last time and the reign of peace have already dawned. All heaven, heaven as such, becomes presence, appearance and word, and proclaims God—God in His highest throne, [506] in His majesty—as the One who has taken earth to Himself. And all heaven, heaven as such, summons man to join the people of His good-pleasure, the community which knows and values and confesses His grace. This is the action or ministry of angels in retrospect of the beginning of the doing of the will of God on earth as this has taken place in the birth of Jesus Christ.

The third Evangelist especially has thus surrounded his account of this event with this account of the angels. It is to be noted again that they have no part in the event as such. They cannot anticipate it. They can only announce that it will take place. They neither see nor

---

EN420 saviour
EN421 God in the highest

hear it taking place. When it has taken place, they can only point to God Himself and His completed act. When they have done this, they return to heaven, and for a long time we hear no more about them. Both before and after the event their function is merely to declare it. They do not issue any summons of their own. It is not they who awaken Mary and Zacharias to obedience. It is not they who set the shepherds on the way to Bethlehem. Indeed, it is particularly emphasised that the shepherds decided to go of themselves. But the angels drew attention to the fact that Christ would come and that He had come, and that it was necessary to be ready for the coming One and to seek in His lowliness the One who had come. Their activity acquires and has its substance in the fact that Christ actually will come and has come, and that the calling of His people—not by their power, but by the shining of that of God— will actually take place. Their ministry consists in making visible and audible on earth this whole happening whose subject and author is God Himself. As the heavenly creation, they are the medium in which this is possible. The third Evangelist regards it as right and necessary, in his account of the beginning of the things fulfilled among us (Lk. 1^1), to lay on this medium the particular stress which he does actually lay on it in chapters 1 and 2. We must consider the impression which this makes on the reader. On the one hand, it increases the surprise and strangeness without which we cannot appraise or understand the event announced by the angels. Unless we see it at an appropriate distance, we cannot see this event or the Saviour and His prophet. We are set at this distance when we read that it was announced by angels. But this is only one side of the matter. For the announcement by the angels also introduces a certain softening. Seen in the mirror of the angelic message, the event is recognisable as one which for all its strangeness is a real event in our cosmic sphere, so that it is possible and meaningful not only to keep our distance but to take up an attitude and enter into a relationship to it. By his visible and audible introduction of heaven, Luke achieves the twofold effect of enabling the reader to see the event at a distance, but at a possible and meaningful distance which includes a relationship, or conversely to see it in a relationship, but in a relationship which entails a suitable distance. It is the ministry of angels on earth which corresponds exactly to this twofold impression. Apart from some traces in Matthew, Luke is the only Evangelist to make this impression. It is a subject for enquiry how far this is of a piece with his distinctive theology. But it may be noted that Matthew really attains the same effect by calling the kingdom of God the kingdom of heaven. At all events, Luke's distinction of the beginning of the history of Jesus by the ministry of angels was intentional and is certainly instructive. Here at least in the New Testament we are made conscious by it of the distinctive atmosphere in which it became true and recognisable that ὁ λόγος σὰρξ ἐγένετο^{EN422}. But there are also good reasons why Luke should stand alone to the extent that this reference is not to be found in the Gospel tradition as a whole and does not seem to correspond to any principle. The angels demand our attention, but they refuse to be set systematically in the foreground of interest.

We pass over the references in the stories of the temptation and the passion, to which allusion has already been made, and turn at once to the opposite pole of the records, the history of the forty days. It is to be noted that in exact correspondence to their appearances before and after the birth of Jesus, and also to the position and function in the whole context [507] of the record, they again appear at the beginning and the end in this part of the tradition. Whenever the Resurrected Himself appears—and His appearances form the heart of the presentation—there is no mention of angels. They are visible and audible as witnesses before and after He Himself is seen and heard and touched by His own. Primarily and decisively they are present before. Only once, at the beginning of Acts, do they make a last appearance in retrospect of the forty days.

---

^{EN422} the word became flesh

As concerns their appearance at or before the beginning of the Easter appearances, all four Evangelists agree that something takes place in the early morning on the first day of the week after the death and burial of Jesus. In respect of the external facts and circumstances, there are from the very first differences which temporarily seem to disappear but then become even more acute. As concerns the participants, for example, John speaks only of Mary Magdalene (20^1), Matthew of Mary and the other Mary (28^1), Mark of these two and a Salome (Mk. 16^1), and Luke of these two and a Joanna (24^{10}). In Matt. 28^4 and Lk. 24^4 the scene was outside the sepulchre, whereas in Mk. 16^5 and Jn. $20^{11f.}$ it was inside. In Matt. 28^2 they met the ἄγγελος κυρίου EN423, in Mk. 16^5 a νεανίσκος EN424, in Lk. 24^4 ἄνδρες δύο EN425 (obviously angels), and in Jn. 20^{12} δύο ἄγγελοι EN426. All four accounts refer to their white robes or radiant appearance. In Matt. $28^{2f.}$ we are told that the angel of the Lord has come down from heaven, rolled away the stone and seated himself upon it. But the meaning of the Evangelist can hardly be that this took place in the presence of the women. The other three all say that the women found the grave open and empty, and were then addressed by the angel or angels. From this point there is almost complete unity in relation to the angelic message. It is true that in Jn. 20^{13} it simply consists in the question to Mary: "Woman, why weepest thou?", but we can recognise the question in what the angel or angels say to the women according to the Synoptists. The question implies that there is no reason to weep, nor to complain: "They have taken away my Lord, and I know not where they have laid him." Why not? In Lk. 24^5 the decisive saying of the angel again has the form of a question, although this time the answer is explicit within the question: "Why seek ye the living among the dead?" The explicit answer as such, which is the whole point of the Johannine account too, is to the following effect: "He is not here: for he is risen, as he said. Come, see the place (but only the place) where he lay" (Mt. 28^6, Mk. 16^6). The final reference is missing in Lk. $24^{6f.}$, and we are given instead an explanation of the ἠγέρθη EN427: "Remember how he spake unto you when he was yet in Galilee, saying. The Son of man must be delivered into the hands of sinful men, and be crucified, and the third day rise again."

The first point, then, is that it is by angels whose radiant appearance and heavenly character is generally emphasised that the fact of the resurrection of the Lord is declared to the first men, to these women. It is to be noted that in none of the accounts is the empty grave as such the theme of their message. Even the rather difficult account which we are given in Jn. 20^{2-9} of Peter and the other disciple running to the sepulchre is obviously not meant to be understood in this way. The open and empty grave is as such a sign which needs explanation (like the unexpected pregnancy of Mary in Mt. $1^{18f.}$). Again, in none of the Evangelists is it the case that the Resurrected appears directly to His own before the appearance and announcement of the angels. Their appearance to the women, their declaration to them, their communication: ἠγέρθη (even in the Johannine form of the question: "Why weepest thou?"), seems to be the inescapable medium for an initial knowledge of this event. The appearance and announcement of the angels cannot, of course, be more than this medium. They have no part at all in the occurrence of the resurrection itself. Even the angel of Matthew who rolls away the stone is not to be thought of as co-operating in the actual resurrection of the Lord.

[508]   But as the medium of the knowledge of this happening the angels must immediately withdraw. The second purpose of their appearance and content of their message is to tell the

---

EN423 angel of the Lord
EN424 young man
EN425 two men
EN426 two angels
EN427 he is risen

women to go to the disciples and let them know that they will see the risen Jesus Himself. This is expressly stated in Mt. 28⁷ and Mk. 16⁷, and it is implicit in the recollection of the prediction of the passion and resurrection in Lk. 24⁷, and everywhere Galilee is explicitly mentioned as the place where this direct encounter between the Resurrected and His disciples will take place. From this point, the accounts are again confused. According to Mk. 16⁸ the women do not seem to have carried out this commission: "They went out quickly, and fled from the sepulchre; for τρόμος καὶ ἔκστασις EN428 seized them: neither said they anything to any man; for they were afraid." According to Lk. 24⁹ᶠ· they faithfully discharged their commission but were not believed by the disciples. What they told them seemed to them ὡσεὶ λῆρος EN429 until confirmed by direct appearances of the risen One to the disciples on the way to Emmaus in 24¹³⁻³², to Simon alone in 24³³ and to all of them (in Jerusalem) in 24³⁶⁻⁴⁹. According to Mt. 28⁹ᶠ· Jesus Himself appeared to the women and repeated the commission, again referring expressly to a direct meeting which the disciples were to expect with Him in Galilee. This commission was undoubtedly fulfilled by the women according to Mt. 28¹⁶, and did not meet with disbelief on the part of the disciples. According to Jn. 20¹³ᶠ·, immediately after the angel had put that question to Mary and received from her that complaint by way of answer, Mary turned and was faced by Jesus Himself. It is He who now gives the order: "Go to my brethren, and say unto them, I ascend unto my Father, and your Father." She carries out the order, and according to this account there is an appearance of the Resurrected to all the disciples (except in the first instance Thomas) on the evening of the same day in Jerusalem. Our present concern is, of course, with the part played by the angels in these happenings. And the remarkable thing is that for all the contradictions there can be no doubt not only that it is they who first announce the fact of the resurrection but also that it is they who initiate the repetition of the announcement. With what success? In John there is no mention of any commission given to the women, and they are immediately crowded out by Jesus Himself. In Mark they do not seem to execute the commission at all, and in Luke they do so to no effect. Possibly the meaning in Matthew is that it was only respected and successful when it had been repeated by Jesus Himself. In all cases the commission given by the angels does not seem to be adequate in itself. In all cases Jesus Himself, His appearance and Word, is the agent who gives power to the commission and its execution, and who finally compels the disciples to recognise His presence as the Resurrected. Without Him there could not have taken place the movement initiated at His empty tomb, just as without Him it would not have been true that He was not in the tomb but risen. And yet angels stand at the beginning as the first witnesses of the fact and therefore as those who set in train the ensuing movement. They do not create anything. They do not accomplish anything. They are simply there. But they cannot fail to be there, not as a condition of what happens or of the knowledge of what happens, but for the characterisation, illumination, emphasising and distinction of what happens and of its knowledge by men. Here, too, they show that where God is present and active on earth heaven is also present and active, thus characterising the absolute uniqueness and mystery of the presence and activity of God. We might well repeat what we said concerning their introduction into the Lucan accounts of the beginning of the history of Jesus. Their introduction into the close of the history intentionally awakens in the reader the twofold impression that, by the appearance and announcement of the angels and the presence of heaven with God Himself, he is both set at an appropriate distance and also placed in a meaningful relationship to the event recorded. If we consider this impression, we are given a characteristic view of what is meant by the ministry of angels both in its greatness and in its limitation. In this connexion it might be

---

EN428 trembling and amazement
EN429 like idle tales

[509] worth further enquiry why at the conclusion, as opposed to the beginning, the four Evangelists agree in making express reference to the ministry of angels.

But in this case, too, we have a particular concluding narrative as well, namely, that at the end of the forty days. At the heart of this period the angels are as little visible as during the birth of Jesus proper or in the central tract of the Gospel record as a whole. Jesus is not accompanied by an angel when He appears. The angels appear again only when His appearances as the Resurrected are over. The account of this post-ascension appearance is to be found in Ac. 1^{10-11} "And while they looked stedfastly toward heaven as he went up, behold, two men stood by them in white apparel." The assertion of the heavenly and therefore the divine character of the event of the forty days is thus an express conclusion from its end as well as its beginning. Nor is it any accident that we owe this account to the author to whom we are also indebted for Lk. 1–2. The framework of mystery closes around this last item in the tradition and therefore around the Gospel record as a whole. The two angels mark this conclusion. Yet it is remarkable that their saying does not as it were seal the conclusion but makes it a new beginning: "Ye men of Galilee, why stand ye gazing up into heaven? This same Jesus, which is taken up from you into heaven, shall so come in like manner as ye have seen him go into heaven."

This is best understood, perhaps, from the consequent action of the disciples. It is strikingly modest. It consists simply in the fact (v. 12f.) that the eleven returned to Jerusalem and there assembled with the women and Mary the mother of Jesus and His brethren in an upper room obviously well-known to them all. Why? "These all continued with one accord in prayer and supplication." That is all. They are not yet the community of Pentecost. But they are this community *in spe*[EN430], the little flock to whom, according to Lk. 12^{32}, there will be given the kingdom, i.e., the presence and grace and power of their Lord, i.e., the Spirit. The two angels have not given them the Spirit. No angels will give them the Spirit. As the angels only marked the conclusion of the Easter account and the whole Gospel record, so their appearance and message only marks that which now begins, the history of the apostles, i.e., Church history in the presence and under the guidance of the Holy Ghost. God Himself has accomplished and revealed what is now accomplished and revealed behind them. And God Himself will establish the results and control the ensuing events. But this new thing from God has not yet commenced. What we are told concerning the disciples and the women, that they continued in prayer, corresponds exactly to the strait in which they found themselves between what God has already done and what He will do but has not yet done. But what we are told concerning the disciples and the women takes place under the sign of, and in correspondence with, that which is said to them by the angels. The saying is retrospective, but also prospective. It refers to the past, but also to the future. It is a saying between the times, reminding us of the sayings to Zacharias and Mary. It is a plain deduction from the actual wording, as well as from the consequent action of the disciples, that it claims those who are addressed for waiting upon God and for willingness and readiness for His future. But the waiting and the willingness and readiness are different from those of Lk. 1. Between them there lies the history of the fulfilment of the Christmas message right up to its revelation in the story of Easter. This history of fulfilment and revelation is now concluded and therefore present in all its fulness to those who are now claimed for waiting upon God and willingness and readiness for His future. "This same Jesus … is taken up from you into heaven." They know for whom they must wait, for whose future they must be willing and ready. They know in whom they are at one. They know to whom they pray, and for whose sake they continue in prayer. It is a matter of the Lord of this history. He has now concluded it. He has brought them (the disciples and the women) into the strait between yesterday and

---

[EN430] in hope

to-morrow. But is it really a strait? Do they not exist already in illimitable freedom? For the [510] concluded yesterday was this Jesus, the Lord of this history. What cannot take place in the history which is just commencing when that which has concluded is this history? What will not be its end and goal when its beginning is the conclusion of this history? Where will it not lead when it begins with the fact that this Jesus is taken up into heaven? Who and what is not to be expected from heaven? The saying of the angels under the sign of which the disciples and the women continue with one accord in prayer must obviously run as it does: "This same Jesus ... shall so come in like manner as ye have seen him go into heaven." It would not be this Jesus, nor would the concluded history be this history, nor would the beginning made with this conclusion, the beginning of the history of the apostles or Church history, be this beginning, if the end and goal to which it moves did not correspond, and the One who had come and gone were not to come again. Who else should come but the One who had come already? He *was*, and therefore who else can be the One who is to be? He was the Alpha, and therefore who else can be the Omega? Where else can those who come from Him go except to Him? How can this One who has come fail to come again? For He did not come in vain. By His coming the doing of the will of God on earth was begun. Indeed, it was achieved once and for all, and perfectly revealed in His person. He Himself became man, and united humanity in Himself. How can He be untrue to Himself? How can He fail to confess His work, His people, the earth on which He has so greatly magnified the mercy of God and therefore the glory of God? But again, how can He come again otherwise than He has gone? How else can all earthly occurrence terminate but in the glory with which the events of the forty days and therefore of His whole epiphany and *parousia* conclude? He is the One who has appeared to His own as the Victor over death and therefore as the Lord. As this Victor and Lord He has gone up into heaven. But as the Victor and Lord He will also come again in the fulness whose $\dot{\alpha}\pi\alpha\rho\chi\dot{\eta}$ or $\dot{\alpha}\rho\rho\alpha\beta\dot{\omega}\nu$ [EN431] is His resurrection, the conclusion of His history and the beginning of that of His community.

This, then, is the purport of the saying of the angels in Ac. 1[11]. With its indication that the frontier of the Gospel story forms the announcement of the final horizon of all earthly occurrence it is perhaps the most powerful and comprehensive of all the sayings attributed to angels in the Bible. For what other saying embraces so fully the mystery of the incarnate Word and therefore the mystery of God? At any rate, it is the most important in practice. Indicating that the frontier of this particular history is the horizon of all history, it is an authoritative direction to the Christian community in every age. It tells it that it belongs to the place where this One who has come is expected as the One who comes. More than angelic appearances and sayings are needed, of course, to awaken and gather the community, to rule it by judgment and grace, continually to conduct it to knowledge and service, continually to quicken and sustain it—the community which will occupy this place, existing in the world in retrospect of this frontier and in prospect of this horizon. Men will also be needed for this purpose, apostles, prophets, evangelists, the bearers of the manifold gifts of the Spirit, all proclaiming with their many voices that it belongs to this place, warning it against any aberration, and calling it back when it is guilty of aberration. But angels are needed to say this first, to tell it that the frontier may and must also be its horizon. Angels are needed to set up the sign under which we may live patiently, cheerfully and confidently *post Christum*[EN432]. And therefore we can say that Luke has introduced these angels at the right place, at the end of the incomparable history of Jesus which is the beginning of that of the apostles and therefore of the Church.

[EN431] first fruits or guarantee
[EN432] after Christ

[511] So much, then, for the ministry and therefore the being of angels in relationship to Jesus Christ. We have not exhausted the theme. For instance, it would be significant and instructive to consider why it is that in so many passages (e.g., Mt. 13^{41}, 24^{31}, 25^{31} and par.; 1 Thess. 4^{16}; 2 Thess. 1^7) we are told that at His second coming, unlike His first, Jesus Christ will manifest Himself with His angels and obviously to some extent with their active participation, after which, if our interpretation of 1 Cor. 15^{24} is correct, there will be that complete suspension of their function. This clearly means that the ministry of angels, the whole participation of heaven in earthly occurrence, although it is necessarily concealed here and now in its distinctive invisibility, will finally be revealed and declared with the lordship of Jesus Christ which is also hidden here and now.

Again, beyond the Christological field in the narrower sense we might consider much that is said about the ministry of angels away from the centre but within its radius in the history of Israel and that of the New Testament community. There are many interesting and pregnant passages upon which we have only touched in passing if at all. But I know of none which would really lead us any further in the subject. Our present purpose is not a complete biblical angelology. We have simply taken the most important examples to illustrate the decisive matters which claim our attention in dogmatics.

And now we have reached a point where we can answer the question of the right name or term for the distinctive reality with which we are concerned. Does it best correspond to the matter itself if we continue to use the word which is current in all modern languages, i.e., "angels," and, if we are to content with the term, how are we to understand it? We must begin by stating that it is not only legitimate but advisable to accept the common title.

From the essay of W. Baumgartner already quoted, I take the following conclusions. The Hebrew has no specific word for the concept. *Maleak* simply means a messenger. In Hebrew, therefore, the general term is used in a particular sense to denote an angel. And in these cases it is usually distinguished either by a genitival connexion with the name of God or by the use of the possessive pronoun. Thus according to Baumgartner the *maleak Yahweh*[EN433] is not a particular angel in distinction from others, but the messenger of Yahweh in distinction from ordinary messengers, i.e., an angel. The facts concerning the introduction of the latter term are as follows. In itself the Greek ἄγγελος[EN434] is not a particular designation. But in the New Testament the secular usage of the word is so strongly pushed into the background that the distinction of the word becomes a *fait accompli*[EN435]. On this basis, perhaps, the Vulgate is fairly consistent in using *nuntius*[EN436] for an ordinary messenger and *angelus*[EN437] for a heavenly, and in this it has been followed not only by English but also by German, Dutch, Swedish, French, Italian, Spanish etc.

There are good material reasons for this procedure. The distinctive matter requires a distinctive term. We evade the problem, or deny the intended reality, if we refuse to accept a distinctive word. And the term "angel" commends itself on three counts.

EN433 angel of the Lord
EN434 messenger or angel
EN435 accomplished fact
EN436 messenger
EN437 angel

First, it describes the reality which calls for description, irrespective of the question of its being, in the light of its function and activity.

Second, it describes this activity as the conveyance of a message, the making of an announcement, the giving of a witness.

Third, it explains this activity (according to the sense which it has acquired in its history) as one which in an emphatic way, unique of its kind, and distinguished by its immediacy from the corresponding activities of other beings, is exercised in the service of God.

According to our previous deliberations this is an outline of the reality [512] which it is our task to describe and name. No other word corresponds so exactly to this outline as the word "angel." If we decide for this word, we do so (in the sense of the statements which we have just made) with the following more precise definitions of our understanding of the term.

What angels are is to be understood wholly and exclusively from their function and activity. They are wholly and utterly angels, messengers. They are beings which are as they are engaged in the action thereby denoted. We grope in the void if we speak of a being of angels presupposed in this action and distinguishable from it. They are heavenly beings. But heaven is the upper cosmos inconceivable to us. We know of it only that it is the intracosmic Whence of the divine speech and action in the conceivable cosmos, and that to this extent it is the upper cosmos in relation to the latter. But we know nothing of its being as such, nor therefore of that of heavenly creatures. We know them only in their action and service as God's messengers. There is thus no place for any questions concerning their person or form or qualities or nature in abstraction from their action as God's messengers. There is no place, as we have seen, for any question of their numbers. We say exactly the same when we speak of one angel as when we speak of an infinite host. For one angel acts and speaks as all and for all, and all can and do only confirm what is spoken and done by one. There is also no place, as we have seen, for any question of the mutual relationship, of an internal order and hierarchy of heaven. Naturally, we cannot deny or suppress the fact that angels exist. But we deny that they exist otherwise than in the execution of their office. Thus the use of the term "angel" excludes the error of so much angelology both ancient and modern, both positive and negative. The basic meaning of the term must be taken in all seriousness when we use it.

Again, the description in the term "angel" of their action as messengers, as bringers of news, as heralds and witnesses, must not be taken in any weak sense, but with all strictness. When as heavenly beings, coming with God Himself from above, they act and speak in the service of God, their speech and action is that of very special messengers, supremely competent, authorised and powerful, and quite incomparable. In the title I have called them "The Ambassadors of God," and in so doing I have had in mind the implications of the word as it is used in diplomacy.

An ambassador does not belong to the government which he represents. He merely represents it. He does not pursue any policy of his own, but only that of his government. He has no independent ideas or initiative. His activity consists wholly in representing as exactly and fully as possible the intentions of the government, with which he has always to identify his own. But while this is the sum of his activity, he represents his government with full authority. [513] He is no mere emissary or official or commissar. Within the limits of his appointment as an ambassador he may and must speak and act in the place and name of his government. Its honour and dignity are his. In his person we have to do with it, and his government will unhesitatingly acknowledge the decisions and steps which he takes. We respect his government by respecting him, and an insult to him is an insult to his government. It is in this way, but in a supreme sense, that the angels are the ambassadors of God.

They have specific messages to give and tasks to perform. They are not God or secondary gods. They are creatures, and as such they are wholly under God. As heavenly creatures they are this in an even stricter sense than is true of earthly, for unlike the latter, as we have seen, they have no autonomy (just as a private citizen pursuings his private concerns enjoys a very different independence of speech and action from the accredited ambassador of his country, although naturally without the privileges of the latter). But while angels as heavenly beings are only under God, and are what they are only in His service, they have behind them and for them the whole authority and glory and power of God in the performance of this service and the execution of this office. Where the angel is, there God Himself is present. Thus an angel never speaks half-truths or does things by halves. We can rely on what an angel says. There can be no contesting what he says, or appeal against his decisions, or opposition to his actions. This is not because he himself is high and infallible and powerful. It is because he represents God in His speech and actions. He is the divine plenipotentiary whom God Himself acknowledges and in whose words and decisions we are dealing directly with the intentions of God Himself. In this way then, in this strong sense of the term, he is the messenger of God. The same cannot be said of any prophet or apostle. If in certain situations a man is the messenger of God with this supreme authority, we can only say that it is an angel who speaks and acts through this man.

There are passages in the Bible which seem to take account of this possibility. For example, we are told in Ac. 6[15] that when the council looked on Stephen "they saw his face as it had been the face of an angel." Again, in Gal. 4[14] Paul reminds his readers that they had received him "as an angel of God, even as Jesus Christ." Again, in Heb. 13[2] we read of some who, exercising Christian hospitality, entertained angels unawares. In the Old Testament we are told in 2 Sam. 14[17] that the wise woman of Tekoah said to David: "For as an angel of God, so is my lord the king to discern good and bad." Again, we read in Zech. 12[8] that in that day the house of David shall be as heavenly beings, "as the angel of the Lord before them." Again, in Hag. 1[13] the prophet is explicitly called "the Lord's messenger." The same is said of the priest in Mal. 2[7], where we read that "his lips keep knowledge, and they seek the law at his mouth." And in Mt. 11[10] John the Baptist is expressly equated with the messenger of Ex. 23[20] who goes before the face of the Lord and prepares the way for His people. Along the same lines we are probably to seek the solution to the riddle of Rev. 2–3, where the human leaders of the communities of Asia Minor are openly called ἄγγελοι EN438

But this only brings out the more clearly the distinction of angelic speech [514] and action. The fact that it has this distinction is the further point which we have to keep in mind and to maintain in our use of the word "angel" in the sense of "messenger."

But a third point is that, if we use the word "angel," we must keep clearly in view the specific meaning of the term "God" with which it stands in such close relationship. The decisive thing about their activity, and therefore about their being as extraordinary ambassadors, is that they are the messengers of God. They are not the manifestations of an idea, or the expressions of a power, or the bearers of any news or announcement or witness. They are not a mere postal service for their message. In the sense stated, they are the messengers of the God attested in Holy Scripture, who in Jesus Christ has made Himself the Lord and Ally and Deliverer of man. Apart from this they are nothing. They either exist in connexion with the history which this involves, or they do not exist at all. They act only according to that which God wills and accomplishes in this history. As heaven is determined by this, so are heavenly beings. As God Himself is not an imaginary or supposedly or genuinely experienced being of supreme perfection, power or dignity, but the One who has acted and revealed Himself in Jesus Christ, so the angels are not hypostases and mediators subordinated to and co-ordinated with this supreme being, and superior to man, but in the sense described messengers of the one true God living, active and revealed as Father, Son and Holy Ghost. If we keep to this fact, it is easy and self-evident to avoid the basic error concerning their being, as though it were to be sought somewhere behind their activity. It is easy and self-evident to cling to the root-meaning of the word "angel" (i.e., messenger). And it is natural to see and maintain the extraordinary force which the word carries in their case. But whatever lies to the right hand or to the left of this concept of a messenger of God—and of this one God—cannot possibly be described by the term "angel," no matter what it may be or however real it may be in itself.

Our reference is, of course, to the Christian use of the term "angel." What has been meant and thought and written and maintained and taught in both ancient and more modern times concerning the being and existence and activity of the possible hypostases and mediators of others gods, we commit into the hands of the inventors and adherents of the relevant systems and messages and writings in which these figures occur. We are obviously unable to prevent them using the term "angel" for what they think they may know and accept and believe in this respect. We insist, however, that whatever lies to the right hand or to the left of the reality whose concept is decisively given by its relationship to the living, active and revealed God of Holy Scripture, does not correspond to the Christian idea of an angel and does not deserve to be called an angel according to the Christian use. In the nature and significance decisively ascribed to them, the angels of Thomas Aquinas are not angels in the Christian sense. Nor are the angels of R. M. Rilke in the various stages of his

---

EN438 angels

[515]   poetry, including the last. Nor are the angels of so many mythical, spiritualistic, occult, theo-
sophical and anthroposophical systems, nor those of the popularly phantastic imagination
of so many individual dreamers or whole circles of such. Nor are the beings which under this
name have met with so much ridicule and scepticism and denial. Whether or not these
beings exist is a matter which need not be decided in the present context. The decision
which has to be made here is that, whether they are real or unreal, maintained or denied,
feared, loved or even scorned, they belong to a different sphere from that in respect of
which Holy Scripture speaks of angels. The decision which has to be made is that as Christians and theologians we must refrain from speaking of such beings as angels, and that we
must certainly not be so foolish as to try to learn from an acquaintance with such beings what
is to be understood by angels in the Christian sense of the term.

By way of appendix to this final explanation of the name and concept of
angels a last question may be explicitly raised and answered which has probably been quietly present in all our previous discussions. I formulate it intentionally in the false form in which it is usually put. Do the reality and ministry
of angels belong only to the history which took place then and there according
to the witness of Holy Scripture, to the history of the establishment of the
divine covenant with the fathers of the Israel, the appearance of Jesus Christ
and the institution of His community? Or do angels belong to cosmic occurrence generally, and therefore to the history of all ages, and therefore to our
own history too, including the life-history of each individual?

The question is wrongly put because there is no such alternative. The history which begins with the patriarchs, has its centre in Jesus Christ and concludes with the apostles, is not enclosed as the history of the covenant of
grace—we must remember what took place at its centre—in a "then and there"
in which it is alien and remote in relation to what did and does and will take
place before and afterwards in other places and on other occasions. If angels
belong to the history of the covenant, they cannot be remote and alien in
relation to other events before and after. Again, world occurrence generally,
including that in which we ourselves participate or will participate, is not
autonomous in relation to the history of the covenant, to the divine speech
and action in Jesus Christ. In this history all history, and therefore our own,
has its meaning and centre. By it the existence of all earthly creatures, of all
humanity and of each individual man past, present and future, is illuminated,
determined and controlled. All existence has its root there, hastening towards
and proceeding from it. The history of the Christian community especially, as
the movement of the inner circle around this centre, proceeds from and hastens towards it to the extent that it recognises the goal of all occurrence in the
revelation of the validity of what took place then and there. Because it lives in
this hope and expectation, it lives—in virtue of the Holy Spirit poured out
thence—in and with what took place there. But all creation unwittingly does
[516]   the same in a wider circle around the Christian community. Hence if what took
place there did not take place without the angels, the same is necessarily true
of the life of the community in every age, of world occurrence generally, and
of all individual and personal occurrence. Where, known or unknown, Jesus

Christ is present, living and powerful by His Spirit, there, known or unknown, the ministry of angels is also executed.

It is clear that this cannot be grasped and expressed as a generally known or recognisable truth. But the same is true of the existence and kingdom of God and His presence, life and power in Jesus Christ. This, too, is a particular truth—*kerygma*, confession, Spirit, revelation—where it is really grasped and expressed. Similarly the ministry of angels in the narrower and wider circle of occurrence distinct from that of the history of the covenant is *kerygma*, confession, Spirit and revelation, and therefore not an element in a general outlook or philosophy of life or history. But the Christian message and therefore Church dogmatics has to do with this particular truth and its universal significance. It is self-evident that the reality of the ministry of angels cannot be restricted to the history attested in the Bible, but that by reason of the central and universal significance of this particular occurrence we must (or may) count on it that this ministry is also rendered, and is genuine and effective, in the narrower and wider circle as well.

Where and when is the problem not raised which we have now seen to be the problem of angelology, i.e., the problem of the mystery of the presence and speech and action of God in our sphere and therefore in the lower cosmos, the problem of heaven on earth, and therefore the problem of the purposeful proximity and distance, distance and proximity, without which God would not encounter earthly creation either in majesty or intimacy, in holiness or grace, and therefore genuinely as God? Where He does this, He always does it through the ministry of angels. For He does it through His Holy Spirit. And the work of His Holy Spirit is to make us participants in the history of the covenant of grace, as fellow-citizens, house-fellows and contemporaries with the patriarchs and prophets, the apostles and evangelists. Life in the Spirit, and under His guidance, consists quite simply in participation in this history. But to have a part in this history is to have a part in the ministry of angels which took place within it. Where the kingdom of God is, there the strict and saving mystery of God is at work, and therefore the kingdom of heaven, and therefore, in all their imperceptibility and humility, in the unreserved selflessness and objectivity which distinguishes them from all earthly creatures, the angels.

In conclusion we must insist with some stringency that where this is the case the real angels attested in the Bible are at their own work in their own way. There is thus no place for speculation. If it were a matter of something else, [517] angelic beings might well be occupied with marvellous works either proper or ascribed to them. On the other hand, they might not. But either way, our own concern is with what is. For real angels the only thing which matters is the glory of God on earth. They serve earthly creatures by showing them the proximity and distance, the distance and proximity, in short the mystery of God, and therefore God Himself. They attest Him to earthly creatures as these require according to the wisdom of God, and it is therefore most unlikely that they should do so as they themselves think desirable, interesting or remarkable according to their own wisdom. In doing this, they do, of course, enlighten and guide, help and keep, protect and save. But this simply means that God does all these things, and they are His witnesses proclaiming His praise and summoning to His praise in great events and small, cosmic and personal, thus ministering not only to Him but to earthly creatures as well. That they are present as His servants in what God does means that they show earthly creatures that it is He who does it, that He is so faithful and gracious and patient. And in so doing they render to earthly creatures, to us, their proper service, the only benefit that we can expect at their hands.

Regard should be had to the context in which Ps. 34$^{6f.}$ speaks of this ministry of angels. First we read: "This poor man cried, and the Lord heard him, and saved him out of all his troubles"; then: "The angel of the Lord encampeth round about them that fear him, and delivereth them"; and finally: "O taste and see that the Lord is good: blessed is the man that trusteth in him." The same is true of Ps. 91$^{9f.}$: "Thou hast made the Lord, which is my refuge, even the most High, thy habitation." It is to the man who does this, to his confirmation in this action, that the continuation applies: "There shall no evil befall thee, neither shall any plague come nigh thy dwelling. For he shall give his angels charge over thee, to keep thee in all thy ways. They shall bear thee up in their hands, lest thou dash thy foot against a stone." In this connexion we recall the misuse which the devil made of this passage in Mt. 4^6. The passage is misused when it is thought that the angels are present to give man sensational help in his own plans by sending things which are pleasant and warding off those which are not. They are indeed present, but in such a way as to make known to him the help of God. They serve him, but in such a way that they set his history in relationship to the history of the covenant of grace as this applies to him and embraces him. They are there for him personally and directly, but in such a way that in the very greatest and the very smallest things they place him before the mystery of God. *In hoc sunt constituti, ut praesentiorem eius opem nobis testentur ..., mediatore Christo nos retinent, ut ab eo prorsus pendeamus, in eo recumbamus, ad eum feramur et ipso acquiescamus*^{EN439} (Calvin, *Instit.* I, 14, 12). If we do not see or try to evade the high objectivity of this service, we do better to confess that we know nothing about angels, and therefore not to call upon them or to think that we can expect anything from or have anything to do with them.

At this point we may say a few words about the so-called national angels. In the days of the Third Reich they figured prominently in the philosophy of history of certain German theologians. But the idea cannot really be proved from Dan. 10^{13}, for in this passage the prince of Persia who opposes Michael and the other angels is clearly depicted as a demonic figure and not as an angel of God. Yet within the divine overruling of the world why should there not be particular angelic relationships to the existence and way and role of historical collectives? In this connexion, however, we are not really to think of nations but of states as the forces of order established by man. The concepts of order and power so often applied to angels in the New Testament Epistles seem to point in this direction. The only thing is that if we look in this direction we should not forget the high objectivity of the angels or plunge into the theology of the Iliad, ascribing to angels the character of protective deities for the representation in heaven of national and political interests. If the angels represent any interests of

[518]

---

^{EN439} who have been so constituted as to testify that his power is present for us ... Christ the Mediator preserves us, so that we might utterly depend on him, lean on him, be brought to him and rest in him order and power in history, they are those of God. We have thus to understand the service which they render to the different historical groupings and their development in the following sense—that, always in the context of the history of the covenant as the guiding thread of the whole, they are witnesses to His mystery in the course of political history and its various combinations. There can be no doubt that we do have to reckon with their ministry in this respect.

And finally we may again refer to the question of what are called guardian angels in relation to individuals. There are passages in the Bible which seem to support this view. The strongest is Job $33^{22f.}$, which unmistakeably refers to the effective advocacy of an angel on behalf of a man before the throne of God. Yet even there we are not told that this one in a thousand is specifically or permanently the angel of this particular man. Again, in Ac. 12^{15} we are told that when the Christians assembled in the house of Mary heard the imprisoned Peter knocking at the door, but did not realise that it was he in person, they expressed the view: ὁ ἄγγελός ἐστιν αὐτοῦ[EN440]. But in this case it is an open question, as Calvin rightly observed (*Instit.* I, 14, 7), whether they are not merely toying with a popular notion. At all events the expression does not force us to conclude that "his" angel is his guardian angel. On the other hand, the angel who in this passage actually frees Peter and might therefore be described as his guardian angel is not described as "his angel" but simply as "the angel of the Lord." The saying in Mt. 18^{10}, however, is the one which is most commonly adduced in favour of this view: "Take heed that ye despise not one of these little ones; for I say unto you ὅτι οἱ ἄγγελοι αὐτῶν[EN441] (ἐν οὐρανοῖς[EN442] is missing in some manuscripts) διὰ παντὸς βλέπουσι τὸ πρόσωπον τοῦ πατρός μου ἐν οὐρανοῖς[EN443]." It is certainly stated here that the heavenly Father of Jesus stands in a particular relationship to these little ones which is mediated by angels. But it does not say, as even Calvin maintained, that each of them has his own angel charged to be a guardian angel. The popularity of this concept in the Early Church and ever since is suspicious. Does it not owe more to the heathen notion of the "genius," usually accompanied even more capriciously by the "daemon," than to the biblical passages quoted in its favour? Most of the older Reformed dogmaticians, in contrast to the more easy-going Lutherans, refused to take up the matter. Quite apart from any questions of disposition, it might be asked why there should not be a particular relationship between angelic reality and each individual. Is not this necessarily the case? Does not the relationship between God and man (by the Word and Spirit of God) always have an individual character? But does this necessarily imply a permanent private angel for each private person? The most forceful, because positive, objection to this view was again brought by Calvin, who maintained that the divine care for an individual is not committed only to one angel, *sed omnes uno consensu vigilantur pro salute nostra*[EN444]. If we do not think it sufficient that all the hosts of heaven keep watch over us, what will be the value of thinking that one angel in particular is our guardian? This is sound angelology. In Ps. $91^{11f.}$, which emphasises most plainly the protective function of angels, the reference is not to one angel but to many. And here, too, we must remember that the protection of angels consists in the fact that by their witness to God they keep those committed to them in fellowship with God, and therefore genuinely keep and secure them. In the life of each man they prosecute the cause of the kingdom of God, and therefore they are the best possible representatives of the cause of this man himself.

[519]

[EN440] because their angels
[EN441] it is his angel
[EN442] in heaven
[EN443] continually see the face of my father in heaven
[EN444] but they all with one accord watch out for our salvation

And now to conclude our consideration of the kingdom of heaven and the ambassadors of God we must take a brief look at a very different sphere.

We are forced to do this because a primitive and fatal association has always brought together these two spheres of angels and demons from the days of the fathers to those of Neo-Protestantism. We shall not bring them into the same close relationship as formerly. But there is good reason to cast a momentary glance at demons immediately after our discussion of the angels, for demons are best considered in contrast to the theme of this discussion.

Why must our glance be brief? Because we have to do at this point with a sinister matter about which the Christian and the theologian must know but in which he must not linger or become too deeply engrossed, devoting too much attention to it in an exposition like our own. In its own way it is very real. "The prospect was neither instructive nor pleasing," was the experience and judgment of Goethe when he stood on the top of Vesuvius and looked for a while into its open crater. And if we do not share this experience and judgment on the edge of the crater where we now find ourselves, we surely cannot see what is to be seen there. Sinister matters may be very real, but they must not be contemplated too long or studied too precisely or adopted too intensively. It has never been good for anyone—including (and particularly) Martin Luther—to look too frequently or lengthily or seriously or systematically at demons (who for Luther were usually compressed into the single figure of the devil). It does not make the slightest impression on the demons if we do so, and there is the imminent danger that in so doing we ourselves might become just a little or more than a little demonic. The very thing which the demons are waiting for, especially in theology, is that we should find them dreadfully interesting and give them our serious and perhaps systematic attention. In this way they can finally catch out, not bad theologians, but good. For this reason, having consciously and intentionally devoted a full discussion to the angels, we shall take only a brief look at this matter. It is not a question of treating them lightly, but of handling them as best befits their nature. A quick, sharp glance is not only all that is necessary but all that is legitimate in their case.

I have called this sphere a very different one from that of angels. This brings us right up against a materially decisive point. Indeed, it brings us right up against *the* decisive point, against the whole problem and its legitimate solu-[520] tion. The two spheres do not belong together either by origin or nature. The demons are not as it were the poor relations, or the vicious, disreputable and troublesome relations of angels. Between heaven and hell, between that which comes from above and its opposite which meets and resists it from below and would like to be above, there is nothing in common. It is thus quite inappropriate to speak of God and the devil or angels and demons in the same breath. They have no common denominator. They do not grow from a common root. If we maintain that they do, or portray them as if this were the case, we obviously do not know what we are talking about when we speak either about angels or demons.

3. *The Ambassadors of God and Their Opponents*

The older theology was responsible for very serious confusion when it spoke about angels and demons under the title *De bonis et malis angelis*[EN445], or simply *De angelis*[EN446], as though they could both be brought under the one concept "angels," like the white and black pieces at chess which are both brought out of the same box and can both be put back in it at the end of the game. To be sure, Mt. 25^{41} speaks of the devil and his angels, Rev. 12^7 of the dragon and his angels, and 2 Cor. 12^7 of the angel of Satan. Again ἄγγελοι[EN447] are obviously to be regarded as hostile powers in the list in Rom. 8^{38}. But when these beings are brought into the same connexion with the διάβολος or δράκων or σατανάς[EN448], as elsewhere ἄγγελος[EN449] is with κύριος or θεός[EN450], it is obvious that this is simply a manner of speech from which we cannot legitimately conclude that there is a genus "angel" and that within this genus there are the two species, the angels of God and the angels of the devil. The genitive of origin and nature obviously divides the two classes of ἄγγελος[EN451] in such a way that there can be no question of any correlation between them but only that of absolute and exclusive antithesis. Just as the word "nonsense " does not denote a particular species of sense, but that which is negated and excluded by sense, so *angeli mali*[EN452] are not a particular species of angels, but the reality which is condemned, negated and excluded by the opposing angels which as such are *angeli boni*[EN453]. In the few biblical passages in which angels and demons are seen together at all (as in the "war in heaven" of Rev. 12^{7f} or the brief encounter at the temptation in Mk. 1^{12}), they are always understood to be in radical conflict. This radical conflict ought to have been regarded as a radical and essential determination on both sides. The devil and demons ought never to have been seen or understood otherwise than in this essential conflict.

The demons are the opponents of the heavenly ambassadors of God, as the latter are the champions of the kingdom of heaven and therefore of the kingdom of God on earth. Angels and demons are related as creation and chaos, as the free grace of God and nothingness, as good and evil, as life and death, as the light of revelation and the darkness which will not receive it, as redemption and perdition, as *kerygma* and myth. Perhaps the last analysis is best adapted to bring out the matter most sharply. At any rate, we cannot exaggerate the sharpness of the antithesis. No concern lest we fall into dualism and the consequent intolerance, no need for synthesis, must prevent us from insisting on the unconditional antithesis of the two spheres. God is the Lord of the demonic sphere, and it derives from Him, just as in a wholly different way He is the Lord of the angelic sphere and it too derives from Him. But we cannot see or say too   [521] clearly that it is in a wholly different way. There can be no question of God Himself and therefore the angelic sphere ceasing to oppose the demonic. There can be no question of the sovereignty of God and therefore the superiority of the angelic sphere over the demonic coming to a kind of agreement

---

EN445 On Good and Evil Angels
EN446 On angels
EN447 angels
EN448 dragon or satan
EN449 angel
EN450 Lord or God
EN451 angel
EN452 evil angels
EN453 good angels

with the latter or concluding a kind of armistice, which entails a certain measure of recognition. To be sure, the latter is brought into subjection and service. But it is not recognised. Its overthrow is a genuine overthrow. In its final
manifestation it will even mean its destruction. According to Matthew 25[41]
there is an eternal fire which the Father of Jesus has prepared for the devil and
his angels. And the demonic sphere for its part, even though it stands under
the sovereignty of God, and in its own way derives from Him, and is subjected
to Him and brought into His service, does not cease to be the demonic sphere
and therefore a sphere of contradiction and opposition which as such can only
be overthrown and hasten to destruction. Thus the glance which we have to
cast at this sphere can only be a sharp glance, a glance of aversion and not in
any sense of secret respect or reverence or admiration. We cannot believe in
the devil and demons as we may believe in angels when we believe in God. We
have a positive relationship to that in which we believe. But there is no positive
relationship to the devil and demons. We cannot ignore them. We must know
about them, but only as the limit of that to which a positive relationship is
possible and legitimate and obligatory. We can know about them only in such a
way that—as and because we believe in God and His angels—we oppose to
them the most radical unbelief. They are *the* myth, the myth of all mythologies.
Faith in God and His angels involves demythologisation in respect of the devil
and demons; but not in the superficial phenomenological sense current
to-day, in which they are grouped with the angels and even with God's own
Word and work as the figures of a world-outlook which has now been super-
seded. It would no doubt suit them very well to be grouped with the angels,
with the wonders of the reconciling act and resurrection of Jesus Christ, and
finally with God Himself, and in this exalted company to be "demythologised,"
to have their reality denied, to be interpreted away. Demons are only the more
magnified if they are placed in the framework of the conflict between a modern and an ancient system, and called in question in this exalted company. The
demythologisation which will really hurt them as required cannot consist in
questioning their existence. Theological exorcism must be an act of the
unbelief which is grounded in faith. It must consist in a resolute denial that
they belong to this exalted company. It must consist in the fact that in the light,
not of a world-outlook but of Christian truth, they are seen to be a myth, the
[522]   myth which lurks in all myths, the lie which is the basis all other lies, so that a
positive relationship to them, an attitude of respect and reverence and obedience, is quite impossible.

There has always flourished in Christianity and its theology a supposedly very realistic
demonology which has suffered from the lack of this safeguard. It begins with respect
instead of aversion, with reverence instead of anger and scorn. It gazes at the poisonous
serpent instead of striking it. It moves from the very outset in the secret respect and admiration, or at least in an atmosphere of curiosity, where distaste is the only possible attitude. It
derives from a kind of awe that there should be anything of this kind. It attests and demands

a priori[EN454] a kind of faith, or seriously and explicitly real faith, in the matter, at the same time and in the same sense as it attests and demands faith in the angels and Christ and God. It proceeds from the fact that there can and must be a positive relationship to the matter. It had already misunderstood the biblical references to this whole sphere by overlooking their consistently critical and even negative character, not noticing that the Bible only touches on this sphere at all as it shows God and His angels to be in conflict with it, that it is concerned with the rejection and ultimate destruction of the devil and demons, that it does not in the least require us to consider or take this sphere seriously in and for itself, that the realism of the Bible in this respect consists exclusively in the clarity and vigour with which we are comforted and warned and set on our guard against this sphere, but called away from it rather than to it, being commanded merely to give it a passing glance and then to turn our backs upon it. The trouble is that this was not perceived when so strong and as it was supposed so scriptural a demonology was set alongside angelology, and then Christology, and then the doctrine of creation and reconciliation, and then eschatology. So great was the honour which it was thought must be paid to this sphere that the doctrine of the devil and demons became an integral part of the Christian message, and in many cases the part in which Christian preachers and theologians believed they should display their zeal and realism. The result was that all Christianity, even when there were no witch-hunts and the like, acquired a more or less pervasive odour of demonism, becoming something which from this dark chamber seemed to spread abroad, and did actually spread abroad, menace, anxiety, melancholy, oppression, or tragic excitement. And this had the consequence that when in the light of witch-hunts a protest was made against this chamber by the Jesuit Friedrich von Spee and the Dutch Reformed Balthasar Bekker (*Die bezauberte Welt*, 1680), it necessarily led to the Enlightenment and thus to a protest against the whole Christian message. And the further consequence has been that in all subsequent discussion the view has had to be taken into account that angelology, Christology and Christian theology generally form a whole with a particular demonology, and that this whole has either to be accepted, rejected, or, in the process of a general demythologisation in the name of the modern outlook, reduced to a definite anthropology. It was fatal that at the time of the Enlightenment the way was entered which led from a criticism of demonology to a contesting of theology generally. But it was even more fatal that orthodoxy gave good cause for following this path. And it is even more fatal still that to this very day attempts are made to champion a demonology which will only give cause to take this path again and again. How remarkable it is that in what Scripture says and does not say about the demonic sphere it could be overlooked that the fear of God and fear of the devil do not belong together but are mutually exclusive, the sole task of theology in this matter being to show and say that it is the fear of God which overcomes and excludes fear of the devil! How remarkable it is that even to-day this is not self-evident!

What is the origin and nature of the devil and demons? The only possible answer is that their origin and nature lie in nothingness. As we have seen in the preceding section, this is the element of contradiction and opposition which exists on the left hand of God and is thus subject to His world-dominion, but which constitutes a threat to His creation. In biblical terms we can also describe it as chaos, or darkness, or evil, or (to the extent that this signifies a power rather than a place) Hades. Or we might call it the being which exists only as it denies all true being, and is denied by it. Everything which had to be said about this element is also to be said of demons as the opponents of God's [523]

[EN454] unconditionally

heavenly ambassadors. They are. As we cannot deny the peculiar existence of nothingness, we cannot deny their existence. They are null and void, but they are not nothing. They are, but only in their own way; they are, but improperly. Their being is neither that of God nor that of the creature, neither that of heavenly creatures nor that of earthly, for they are neither the one nor the other. They are not divine but non-divine and anti-divine. On the other hand, God has not created them, and therefore they are not creaturely. They are only as God affirms Himself and the creature and thus pronounces a necessary No. They exist in virtue of the fact that His turning to involves a turning from, His election a rejection, His grace a judgment. They are as they are judged, repudiated and excluded by God, and as always and everywhere and in every way, with all the expressions of their being, they can only prove that they are not condemned accidentally or capriciously, but legitimately. They can only hate God and His creation. They can only exist in the attempt to rage against God and to spoil His creation. They can only be disruptive in relation to Himself and His creation, His history with it and His work upon it. For this very reason they are improperly. This disruptive being is what God naver willed, and never does nor will. It is that which, because its being is improper being, can only stand to all eternity under His non-willing, on His left hand, condemned by Him and hastening to destruction.

This is all to be said of demons as of nothingness. They are not different from the latter. They do not stand apart. They derive from it. They themselves are always nothingness. They are nothingness in its dynamic, to the extent that it has form and power and movement and activity. This is how Holy Scripture understands this alien element. Hence it does not understand it as a being which is somewhere and somehow at repose in its improper nature, which in greater or lesser proximity can be considered and assessed with corresponding calm, which can be integrated into a total picture of God and the world, and which can be theoretically mastered and held at a distance. Holy Scripture regards nothingness as a kingdom, based upon a claim to power and a seizure of power, yet not consisting anywhere, but always on the march, always invading and attacking. Its decisive insight is that God Himself is the superior and [524] victorious Opponent of nothingness, the One who has taken up this problem and made it His own, and whose kingdom confronts nothingness and contains it within its frontiers. Hence it does not render it innocuous by viewing it in the theoretical way in which man would like to see it, nor does it adopt the defeatist attitude of absolutising it as man feels impelled to do when for some reason or other he finds it impossible to rob it of its sting by treating it theoretically. It sees it as God Himself sees it, and especially as God Himself treats it, as He deals with it. It thus sees it as a kingdom. And because it starts from the view that God sees and therefore treats all things, including nothingness, with justice, i.e., according to their true being, it is for the Bible no mere figure of speech or poetic fancy or expression of human concern but the simple truth that nothingness has this dynamic, that it is a kingdom on the march and

engaged in invasion and assault: not a kingdom which has to be feared; a kingdom of that which is improper; a kingdom which by the very fact that God
confronts it is characterised from the very outset as weak and futile; a kingdom
which is usurped and not legitimate, transitory and not eternal; yet a real kingdom, a nexus of form and power and movement and activity, of real menace
and danger within its appointed limits. This is how Holy Scripture sees nothingness. And this is how it also sees demons. In this sense it reckons with their
actuality.

We can see at once the similarity of this sphere with that of angels, with the
kingdom of God, the kingdom of heaven. We can see the reason for the misunderstanding in which it could be thought necessary not merely to contrast but
to co-ordinate the two kingdoms, regarding demons not merely as opponents
but as relatives and colleagues of the angels. For do we not have to do here
with accredited ambassadors, with principalities and powers? Is not our earthly
sphere visited in this case, too, by an alien and mysterious dominion? Is not
man placed in both cases under a real mystery? Is there not, then, a final relationship of being, a final similarity? Yet this is the very thing which we must
never say, but resolutely oppose, in relation to these two kingdoms, the kingdom of heaven and that of demons. In relation to these two kingdoms means
in relation to the attitude of God, and therefore of His creature, to these two
kingdoms. Where God says Yes and No, where He is affirmed and denied,
where He is praised and blasphemed, where He is served and hampered,
where His will is done and sabotaged, for all the similarity there is no relationship or homogeneity. And the same is true with reference to the creature.
Where its Creator and therefore its own being are proclaimed and where they
are both denied and plunged in darkness, where it is a matter of its salvation
and of its corruption, where it is affirmed and denied, where it is helped and   [525]
hampered and even destroyed, for all the similarity there is no re lationship or
homogeneity. God Himself, and the creature bound to Him and blessed and
enlightened by Him, comes between the two kingdoms, separating and distinguishing them, so that there can be no real question of any conspectus or
confusion. This is possible only where God is forgotten (or where it is forgotten who and what God is) and it is thought necessary to see and compare an
abstract kingdom of good and an equally abstract kingdom of evil, and angels
and demons no less abstractly as the champions of these two spheres. This
misfortune ought to be quite impossible in a Christian theology. The similarity
of the two spheres ought not to prevent a radical prohibition of their
co-ordination.

What is the basis of this similarity? It rests on the fact that *in se*EN455 nothingness is falsehood. As such it fashions and gives itself similarity with the kingdom of God. It ascribes and arrogates to itself a being which, because it is
neither God nor an earthly nor heavenly creature, cannot belong to it. In so

---

EN455 in itself

237

doing, it is falsehood in its very being. It lies against God by desiring to rule and reveal itself alongside Him, to be as great and important as He is. And it lies against the creature by desiring to play in relation to it the role of a fellowruler. It lies by pretending, in all its nothingness, that it is for God and the creature a relevant and serious factor which has to be taken into significant account. It lies by proclaiming that it can intervene between the grace of God and the salvation of the creature, rendering the grace of God weak and ineffective and hampering and retarding the salvation of the creature. It lies by attempting to ingratiate itself with God and to impose upon the creature. It lies by pretending to be glorious and attractive on the one side or terrifying on the other. It lies by assuming form and power for a particular purpose. It lies in its whole movement and activity, in its whole march, in its whole invasion and assault. It lies in its representation of itself as a kingdom with a leader and subjects, as a system of government with legislative, executive and judicial organs. It lies by opposing itself as such to the kingdom of God. And in so doing—and this is our present concern—it lies by opposing its own messengers, the demons, to the angels of God, attempting to give them the same names and appearance and activity. It lies when it does this, when it pretends that it, too, comes down from heaven to earth as a superior power or a whole host of superior powers, that it, too, has something to institute on earth, that its will is to be done on earth in opposition to the will of God.

We must not deceive ourselves and say that it does not really do all these things, or is not real in all these things. One form of the triumph which nothingness can achieve is to represent itself as a mere appearance with no genuine reality. Let us only be proud and enlightened and unafraid and unconcerned in face of it! Let us only persuade ourselves that there is nothing in it, that [526] there is no devil and no kingdom of evil and demons as his plenipotentiaries, as effective powers and forces in the life of nations and societies, in the psychical and physical life of men and their relationships, that we can control our being without having to take into account this alien lordship or considering that where it is not broken all being and enterprise and achievement on earth is fundamentally corrupt and worthless! Nothingness lies also and supremely by trivialising and concealing itself, spreading abroad a carefree optimism, being content simply to be present, to be in fact a powerful kingdom subtly controlled, and thus to declare, express and maintain its power. Nothingness rejoices when it notices that it is not noticed, that it is boldly demythologised, that humanity thinks it can tackle its lesser and greater problems with a little morality and medicine and psychology and aesthetics, with progressive politics or occasionally a philosophy of unprecedented novelty—if only its own reality as nothingness remains beautifully undisclosed and intact.

But there is another side to the matter. We must not dream and say that in all that it does and is nothingness can be anything but falsehood. The other form of its triumph is to present itself as though it were no lie, as though it really had something to proclaim, as though it could really found and organise a kingdom, as though it could really come down from heaven to earth, as though its powers and forces were really agents which could contradict and withstand the grace of God and the salvation of the creature, as though it had rights over against God and the creature which entitled it to fear and respect. Let us only admire it for its independent truth! Let us only integrate the devil and the kingdom of demons and evil into the same system in which elsewhere and according to their different character we also treat of God and Christ and true man and the angels! Let us only do this kingdom the honour of taking it seriously in this sense! If nothingness can only succeed in making itself noticeable in this way as the truth, it is jubilant on the other side. Nothing could suit it better than to find a sure place in the philosophical outlook of man or the world of human thought, securing recognition as a serious co-worker and opponent of God and man. But it may be that as such it again falls under suspicion, that its truth becomes a matter of doubt, that man grows tired of treating it with too great trepidation and respect. In these circumstances, there is always scope for a new cycle of enlightenment and demythologisation, for morality, medicine, psychology, aesthetics, politics, philosophy or even piety and religion to take the stage as the true liberators, and for a reassertion of the undisclosed and intact dominion of negated nothingness. There is alternation in this matter. If we ignore demons, they deceive us by concealing their power until we are again constrained to respect and fear them as powers. If we absolutise them, respecting and fearing them as true powers, they have   [527] deceived us by concealing their character as falsehood, and it will be only a little while before we try to ignore and are thus deceived by them again.

Nothingness is falsehood. It exists as such, having a kind of substance and person, vitality and spontaneity, form and power and movement. As such it founds and organises its kingdom. And demons are its exponents, the powers of falsehood in a thousand different forms. Its kingdom is indeed very similar to the kingdom of heaven with its angels. And this imitation of the kingdom of heaven and its angels, the uncanny resemblance to this very different sphere in which it dares to present itself, is the crown of its existence as falsehood. It, too, is an invisible and incomprehensible kingdom. It, too, is undoubtedly superior to man and the whole earthly creation. It, too, has in its midst a kind of throne and ruler. It, too, has an enterprise and movement aimed at earth and man. It, too, has powerful messengers who attest and proclaim a kind of mystery, who do this with a kind of humility and objectivity, and who obviously stand in its service. The word "too" is the real mark of this kingdom as the kingdom of falsehood. Nothingness wants to do everything *too*, and not only what creatures are and can do and accomplish, but also and supremely what God is and wills and does. Nor does it merely want to do, but it actually does, or tries to do, what God does. It plays at creation and redemption, providence and dominion. It plays at Law and Gospel, grace and judgment. All falsehood! It constructs a false heaven with a false God, a false throne from which false messengers are despatched, to proclaim a false mystery with all the humility and objectivity of falsehood. There is no other word for it—it is all a mimicry.

But we must not overlook or deny the fact that the performance is real and constantly successful. We cannot deny the power and powers of falsehood in a thousand different forms. We cannot deny that in their infamous way they are real and brisk and vital, often serious and solemn, but always sly and strong, and always present in different combinations of these qualities, forming a dreadful fifth or sixth dimension of existence. Where? But surely the real question is: Where not? They are there in the depths of the soul which we regard as most properly our own. They are there in the relationships between man and man, and especially between man and woman. They are there in the developments of individuals and their mutal relationships. They are there in the concern and struggle for daily bread, and especially for that which each thinks is also necessary in his case. They are there in that in which man seeks his satisfaction or which he would rather avoid as undesirable, in his care and carelessness, in the flaming up and extinguishing of his passions, in his sloth and zeal, in his inexplicable stupidity and astonishing cleverness, in his systematisation [528] and anarchism, in his progress, equilibrium and retrogression, in the great common ventures of what is called culture, science, art, technics and politics, in the conflict and concord of classes, peoples and nations, in the savage dissensions but also the beautiful agreements and tolerances in the life of the Church, and not least in the *rabies*[EN456] and even more so the *inertia theologorum*[EN457]. We cannot really deny but must see and recognise and know that in, with and under all these things there is constantly played out the mimicry of nothingness—the play of that which is absolutely useless and worthless, yet which is not prepared to allow that this is the case, but pretends to be vitally necessary and of supreme worth. We cannot deny but must soberly recognise that in all these things the demons are constantly present and active like the tentacles of an octopus. Fortunately the angels are also present and active. But there can be no doubt that the demons are there too, beings which betray their nature by this fatal "too."

Yet it is as well not to consider this without recognising that they are only the powers of falsehood. As falsehood they are really powerful. Indeed, because they are so thorough, because they imitate no less than God and His kingdom and angels, because nothingness always masquerades as the highest and deepest, the first and the last, they are always much more powerful than we expect or concede, and can always turn our defences or cut off our escape, seizing us at the very point from which we try to resist them or where we try to find refuge from them. They are powers indeed, and yet they are only the powers of falsehood. Hence we must not regard them as real powers, or the mimicry with

---

[EN456] frenzy
[EN457] laziness of theologians

which they make fools of us as reality. They work so long and extensively and deeply as they can work as lies, and are not shown to be such, or set over against the truth, and thus dispelled as lies. Anything other or less than the truth is no match for them, whether it takes the form of mental purification, zealous good will, knowledge or technics. Because they are the powers of falsehood, of the great and comprehensive falsehood which imitates even God and His angels, it is child's play for them to surround and imprison the man who encounters them armed only with these weapons. Only the truth is strong enough to meet them. This is so immediately, basically and conclusively. Yet it must be the whole truth, the real truth, the truth of God and His kingdom and angels, the truth which they have attempted to imitate and in the imitation of which they are so powerful. Other truths may be most profound and excellent, but they are of no value because they cannot touch, let alone destroy, their power, the power of imitation and falsehood which makes them so great and dangerous.

The truth of God dispels them as and because in confrontation with it they are disclosed, unmasked and stripped as the powers of falsehood. This is the insight which is even more important in relation to demons than the fact that they exist, and exist always and everywhere as forces. The fact is that they exist [529] always and everywhere where the truth of God is not present and proclaimed and believed and grasped, and therefore does not speak and shine and rule. This is the limit and destruction of demons. This extinguishes them as lies and therefore as forces. This negates, condemns and rejects nothingness and all its representatives. This contradicts the contradiction and opposes the opposition; and it does so radically and definitively. It does so simply by speaking for itself as the truth, and thus separating from itself the lie as such and showing it to be a lie. It reveals the devil and all devils for what they are. It shows that they are tempters falsely suggesting that there is something better than the obedience to which we are summoned and for which we are empowered by the Word and work of God. It shows that they are accusers who falsely charge us when, in spite of all that speaks against us, we see ourselves set with quiet consciences on the right way by the Word and work of God. It shows that they are tyrants who falsely pretend to have the right and power to make us their prisoners and slaves, puppets who must dance on their wires, when we are really placed in the freedom of the children of God by His Word and work. It shows that they are spirits of complaint which falsely depress us and rob us of our humour by persuading us that the natural limits of our physical and psychical existence are a constriction, curse and misfortune, when we are really borne, sustained and even uplifted by God within these limits. It shows that they are poltergeists which falsely alarm us when we may really have a total and radical peace on the basis of the Word and work of God. As the truth of God shows nothingness and its representatives the demons in their true nature, and thus shows the falsity of their claim and enterprise, it disarms them and makes them impotent. That the lie should be exposed is what is most appropriate to the lie

241

itself and most helpful to those who are threatened, oppressed and tormented by its power. This is what is done by the truth of God. And as it is done the lie loses the vital breath which enables it to threaten, oppress and torment. It is vanquished and driven from the field.

This, then, is what Holy Scripture has to tell us concerning demons. It certainly does not say that they do not exist or have no power or do not constitute this threat. It is quite evident that their existence and nature are very definitely taken into account, and it is surprising that this is more expressly the case in the New Testament than the Old. But this is inevitable, for in the light of the fulfilled and completed covenant of grace, of the kingdom of God coming from heaven to earth, that which contradicts and resists it, as it is driven from the field, is seen much more clearly than where there is only a movement towards the fulfilment and the kingdom is only announced. But the contradiction and resistance are now seen to be nothingness, and its representatives the

[530]   powers of falsehood, unreal beings unmasked as falsehood and thus robbed of their powers. What might be called biblical demonology is in fact only a negative reflection of biblical Christology and soteriology. What is revealed is the kingdom of Satan and his angels as this is already assaulted and mortally threatened, and indeed radically destroyed; demonic being, not in its concealment and therefore powerful, but unmasked and therefore disarmed; not its march and attack and even victory, but its defeat and withdrawal and flight; not an earth and humanity controlled, visited and plagued by demons, but liberated from them; not a world bewitched but exorcised; not a community and Christendom believing in demons but opposing to them in faith that resolute disbelief; in short, the triumph of truth over falsehood. But it is the truth of God which triumphs; it is really His Word and work. It is Jesus Christ, God in His person, who as the Lord and Victor overthrows nothingness and its lying powers. It is in the history of His conflict, of the kingdom of God dawning in Him, and therefore in the history of His humiliation to the death of the cross and His resurrection and exaltation to the right hand of the Father, that it is not merely true, but at the cost of the sacrifice of the Son of God and therefore in glory it becomes true, that nothingness and the demons have nothing to declare. The reference is thus to faith in Him, to obedience to Him as Lord and Saviour, to life in His community, to the proclamation and hearing of the message of the salvation which has appeared in Him, when we are summoned in the New Testament to follow His triumph over demonic being. In Jesus Christ Himself this triumph is won only in the history of that conflict. And our celebration of it, our liberation from demons, can take place only as we participate in this history. And as the angels were witnesses of this history, encountering demons as witnesses of the victory, they are always present as described when it is a matter of summoning men, and making them able and willing, to participate in this history, in this conflict and triumph. They witness for the truth which has fought and conquered and will continually be revealed and known in the light of that conflict and victory. And in the genuine power of

this truth they are for us continually the counter-witnesses to the lying messengers of the kingdom of falsehood.

We may conclude with a short observation on the doctrine of the Early Church concerning the relationship between angels and demons. We refer to the view constantly held in ancient and modern times that the demons are "fallen angels." At an earlier date this was linked with the saying in Is. 14^{12} which describes the king of Babylon as the radiant star of the morning (*lucifer*) cast down from heaven. The remarkable passage in Gen. 6$^{1-14}$ was related to this verse. Most strongly of all Jude 6 seemed and seems to point in this direction, with its mention of angels which did not keep their ἀρχή EN458 and lost their ἴδιον οἰκητήριον EN459. We might also refer to 2 Pet. 2^4 with its reference to angels who sinned. But these texts are so uncertain and obscure that it is inadvisable to allow them to push us in this direction. However they may have to be expounded, against their exposition along these lines there has to be set the intolerable artificiality with which attempts have been made to use them as a basis for the development of the doctrine of a fall of angels and therefore of an explanation of the existence of the devil and demons. And literally all the insights which we have gained concerning the being and ministry of angels, and developed at least concerning the character and activity of demons, are necessarily false if this doctrine is correct. It is, in fact, one of the bad dreams of the older dogmatics. It arises from the superfluous need to ground our knowledge of the fall of man upon the notion of a metaphysical prelude which it was quite inappropriately thought should be located in heaven. It derives from the definitely illegitimate attempt not to allow nothingness to be what it is but to bring it into systematic connexion with God and the creature, to understand, explain and deduce its possibility (the possibility of the impossible) and essence (the essence of non-essence). And it stems from a frightful misunderstanding of the kingdom of heaven and angels, as though the freedom of these creatures were not a real freedom if it were not for them too, or had not been once in some primal epoch, the so-called *liberum arbitrium* EN460, i.e., the freedom to become fools. Along these lines we do not rightly understand the freedom of the earthly creature, of man, let alone of the heavenly. To bring angels and demons under the common denominator of this fatal concept of freedom is to confuse and obscure everything that is to be said of both. A true and orderly angel does not do what is ascribed to some angels in this doctrine (in obscure speculation concerning this derivation). And on the other hand it cannot be said that a real demon has ever been in heaven. The demons merely act as if they came from heaven. But the devil was never an angel. He was a murderer ἀπ᾽ ἀρχῆς EN461. He never stood in the truth. No truth was ever in him. He speaks falsehood, and he does so ἐκ τῶν ἰδίων EN462, because he is a liar and the father of lies. This is how he is described in Jn. 8^{44}, and it agrees with everything else that we are told in the New Testament concerning him and demons. But of angels we must say with Jas. 1^{17}: "Every good gift and every perfect gift is from above, and cometh down from the Father of lights, with whom is no variableness, neither shadow of turning." And reference may also be made to the preceding verse (v. 16): "Do not err, my beloved brethren."

[531]

EN458 position of authority
EN459 their own habitation
EN460 freedom of the will
EN461 from the beginning
EN462 of his own

INDEX OF SCRIPTURE REFERENCES

INDEX OF SUBJECTS

INDEX OF NAMES